W9-BUJ-373

Traveler's World Atlas & Guide

Quick Reference Contents

World Time Zones **6**

Air Distances Between World Cities **8**

Travel Information **11**

City Maps **33**

Guide to Selected Cities **70**

World Travel Maps **81**

World Comparisons **145**

Map Index **153**

World Flags **209**

Country Profiles **214**

Traveler's Personal Diary **241**

© 1996, 1994, 1993 Rand McNally & Company
1998 Revised Edition
All rights reserved.
Printed in the United States of America

Library of Congress Cataloging-in-Publication Data
Rand McNally & Company.
    Traveler's world atlas and guide.
        p.   cm.
    At head of title: Rand McNally.
    Includes travel information, guide to selected cities, and country
profiles.
    Includes index.

    1. Atlases.   I. Title.   II. Title: Traveler's world atlas and
guide.   III. Title: Rand McNally traveler's world atlas & guide.
G1021.R487   1993 < G&M >
912—dc20   93–11580
                                         CIP
                                         MAP

Contents

World Time Zones 6

Air Distances Between World Cities 8

Travel Information 11

Dialing Codes, U.S. Embassy addresses and telephone numbers,
Holidays, Entry Requirements, Travel Advisories, Climates, etc.

City Maps 33

Legend, 33
Athens, Greece, 59
Baltimore, U.S.A., 38
Bangkok, Thailand, 63
Barcelona, Spain, 57
Beijing, China, 60
Berlin, Germany, 56
Boston, U.S.A., 35
Budapest, Hungary, 59
Buenos Aires, Argentina, 47
Buffalo, U.S.A., 40
Cairo, Egypt, 69
Calcutta, India, 60
Caracas, Venezuela, 48
Chicago, U.S.A., 43
Cleveland, U.S.A., 39
Delhi, India, 61
Detroit, U.S.A., 41
Havana, Cuba, 46
Ho Chi Minh City (Saigon), Vietnam, 63
Istanbul, Turkey, 59
Jakarta, Indonesia, 63
Johannesburg, South Africa, 68
Kinshasa, Dem. Rep. of the Congo and
    Brazzaville, Congo, 68
Kyōto, Japan, 62
Lagos, Nigeria, 68
Lima, Peru, 46
Lisbon, Portugal, 57
Liverpool, England, 54
London, England, 50–51
Los Angeles, U.S.A., 44–45

Madrid, Spain, 57
Manchester, England, 54
Manila, Philippines, 63
Melbourne, Australia, 67
Mexico City, Mexico, 46
Milan, Italy, 57
Montréal, Canada, 34
Moscow, Russia, 58
Mumbai (Bombay), India, 61
New York, U.S.A., 36–37
Ōsaka-Kōbe, Japan, 65
Paris, France, 55
Philadelphia, U.S.A., 39
Pittsburgh, U.S.A., 40
Rio de Janeiro, Brazil, 49
Rome, Italy, 58
Ruhr Area, Germany, 52–53
St. Petersburg, Russia, 58
San Francisco, U.S.A., 42
Santiago, Chile, 48
São Paulo, Brazil, 49
Seoul, South Korea, 62
Shanghai, China, 62
Singapore, 61
Sydney, Australia, 66
T'aipei, China, 62
Tehrān, Iran, 63
Tōkyō-Yokohama, Japan, 64
Toronto, Canada, 34
Vienna, Austria, 59
Washington, D.C., U.S.A., 38
Xianggang (Hong Kong), 62

Guide to Selected Cities 70

Amsterdam, 70
Athens
Atlanta

Beijing
Berlin, 71
Boston

Brussels
Buenos Aires

Cairo
Calcutta, 72

4 Contents

Guide to Selected Cities (cont'd)

Chicago
Dallas-Ft. Worth
Denver, 73
Detroit
Frankfurt
Hong Kong
 (Victoria)
Honolulu, 74
Istanbul

Johannesburg
Kuala Lumpur
London, 75
Los Angeles
Madrid
Manila
Mexico City, 76
Miami
Milan

Montréal
Moscow, 77
New Orleans
New York
Ōsaka
Paris
Rio de Janeiro, 78
Rome
San Francisco

São Paulo
Singapore, 79
Stockholm
Sydney
Tel Aviv
Tōkyō, 80
Toronto
Vienna
Zurich

World Travel Maps 81

Legend, 81
World Political, 82–83
Arctic Region, 84
Antarctic Region, 85
Europe, 86–87
British Isles, 88
Scandinavia, 89
Central Europe, 90–91
France and the Alps, 92–93
Spain and Portugal, 94–95
Italy, 96–97
Southeastern Europe, 98–99
Baltic and Moscow Region, 100–101
Northeast Asia, 102–103
Western North Africa, 104–105
Southern Africa and Madagascar, 106–107
Northeastern Africa and Arabia, 108
The Middle East, 109
India, 110
Southern India and Sri Lanka, 111

Northern India and the Himalayas, 112–113
China, Japan and Korea, 114–115
Japan, 116–117
Southeast Asia, 118–119
Indochina, 120–121
Australia, 122–123
Southeastern Australia, 124–125
New Zealand, 126
Pacific Islands, 127
Mexico, 128–129
Central America and the Caribbean, 130–131
Northern South America, 132–133
Southern South America, 134
Southeastern Brazil, 135
Canada, 136–137
United States, 138–139
Northeastern United States, 140–141
California, Nevada and Hawaii, 142–143
Alaska, 144

World Comparisons 145

The Continents, 145
Principal Mountains, 146
Oceans, Seas, and Gulfs, 147
Principal Islands, 147
Principal Lakes, 148
Principal Rivers, 148
Countries by Area, 149

Countries by Population, 150
Urban Population, 151
Life Expectancy, 151
Literacy, 152
GDP (Gross Domestic Product) per Capita, 152

Map Index 153

Introduction to the Index 153

List of Abbreviations 154

Key to Symbols 158

Index to the Maps 158

World Flags 209

Country Profiles 214

Afghanistan, 214
Albania
Algeria
Angola
Antigua and
  Barbuda
Argentina
Armenia
Australia, 215
Austria
Azerbaijan
Bahamas
Bahrain
Bangladesh
Barbados
Belarus, 216
Belgium
Belize
Benin
Bhutan
Bolivia
Bosnia and
  Herzegovina
Botswana, 217
Brazil
Brunei
Bulgaria
Burkina Faso
Burundi
Cambodia
Cameroon
Canada, 218
Cape Verde
Central African
  Rep.
Chad
Chile
China
Colombia, 219
Comoros
Congo
Congo, Dem. Rep.
  of the
Costa Rica
Cote d'Ivoire
Croatia
Cuba, 220
Cyprus
Czech Rep.
Denmark
Djibouti

Dominica
Dominican Rep.
Ecuador
Egypt, 221
El Salvador
Equatorial Guinea
Eritrea
Estonia
Ethiopia
Fiji
Finland, 222
France
French Guiana
French Polynesia
Gabon
Gambia
Georgia
Germany, 223
Ghana
Greece
Greenland
Grenada
Guatemala
Guinea
Guinea-Bissau, 224
Guyana
Haiti
Honduras
Hong Kong
  (Xianggang)
Hungary
Iceland
India, 225
Indonesia
Iran
Iraq
Ireland
Israel
Italy
Jamaica, 226
Japan
Jordan
Kazakhstan
Kenya
Kiribati
Korea, North
Korea, South
Kuwait, 227
Kyrgyzstan
Laos
Latvia

Lebanon
Lesotho
Liberia
Libya, 228
Liechtenstein
Lithuania
Luxembourg
Macao
Macedonia
Madagascar
Malawi, 229
Malaysia
Maldives
Mali
Malta
Mauritania
Mauritius
Mexico, 230
Moldova
Monaco
Mongolia
Morocco
Mozambique
Myanmar
Namibia, 231
Nepal
Netherlands
New Caledonia
New Zealand
Nicaragua
Niger
Nigeria, 232
Norway
Oman
Pakistan
Panama
Papua New Guinea
Paraguay
Peru, 233
Philippines
Poland
Portugal
Puerto Rico
Qatar
Romania
Russia, 234
Rwanda
St. Kitts and Nevis
St. Lucia
St. Vincent and the
  Grenadines

Samoa
Sao Tome and
  Principe
Saudi Arabia
Senegal, 235
Seychelles
Sierra Leone
Singapore
Slovakia
Slovenia
Solomon Islands
Somalia, 236
South Africa
Spain
Sri Lanka
Sudan
Suriname
Swaziland
Sweden, 237
Switzerland
Syria
Taiwan
Tajikistan
Tanzania
Thailand
Togo, 238
Tonga
Trinidad and
  Tobago
Tunisia
Turkey
Turkmenistan
Uganda
Ukraine, 239
United Arab
  Emirates
United Kingdom
United States
Uruguay
Uzbekistan
Vanuatu
Vatican City, 240
Venezuela
Vietnam
Xianggang (see
  Hong Kong)
Yemen
Yugoslavia
Zambia
Zimbabwe

Traveler's Personal Diary 241

6

75° 90° 105° 120° 135° 150° 165° 180° 165° 150° 135°

Longitude East of Greenwich   Longitude West of Greenwich

(16) (17) (18) (19) (20) (21) (22) (23) (24) (1) (2) (3)

ARCTIC OCEAN

ZEML'A FRANCA-IOSIFA

NOVAJA ZEML'A

Kara Sea

Laptev Sea

NOVOSIBIRSKIJE OSTROVA

Beaufort Sea

75°

Nordvik

(19)

Tiksi

Inuvik

Vorkuta   Igarka   Arctic Circle   Verchojansk

Salechard

RUSSIA

Anadyr'

Nome   Fairbanks
UNITED
STATES   Anchorage   Juneau

Jekaterinburg

Ochotsk

Magadan

Bering

Gulf of Alaska

60°

Cel'abinsk   Novosibirsk (20)   Lake Baykal   Sea of Okhotsk   Petropavlovsk   Sea

KAZAKHSTAN

Ulaanbaatar   MONGOLIA   Harbin   Khabarovsk   SAKHALIN   ALEUTIAN ISLANDS   Vancouver

45°   Ürümqi   GOBI   KURIL ISLANDS   PACIFIC   Portland

UZBEK. KYRG.   P'yongyang   HONSHU

TURK. TAJIK.   BEIJING   SEOUL   TOKYO   SAN FRANCISCO

AFG.   CHINA   KOREA   JAPAN   LOS ANGE

30°   DELHI   Chongqing   Nanjing   OSAKA   San

PAK.   NEP.   BHU.   SHANGHAI   International Date Line

Karachi   (18)   Canton   T'aipei   Tropic of Cancer   OCEAN

INDIA   MYA.   HONG KONG   TAIWAN   WAKE ISLAND (U.S.)   Honolulu   HAWAIIAN ISLANDS (U.S.)

MUMBAI (17½)   Hanoi   MARIANA ISLANDS (U.S.)

15°   Chennai   (18½)   THAI.   VIET-NAM   MANILA (21)   GUAM (U.S.)   MARSHALL ISLANDS

Colombo   SRI LANKA   CAMB.   Thanh-pho Ho Chi Minh   PHILIPPINES   CAROLINE ISLANDS

MALDIVES   MALAYSIA

SINGAPORE   (23½)   NAURU   KIRIBATI   Equato

0°   Equator   SUMATERA   SULAWESI   PAPUA NEW GUINEA   TUVALU   (2½)   ILES MARQUISES (Fr.)

JAKARTA   INDONESIA   ILES

JAWA   SOLOMON ISLANDS   SAMOA AM. SAMOA   TUAMOTU (Fr.)

15°   INDIAN   COCOS ISLANDS (Austl.)   VANUATU FIJI

Tropic of Capricorn   (18½)   (21½)   Cairns   Coral Sea   NEW (NEW HEBRIDES)   TONGA   COOK ISLANDS (N.Z.)   Tropic

OCEAN   AUSTRALIA   Brisbane   NEW CALEDONIA (Fr.)   PITCAIRN (U.K.)

30°   Perth   Adelaide   Sydney (23½)   Auckland   PACIF

Melbourne   Canberra   NEW

TASMANIA   ZEALAND   Wellington

45°   Hobart   Christchurch   OCE

ILES DE KERGUELEN (Fr.)

HEARD ISLAND (Austl.)   Antarc

60°   B-510000-1T23-8-17-7-13 TW1
Copyright by
RAND McNALLY & COMPANY
Made in U.S.A.

WILKES   LAND

75°   ANTARCTICA   Ross Sea

(16) (17) (18) (19) (20) (21) (22) (23) (24) (1) (2) (3)

4:00 5:00 6:00 7:00 8:00 9:00 10:00 11:00 NOON 1:00 2:00 3:00

Longitude West of Greenwich | Longitude East of Greenwich

ARCTIC OCEAN

ZEMLʼA FRANCA-IOSIFA
SVALBARD (Nor.)
NOVAJA ZEMLʼA

GREENLAND (Den.)
Greenland Sea
Thule
Baffin Bay
JAN MAYEN (Nor.)
Hammerfest
Murmansk
Barents Sea

VICTORIA ISLAND
BAFFIN ISLAND
Godhavn
Godthåb
ICELAND
Reykjavik
FAEROE ISLANDS (Den.)
Oslo
Stockholm
Archangelʼsk
SANKT-PETERBURG
RUSSIA

NORTH AMERICA
Yellowknife
Hudson Bay
Churchill
KAP FARVEL
UNITED KINGDOM
IRELAND
DEN.
BERLIN
MOSCOW
Nizhnij Novgorod

CANADA
Edmonton
Calgary
Winnipeg
Québec
Toronto
Ottawa
Montréal
NEW YORK
NEWFOUNDLAND
ATLANTIC
LONDON
PARIS
FRANCE
SWITZ. AUS. HUNG.
Warsaw
UKRAINE
Volgograd
KAZAKH.

Seattle
Minneapolis
UNITED STATES
CHICAGO
DETROIT
PHILADELPHIA
St. Louis
Washington
AZORES (Port.)
PORT. SPAIN
Lisbon
Rome
ALB.
GREECE
TURKEY
Ankara
IRAN

Phoenix
Dallas
New Orleans
BERMUDA (U.K.)
OCEAN
Rabat
Casablanca
MOROCCO
Algiers
TUN.
Mediterranean Sea
SYRIA
LEB.
IRAQ
JOR.
KUWAIT
PAK.

MEXICO
Gulf of Mexico
Miami
BAHAMAS
CUBA
DOM. REP.
Tropic of Cancer
CANARY IS. (Sp.)
ALGERIA
LIBYA
CAIRO
EGYPT
SAUDI ARABIA
OMAN
U.A.E.

MEXICO CITY
GUAT.
BELIZE
HOND.
EL SAL.
NIC.
JAM.
HAITI
PUERTO RICO (US)
CAPE VERDE
SENEGAL
MAURITANIA
MALI
NIGER
CHAD
Al-Khartum
SUDAN
YEM.
Adis Abeba

CLIPPERTON (Fr.)
COSTA RICA
PANAMA
COL.
VEN.
Santa Fe de Bogota
GUYANA
SURINAME
FR. GUIANA
GAMBIA
GUINEA-BISS.
SIERRA LEONE
LIBERIA
GUINEA
C. dʼI.
NIGERIA
CAM.
CENT. AFR. REP.
ETH.

ECUADOR
PERU
Lima
SOUTH AMERICA
BRAZIL
Recife
Belém
Equator
GABON
CONGO
D. RRW.
CONGO
BDI.
KENYA
TANZANIA
INDIAN

BOL.
Brasília
Salvador
ANGOLA
ZAMBIA
MADAG.
OCEAN

Capricorn
Antofagasta
PARA.
RIO DE JANEIRO
Asunción
Tropic of Capricorn
NAMIBIA
BOTS.
MOZ.
SWAZ.

Santiago
CHILE
ARGENTINA
URUGUAY
Montevideo
BUENOS AIRES
ATLANTIC
OCEAN
Johannesburg
SOUTH AFRICA
Cape Town
LESO.

Graphic Linear Scale

Punta Arenas
FALKLAND ISLANDS (U.K.)
SOUTH GEORGIA (U.K.)
0° 1000
15° 75°
30° 30°
45° 45°
60° 60°
76° 76°
0 100 200 300 400 500 600 700 800 900 1000
Statute Miles
Miller Cylindrical Projection

CABO DE HORNOS
CAPE HORN
SOUTH ORKNEY ISLANDS (U.K.)

Circle
Bellingshausen Sea
Weddell Sea
ENDERBY LAND

ANTARCTICA

5 | 6 | 7 | 8 | 9 | 10 | 11 | 12 | 13 | 14 | 15 | 16
5:00 | 6:00 | 7:00 | 8:00 | 9:00 | 10:00 | 11:00 | MIDNIGHT | 1:00 | 2:00 | 3:00 | 4:00

8

Air Distances Between World Cities
Given in statute miles

	Apia, Samoa	Azores Islands	Beijing, China	Berlin, Germany	Bombay (Mumbai), India	Buenos Aires, Argentina	Calcutta, India	Cape Town, South Africa	Cape Verde Islands	Chicago, U.S.A.	Darwin, Australia	Denver, U.S.A.	Gibraltar	Hong Kong (Xiangang)
Apia		9644	5903	9743	8154	6931	7183	9064	10246	6557	3843	5653	10676	5591
Azores Islands	9644		6565	2185	5967	5417	6549	5854	1499	3093	10209	3991	1249	7572
Beijing	5903	6565		4567	2964	11974	2024	8045	7763	6592	3728	6348	6009	1226
Berlin	9743	2185	4567		3910	7376	4376	5977	3194	4402	8036	5077	1453	5500
Bombay (Mumbai)	8154	5967	2964	3910		9273	1041	5134	6297	8054	4503	8383	4814	2673
Buenos Aires	6931	5417	11974	7376	9273		10242	4270	4208	5596	9127	5928	5963	11463
Calcutta	7183	6549	2024	4376	1041	10242		6026	7148	7981	3744	8050	5521	1534
Cape Town	9064	5854	8045	5977	5134	4270	6026		4509	8449	6947	9327	5076	7372
Cape Verde Is.	10246	1499	7763	3194	6297	4208	7148	4509		4066	10664	4975	1762	8539
Chicago	6557	3093	6592	4402	8054	5596	7981	8449	4066		9346	920	4258	7790
Darwin	3843	10209	3728	8036	4503	9127	3744	6947	10664	9346		8557	9265	2642
Denver	5653	3991	6348	5077	8383	5928	8050	9327	4975	920	8557		5122	7465
Gibraltar	10676	1249	6009	1453	4814	5963	5521	5076	1762	4258	9265	5122		6828
Hong Kong (Xiang.)	5591	7572	1226	5500	2673	11463	1534	7372	8539	7790	2642	7465	6828	
Honolulu	2604	7180	5067	7305	8020	7558	7037	11532	8311	4244	5355	3338	8075	5537
Istanbul	10175	2975	4379	1078	2991	7568	3646	5219	3507	5476	7390	6154	1874	4980
Juneau	5415	4526	4522	4560	6866	7759	6326	10330	5911	2305	7105	1831	5273	5634
London	9789	1527	5054	574	4462	6918	4954	6005	2731	3950	8598	4688	1094	5981
Los Angeles	4828	4794	6250	5782	8701	6118	8148	9969	5772	1745	7835	831	5936	7240
Manila	4993	8250	1770	6128	3148	11042	2189	7525	9221	8128	1979	7661	7483	693
Melbourne	3113	12101	5667	9919	6097	7234	5547	6412	10856	9668	1964	8759	10798	4607
Mexico City	5449	4385	7733	6037	9722	4633	9495	8511	4857	1673	9081	1434	5629	8776
Moscow	9116	3165	3507	996	3131	8375	3506	6294	3982	4994	7046	5485	2413	4439
New Orleans	6085	3524	7314	5116	8865	4916	8803	8316	4194	833	9545	1082	4757	8480
New York	7242	2422	6823	3961	7794	5297	7921	7801	3355	713	9959	1631	3627	8051
Nome	5438	4954	3428	4342	5901	8848	5271	10107	6438	3314	6235	2925	5398	4547
Oslo	9247	2234	4360	515	4130	7613	4459	6494	3444	4040	8022	4653	1791	5337
Panamá	6514	3778	8906	5849	9742	3381	10114	7014	3734	2325	10352	2636	4926	10084
Paris	9990	1659	5101	542	4359	6877	4889	3841	2666	4133	8575	4885	964	5956
Port Said	10485	3391	4584	1747	2677	7362	3506	4590	3672	6103	7159	6819	2179	4975
Quebec	7406	2240	6423	3583	7371	5680	7481	7857	3355	878	9724	1752	3383	8650
Reykjavik	8678	1777	4903	1479	5191	7099	5409	7111	3248	2954	8631	3596	2047	6031
Rio de Janeiro	8120	4428	10768	6144	8257	1218	9376	3769	3040	5296	9960	5871	4775	10995
Rome	10475	2125	5047	734	3843	6929	4496	5249	2772	4808	8190	5561	1034	5768
San Francisco	4786	4872	5902	5657	8392	6474	7809	10241	5921	1858	7637	949	5936	6894
Seattle	5222	4501	5396	5041	7741	6913	7224	10199	5714	1737	7619	1021	5462	6471
Shanghai	5399	7229	662	5215	3133	12197	2112	8059	8443	7053	3142	6698	6646	772
Singapore	5850	8326	2774	6166	2429	9864	1791	6016	8700	9365	2075	9063	7231	1652
Tokyo	4656	7247	1307	5538	4188	11400	3186	9071	8589	6303	3367	5795	6988	1796
Valparaíso	6267	5678	11774	7795	10037	761	10993	4998	4649	5268	8961	5452	6408	11607
Vienna	10010	2291	4639	328	3718	7368	4259	5671	3147	4694	7974	5383	1386	5429
Washington, D.C.	7066	2667	6922	4167	7988	5216	8088	7894	3486	597	9923	1464	3822	8148
Wellington	2062	11269	6698	11265	7677	6260	7042	7019	10363	8349	3310		12060	5853
Winnipeg	6283	3389	5907	4286	7644	6297	7424	9054	4556	714	8684	798	4435	7096
Zanzibar	9892	5323	5803	4309	2855	6421	3859	2346	4635	8358	6409	9221	4103	5414

Honolulu, Hawaii, U.S.A.	Istanbul, Turkey	Juneau, Alaska, U.S.A.	London, United Kingdom	Los Angeles, U.S.A.	Manila, Philippines	Melbourne, Australia	Mexico City, Mexico	Moscow, Russia	New Orleans, U.S.A.	New York, U.S.A.	Nome, Alaska, U.S.A.	Oslo, Norway	Panamá, Panama	Paris, France	Port Said, Egypt	Quebec, Canada
2604	10175	5415	9789	4828	4993	3113	5449	9116	6085	7242	5438	9247	6514	9990	10485	7406
7180	2975	4526	1527	4794	8250	12101	4385	3165	3524	2422	4954	2234	3778	1659	3391	2240
5067	4379	4522	5054	6250	1770	5667	7733	3597	7314	6823	3428	4360	8906	5101	4584	6423
7305	1078	4560	574	5782	6128	9919	6037	996	5116	3961	4342	515	5849	542	1747	3583
8020	2991	6866	4462	8701	3148	6097	9722	3131	8865	7794	5901	4130	9742	4359	2659	7371
7558	7568	7759	6918	6118	11042	7234	4633	8375	4916	5297	8848	7613	3381	6877	7362	5680
7037	3646	6326	4954	8148	2189	5547	9495	3447	8803	7921	5271	4459	10114	4889	3506	7481
11532	5219	10330	6005	9969	7525	6412	8511	6294	8316	7801	10107	6494	7014	5841	4590	7857
8311	3507	5911	2731	5772	9221	10856	4857	3982	4194	3355	6438	3444	3734	2666	3672	3355
4244	5476	2305	3950	1745	8128	9668	1673	4984	833	713	3314	4040	2325	4133	6103	878
5355	7390	7105	8598	7835	1979	1964	9081	7046	9545	9959	6235	8022	10352	8575	7159	9724
3338	6154	1831	4688	831	7661	8759	1434	5485	1082	1631	2925	4653	2636	4885	6819	1732
8075	1874	5273	1094	5936	7483	10798	5629	2413	4757	3627	5398	1791	4926	964	2179	3383
5537	4980	5634	5981	7240	693	4607	8776	4439	8480	8051	4547	5337	10084	5956	4975	7650
	8104	2815	7226	2557	5296	5513	3781	7033	4207	4959	3004	6784	5245	7434	8738	5000
8104		5498	1551	6843	5659	9088	7102	1088	6171	5009	5101	1518	6750	1401	693	4644
2815	5498		4418	1842	5869	8035	3219	4534	2905	2854	1094	4045	4460	4628	6215	2660
7226	1551	4418		5439	6667	10501	5541	1549	4627	3459	4381	714	5278	213	2154	3101
2557	6843	1842	5439		7269	7931	1542	6068	1673	2451	2876	5325	3001	5601	7528	2579
5296	5659	5869	6667	7269		3941	8829	5130	8724	8493	4817	6016	10283	6673	5619	8124
5513	9088	8035	10501	7931	3941		8422	8963	9275	10355	7558	9926	9022	10396	8658	10497
3781	7102	3219	5541	1542	8829	8422		6688	934	2085	4309	5706	1495	5706	7671	2454
7033	1088	4534	1549	6068	5130	8963	6688		5756	4662	4036	1016	6711	1541	1710	4242
4207	6171	2905	4627	1673	8724	9275	934	5756		1171	3937	4795	1603	4788	6756	1534
4959	5009	2854	3459	2451	8493	10355	2085	4662	1171		3769	3672	2231	3622	5590	439
3004	5101	1094	4381	2876	4817	7558	4309	4036	3937	3769		3836	5541	4574	5745	3489
6784	1518	4045	714	5325	6016	9926	5706	1016	4795	3672	3836		5691	832	2211	3263
5245	6750	4460	5278	3001	10283	9022	1495	6711	1603	2231	5541	5691		5382	7146	2659
7434	1401	4628	213	5601	6673	10396	5706	1541	4788	3622	4574	832	5382		1975	3235
8738	693	6215	2154	7528	5619	8658	7671	1710	6756	5590	5745	2211	7146	1975		5250
5000	4644	2660	3101	2579	8124	10497	2454	4242	1534	439	3489	3263	2659	3235	5250	
6084	2558	3268	1171	4306	6651	10544	4622	2056	3711	2576	3366	1083	4706	1380	3227	2189
8190	6395	7598	5772	6926	11254	4181	4770	7179	4796	4820	8586	6482	3294	5703	6244	5125
8022	854	5247	887	6326	6457	9934	6353	1474	5439	4273	5082	1243	5903	682	1317	3943
2392	6700	1525	5355	347	6963	7854	1885	5868	1926	2571	2547	5181	3322	5441	7394	2642
2678	6063	899	4782	959	6641	8186	2337	5199	2101	2408	1976	4591	3651	4993	6759	2353
4934	4959	4869	5710	6477	1152	5005	8039	4235	7720	7357	3784	5020	9324	5752	5132	6981
6710	5373	7235	6744	8767	1479	3761	10307	5238	10082	9630	6148	6246	11687	6671	5088	9097
3850	5556	4011	5938	5470	1863	5089	7035	4650	6858	6735	2983	5221	8423	6033	5842	6417
6793	8172	7271	7263	5527	10930	6998	4053	8792	4514	5094	8360	7914	2943	7251	8088	5504
7626	783	4895	772	6108	6120	9792	6306	1044	5385	4224	4657	850	6026	644	1429	3858
4829	5216	2834	3665	2300	8560	10173	1878	4883	966	205	3792	3870	2080	3828	5796	610
4708	10663	7475	11682	6714	5162	1595	6899	10279	7794	8946	7383	10974	7433	11791	10249	9228
3806	5361	1597	3918	1525	7414	9319	2097	4687	1418	1281	2599	3854	2998	4118	6032	1199
10869	3312	8795	4604	10021	5763	6802	9484	4270	8754	7698	8209	4803	8245	4396	2729	7443

Reykjavik, Iceland	Rio de Janeiro, Brazil	Rome, Italy	San Francisco, U.S.A.	Seattle, U.S.A.	Shanghai, China	Singapore, Singapore	Tokyo, Japan	Valparaiso, Chile	Vienna, Austria	Washington, D.C. U.S.A.	Wellington, New Zealand	Winnipeg, Canada	Zanzibar, Tanzania	
8678	8120	10475	4786	5222	5399	5850	4656	6267	10010	7066	2062	6283	9892	Apia
1777	4428	2125	4872	4501	7229	8326	7247	5678	2291	2667	11269	3389	5323	Azores Islands
4903	10768	5047	5902	5396	662	2774	1307	11774	4639	6922	6698	5907	5803	Beijing
1479	6114	734	5657	5041	5215	6166	5538	7795	328	4167	11265	4285	4309	Berlin
5191	8257	3843	8392	7741	3133	2429	4188	10037	3718	7988	7677	7644	2855	Bombay (Mumbai)
7099	1218	6929	6474	6913	12197	9864	11400	761	7368	5216	6260	6297	6421	Buenos Aires
5409	9376	4496	7809	7224	2112	1791	3186	10993	4259	8088	7042	7424	3859	Calcutta
7111	3769	5249	10241	10199	8059	6016	9071	4998	5671	7894	7019	9054	2346	Cape Town
3248	3040	2772	5921	5714	8443	8700	8589	4649	3147	3486	10363	4556	4635	Cape Verde Is.
2954	5296	4808	1858	1737	7053	9365	6303	5268	4694	597	8349	714	8358	Chicago
8631	9960	8190	7637	7619	3142	2075	3367	8961	7974	9923	3310	8684	6409	Darwin
3596	5871	5561	949	1021	6698	9063	5795	5452	5383	1494	7516	798	9921	Denver
2047	4775	1034	5936	5462	6646	7231	6988	6408	1386	3822	12060	4435	4103	Gibraltar
6031	10995	5768	6894	6471	772	1652	1796	11607	5429	8148	5853	7096	5414	Hong Kong (Xiang.)
6084	8190	8022	2392	2678	4934	6710	3850	6793	7626	4829	4708	3806	10869	Honolulu
2558	6395	854	6700	6063	4959	5373	5556	8172	783	5216	10663	5361	3312	Istanbul
3268	7598	5247	1525	899	4869	7235	4011	7271	4895	2834	7475	1597	8795	Juneau
1171	5772	887	5355	4782	5710	6744	5938	7263	772	3665	11682	3918	4604	London
4306	6296	6326	347	959	6477	8767	5470	5527	6108	2300	6714	1525	10021	Los Angeles
6651	11254	6457	6963	6641	1152	1479	1863	10930	6120	8560	5162	7414	5763	Manila
10544	8186	9934	7854	8186	5005	3761	5089	6998	9792	10173	1595	9319	6802	Melbourne
4622	4770	6353	1885	2337	8039	10307	7035	4053	6306	1878	6899	2097	9484	Mexico City
2056	7179	1474	5868	5199	4235	5238	4650	8792	1044	4883	10279	4687	4270	Moscow
3711	4796	5439	1926	2101	7720	10082	6858	4514	5385	966	7794	1418	8754	New Orleans
2576	4820	4273	2571	2408	7357	9630	6735	5094	4224	205	8946	1281	7698	New York
3366	8586	5082	2547	1976	3784	6148	2983	8360	4657	3792	7383	2599	8209	Nome
1083	6482	1243	5181	4591	5020	6246	5221	7914	859	3870	10974	3854	4803	Oslo
4706	3294	5903	3322	3651	9324	11687	8423	2943	6026	2080	7433	2998	8245	Panamá
1380	5703	682	5441	4993	5752	6671	6033	7251	644	3828	11791	4118	4396	Paris
3227	6244	1317	7394	6759	5132	5088	5842	8088	1429	5796	10249	6032	2729	Port Said
2189	5125	3943	2642	2353	6981	9097	6417	5504	3858	610	9228	1199	7443	Quebec
	6118	2044	4199	3614	5559	7160	5472	7225	1805	2800	10724	2804	5757	Reykjavik
6118		5684	6619	6891	11340	9774	11535	1855	6136	4797	7349	6010	5589	Rio de Janeiro
2044	5684		6240	5659	5677	6232	6124	7420	463	4435	11524	4803	3712	Rome
4199	6619	6240		678	6132	8479	5131	5876	5988	2442	6739	1504	9958	San Francisco
3614	6891	5639	678		5703	8057	4777	6230	5376	2329	7242	1150	9359	Seattle
5559	11340	5677	6132	5703		2377	1094	11650	5270	7442	6054	6350	5971	Shanghai
7160	9774	6232	8479	8057	2377		3304	10226	6036	9834	5292	8685	4480	Singapore
5472	11535	6124	5131	4777	1094	3304		10635	5679	6769	5760	5575	7040	Tokyo
7225	1855	7420	5876	6230	11650	10226	10635		7783	4977	5785	5931	7184	Valparaíso
1805	6136	463	5988	5376	5270	6036	5679	7783		4429	11278	4604	3983	Vienna
2800	4797	4435	2442	2329	7442	9834	6769	4977	4429		8745	1243	7884	Washington, D.C.
10724	7349	11524	6739	7242	6054	5292	5760	5785	11278	8745		8230	8122	Wellington
2804	6010	4803	1504	1150	6350	8685	5575	5931	4604	1243	8230		8416	Winnipeg
5757	5589	3712	9958	9359	5971	4480	7040	7184	3983	7884	8122	8416		Zanzibar

Travel Information

Entry requirements and travel advisories are subject to change. Travelers are advised to contact a travel agent, the State Department, a passport office, and/or the embassy of the destination for definitive travel information. In Islamic countries, when appearing in public, women should cover their arms, legs, and, in some places, their heads. Holidays for which a date is not given change from year to year; contact the country's embassy for exact dates.

Country	Argentina	Australia	Austria
Int'l Dialing Code	54	61	43
City Codes	Buenos Aires 1, Córdoba 51, La Plata 21, Mar Del Plata 23, Mendoza 61, Rosario 41, San Juan 64	Adelaide 8, Brisbane 7, Canberra 62, Darwin 89, Hobart 02, Melbourne 3, Perth 9, Sydney 2	Graz 316, Innsbruck 512, Linz 732, Salzburg 662, Wien (Vienna) 222
Consulate Phone	(202) 939-6400	(202) 797-3000	(202) 895-6700
Climate	Climate ranges from hot, subtropical lowlands of the north to cold and rainy in the south. Buenos Aires has warm humid summers, mild winters and no pronounced rainy season.	Arid to semiarid in the interior, west and south; temperate in the southeast and east; monsoon season is January to March in the north. Most of southern Australia has warm summers and mild winters.	Cold winters with frequent rain in the lowlands and snow in the mountains; cool summers with occasional showers.
Clothing	Lightweight cottons are advisable for the north; woolens are needed during the winters and year-round in the extreme south. Dress is more formal than in the U.S. Shorts are not universally acceptable.	Wear lightweight clothing year-round. In the temperate regions during the winter warmer clothes and an overcoat are required. Casual clothing is usually appropriate.	Clothing needs and tastes are about the same as the northeastern United States. Bring sweaters and light woolens for possible cool spells in the summer. Many restaurants in Vienna have dress codes.
Entry Requirements	Passport, visa	Passport, visa, ticket to leave, sufficient funds	Passport, ticket to leave
Holidays	New Year's Day, Jan. 1; Maundy Thursday; Good Friday; Labor Day, May 1; National Day, May 25; Flag Day, June 20; Independence Day, July 9; Anniversary of San Martin's Death, Aug. 17; Columbus Day, Oct. 12; Immaculate Conception, Dec. 8; Christmas Day, Dec. 25	New Year's Day, Jan. 1; Australia Day, late Jan.; Good Friday; Holy Saturday; Easter Monday; ANZAC Day, Apr. 25; Queen's Birthday, June; Christmas Day, Dec. 25; Boxing Day, Dec. 26; States also have separate public holidays.	New Year's Day, Jan. 1; Epiphany, Jan. 6; Easter Monday; Labor Day, May 1; Ascension Day; Whitmonday; Corpus Christi; Assumption Day, Aug. 15; National Day, Oct. 26; All Saints' Day, Nov. 1; Immaculate Conception, Dec. 8; Christmas Day, Dec. 25
Special Notes	Tapwater is safe. It is advisable to sterilize water outside of main cities. Dairy products, fruits, vegetables and meats are considered safe.		Alpine weather can change quickly and vary dramatically with elevation.

Country	Bahamas	Barbados	Belarus
Int'l Dialing Code	809	809	375
City Codes	809 is area code, dial 1 + 809	809 is area code, dial 1 + 809	Minsk 172, Mogil'ev 222
Consulate Phone	(202) 319-2660	(202) 939-9200	(202) 986-1604
Climate	Tropical marine. Warm and humid year-round with a summer rainy season. Hurricane season is from June to October.	Subtropical to tropical; rainy season is from June to October; hurricane season is from July to November.	Temperate; warm summers and cold winters. Rain heaviest in the summer; snow in winter.
Clothing	Lightweight clothing is worn year-round. Beachwear should be confined to resort areas. Daytime dress is casual, evening clothes are more formal.	Lightweight clothing is worn year-round; rainwear is needed for the rainy season. Casual clothes are usually acceptable. Beachwear is not worn in towns.	Lightweight clothing is appropriate for summer. In winter medium to heavy clothing is needed. Rainwear is advised throughout the year.
Entry Requirements	Passport; U. S. citizens must have proof of citizenship, ticket to leave	Passport, ticket to leave	Passport, visa, ticket to leave; letter of invitation is recommended
Holidays	New Year's Day, Jan. 1; Good Friday; Easter Monday; Whitmonday; Labor Day, early June; Independence Day, July 10; Emancipation Day, early Aug.; Discovery Day, Oct. 12; Christmas Day, Dec. 25; Boxing Day, Dec. 26	New Year's Day, Jan. 1; Errol Barrow Day, Jan 22; Good Friday; Easter Monday; Labor Day, May 1; Whitmonday; Kadooment Day; United Nations Day ; Independence Day, November 30; Christmas Day, Dec. 25; Boxing Day, Dec. 26	New Year's Day, Jan. 1; Orthodox Christmas, Jan.7; International Women's Day, Mar. 8; Labor Day, May 1; Victory Day, May 9; Independence Day, July 27; Day of Commemoration, Nov. 2; Catholic Christmas, Dec. 25
Special Notes	Water is potable but saline, and many people use bottled water. Local meat, seafood, poultry, fruits and vegetables are generally considered safe to eat.		Foreigners and foreign cars tend to be the targets of crime.

Belgium	Bermuda	Botswana	Brazil
32	809	267	55
Antwerpen 3, Brugge 50, Bruxelles 2, Charleroi 71, Gent 91, Liège 41, Namur 81	809 is area code, dial 1 + 809	Francistown 21, Gaborone 31, Serowe 43	Belém 91, Belo Horizonte 31, Brasília 61, Rio de Janeiro 21, Salvador 71, São Paulo 11
(202) 333-6900	(202) 462-1340	(202) 244-4990	(202) 745-2700
Mild winters with little snow; cool summers; rainy, humid, cloudy.	Subtropical; mild, humid; gales, winds are common during the frost-free but chilly winter. Hurricane season is from June to November.	Semiarid with hot summers. Frost may occur in winter.	In most of the country, days range from warm to hot; rainy season from November to February; cool winters in the extreme south; seasons are reversed from North America.
Clothing and shoe needs in Belgium are about the same as for the Pacific Northwest. Raincoat, umbrellas, and low-heeled, thick-soled walking shoes are necessary.	Warm-weather clothing is suitable April-November; moderately heavy clothing is needed during the winter. Swimwear should be worn only on the beach. Most restaurants have evening dress codes.	Lightweight clothing is worn most of the year. Spring clothing for cool evenings and winter months is recommended.	Spring or summer clothes are appropriate year-round. In tropical regions rainwear is advised.
Passport, ticket to leave, sufficient funds	Proof of citizenship, visa (for stays of more than 21 days), ticket to leave	Passport	Passport, visa, ticket to leave, sufficient funds, yellow fever and other inoculations are recommended
New Year's Day, Jan. 1; Easter Monday; Labor Day, May 1; Ascension Day; Whitmonday; National Day, July 21; Assumption Day, Aug. 15; All Saints' Day, Nov. 1; Armistice Day, Nov. 11; Christmas Day, Dec. 25	New Year's Day, Jan. 1; Good Friday; Bermuda Day, May 24; Queen's Birthday, June; Cup Match Day, late July; Labor Day, early Sept.; Remembrance Day, Nov. 11; Christmas Day, Dec. 25; Boxing Day, Dec. 26	New Year's Day, Jan. 1; Easter Monday; Ascension Day; President's Day, July 19; Independence Day, Sept. 30; Public Holiday, Oct. 1; Christmas Day, Dec. 25; Boxing Day, Dec. 26	New Year's Day, Jan. 1; Carnival, Feb./Mar.; Good Friday; Tiradentes Day, Apr. 21; Labor Day, May 1; Corpus Christi; Independence Day, Sept. 7; Our Lady of Aparecida, Oct. 12; All Souls' Day, Nov 2; Proclamation of the Republic, Nov. 15; Christmas Day, Dec. 25
Tapwater is potable.		Tapwater is potable in the major towns. Local foods, including fruits, vegetables, meats and dairy products, are generally considered safe to eat. Travel by automobile outside of major towns may be dangerous, especially at night.	All water should be regarded as potentially contaminated. Carefully prepared and thoroughly cooked foods are safe for consumption. Street crime is common in Brazil's larger cities and airports. There is tension between natives and developers.

14 Travel Information

Country	Bulgaria	Canada	Chile
Int'l Dialing Code	359		
City Codes	Kârdžali 361, Pazardžik 34, Plovdiv 32, Sofija 2, Varna 52		Concepción 41, San Bernardo 2, Santiago 2, Talcahuano 41, Valparaíso 32, Viña del Mar 32
Consulate Phone	(202) 387-7969	(202) 682-1740	(202) 785-1746
Climate	Cold, damp winters with considerable snowfall; hot, dry, summers.	Varies from temperate in the south to subarctic and arctic in the north.	Climate ranges from desert in the north to cold and damp in the south; summers are dry and hot with cool nights; winters are cold and rainy. Seasons are reversed from North America.
Clothing	Summer clothing should include sweaters for cool evenings. Warm clothing advisable for cold winters. Formal wear is seldom required.	Lightweight clothes for summer months with a sweater for cool evenings; heavy clothing for winter months. In coastal areas, rainwear is advisable.	Sweaters are useful for cool summer nights; a jacket or coat is needed in the winter. Rainwear is advised during the rainy season, especially in the south. Shorts should not be worn outside resort areas.
Entry Requirements	Passport, visa	Proof of citizenship, sufficient funds	Passport, ticket to leave
Holidays	New Year's Day, Jan. 1; Independence Day, Mar. 3; Labor Day, May 1; Education Day, May 24; Liberation Days, Sept. 9,10; Christmas, Dec. 24, 25	New Year's Day, Jan. 1; Good Friday; Easter Monday; Victoria Day; Canada Day, July 1; Labor Day; Thanksgiving; Remembrance Day, Nov. 11; Christmas Day, Dec. 25; Boxing Day, Dec. 26	New Year's Day, Jan. 1; Good Friday; Easter Saturday; Labor Day, May 1; Battle of Iquique, May 21; Corpus Christi; St. Peter's and Paul's Day; Assumption Day, Aug. 15; National Liberation Day, Sept. 11; Independence Day, Sept. 18; Armed Forces Day, Sept.19; Day of the Race, Oct. 12; All Saints' Day, Nov. 1; Immaculate Conception, Dec. 8; Christmas Day, Dec. 25
Special Notes	Tapwater is potable in the capital. Outside of main cities, use of bottled water is advised. Eating in larger restaurants is advised. There has been a recent rise in street crime. Insist on a pre-agreed taxi fare to avoid excessive overcharges.	Firearms are strictly controlled, especially handguns. Driving Under the Influence (DUI) of alchohol is a serious offense. A prior DUI conviction is grounds for exclusion from Canada. There is a strong separatist movement in Quebec.	All water may be contaminated and should be sterilized. Only well-cooked foods should be eaten, preferably when hot. Fruit should be peeled. There have been sporadic attacks against businesses and institutions identified with the United States.

China	Colombia	Costa Rica	Czech Republic
86	57	506	42
Beijing (Peking) 1, Fuzhou 591, Guangzhou (Canton) 20, Shanghai 21	Barranquilla 58, Cali 23, Cartagena 59, Cúcuta 70, Medellin 4, Santa Fe de Bogotá 1		Brno 5, Havirov 6994, Ostrova 69, Prague 2
(202) 328-2500	(202) 387-8338	(202) 234-2945	(202) 363-6315
Extremely diverse; tropical in the south to subarctic in the north.	Tropical along the coast and eastern plains; cooler in the highlands.	Tropical; hurricane and rainy season from May to November; dry season from December to April. Highland regions are cooler than coastal areas.	Cool, pleasant summers; cold, cloudy, humid winters.
In the north, lightweight clothing is required for the summer and heavy woolens for the harsh winters. In the south, tropical clothing is suitable for summer and spring-like clothing is worn in the winter. Clothing should be casual but conservative.	Knits and lightweight woolens are suitable in Bogotá. Tropical clothing is worn in the lowlands. Rainwear is recommended during the May to November rainy season.	Spring-weight clothing, with a sweater for cool evenings, is recommended. Beachwear should be confined to resorts. Rainwear is necessary during the rainy season.	Bring rainwear and light or heavy woolens depending on the season. Casual but conservative dress is appropriate.
Passport, visa, ticket to leave, sufficient funds	Passport, visa (for stays of more than 30 days), ticket to leave, inoculations recommended	Passport, ticket to leave, sufficient funds	Passport, visa (for stays of more than 30 days)
New Year's Day, Jan. 1; Chinese New Year; International Women's Day, Mar. 8; Labor Day, May 1; Army Day, Aug. 1; Teacher's Day, Sept. 9; National Day, Oct. 1	New Year's Day, Jan. 1; Epiphany, Jan. 6; St. Joseph's Day; Maundy Thursday; Good Friday; Labor Day, May 1; Ascension Day; Corpus Christi; Feast of the Sacred Heart; St. Peter's and Paul's Day; Independence Day, July 20; Battle of Boyaca, Aug. 7; Assumption Day; Day of the Race, Oct. 12; All Saints' Day, Nov. 1; Independence of Cartagena, Nov. 11; Immaculate Conception, Dec. 8; Christmas Day, Dec. 25	New Year's Day, Jan. 1; St. Joseph's Day, Mar. 19; Maundy Thursday; Good Friday; Anniversary of the Battle of Rivas, Apr. 11; Labor Day, May 1; Corpus Christi; St Peter's and Paul's Day; Annexation of Guanacaste, July 5; Our Lady of the Angels, Aug. 2; Assumption Day, Aug 15; Independence Day, Sept. 15; Columbus Day, Oct. 12; Abolition of the Armed Forces Day, Dec. 1; Immaculate Conception, Dec. 8; Christmas Day, Dec. 25	New Year's Day, Jan. 1; Easter Monday; Labor Day, May 1; Apostles St. Cyril and St. Methodius Day, July 5; Martyrdom of Jan Hus, July 6; Christmas Eve, Dec. 24; Christmas, Dec. 25; Boxing Day, Dec. 26
Use bottled water. Eat only well-cooked foods and peel fruit. Travel to Tibet or restricted areas requires advance permission. Tourists have been robbed in remote areas near Mt. Everest and the Nepal border. Tension between China and Taiwan has increased.	All water may be contaminated. Milk is unpasteurized, and only well-cooked and carefully prepared foods should be eaten. Violence, including bomb attacks and kidnapping, are serious problems. Travel by automobile can be dangerous due to road conditions.	Drinking water in major San Jose hotels and restaurants is purified; outside the capital drinking water should be purified. Crime is increasing and becoming more violent.	Tapwater is generally safe.

Country	Denmark	Egypt	Fiji
Int'l Dialing Code	45	20	679
City Codes		Al-Iskandarīyah (Alexandria) 3, Al-Qāhirah (Cairo) 2, Aswān 97, Asyūṭ 88, Ṭahṭa 40	
Consulate Phone	(202) 234-4300	(202) 895-5400	(202) 337-8320
Climate	Humid and overcast; mild, windy winters; cool, sunny summers.	Desert; hot, dry summers with moderate winters.	Tropical with high humidity; rainfall is abundant in Suva; little temperature variation; rainy season from December to April.
Clothing	Woolen clothes are worn most of the year. Lightweight clothes may be required in the summer. Winter requires heavy clothing.	Lightweight summer clothing is needed for the summer; light woolens for the winter and cool evenings. Casual dress is appropriate, but revealing clothing is not appreciated.	Lightweight clothing is appropriate; dress is generally casual. Swimwear should not be worn in towns.
Entry Requirements	Passport, ticket to leave	Passport, visa, ticket to leave; yellow fever and cholera inoculations recommended	Passport, ticket to leave, sufficient funds
Holidays	New Year's Day, Jan. 1; Thurs.-Mon. surrounding Easter; Prayer Day; Ascension Day; Whitmonday; Constitution Day, June 5; Christmas Day, Dec. 25; Boxing Day, Dec. 26	Union Day, Feb. 22; Ramadan and Id al-Fitr; Coptic Easter Monday; Id al-Adha; Labor Day, May 1; Islamic New Year; Evacuation Day, June 18; Revolution Day, July 23; Prophet's Birthday; Armed Forces Day, Oct. 6; Suez Day, Oct. 24; Leilat al-Meiraj; Victory Day, Dec.23	New Year's Day, Jan. 1; National Youth Day, Mar. 8; Good Friday; Holy Saturday; Easter Monday; Queen's Birthday, June; Constitution Day, July 22; Prophet's Birthday; Independence Day, Oct. 10; Diwali (Festival of Lights); Prince of Wales's Birthday; Christmas, Dec. 25; Boxing Day, Dec. 26
Special Notes		Water in Cairo and Alexandria is generally safe, but milk should be boiled. Eat only well-cooked foods and peel fruit. Islamic fundamentalists have attacked tourists in southern Egypt and in Cairo.	Drinking water is safe in all cities and major tourist resorts.

Finland	France	French Polynesia	Germany
358	33	689	49
Espoo 0, Helsinki 0, Tampere 31, Turku 21, Vantaa 0	Bordeaux 56, Grenoble 76, Lyon 7, Marseille 91, Nancy 8, Nice 93, Paris 1, Rouen 35, Tours 47		Berlin 30, Bonn 228, Dresden 351, Frankfurt am Main 69, Hamburg 40, München (Munich) 89
(202) 298-5800	(202) 944-6000	(202) 944-6000	(202) 298-4000
Cold winters; mild summers. Precipitation is year-round but light. Helsinki's winter climate is similar to Boston's.	Cool winters and mild summers inland; mild winters and hot summers along the Mediterranean. High mountain regions have highly variable climate with heavy snows in winter.	Tropical, but moderate. Hot and wet from November through February and cool and dry March through October.	Cool, cloudy, wet winters and summers; high relative humidity.
Warm outdoor clothing for winter and light woolens for summer are necessary. Rainwear is required year-round.	Casual clothing, light to medium in summer and medium in the cooler months is appropriate. At high elevations, heavy clothing may be necessary. Some restaurants and evening events require formal attire.	Lightweight clothing is worn throughout the year. Rainwear is advisable.	Germany is cooler than much of the United States, especially in summer. Lightweight summer clothing is seldom needed. Very warm clothing is needed in the winter.
Passport	Passport	Passport	Passport, ticket to leave, sufficient funds
New Year's Day, Jan. 1; Epiphany; Good Friday; Easter; Easter Monday; May Day Eve, Apr. 30; May Day, May 1; Ascension Day; Whitsunday; Whitmonday; Midsummer's Day; All Saints' Day; Independence Day, Dec. 6, Christmas Day, Dec. 25; Boxing Day, Dec. 26	New Year's Day, Jan. 1; Easter Monday; Labor Day, May 1; Liberation Day; Ascension Day; Whitmonday; Bastille Day, July 14; Assumption Day, Aug. 15; All Saints' Day, Nov. 1; Armistice Day, Nov. 11; Christmas Day, Dec. 25	New Year's Day, Jan. 1; Good Friday; Easter Monday; Labor Day; Liberation Day; Ascension Day; Whitmonday; Bastille Day, July 14; All Saints' Day, Nov. 1; Armistice Day, Nov. 11; Christmas, Dec. 25, 26	New Year's Day, Jan. 1; Good Friday; Easter Monday; Labor Day, May 1; Ascension Day; Whitmonday; Day of Unity, Oct. 3; All Saints' Day, Nov. 1; Christmas Day, Dec. 25; Boxing Day, Dec. 26.
Insects can be a hazard in the summer; repellent is necessary, especially in the north.		Water outside of main cities and towns may be contaminated, and sterilization is advised.	Tapwater is considered safe to drink.

Country	Greece	Guatemala	Hong Kong
Int'l Dialing Code	30	502	852
City Codes	Athínai (Athens) 1, Iráklion 81, Lárisa 41, Pátrai 61, Piraiévs 1, Thessaloníki 31	Guatemala 2, all other cities 9	
Consulate Phone	(202) 939-5800	(202) 745-4952	(202) 328-2500
Climate	Mild, wet winters; hot, dry, summers.	Hot and humid in the lowlands; cooler in the highlands. The rainy season is from June through October.	Cool, humid winters; hot, rainy summers. Spring and autumn are warm with occasional showers. A risk of typhoons exists from July to September.
Clothing	Lightweight clothing from May through September; woolens from October through April.	Spring or summer-weight clothing is needed most of the year; woolens are practical from November through February.	Cottons and rainwear are advisable for the summer; warmer clothes are needed for the winter. Sports clothes are good for daytime, evening clothes are more formal.
Entry Requirements	Passport, sufficient funds	Passport, visa or tourist card, ticket to leave, inoculations recommended	Passport, visa (for stays of more than 30 days), ticket to leave
Holidays	New Year's Day, Jan. 1; Epiphany, Jan. 6; Clean Monday, Feb. 26; Independence Day, Mar. 25; Good Friday; Easter Monday; Labor Day, May 1; Whitmonday; Assumption Day, Aug. 15; Ochi Day, Oct. 28; Christmas Day, Dec. 25; Boxing Day, Dec. 26	New Year's Day, Jan. 1; Epiphany, Jan. 6; Maundy Thursday; Good Friday; Holy Saturday; Labor Day, May 1; Army Day, June 30; Assumption Day, Aug. 15; Independence Day, Sept. 15; Columbus Day, Oct. 12; Revolution Day, Oct. 20; All Saints' Day, Nov. 1; Christmas Eve Day, Dec 24; Christmas, Dec. 25; New Year's Eve, Dec. 31	New Year's Day, Jan. 1; Chinese New Year, Jan. or Feb.; Ching Ming Festival; Good Friday; Easter Monday; Dragon Boat Festival; Liberation Day, Aug. 26; Mid-Autumn Festival; Chung Yeung Festival; Christmas Day, Dec. 25; Boxing Day, Dec. 26
Special Notes	Tapwater is safe though it may cause mild abdominal distress. Local foods are considered safe to eat. Driving defensively is strongly advised.	Tapwater is not potable, and fruits and vegetables should be prepared carefully. Eat only well-cooked foods; fruit should be peeled. Children should be approached cautiously due to rumors of abduction of children by foreigners.	Water direct from government mains is potable. On July 1, 1997 Hong Kong was returned to the People's Republic of China.

Hungary	India	Indonesia	Ireland
36	91	62	353
Budapest 1, Debrecen 52, Győr 96, Miskolc 46, Székesfehérvár 22	Ahmadābād 79, Bangalore 80, Calcutta 33, Chennai 44, Hyderābād 40, Mumbai (Bombay) 22, New Delhi 11	Bandung 22, Jakarta 21, Medan 61, Semarang 24, Surabaya 31	Cork 21, Dublin 1, Galway 91, Waterford 51
(202) 362-6730	(202) 939-7000	(202) 775-5200	(202) 462-3939
Cold, cloudy, humid winters; warm, pleasant summers. Spring and autumn are mild.	Varies from tropical monsoon in the south to temperate in the north. Monsoon occurs between June and September. In the mountains, weather conditions can change rapidly. Waterproof clothing is necessary.	Tropical; hot, humid; more moderate in the highlands; rainy season from November to April.	Humid and overcast; mild winters; cool summers.
Lightweight clothing is needed for the summer and heavy woolens for the winter.	Summer clothing is suitable year-round in the south. In the north, lightweight woolens are necessary from mid-December to mid-February. Women should wear modest, loose-fitting clothing.	Tropical; hot, humid; more moderate in the highlands; rainy season from November to April.	Medium to heavy-weight clothing is worn most of the year. Rainwear is advisable.
Passport, sufficient funds	Passport, visa, sufficient funds; inoculations recommended	Passport, visa (for stays of more than 60 days), ticket to leave, sufficient funds; inoculations recommended	Passport, ticket to leave
New Year's Day, Jan. 1; National (Liberation) Day, Apr. 4; Easter Monday; Labor Day, May 1; Constitution Day, Aug. 20; Proclamation of the Republic, Oct. 23; Christmas Day, Dec. 25; Boxing Day, Dec. 26	Republic Day, Jan. 26; Holi; Independence Day, Aug. 15; Dashara; Mahatma Gandhi's Birthday, Oct. 2; Diwali; Christmas Day, Dec. 25; Boxing Day, Dec. 26	New Year's Day, Jan. 1; Good Friday; Ramadan and Id al-Fitr; Id al-Adha; Ascension Day; Islamic New Year; Independence Day, Aug. 17; Prophet's Birthday; Ascension of the Prophet; Christmas Day, Dec. 25	New Year's Day, Jan. 1; St. Patrick's Day, Mar. 17; Good Friday; Easter Monday; Bank Holiday, early June; Bank Holiday, early August; Bank Holiday, late October; Christmas Day, Dec. 25; St. Stephen's Day, Dec. 26
Tapwater is relatively safe to drink, and bottled water is available. Avoid unpasteurized milk and food products that lack preservatives.	Tapwater is unsafe throughout India. In hotels and restaurants, drink only bottled or carbonated water and avoid ice cubes. Eating foods sold by street vendors can be risky. Travel to Kashmir is not advised. Sectarian and ethnic violence is increasing.	Water and milk should be boiled before use. Eat only well-cooked foods, preferably served hot. Fruit should be peeled. Civil unrest in North Sumatra and East Timor make travel to these areas potentially dangerous.	

Country	Israel	Italy	Jamaica
Int'l Dialing Code	972	39	809
City Codes	Hefa (Haifa) 4, Holon 3, Ramat Gan 3, Tel Aviv-Yafo 3, Yerushalayim (Jerusalem) 2	Bologna 51, Firenze (Florence) 55, Genova (Genoa) 10, Milano (Milan) 2, Napoli (Naples) 81, Palermo 91, Roma (Rome) 6, Venezia (Venice) 41	809 is area code, dial 1 + 809
Consulate Phone	(202) 364-5500	(202) 328-5500	(202) 452-0660
Climate	Temperate; hot and dry in desert areas; cooler and more rainy December through March.	Predominantly hot, dry summers and cool, wet winters; alpine in the far north; winter in the south is warmer and drier than in the north.	Tropical; hot, humid; temperatures are more moderate in the interior highlands. Hurricane season is from June to November.
Clothing	Clothing and shoe needs are about the same as for the American Southwest. Dress at religious sites should be appropriately modest.	Woolens and sweaters are practical most of the year; cottons are recommended for the hot summers.	Summer clothes are suitable year-round. The evenings can be chilly, especially from November to March, and light wraps or sweaters are recommended. Dress is informal, but swimsuits should be worn only at the beach or poolside.
Entry Requirements	Passport, ticket to leave, sufficient funds	Passport, sufficient funds	Proof of citizenship, ticket to leave, sufficient funds
Holidays	Purim; Passover; Independence Day, April 24; Yom Kippur; Rosh Hashana; Tabernacles; Hanukka; Succot; Simhat Torah	New Year's Day, Jan. 1; Epiphany, Jan. 6; Easter Monday; Liberation Day, Apr. 25; Labor Day, May 1; Anniversary of the Republic, June 2; Assumption Day, Aug. 15; All Saints' Day, Nov. 1; National Unity Day, Nov. 5; Immaculate Conception, Dec. 8; Christmas Day, Dec. 25; St. Stephen's Day, Dec. 26	New Year's Day, Jan. 1; Ash Wednesday; Good Friday; Easter Monday; Labor Day, May 23; Independence Day, early August; National Heroes' Day, late Oct.; Christmas Day, Dec. 25; Boxing Day, Dec. 26
Special Notes	Tapwater is generally potable. Outside of urban areas, water should be sterilized. Terrorist attacks continue in Israel, especially along the Lebanese border.	Tapwater is safe. Local meat, fruit, vegetables, and seafood are considered safe to eat.	Municipal water supplies are potable. Fruits and vegetables are safe. Crime is a serious problem in Kingston. Nighttime travel is discouraged.

Japan	Kazakhstan	Kenya	Korea, South
81	7	254	82
Kawasaki 44, Kyōto 75, Nagoya 52, Naha 988, Ōsaka 6, Sapporo 11, Tōkyō 3, Yokohama 45	Almaty 3272, Cimkent 325, Guryev (Atyraū) 312, Petropaul 315	Kisumu 35, Mombasa 11, Nairobi 2, Nakuru 37	Inch'ŏn 32, Kwangju 62, Pusan 51, Sŏul (Seoul) 2, Taegu 53
(202) 939-6700	(202) 244-4305	(202) 387-6101	(202) 939-5600
Varies from tropical in the south to cool temperate in the north. Typhoon season is September and October.	Arid to semiarid; cold winters and hot summers.	Varies from tropical along the coast to arid in the interior. Rainy seasons are from March to June and from October to December.	Temperate, four season climate, with rainfall heavier in summer than winter.
Lightweight clothing is worn in the summer throughout the country. Medium to heavy-weight clothing is needed for the winter. Very heavy clothing is needed for the mountains.	Shorts are not acceptable except for sports. Heavy clothing is needed in winter; in summer, light clothing in the daytime and warmer clothing at night.	Light and medium weight clothing is worn most of the year. Sweaters and light raincoats are needed during the rainy seasons. Some restaurants have evening dress codes.	Clothing requirements are similar to those of the eastern U.S. Dress is more conservative than in the U.S.
Passport, ticket to leave	Passport, visa (requires letter of invitation), ticket to leave	Passport, visa, ticket to leave; cholera and other inoculations recommended	Passport, ticket to leave
New Year's Day Jan. 1; Coming of Age Day, Jan. 15; National Foundation Day, Feb. 11; Vernal Equinox Day, Mar. 21; Constitution Day, May 3; Children's Day, May 5; Respect for the Aged Day, Sept. 15; Autumnal Equinox Day, Sept.; Health and Sports Day, Oct. 10; Culture Day, Nov. 3; Labor Thanksgiving Day, Nov. 23; Emperor's Birthday, Dec. 23	New Year, Jan. 1; Constitution Day, Jan. 28; International Women's Day, Mar. 8; Kazakh New Year, Mar. 22; Solidarity Day, May 1; Victory Day, May 9; State Sovereignty Day, October 25; New Year, Dec. 31	New Year's Day, Jan. 1; Ramadan and Id al-Fitr; Good Friday; Easter Monday; Labor Day, May 1; Id al-Adha; Madaraka Day, June 1; Kenyatta Day, Oct. 20; Independence Day, Dec. 12; Christmas Day, Dec. 25; Boxing Day, Dec. 26	New Year, Jan. 1-3; Lunar New Year, Jan. or Feb.; Independence Day, Mar. 1; Buddha's Birthday, May; Memorial Day, June 6; Constitution Day, July 17; Liberation Day, Aug. 15; Chusok (Thanksgiving), Aug. or Sept.; Armed Forces Day, Oct. 1; Foundation Day, Oct. 3; Christmas Day, Dec. 25
	All water should be considered contaminated. Eat only well-cooked foods, preferably hot, and fruit should be peeled. Common street crime has increased and become violent more frequently. Travel at night can be dangerous as robbers congregate near hotels.	Avoid tapwater outside the capital. Local meat, vegetables and fruits are considered safe to eat. Anti-malarial drugs are recommended. Street crime against tourists is increasing. The Kenyan mail system can be unreliable.	Outside of the major hotels, water is generally not potable. Milk is unpasteurized and should be boiled. Eat only well-cooked foods. Fruit should be peeled. Several shooting incidents have occurred recently along the demilitarized zone.

Country	Luxembourg	Malaysia	Malta
Int'l Dialing Code	352	60	356
City Codes		Ipoh 5, Johor Baharu 7, Kajang 3, Kuala Lumpur 3, Seremban 6	
Consulate Phone	(202) 265-4171	(202) 328-2700	(202) 462-3612
Climate	Mild winters; cool summers. Rain falls in all seasons.	Tropical; hot summers and winters; heavy summer rainfall, moderate winter rainfall. Rainy seasons differ on east and west coasts due to monsoon winds.	Mild, rainy winters; hot, dry summers.
Clothing	Fall and light winter clothing is worn. Some restaurants have evening dress codes. Rainwear is advisable.	Lightweight clothing is suitable for the tropical climate, except in the highland resort areas. Rainwear is advisable year-round.	City casual dress is appropriate. Lightweight apparel for the summer and woolens for the winter are required. Modest dress is required when visiting religious sites.
Entry Requirements	Passport, ticket to leave, sufficient funds	Passport, ticket to leave, sufficient funds; inoculations recommended	Passport, ticket to leave
Holidays	New Year's Day, Jan. 1; Easter Monday; Labor Day, May 1; Ascension Day; Whitmonday; National Day, June 23; Assumption Day, Aug. 15; All Saints' Day, Nov. 1; Christmas Day, Dec. 25; St. Stephen's Day, Dec. 26	Ramadan and Id al-Fitr; Chinese New Year, Jan. or Feb.; Labor Day, May 1; Wesak Day, May 30; Monarch's Day, June 1; Id al-Adha; National Day, Aug. 31; Prophet's Birthday; Diwali; Christmas, Dec. 25	New Year's Day, Jan. 1; St. Paul's Shipwreck, Feb. 10; St. Joseph, Mar. 19; Freedom Day, Mar. 31; Good Friday; Easter Monday; St. Joseph the Worker and May Day, May 1; 1919 Memorial, June 7; Assumption Day, Aug. 15; Our Lady of Victories, Sept. 8; Independence Day, Sept, 21; Immaculate Conception, Dec. 8; Republic Day, Dec 13; Christmas, Dec. 25
Special Notes	Tapwater and local foods are considered safe for consumption.	All water should be regarded as being potentially contaminated. Milk is unpasteurized. Eat only well-cooked foods. Fruit should be peeled. Credit card fraud is a serious problem.	Tapwater is very saline; bottled water is advised and available.

Martinique	Mauritius	Mexico	Morocco
596	230	52	212
		Acapulco 74, Cancún 988, Chihuahua 14, Ciudad de México (Mexico City) 5, Monterrey 83, Puebla 22, Tijuana 66	Agadir 88, Casablanca 2, Fes 5, Marrakech 4, Oujda 668, Rabat 7, Tanger 99
(202) 944-6000	(202) 244-1491	(202) 728-1600	(202) 462-7979
Tropical; hurricane and rainy season is from June to November.	Warm winter rainy season; hot, humid summers. Seasons are reversed from those in North America.	Varies from tropical to desert; cooler at higher elevations. Guadalajara and Mexico City are pleasant year-round. Monterrey, the Yucatan Peninsula, and desert areas are very hot in the summer.	Mild winters; hot summers; moderate winter rainfall along the coast; interior dry all year; wide daily temperature variations. Snow in the mountains in winter.
Lightweight clothing and rainwear are advisable. Some restaurants have evening dress codes.	Lightweight cottons are worn with a sweater for cooler evenings. Woolens are needed for winter months.	Wear tropical clothing in desert areas and lowlands. In Mexico City and other mountainous areas, medium-weight clothing is comfortable. Shorts are worn only on the beaches.	Wear clothing suitable for the eastern central U.S., but more conservative. Bring a jacket or sweater for cool evenings. Swimsuits and shorts should be confined to the beach or poolside.
Passport, ticket to leave	Passport, ticket to leave	Proof of citizenship, business pass or tourist card	Passport, ticket to leave, sufficient funds
New Year's Day, Jan. 1; Carnival, Feb.; Ash Wednesday; Good Friday; Easter Monday; Labor Day, May 1; Victory Day, May 8; Ascension Day; Whitmonday; National Day, July 14; Schoelcher Day, July 21; Assumption Day, Aug. 15; All Saints' Day, Nov. 1; Armistice Day, Nov. 11; Christmas Day, Dec. 25	New Year, Jan. 1, 2; Chinese Spring Festival; Thaipoosam Cavadee; Maha Shivaratri; Independence Day, Mar. 12; Ougadi; Ramadan and Id al-Fitr; Easter Monday; Labor Day, May 1; Assumption Day, Aug. 15; Ganesh Chaturthi, Sept. 14; Diwali; All Saints' Day, Nov. 1; Christmas Day, Dec. 25	New Year's Day, Jan. 1; Constitution Day, Feb. 5; Birthday of Benito Juarez, Mar. 21; Maundy Thursday; Good Friday; Holy Saturday; Labor Day, May 1; Battle of Puebla, May 5; Sept. 1; Independence Day, Sept. 16; Columbus Day, Oct. 12; All Saints' Day, Nov. 1; All Souls' Day, Nov. 2; Revolution Anniversary, Nov. 20; Our Lady of Guadalupe, Dec. 12; Christmas Day, Dec. 25	New Year's Day, Jan. 1; Prophet's Ascension; Ramadan and Id al-Fitr; Feast of the Throne, Mar. 3; Labor Day, May 1; Id al-Adha; Islamic New Year; Ashurah; Sahara Annexation Day, Aug. 14; Prophet's Birthday; Green March Day, Nov. 6; Independence Day, Nov. 16
Tapwater is generally safe. Outside main cities water should be sterilized.	Drinking water and milk should be sterilized. Avoid uncooked vegetables. Fruit should be peeled.	Tapwater may not be safe. Cooked food is safe to eat; raw vegetables often are not. Fruit should be peeled. Travel after dark is not advised due to bandit and rebel activity. Caution is advised for daytime travel. Chiapas remains an area of tension.	When outside the large cities and resorts, carry water purification tablets or a supply of purified drinking water. Eat only carefully prepared foods, preferably served hot. Access to Western Sahara is restricted. Tourists are targeted by criminals.

Country	Netherlands	New Zealand	Norway
Int'l Dialing Code	31	64	47
City Codes	Amsterdam 20, Rotterdam 10, 's-Gravenhage (The Hague) 70, Utrecht 30	Auckland 9, Christchurch 3, Dunedin 24, Hamilton 71, Wellington 4	Bergen 5, Stavanger 4, Trondheim 7
Consulate Phone	(202) 244-5300	(202) 328-4800	(202) 333-6000
Climate	Mild winters, cool summers. Rainy year-round.	Temperate; wet, windy, cool; warm summers; mild winters; seasons are reversed from North America.	Temperate along coast, colder in interior; rainy year-round on west coast.
Clothing	Clothing needs are similar to those of the U.S. Pacific Northwest. Some restaurants have evening dress codes. Rainwear is advisable all year.	Warm clothing is comfortable most of the year. Raincoats are essential.	Lightweight clothing and light woolens are worn in the summer, and heavy clothing in the winter. Rainwear is advisable all year.
Entry Requirements	Passport	Passport, ticket to leave, sufficient funds	Passport
Holidays	New Year's Day, Jan. 1; Good Friday; Easter Monday; Queen's Birthday, Apr. 30; Liberation Day, May 5; Ascension Day; Whitmonday; Christmas Day, Dec. 25; Boxing Day, Dec. 26	New Year, Jan. 1, 2; New Zealand Day, Feb. 6; Good Friday; Easter Monday; ANZAC Day, Apr. 25; Queen's Birthday, June; Labor Day, late Oct.; Christmas Day, Dec. 25; Boxing Day, Dec. 26	New Year's Day, Jan. 1; Maundy Thursday; Good Friday; Easter Monday; May Day, May 1; Constitution Day, May 17; Ascension Day; Whitmonday; Christmas Day, Dec. 25; Boxing Day, Dec. 26
Special Notes			Because of narrow, winding mountain roads, driving conditions can be hazardous.

Pakistan	Peru	Philippines	Poland
92	51	63	48
Faisalabad 411, Hyderābād 221, Islāmābād 51, Karāchi 21, Lahore 42, Multān 61	Arequipa 54, Callao 14, Chiclayo 74, Chimbote 44, Cuzco 84, Lima 14, Trujillo 44	Bacolod 34, Baguio 74, Cebu 32, Davao 82, Iloilo 33, Manila 2	Gdańsk 58, Katowice 32, Łódź 42, Poznań 61, Kraków 12, Warszawa (Warsaw) 22
(202) 939-6200	(202) 833-9860	(202) 467-9300	(202) 234-3800
Mostly hot, dry, desert; temperate in the northwest; arctic in the mountains of the north; monsoon season during July and August.	Varies from tropical in the east to dry desert in the west; winters are damp; seasons are reversed from those in North America.	Hot and humid; cooler in mountainous areas. Typhoons occasionally occur from June through September.	Cold, cloudy, moderately severe winters with frequent precipitation; mild summers with showers and thundershowers.
Lightweight clothing for most of the year; medium weight clothing for the winter, with woolens needed in the north. Women should dress conservatively.	Medium-weight clothing is suitable in the winter; in summer, wear lightweight clothing. Fashions are similar to those in the U.S., but shorts should be worn only in resort areas.	Cotton and other lightweight clothing is worn all year. If traveling to the popular mountain resorts in northern Luzon, light sweaters are appropriate. Some restaurants have evening dress codes.	Spring-weight clothing is worn in the summer and heavy clothing in the winter. Rainwear is advisable throughout the year.
Passport, visa, ticket to leave	Passport, business visa, ticket to leave; inoculations recommended	Passport, ticket to leave, sufficient funds	Passport
Ramadan and Id al-Fitr; Pakistan Day, Mar. 23; Labor Day, May 1; Id al-Adha; Islamic New Year; Ashoura; Prophet's Birthday; Independence Day, Aug. 14; Defense Day, Sept. 6; Anniversary of the Death of Quaid-i-Azam, Sept. 11; Dr. Allama Muhammad Iqbal's Birthday, Nov. 9; Birthday of Quaid-i-Azam, Christmas, Dec. 25	New Year's Day, Jan. 1; Maundy Thursday; Good Friday; Labor Day, May 1; St. Peter's and St. Paul's Day, June 29; Independence Days, July 28, 29; Saint Rose of Lima, Aug. 30; National Dignity Day, early Oct.; All Saints' Day, Nov. 1; Immaculate Conception, Dec. 8; Christmas Day, Dec. 25	New Year's Day, Jan. 1; Freedom Day, Feb. 25; Maundy Thursday; Good Friday; Labor Day, May 1; Kagatingan, May 6; Independence Day, June 12; Philippine-American Friendship Day, July 4; Barangay; National Thanksgiving Day, Sept. 21; All Saints' Day, Nov. 1; Bonifacio Day, Nov. 30; Christmas Day, Dec. 25; Rizal Day, Dec. 30	New Year's Day, Jan. 1; Easter Monday; Labor Day, May 1; Constitution Day, May 3; Victory Day, May 9; Corpus Christi; Assumption, Aug. 15; All Saints' Day, Nov. 1; Independence Day, Nov 11; Christmas Day, Dec. 25; Boxing Day, Dec. 26
Travel to many areas outside Karachi is dangerous. Armed battles between factions occur and police and foreigners are targeted. All water may be contaminated. Eat only well-cooked foods. Peel all fruit.	Although Lima's tapwater is treated, many people drink bottled water, and elsewhere it should be sterilized. Milk is unpasteurized and should be boiled. Do not eat uncooked fruits or vegetables. Sporadic terrorist attacks against the government continue.	The Manila water supply is generally safe. Untreated water should not be drunk outside the city. Eat only fruits that can be peeled and avoid fresh vegetables unless cleaned with safe water. Guerrilla activity may make travel in some regions dangerous.	Tapwater is treated and considered safe but may cause minor abdominal upsets. Bottled water is available. Roads are narrow, poorly lit and in need of repair. Driving after dark is hazardous.

Country	Portugal	Puerto Rico	Romania
Int'l Dialing Code	351		40
City Codes	Coimbra 39, Lisboa (Lisbon) 1, Porto 2, Setúbal 65		Braşov 21, Bucureşti (Bucharest) 1, Cluj-Napoca 951, Constanţa 916, Iaşi 81, Timi şoara 61
Consulate Phone	(202) 328-8610		(202) 232-4747
Climate	Mild, damp winters; hot, dry summers; climate is more moderate along the coast.	Warm and tropical, little seasonal temperature variation; hurricane season is from July to November.	Temperate; cold, cloudy winters with frequent snow and fog; sunny summers with frequent showers and thunder-storms.
Clothing	Wear summer clothing during the temperate sunny days and cool nights. Fall-weight clothing and a topcoat or warm raincoat are appropriate for winter. A rain hat or umbrella is recommended. Swimsuits should be confined to the beach.	Lightweight clothing is worn throughout the year, with a sweater or jacket for cooler evenings. Some restaurants have evening dress codes.	Dress is conservative but casual wear is acceptable. Lightweight clothing is worn in the summer. Warm clothing is needed in the winter and throughout the year in the highlands.
Entry Requirements	Passport, visa (for stays of more than 60 days)	Proof of citizenship, ticket to leave	Passport, visa (for stays of more than 30 days), ticket to leave, sufficient funds
Holidays	New Year's Day, Jan. 1; Shrove Tuesday; Good Friday; Anniversary of the Revolution, Apr. 25; Labor Day, May 1; Portugal Day, June 10; Corpus Christi; Assumption Day, Aug. 15; Republic Day, Oct. 5; All Saints' Day, Nov. 1; Independence Day, Dec. 1; Immaculate Conception, Dec. 8; Christmas Day, Dec. 25.	New Year's Day, Jan. 1; Epiphany, Jan. 6; De Hostos' Birthday, Jan. 11; Martin Luther King's Birthday, Jan. 15; Presidents' Day, Feb.; Emancipation Day, Mar. 22; De Diego's Birthday, Apr. 16; Memorial Day, late May; Independence Day, July 4; Muñoz Rivera's Birthday, July 17; Constitution Day, July 25; Barbosa's Birthday, July 27; Labor Day, early Sept.; Columbus Day, Oct.; Veterans Day, Nov. 11; Discovery of Puerto Rico, Nov. 19; Thanksgiving, late Nov.; Christmas Day, Dec. 25	New Year, Jan. 1, 2; Good Friday; Easter Monday; Labor Day, May 1, 2; National Day, Dec. 1; Christmas, Dec. 25
Special Notes	Tapwater is potable year-round in large cities, and in outlying areas during rainy seasons. Bottled water is available. Outside of main cities, water should be treated or boiled.	Tapwater is considered safe to drink.	Tapwater is treated and relatively safe. Bottled water is available. Street crime against tourists is a growing problem.

Russia	Saudi Arabia	Singapore	South Africa
7	966	65	27
Magadan 413, Moskva (Moscow) 095, St. Petersburg 812	Ad-Dammān 3, Al-Madīnah 4, Ar-Riyāḍ (Riyadh) 1, Jiddah 2, Makkah (Mecca) 2		Bloemfontein 51, Cape Town 21, Durban 31, Johannesburg 11, Port Elizabeth 41, Pretoria 12
(202) 939-8918	(202) 342-3800	(202) 537-3100	(202) 232-4400
Mostly temperate to arctic continental; winters vary from cool along the Black Sea to frigid in Siberia; summers vary from hot in the south to cool along the Arctic coast.	Dry desert with hot days and cool nights. Winter months in the interior can be quite cool.	Tropical; hot, humid, rainy.	Mostly semiarid; subtropical along coast; sunny days, cool nights. Seasons are reversed from those in North America.
Clothing requirements are as varied as in the United States, although the weather tends to be cooler. Public buildings, hotels and homes are well-heated. Hot weather occurs from June through August.	Lightweight clothing is essential for the hot climate. However, warmer clothing is recommended during the winter months in the interior. The coastal areas are more humid than the interior. Both men and women should dress conservatively.	Light cotton clothing is worn throughout the year. An umbrella is needed. Some restaurants have evening dress codes.	Clothing suitable for central and southern California is appropriate for South Africa's mild climate. Many restaurants have evening dress codes.
Passport, visa, ticket to leave	Passport, visa, ticket to leave, cholera inoculation; sponsorship by a Saudi citizen or employer required	Passport, ticket to leave, sufficient funds	Passport, ticket to leave, sufficient funds; cholera inoculation recommended
New Year's Day, Jan 1; International Women's Day, Mar. 8; Labor Day May 1, 2; Victory Day, May 9; Constitution Day, Oct. 7; Revolution Day, Nov 7, 8	Ramadan and Id al-Fitr; Id al-Adha; Hijra; Muharram; Ashoura; Prophet's Birthday, Ascension of the Prophet	New Year's Day, Jan. 1; Chinese New Year, Jan. or Feb.; Ramadan and Id al-Fitr; Good Friday; Id al-Adha; Labor Day, May 1; Wesak Day, May; National Day, Aug. 9; Diwali; Christmas Day, Dec. 25	New Year's Day, Jan. 1; Human Rights Day, Mar. 21; Good Friday; Easter Monday; Freedom Day, Apr. 27; Worker's Day, May 1; Youth Day, June 16; National Women's Day, Aug. 9; Heritage Day, Sept. 24; Kruger Day, Oct. 10; Reconciliation Day, Dec. 16; Christmas Day, Dec. 25; Boxing Day, Dec. 26
Avoid tapwater, especially in St. Petersburg, and drink bottled water. Avoid cold foods, such as salads. Travel to the Caucasus region is extremely dangerous due to armed conflict and political tensions. Terrorist activity is also possible.	All water should be considered potentially contaminated. Eat only well-cooked meals, preferably while hot. Fruit should be peeled. Women should be especially conscious of behavior and customs because religious police enforce Islamic standards.	Tapwater is considered relatively safe, and bottled water is available. There are strict penalties for offenses, such as jaywalking or chewing gum, which are considered minor elsewhere.	Drinking water is generally safe in urban areas but should be sterilized elsewhere. Avoid bathing in lakes or streams. Antimalarial pills are recommended in rural areas. Sporadic political violence occurs and avoidance of demonstrations is advised.

Country	Spain	Sweden	Switzerland
Int'l Dialing Code	34	46	41
City Codes	Barcelona 3, Bilbao 4, Granada 58, Madrid 1, Sevilla 54, Valencia 6	Göteborg 31, Helsingborg 42, Malmö 40, Norrköping 11, Stockholm 8, Uppsala 18, Västerås 21	Basel 61, Bern 31, Genève 22, Lausanne 21, Lucerne 41, Zürich 1
Consulate Phone	(202) 728-2330	(202) 467-2600	(202) 745-7900
Climate	Interior has hot, clear summers and cold winters; coast has moderate, cloudy summers and cool winters.	Temperate in the south with cold, cloudy winters and cool, partly cloudy summers; subarctic in the north	Varies with altitude; cold, cloudy, snowy winters; cool to warm, cloudy, humid summers with occasional showers.
Clothing	Light- or medium-weight clothing is suitable, depending on the season. Slacks, but not shorts, are worn in public. Sweaters and raincoats are advisable.	Lightweight clothing is worn in the summer, with heavy clothing for winter.	Light woolens may be worn in the summer, and heavy clothing in the winter. Rainwear is recommended.
Entry Requirements	Passport, ticket to leave, sufficient funds	Passport	Passport, ticket to leave, sufficient funds
Holidays	New Year's Day, Jan. 1; Epiphany, Jan. 6; St. Joseph's Day, Mar. 19; Good Friday; St. Joseph the Workman, May 1; Corpus Christi; St. John's Day, June 24; St. James' Day, July 25; Assumption Day, Aug. 15; National Day, Oct. 12; All Saints' Day, Nov. 1; Constitution Day, Dec. 6; Immaculate Conception, Dec. 8; Christmas Day, Dec. 25	New Year's Day, Jan. 1; Good Friday; Easter Monday; May Day, May 1; Ascension Day; Whitmonday; Midsummer's Day, late June; All Saints' Day, early November; Christmas Day, Dec. 25; St. Stephen's Day, Dec. 26	New Year, Jan. 1, 2; Good Friday; Easter Monday; Whitmonday; Labor Day, May 1; Ascension Day; National Day, Aug. 1; Christmas Day, Dec. 25; St. Stephen's Day, Dec. 26
Special Notes	Water from mains is considered relatively safe. Use bottled water outside of main cities. Local meats, seafood, vegetables and fruits are considered safe to eat. In summer 1996 several small bombs exploded in areas frequented by tourists.		

Taiwan	Tanzania	Thailand	Trinidad and Tobago
886	255	66	809
Kaohsiung 7, T'aichung 4, T'ainan 6, T'aipei 2	Dar es Salaam 51, Dodoma 61, Mwanza 68, Tanga 53	Chiang Mai 53, Krung Thep (Bangkok) 2, Nakhon Sawan 56	809 is area code, dial 1 + 809
(202) 895-1800	(202) 939-6125	(202) 483-7200	(202) 467-6490
Chilly, damp winters; hot, humid summers; rainy season from June to August; often cloudy. Typhoon season is from June to October.	Varies from tropical along the coast to temperate in the highlands; rainy season from November to April; dry season from May to October.	Tropical; dry, cooler winters; warm, rainy, cloudy summers; southern isthmus is always hot and humid. Monsoon season is from May to October.	Tropical; rainy season from June to December.
In winter, light jackets and sweaters are recommended; in summer, lightweight garments are essential. An umbrella is useful year-round.	Lightweight, tropical clothing is worn year-round, although in the cooler season, a light wrap is useful in the evenings. Conservative dress is required. Bring sunglasses and a hat.	Lightweight, washable clothing is comfortable and practical for Bangkok's tropical climate. In northern Thailand, a jacket or sweater is needed during the cool season. Swimwear should be worn only on the beach.	Summerweight clothing is worn year-round. Beachwear should be confined to the beach. Restaurants may have evening dress codes.
Passport, visa, ticket to leave	Passport, visa, ticket to leave, cholera and yellow fever inoculations	Passport, visa (for stays of more than 30 days), ticket to leave; inoculations recommended	Passport, visa (for stays of more than 2 months), ticket to leave, sufficient funds
Founding of the Republic, Jan. 1; Chinese New Year, Jan. or Feb.; Youth Day, Mar. 29; Ching Ming, Apr. 5; Labor Day, May 1; Teacher's Day/Confucius' Birthday, Sept. 28; National Day, Oct. 10; Taiwan Restoration Day, Oct. 25; Chiang Kaishek's Birthday, Oct. 31; Sun Yat-sen's Birthday, Nov. 12; Constitution Day, Dec. 25	Zanzibar Revolution Day, Jan. 12; CCM Day, Feb. 5; Good Friday; Easter Monday; Ramadan and Id al-Fitr; Union Day, Apr. 26; Id el Haji; Labor Day, May 1; Peasants' Day, July 7; Hijra; Prophet's Birthday; Independence Day, Dec. 9; Christmas Day, Dec. 25	New Year's Day, Jan. 1; Makhabuja; Chakri Day; Songkran Festival, Apr. 13; Coronation Day, May 5; Visakhja Puja, May; Ploughing Ceremony; Buddhist Lent, June or July; Queen's Birthday, Aug. 12; Chulalongkorn Day, Oct. 23; King's Birthday, Dec. 5; Constitution Day, Dec. 10; New Year's Eve, Dec. 31	New Year's Day, Jan. 1; Carnival, Feb.; Ramadan and Id al-Fitr; Good Friday; Easter Monday; Whitmonday; Corpus Christi; Labor Day, June 19; Emancipation Day, Aug. 1; Independence Day, Aug. 31; Republic Day, Sept. 24; Diwali (Festival of Lights); Christmas Day, Dec. 25; Boxing Day, Dec. 26
Drinking water is safe at Taipei's major hotels, but when dining elsewhere, drink only bottled water. Vegetables should be cooked and fruit peeled. Tension between China and Taiwan has increased.	Tapwater is not potable. All water should be boiled or otherwise sterilized and fruits and vegetables carefully prepared. Do not swim or paddle in lakes or streams. Anti-malarial drugs are recommended. Do not go barefoot.	Thailand strictly enforces its drug laws. Severe sentences are meted out for narcotics convictions. Avoid tap water, raw milk, ice cream, uncooked meats, and unwashed raw fruits and vegetables. HIV infection and AIDS are growing problems.	Tapwater is safe, but do not drink water from an unknown source. Wash fruits and vegetables carefully. Outside main cities and towns, water should be sterilized.

Country	Tunisia	Turkey	Ukraine
Int'l Dialing Code	216	90	380
City Codes	Béja 8, Bizerte 2, El Kairouan 7, Sousse 3, Tunis 1	Adana 711, Ankara 4, Bursa 241, Eskişehir 222, İstanbul 1, İzmir 51	Kharkiv 572, Kyyiv (Kiev) 44, L'viv 322
Consulate Phone	(202) 862-1850	(202) 659-8200	(202) 333-0606
Climate	Temperate in the north with mild, rainy winters and hot, dry summers; desert in the south.	Mild, wet winters; hot, dry summers. Climate is more severe in the interior.	Temperate; warm summers; cold winters in the north; milder winters in the far south.
Clothing	Wear lightweight clothes in the summer, light woolens and rainwear in the winter. Women should dress conservatively. Beachwear should not be worn outside of tourist resort areas.	Summer requires lightweight clothing in the northern areas and tropical clothing in the south. Warm woolens are necessary for the winter months. Beachwear should be confined to the beach or poolside.	Lightweight clothing is worn in the summer, woolens in fall and spring, and heavy clothing for the cold winters.
Entry Requirements	Passport, ticket to leave	Passport, visa, ticket to leave	Passport, visa, ticket to leave
Holidays	New Year's Day, Jan. 1; National Revolution Day, Jan. 18; Ramadan and Id al-Fitr; Independence Day, Mar. 20; Youth Day, Mar. 21; Martyrs' Day, Apr. 9; Labor Day, May 1; Id al-Adha; Republic Day, July 25; Islamic New Year; Women's Day, Aug. 13; Evacuation Day, Oct. 15	New Year's Day, Jan. 1; Ramadan and Id-al Fitr; National Sovereignty and Children's Day, Apr. 23; Id al-Adha; Spring Day, May 1; Youth Day, May 19; Constitution Day, May 27; Victory Day, Aug. 30; Republic Day, Oct. 29	New Year's Day, Jan. 1-2; Christmas, Jan. 7; International Women's Day, Mar. 8; Spring and Labor Day, May 1-2; Victory Day, May 9; Independence Day, Aug. 24
Special Notes	Drinking water outside main cities and towns may be contaminated. Eat only well-cooked meats and vegetables. Fruit should be peeled.	Intermittent terrorist activity makes travel in eastern Turkey dangerous. Tapwater should be sterilized.	All water may be contaminated and should be boiled or otherwise sterilized. Internal flight and train schedules can be irregular. Westerners are choice targets for criminals.

United Arab Emirates	United Kingdom	United States	Uruguay
971	44		598
Abū Zaby (Abu Dhabi) 2, Al-'Ayn 3, Dubayy 4	Belfast 232, Birmingham 21, Cardiff 222, Glasgow 41, Liverpool 51, London 71 or 81		Minas 442, Montevideo 2
(202) 338-6500	(202) 462-1340		(202) 331-1313
Desert; hot and dry; cooler in the eastern mountains and during the winter.	Temperate; mild winters, cool summers; cloudy with rainfall in all seasons.	Mostly temperate, but varies from tropical to arctic; arid to semiarid in west.	Warm and temperate; winters are mild, with the temperature seldom dropping below freezing. Seasons are reversed from those in North America.
Lightweight attire is necessary during the summer. From mid-October through April, spring or fall clothing is suitable. Everyone should dress modestly.	Fall and winter clothing is needed from about September through April; spring and summer clothing is useful the rest of the year. Always bring a raincoat and umbrella. Some restaurants have dress codes.	Clothing ranges from very lightweight to very heavy, depending on the region and time of year.	Seasonal clothing, as in the U.S., is recommended. Warm clothing is essential in winter. Rainwear is useful.
Passport, visa, ticket to leave	Passport	Passport, visa, ticket to leave, sufficient funds	Passport, ticket to leave
New Year's Day, Jan. 1; Ramadan and Id al-Fitr; Id al-Adha; Islamic New Year; Hijra; Prophet's Birthday; Abu Dhabi's Day; National Day, Dec. 2; Ascension of The Prophet; Christmas Day, Dec. 25	New Year's Day, Jan. 1; Good Friday; Easter Monday; May Day, early May; Spring Bank Holiday, late May; Summer Bank Holiday; Late Summer Holiday; Christmas Day, Dec. 25; Boxing Day, Dec. 26	New Year's Day, Jan. 1; Martin Luther King's Birthday, Jan. 15; Presidents' Day, late Feb.; Memorial Day, late May; Independence Day, July 4; Labor Day, early Sept.; Columbus Day, early Oct.; Veterans Day, Nov. 11; Thanksgiving Day, late Nov.; Christmas Day, Dec. 25	New Year's Day, Jan. 1; Epiiphany, Jan. 6; Carnival; Holy Week; Landing of the 33 Patriots, Apr. 19; Labor Day, May 1; Battle of Las Piedras, May 18; Birth of Don Jose Artigas, June 19; Constitution Day, July 18; Independence Day, Aug. 25; Columbus Day, Oct. 12; All Souls' Day, Nov. 2; Blessing of the Waters, Dec. 8; Christmas Day, Dec. 25
Water is potable in major cities. In other areas, filtering or the use of bottled water is advised. Vegetables should be cooked and fruit peeled. Legal penalties are generally assessed according to Islamic law.	There is a threat of terrorist activity, though not directed against tourists.	Recently there has been an increase in paramilitary activity targeted at government facilities.	The water supply in main cities is well-maintained. Outside main cities and towns, water may be contaminated.

Country	Venezuela	Vietnam	Zimbabwe
Int'l Dialing Code	58	84	263
City Codes	Barquisimeto 51, Caracas 2, Maracaibo 61, Maracay 43, San Cristobol 76, Valencia 41	Ha Noi 9, Thanh Pho Ho Chi Minh (Saigon) 8	Bulawayo 9, Harare 4, Mutare 20
Consulate Phone	(202) 342-2214	(202) 861-0737	(202) 332-7100
Climate	Tropical; hot, humid; more moderate in the highlands; rainy season from May to November.	Tropical in the south; warm, dry winters and hot, rainy summers in the north. Monsoon season is from May to October.	Temperate; moderated by altitude; rainy season from November to March.
Clothing	Spring-weight clothing is appropriate in Caracas. Elsewhere temperatures vary with altitude, from tropics to freezing. Many restaurants have dress codes. Beachwear and shorts should be worn only on the beach or at poolside.	Lightweight clothing is worn throughout the year in the south and during the summer in the north. Shorts are not considered to be appropriate adult attire.	Light, summer apparel is appropriate from October to May. Fall or spring clothing is suitable the rest of the year. Some urban restaurants have evening dress codes.
Entry Requirements	Passport, business visa or tourist card, ticket to leave; inoculations recommended	Passport, visa, ticket to leave	Passport, ticket to leave, sufficient funds; inoculations recommended
Holidays	New Year's Day, Jan. 1; Carnival; Maundy Thursday; Good Friday; Holy Saturday; Declaration of Independence Day, Apr. 19; Labor Day, May 1; Battle of Carabobo, June 24; Independence Day, July 5; Bolivar's Birthday, July 24; Civil Servant's Day, Sep. 4; Columbus Day, Oct. 12; Christmas Eve, Dec. 24; Christmas Day, Dec. 25; New Year's Eve, Dec. 31	New Year's Day, Jan. 1; Lunar New Year; Liberation of South Vietnam, Apr. 30; May Day, May 1; National Days, Sept. 2-3	New Year's Day, Jan. 1; Good Friday; Easter Monday; Independence Day, Apr. 18; Worker's Day, May 1; Africa Day; May 25; Heroes' Days, Aug. 11-12; Christmas Day, Dec. 25; Boxing Day, Dec. 26
Special Notes	Tapwater in the cities is chlorinated and relatively safe. Outside of larger cities, water should be boiled. Vegetables and other foods should be carefully prepared. Travel to the border area with Colombia is restricted.	All water may be contaminated. Meat, fish and other foods should be well-cooked. Political or other activities or possession of books, tapes, etc., can result in detention and/or expulsion. Security personnel may place foreigners under surveillance.	All water should be regarded as a potential health risk. Avoid swimming and paddling in fresh water. Hotels accept only credit cards or internationally convertible currency. Street crime is increasing in Harare and Bulawayo.

City Maps

Legend

For easy comparison of the major cities of the world, all the metropolitan maps are drawn at a consistent scale of 1:350,000. One inch on the map represents 5.5 miles on the earth's surface.

Inhabited Localities

The symbol represents the number of inhabitants within the locality

•	0–10,000
○	10,000–25,000
◉	25,000–100,000
▣	100,000–250,000
▣	250,000–1,000,000
■	>1,000,000

The size of type indicates the relative economic and political importance of the locality

Écommoy
Trouville
Lisieux

St.-Denis

PARIS

Hollywood ■ **Section of a City,**
Westminster **Neighborhood**
Northland ■ **Major Shopping Center**
Center

Urban Area (area of continuous industrial, commercial, and residential development)

Major Industial Area

Wooded Area

Political Boundaries

International
(First-order political unit)

Demarcated, Undemar-cated, and Administrative

Demarcation Line

Internal

State, Province, etc.
(Second-order political unit)

County, Oblast, etc.
(Third-order political unit)

Okrug, Kreis, etc.
(Fourth-order political unit)

City or Municipality
(may appear in combination with another boundary symbol)

Capitals of Political Units

BUDAPEST — Independent Nation
Recife — State, Province, etc.
White Plains — County, Oblast, etc.
Iserlohn — Okrug, Kreis, etc.

Transportation

Road

PASSAIC EXPWY. (I-80) — **Primary**
BERLINER RING — **Secondary**
Tertiary

Railway

CANADIAN NATIONAL — **Primary**
Secondary
Rapid Transit

Airport

 LONDON (HEATHROW) AIRPORT

Rail or Air Terminal

■ SÜD BAHNHOF

 REICHS-BRÜCKE **Bridge**
Tunnel
GREAT ST. BERNARD TUNNEL

Other Features

SORBONNE ▲ **Point of Interest** (Battlefield, museum temple, university, etc.)
STEPHANSDOM ♦ **Church, Monastery**
UXMAL ∴ **Ruins**
WINDSOR CASTLE ♥ **Castle**
♠ **Lighthouse**
ASWĀN DAM \ **Dam**
<> **Lock**
Mt. Kenya △ **Elevation Above Sea Level**
5199
★ **Rock**

Elevations are given in meters

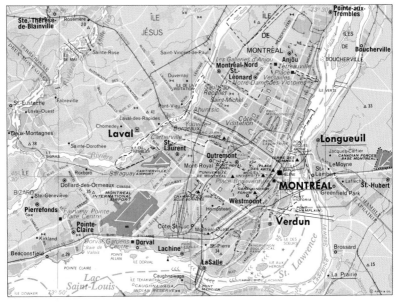

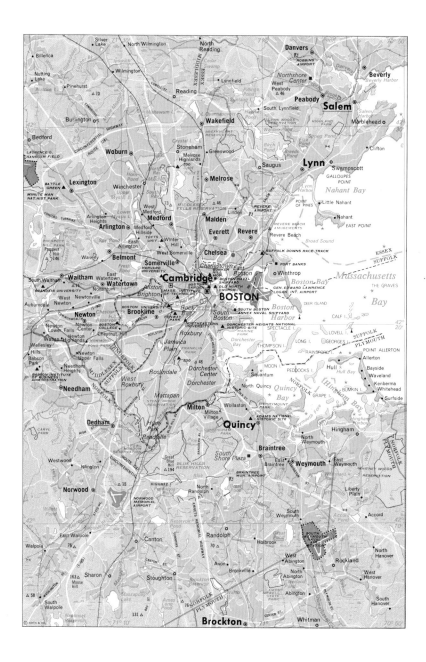

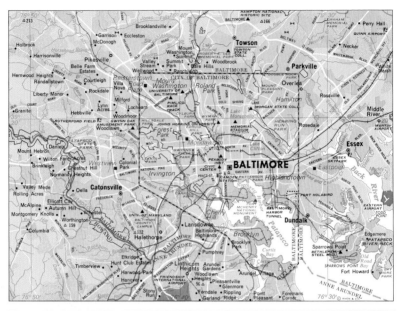

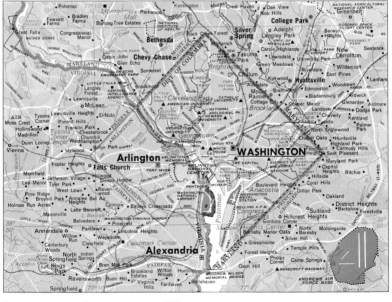

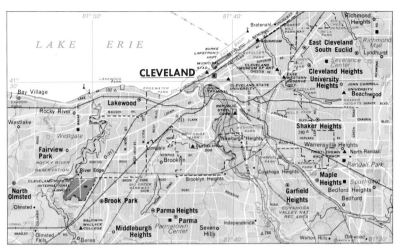

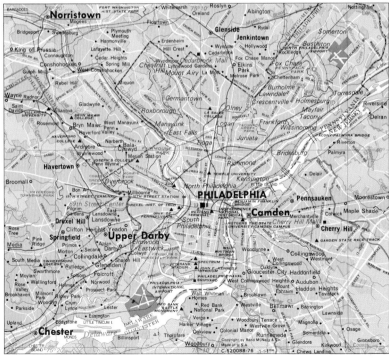

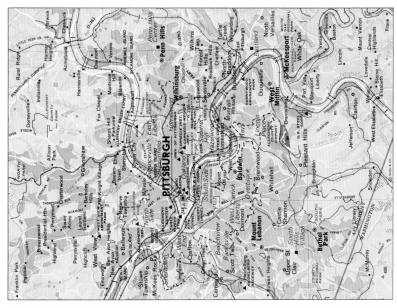

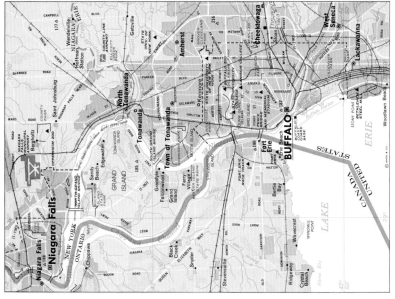

0				5					10 Miles

0			5			10 Kilometers

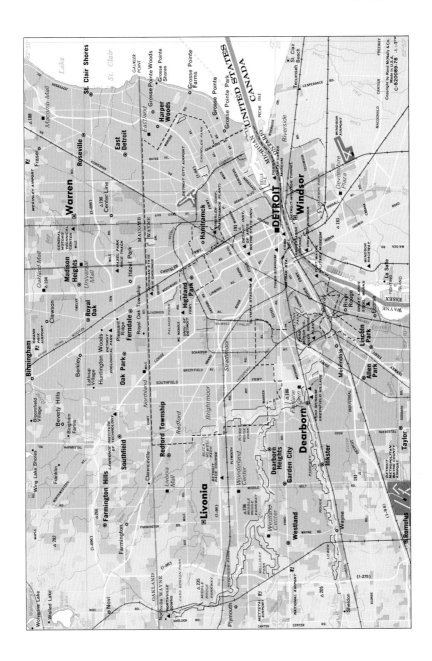

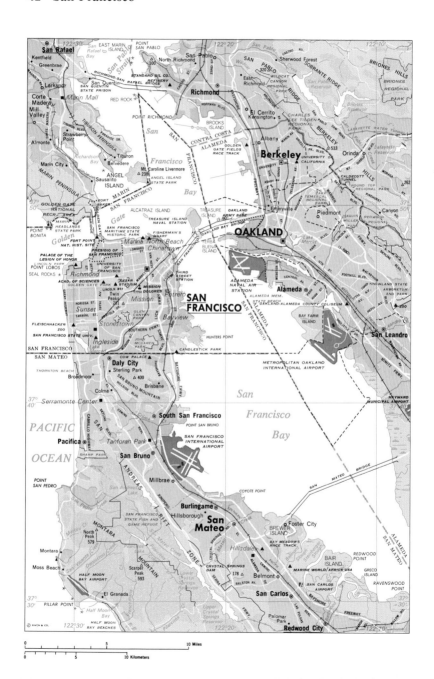

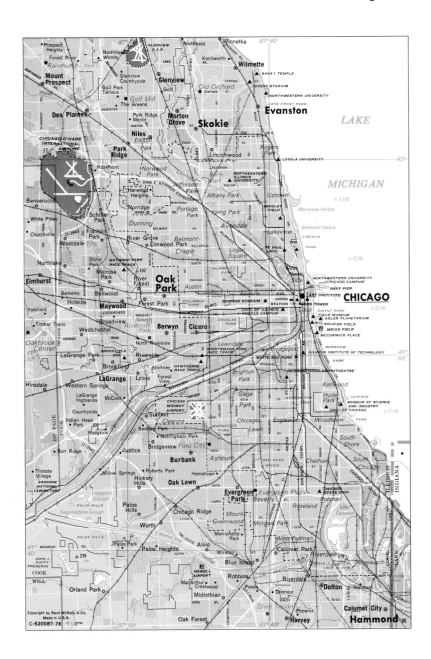

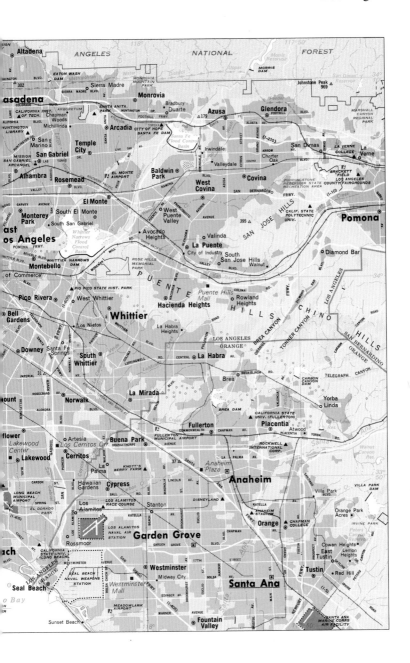

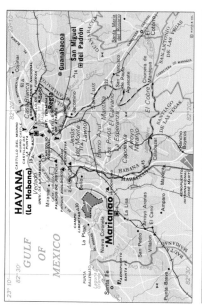

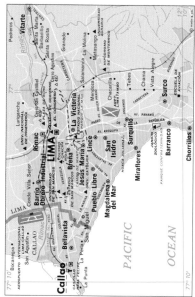

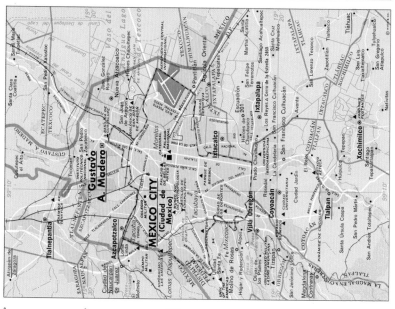

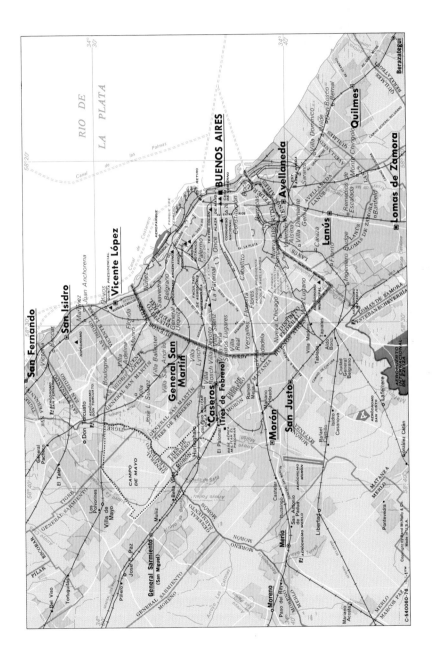

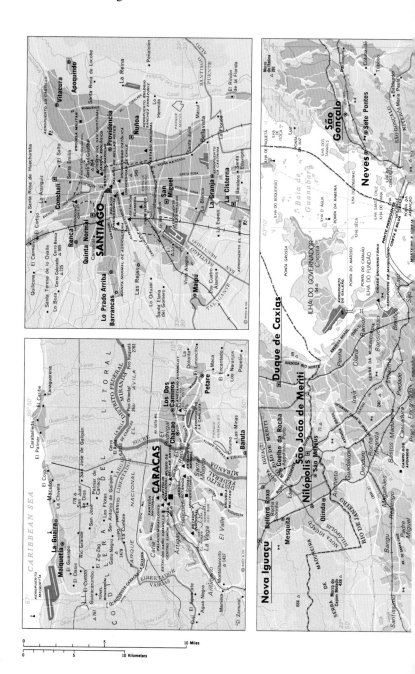

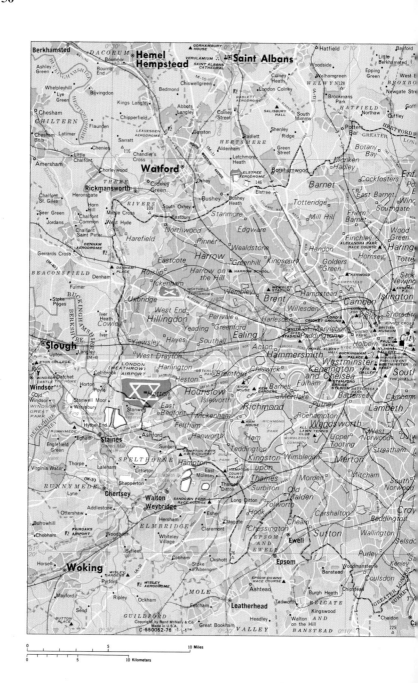

0   5   10 Miles

0   5   10 Kilometers

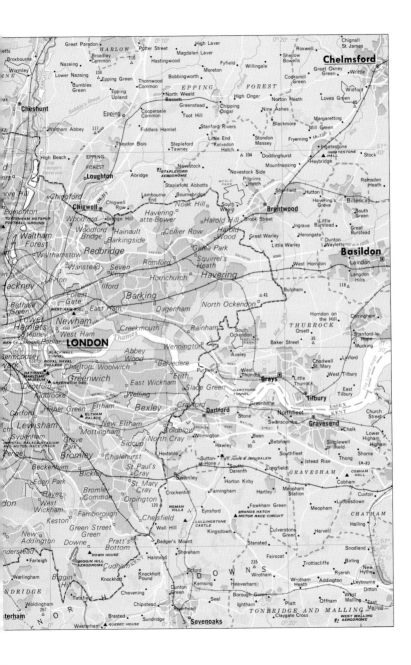

52

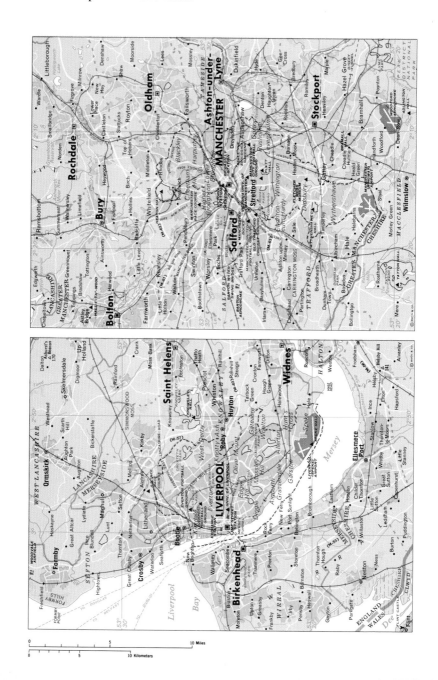

0   5   10 Miles

0   5   10 Kilometers

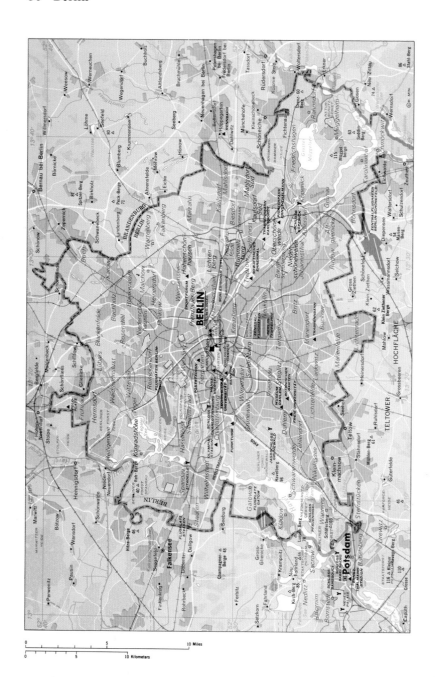

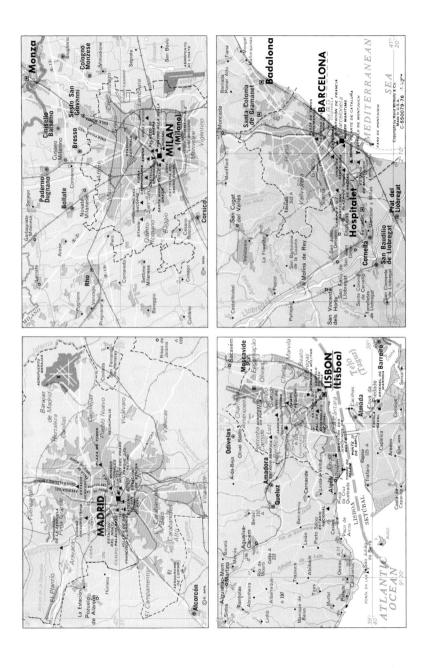

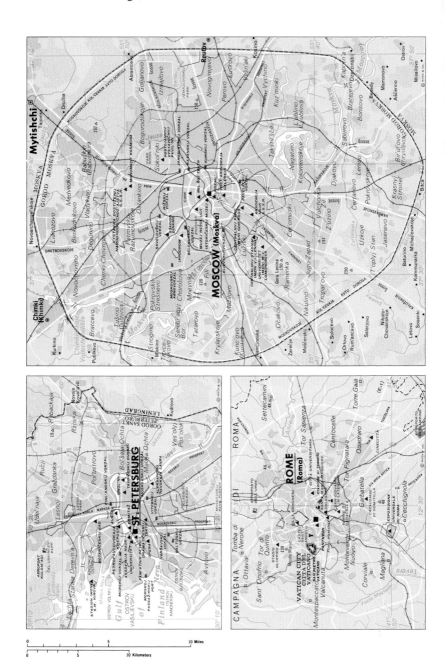

0   5   10 Miles
0   5   10 Kilometers

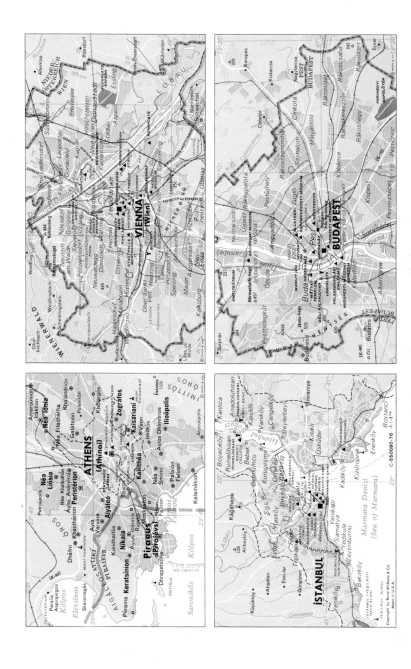

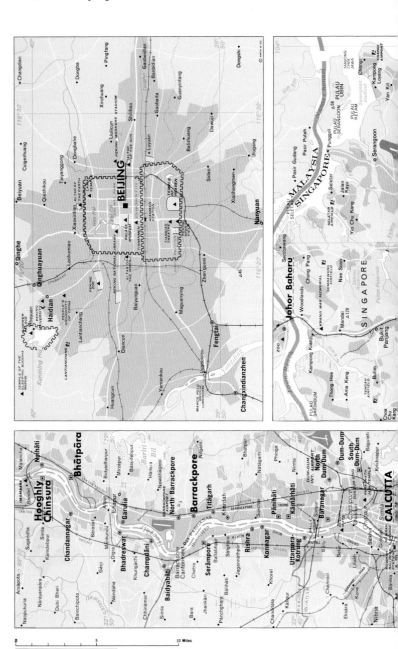

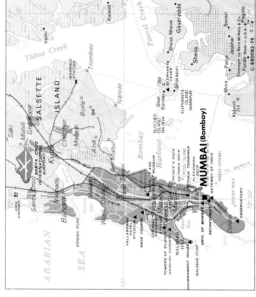

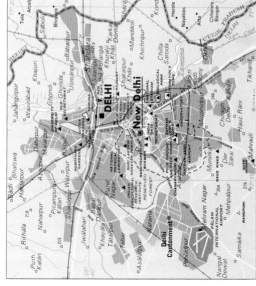

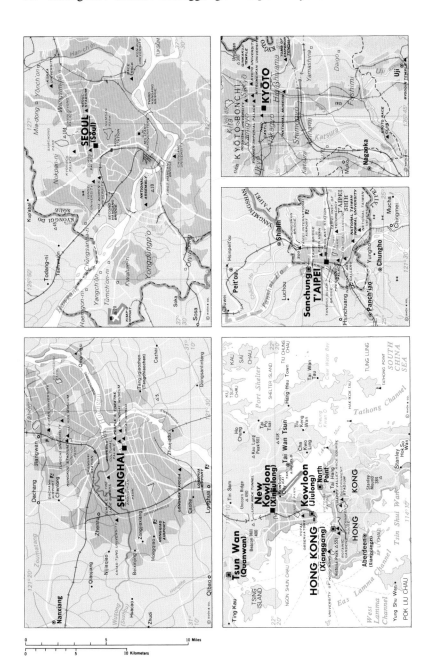

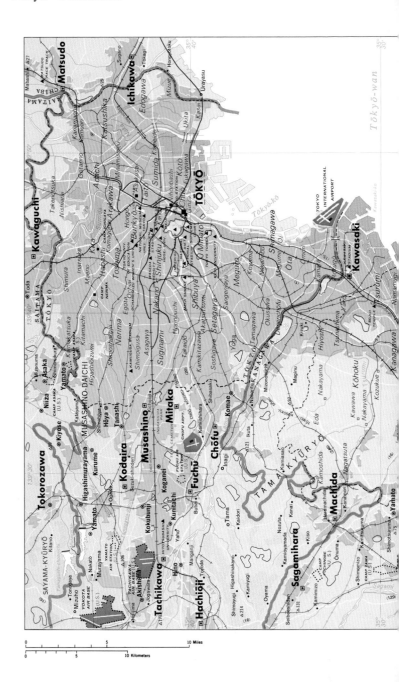

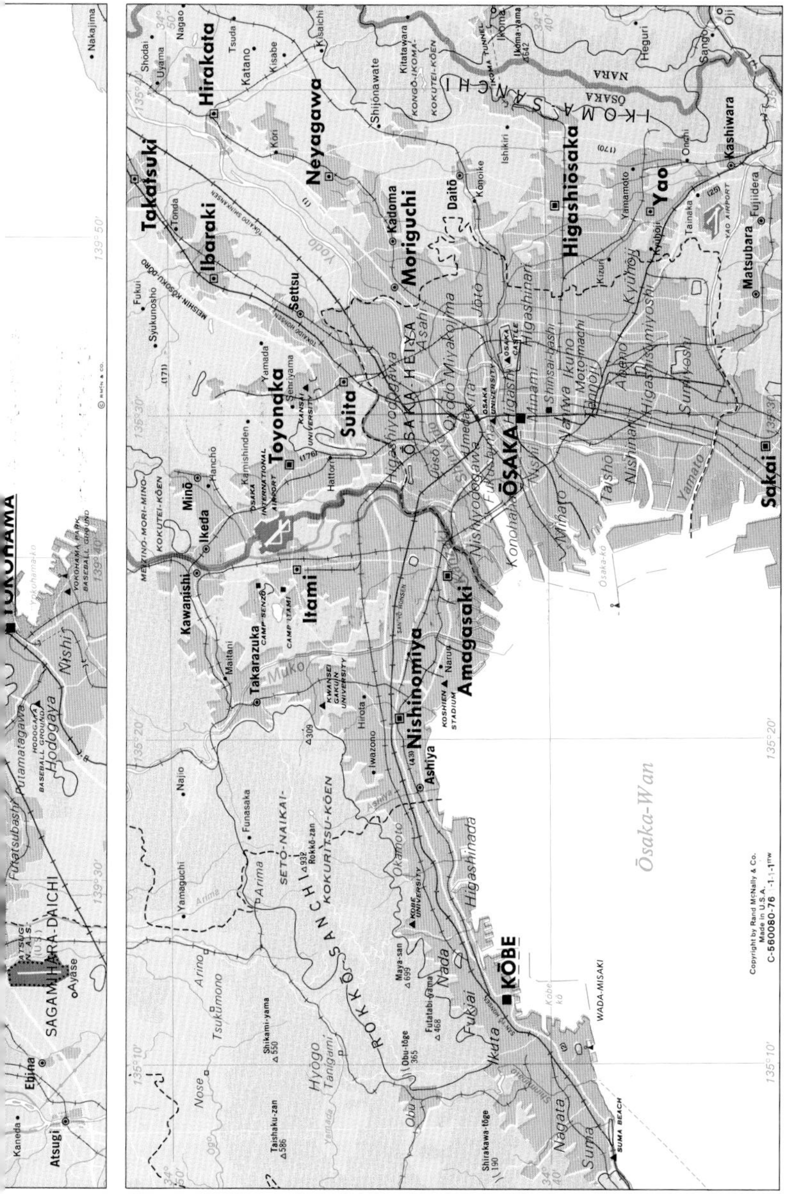

YOKOHAMA

Kaneda •
Atsugi ●
Ebina •
Nakajima •
SAGAMIHARA-DAICHI
Ayase ○
Futatsubashi Putamategawa
HODOGAYA
BASEBALL GROUND
Hodogaya
Nishi
Totsuka

Shioda •
Shiodai •
Nago •
Hirakata
Tsuda •
Katano •
Kisabe •
Kōri •
Ujiama •
Daiichi •
NARA
IKOMA-SANCHI
ŌSAKA
IKOMA TUNNEL
Ikoma-yama 642
Ōji •
Heguri •
Sango •
Kashiwara
Kashiwara •
Fujiidera
Matsubara •
Yao
Higashiōsaka
Daitō •
Kadoma •
Moriguchi
Neyagawa
Takatsuki
Ibaraki
Settsu
Suita
Toyonaka
Minō
Ikeda
Kawanishi
Itami
Takarazuka
Nishinomiya
Ashiya
Amagasaki
ŌSAKA
ŌSAKA-HEIYA
SAKAI
Sakai
Ōsaka-Wan
KŌBE
Nada
Fukiai
Nagata
Suma
SUMA BEACH
WADA-MISAKI
ROKKŌ SANCHI
KOKURITSU-KŌEN
Maya-san
Rokkō-zan 932
Arima
Hyogo Tanigami
SETO-NAIKAI
Yamaguchi •
Funasaka •
Najio •
Taishaku-zan 586
Shihami-yama 550
Ōbu-tōge 965
Futatabi-Gaten 468
Shirakawa-tōge 190
Noze
Tsukimono
Ōtsuki
Nose
Ayase ○

Copyright by Rand McNally & Co.
Made in U.S.A.
C-560080-76

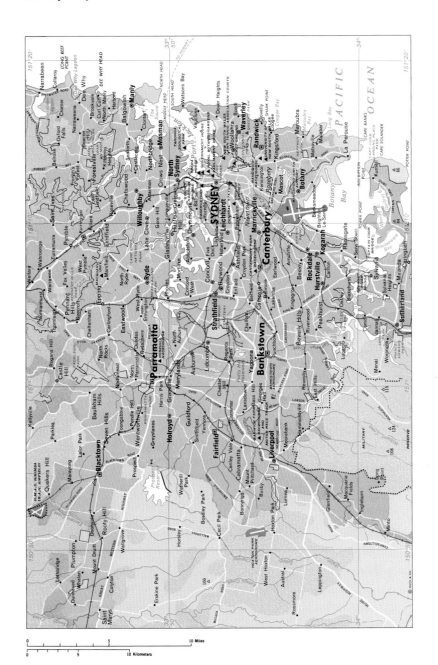

0   5   10 Miles

0   5   10 Kilometers

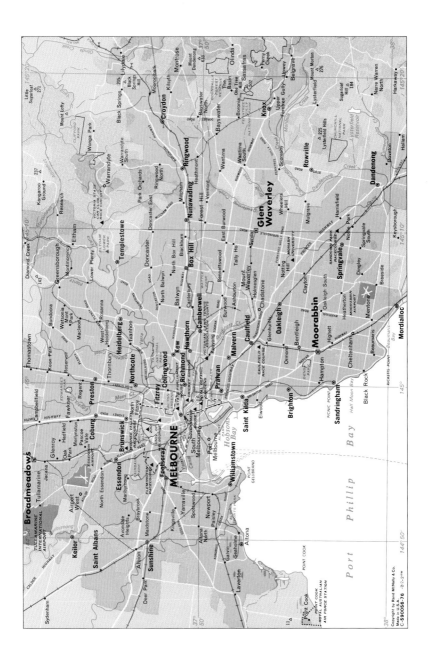

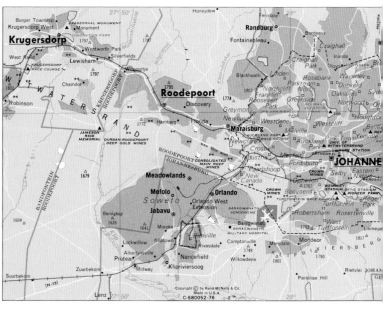

```
0                    5              10 Miles
0          5              10 Kilometers
```

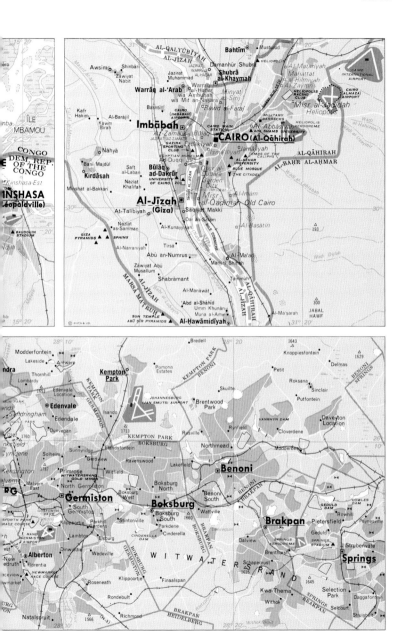

Cairo map

AL-QALYŪBĪYAH
AL-JĪZAH
Bahtīm°   Mustarud
Awsim°   Shinbāri
Zāwiyat
Nabit   Jazirat   WARRĀQ   Damanhūr Shubrā   HELIOPOLIS
Muhammad   WARRĀQ   Shubrā
al-HADAR   al-Khaymah   Al-Matariyah
Warrāq al-'Arab°   Warrāq   Minyat   Mahattat   CAIRO
wa al-Hadar   Sirj   Al-Zaytūn   INTERNATIONAL
wa Ambubah   HELIOPOLIS   AIRPORT
wa Mit an-Nasara   RACING   CAIRO
Kafr   Bāstīli   Rawd al-Faraj   CLUB   ALMAZA
Hakim°   Al-Barajil   CAIRO   °Misr al-Jadidah   AIRPORT
(IMBABAH)   Heliopolis
AIRPORT   MILITARY
Imbābah   BARRACKS   Wādī
Nāhyā°   Al-Duqqi   CAIRO MAIN   °AL-'Abbāsīyah   HELIOPOLIS   al-Hatūrah
STATION   AERODROME
GAZIRAT AL-ZAMALEK   AL-AZHAR   HELIOPOLIS
Bani Majdul   GAZIRA   Būlāq   CAIRO (Al-Qāhirah)   AIN SHAMS UNIVERSITY   AL-QĀHIRAH
Kirdāsah°   Safi   SPORTING   Ishā'īyah   Jamālīyah   AL-BAHR AL-AHMAR
al-Laban   CLUB   TOMBS OF THE
EGYPTIAN MUSEUM   AL-AZHAR   CALIPHS
Nazlat   Al-Duqqi   UNIVERSITY
Minshat al-Bakkāri°   Khalifah   Būlāq   BLUE MOSQUE   Wādi az-Zabbālah
ad-Dakrūr   Qasr al-   THE CITADEL
UNIVERSITY   'Ubārā
OF CAIRO   Garden   °Al-Imam
At-Tālibiyah°   Al-Jīzah   ZOO
(Giza)   Sāqiyat Makki   Misr
At-Talibiyah   °Al-Qadimah   Old Cairo
Dar as-Salam   °Al-Basātin
GIZA   Nazlat   Al-Kunayyisah
PYRAMIDS   'as-Samman   △193
Al-Narranīyah   SPHINX   Tirsa
Abū an-Numrus   °Al-Ma'adi
Zāwiyat Abū   Manyal Shirah
Musallum   Wādī Dulah
Shabrāmant   °Al-Ma'āsarah   △300   JABAL
Al-Manawat   HAWF
'Abd al-Shāhid
Umm Khunan   SUN TEMPLE   Muna al-Amir
ABŪ SĪR PYRAMIDS   Al-Hawāmidīyah°   AL-QĀHIRAH   AL-JĪZAH

ÎLE
MBAMOU
CONGO
DEM. REP.
OF THE
CONGO
°Kinshasa-Est
INSHASA
(Léopoldville)
BAUDOUIN
STADIUM

Johannesburg area map

Modderfontein   Bredell   1643   Knoppiesfontein   1629
Lakeside   Antwerp   Pomona   BENONI
ndra   Thornhill   KEMPTON   Estates   Petit   SPRINGS
Lombardy   PARK   Delmas
1653   Edenvale   Kempton°   Skuilte   Roksana   Sinclair
Edenvale   Location   Park   Putfontein
Edenvale   JOHANNESBURG   Brentwood   Rynfield   Daveyton
JAN SMUTS AIRPORT   Park   VANRHYN DAM   Location
Dunvegan   Isando
1713   KEMPTON PARK   Rusville   Cloverdene
BOKSBURG   Northmead   Modderbee
Solheim   Handsfontein
nksfield   Sunnyridge   Lakefield
Primrose   Gerdview   Ravenswood   Benoni
WITWATERSRAND   Witfield   Benoni   BENONI
North Germiston   GOLD MINES   South   BRAKPAN
RG   Malvern   Boksburg   COWLES
East   North   GEDULD   DAM
Germiston   Boksburg   Boksburg   DAM
GOSFORTH   South   Wattville   Brakpan   Rownhill
RACE COURSE   West   Boksburg   Pietersfield
Alberton   Kingsway   South   1660   Geduld   Paynesville
RAND   Parkhill   Parkdene   SPRINGS   Strubenvale
SPORTH PARK   Gardens   Cinderella   AERODROME   SPRINGS
RACE COURSE   Stintonville   CINDERELLA   Dalview   STADIUM   Springs
New   Lambton   Elsburg   DAM   Schapenrust   Selcourt
edruth   Florentia   Wadeville   1635   1645   Selection
aceview   Dinwiddie   WITWATERSRAND   Park
market   NEWMARKET   Kwa-Thema   SPRINGS
RACE COURSE   Roseneath   Withok   BRAKPAN   Daggafontein
URG   Rondebult   BRAKPAN   Finaalspan
Natalspruit   1566   (N-3)   Richmond   HEIDELBERG   Selcourt

Guide to Selected Cities

This alphabetical guide shows geographical and travel information for major international cities. The list includes metro area population figures, hotels, restaurants, additional information sources, and other details.

The population figures quoted represent the populations of entire metropolitan areas, which include one or more central cities, as well as socially and economically integrated surrounding areas.

Amsterdam, Netherlands
Population: 1,860,000
Altitude: 5 ft. (1.5m.) below sea level
Average Temp.: Jan., 35°F (2°C); July, 64°F (18°C)
Selected Hotels:
American, Leidseplein 28
Amstel Intercontinental, Professor Tulpplein 1
De l'Europe, Nieuwe Doelenstraat 2-8
Excelsior, Hardenberge
Forum, Alexander Platz
Grand Amsterdam, Oude Zijds Voorburgwal 197
Grand Hotel Krasnapolsky, Dam 9
Marriott, Stadshouderskade 19-21
Okura Amsterdam, Ferd. Bolstraat 333
Renaissance, Kattengat 1
Selected Restaurants:
Bali, Beddington's, Brasserie Lido, Cafe Americain, Christophe, De Kersentuin, De Silvern Spieghel, De Trechter, D'Vijff Vlieghen, Dynasty, Het Tuynhuys, La Rive, Lucius, Oyster Bar, Sama Sebo, 't Swarte Schaep, Tom Yam, Tout Court
Banking: Hours are 9 A.M. to 4 P.M., Monday through Friday.
Information Sources:
Netherlands Board of Tourism
355 Lexington Avenue, 21st Floor
New York, New York 10017
212-370-7367

Athens (Athínai), Greece
Population: 3,027,331
Altitude: 230 ft. (70m.)
Average Temp.: Jan., 52°F (11°C); July, 80°F (27°C)
Selected Hotels:
Andromeda Athens, Timoleondos Vassou 22
Athenaeum Inter-Continental, 89-93 Syngrou Ave.
Electra, Hermou St. 5
Grande Bretagne, Constitution Square
Holiday Inn, Michalakopoulou 50
Marriott, Syngrou Ave.
Meridien, Constitution Square
Park, Leoforos Alexandras Ave. 10
St. George Lycabettos, Kleomenous 2
Selected Restaurants:
Aglamair, Athinaikon, Bajazzo, Botsaris, Dionyssos, Floca, Fourtouna, Ideal, Kaldera, Mavri Gida, Papakia, Rose, Symposio, Varoulko, Zonars
Banking: Hours are 8:30 A.M. to 2:30 P.M., Monday through Thursday; 8:30 A.M. to 2 P.M. Friday.
Information Sources:
Greek National Tourist Organization
645 5th Avenue
New York, New York 10022
212-421-5777

Atlanta, Georgia
Population: 2,833,511
Altitude: 1,050 feet
Average Temp.: Jan., 52°F (11°C); July, 85°F (29°C)
Telephone Area Code: 404
Time Zone: Eastern
Selected Hotels:
Atlanta Hilton & Towers, 255 Courtland St. NE, 659-2000
Holiday Inn-Airport North, 1380 Virginia Ave., 762-8411
Hyatt Regency Atlanta, 265 Peachtree St. NE, 577-1234
Marriott Perimeter Center, 246 Perimeter Center Pkwy. NE, 394-6500
Omni Hotel at CNN Center, 100 CNN Center, 659-0000
Radisson Hotel Atlanta, 165 Courtland St., 659-6500
Sheraton Colony Square Hotel, 188 14th St. NE, 892-6000
The Westin Peachtree Plaza, 210 Peachtree St. NW, 659-1400
Selected Restaurants:
The Abbey, 163 Ponce de Leon Ave., 876-8831
Bugatti's, Omni Hotel at CNN Center, 659-0000
Coach and Six, 1776 Peachtree St. NW, 872-6666
Dante's Down the Hatch, 3380 Peachtree Rd., 266-1600
La Grotta, 2637 Peachtree Rd. NE, 231-1368
Nikolai's Roof Restaurant, Atlanta Hilton & Towers, 659-2000
Pano's and Paul's, 1232 W. Paces Ferry Rd. NW, 261-3662
Terrace Garden Inn, 3405 Lenox Rd. NE, 261-9250
Information Sources:
Atlanta Convention & Visitors Bureau
233 Peachtree St. NE, Suite 2000
Atlanta, Georgia 30303
404-521-6600

Beijing, China
Population: 7,320,000
Altitude: 165 ft. (50m.)
Average Temp.: Jan., 23°F (-5°C); July, 79°F (26°C)
Selected Hotels:
Although all travel arrangements are made by the China International Travel Service, here are the leading hotels and their telephone numbers:
Beijing, 33 Chang An Ave. East
Beijing Hilton, 4 Dong San Huan Rd. N.
Beijing-Toronto, 3 Jiangou Men Wai Da Jie
Changfugong, Jianguo Men Wai Da Jie
Grand, 35 Donchanganjie Ave.
Holiday Inn Crowne Plaza, 48 Wangfujing
Kempinski Lufthansa Center, 50 Liangmaqiao Rd.

Peninsula Palace, 8 Goldfish Lane, Wangfujing
SAS Royal, 6A Beisanhuan Rd. E.
Shangri-La, 29 Zizhuyuan Rd.
Sheraton Great Wall, 6A Dongsanhuangbeilu Rd.
Swissotel Beijing, Dongsi Shitiao Li Jiao Qiao
Selected Restaurants:
Chiu Chow Garden, Cui Hua Lou, Dong Lai Shun,
  Fang Shan, Feng Ze Yuan, Fortune Garden, Huai
  Yang Fan Zhuang, Jianguomen Roast Duck, Jin
  Yang, Kang Le, Lili, Kou Rou Ji, Quanjude
  Roast Duck, Sichuan, Temple of the Sun Park
Banking: Hours are 8 A.M. to noon and 2 P.M. to
  5 P.M., Monday through Friday.
Information Sources:
China National Tourist Office
Empire State Building
350 5th Avenue, Suite 6413
New York, New York 10108
212-760-9700

Berlin, Germany

Population: 3,825,000
Altitude: 115 ft. (35m.)
Average Temp.: Jan., 31°F (-1°C); July, 66°F (19°C)
Selected Hotels:
Bristol Hotel Kempinski, Kürfurstendamm 27
Grand Hotel Esplanade, Lutzowufer 15
Inter-Continental, Budapester Str. 2
Maritim Grand, Friedrich Str. 158-164
Maritim ProArte, Friedrich Str. 150-153
Radisson Plaza, Karl-Liebknecht Str. 5
Schweizerhof Inter-Continental, Budapester Str.
  21-31
Steigenberger, Los Angeles Platz 1
Selected Restaurants:
Alt Luzembourg, Alt Nürnberg, Bamberger Reiter,
  Blockhaus Nikolskoe, Borchardt, Ermeler-Haus,
  Frühsammers an der Rehwiese, Marz am Ufer,
  Ponte Vecchio, Rockendorf's, Turmstuben
Banking:
Hours are 9 A.M. to 4 P.M., Monday through
  Friday, with the exception of Thursday, when
  most banks remain open until 5:30 or 6 P.M.
Information Sources:
German National Tourist Office
122 E. 42nd St., 52nd Floor
New York, New York 10168
212-661-7200

Boston, Massachusetts

Population: 4,171,643
Altitude: Sea level to 330 feet
Average Temp.: Jan., 29°F (-2°C); July, 72°F (22°C)
Telephone Area Code: 617
Time Zone: Eastern
Selected Hotels:
The Colonnade, 120 Huntington Ave., 424-7000
Copley Plaza Wyndham Hotel, 138 St. James Ave.,
  267-5300
Le Meridien, 250 Franklin St., 451-1900
Logan Airport Hilton, 75 Service Rd., Logan
  International Airport, 569-9300
Omni Parker House Hotel, 60 School St., 227-8600
Selected Restaurants:
Anthony's Pier 4, 140 Northern Ave., 423-6363
The Cafe Budapest, 90 Exeter St., 266-1979

Copley's Restaurant, Copley Plaza Hotel, 267-5300
The Dining Room, in The Ritz-Carlton, 536-5700
Felicia's, 145A Richmond St., up one flight,
  523-9885
Hampshire House, 84 Beacon St., 227-9600
Julien, in Le Meridien, 451-1900
Locke-Ober Cafe, 3 Winter Pl., 542-1340
Maison Robert, Old City Hall, 45 School St.,
  227-3370
Information Sources:
Greater Boston Convention & Visitors Bureau, Inc.
Prudential Tower, Suite 400
800 Boylston St.
Boston, Massachusetts 02199
617-536-4100

Brussels (Bruxelles), Belgium

Population: 2,385,000
Altitude: 53 ft. (16m.)
Average Temp.: Jan., 38°F (3°C); July, 66°F (19°C)
Selected Hotels:
Amigo, Rue de l'Amigo 1-3
Chateau du Lac, Av. du Lac 87
Conrad, Av. Louise 71
Hilton, Blvd. de Waterloo 38
Metropole, Pl. de Brouckère 31
Montgomery, Av. de Tervueren 134
Royal Windsor, 5-7 Rue Duquesnoy
SAS Royal, Rue du Fosse-aux-Loups 47
Stanhope, Rue du Commerce 9
Selected Restaurants:
Castello Banfi, Comme Chez Soi, L'Ecailler Du
  Palais Royal, La Maison du Cygne, La Truffe
  Noir, Les Brigittines, Les Capucines, Les Delices
  de la Mer, Michel Meyers, Villa Lorraine
Banking: Hours are 9 A.M. to 4 P.M., Monday
  through Friday; 9 A.M. to noon on Saturday.
Information Sources:
Belgian Tourist Office
780 3rd Avenue, Suite 1501
New York, New York 10017
212-758-8130

Buenos Aires, Argentina

Population: 10,750,000
Altitude: 65 ft. (20m.)
Average Temp.: Jan., 75°F (24°C); July, 51°F (11°C)
Selected Hotels:
Alvear Palace, Av. Alvear 1891
Bauen, Av. Callao 360
Bisonte, Calle Paraguay 1207
Caesar Park, Calle Posadas 1232
Claridge, Calle Tucuman 535
El Conquistador, Calle Suipacha 948
Libertador Kempinski, Av. Cordoba 680
Marriott Plaza, Calle Florida
Park Hyatt, Calle Posados 1086
Sheraton, Calle San Martin 1225
Selected Restaurants:
A Los Amigos, Alexanders, Au Bec Fin, Blab,
  Catalinas, Clark's, Downtown Matios, El
  Repecho de San Telmo, Gato Dumas, Harper's,
  Hippopotamus, La Cabaña, La Herradura,
  London Grill, Pedemonte, Plaza Hotel Grill
Banking: Hours are 10 A.M. to 3 P.M., Monday
  through Friday.

Information Sources:
Argentina National Tourist Office
12 West 56th Street, 5th Floor
New York, New York 10019
212-603-0443

Cairo (Al-Qāhirah), Egypt
Population: 9,300,000
Altitude: 65 ft. (20m.)
Average Temp.: Jan., 57°F (14°C); July, 82°F (28°C)
Selected Hotels:
Forte Grand Pyramids, Desert Rd., Giza
Heliopolis Sheraton, Sharia el-Uraba, Heliopolis
Helnan Shepheard, Corniche el-Nil, Garden City
Le Meridien, Corniche el-Nil, Garden City
Marriott, Sharia Saray el-Gezira, Zamalek
Mena House Oberoi, Pyramids Rd., el-Ahram
Movenpick Concorde, Int'l. Airport Rd., Heliopolis
Nile Hilton, Corniche el-Nil, Midan Tahir
Pyramids Park Sofitel, Desert Rd., Giza
Ramses Hilton, 1114 Corniche el-Nil, Maspero
Semiramis Inter-Continental, Corniche el-Nil,
  Garden City
Sheraton, Midan Gala, Giza
Selected Restaurants:
Al-Adin, Al-Saraya, Ali Hassan el-Hati, Arabesque,
  Cairo Tower, Cellar, Chin Chin, El-Dar, Felfela,
  Justine's, La Mamma, Moghul Room, Starlight
Banking: Hours are 8:30 A.M. to 1 P.M., Monday
  through Thursday; 10 A.M. to noon on Sunday.
  Banks are closed on Friday and Saturday.
Information Sources:
Egyptian Tourist Authority
630 5th Avenue
New York, New York 10111
212-332-2570

Calcutta, India
Population: 11,100,000
Altitude: 20 ft. (6m.)
Average Temp.: Jan., 68°F (20°C); July, 84°F (29°C)
Selected Hotels:
Airport Ashok, Calcutta Airport
Best Western Kenilworth, 1-2 Little Russell St.
Great Eastern, 1 Old Court House St.
Hindustan International, 235-1 A.J.C. Bose Rd.
Oberoi Grand, 15 J. L. Nehru Rd.
Park, 17 Park St.
Quality Inn, 15 J.L. Nehru Rd.
Taj Bengal, 34-B Bellvedere Rd., Alipur
Selected Restaurants:
Aheli, Amber, Bar-B-Q, Blue Fox, Kebob e Que,
  Ming Court, Moghul Room, Sonorgaon, Zen
Banking: Hours are 10 A.M. to 2 P.M., Monday
  through Friday; 10 A.M. to noon on Saturday.
  Banks are closed on government holidays.
Information Sources:
Government of India Tourist Office
30 Rockefeller Plaza, Room 15 - North Mezzanine
New York, New York 10112
212-586-4901

Chicago, Illinois
Population: 8,065,633
Altitude: 579 to 672 feet
Average Temp.: Jan., 27°F (-3°C); July, 75°F (24°C)

Telephone Area Code: 312
Time Zone: Central
Selected Hotels:
The Ambassador West, 1300 N. State Pkwy.,
  787-3700
The Barclay, 166 E. Superior, 787-6000
Chicago Marriott Downtown, 540 N. Michigan
  Ave., 836-0100
Days Inn, 644 N. Lake Shore Dr., 943-9200
The Fairmont Hotel-Chicago, 200 N. Columbus Dr.
  at Illinois Center, 565-8000
Holiday Inn Mart Plaza, 350 N. Orleans St.,
  836-5000
Hotel Nikko, 320 N. Dearborn, 744-1900
Hyatt Regency O'Hare, 9300 W. Bryn Mawr Ave.,
  Rosemont, 847-696-1234
Palmer House Hilton, 17 E. Monroe St., 726-7500
Park Hyatt Chicago, 800 N. Michigan Ave.,
  280-2222
The Westin Hotel, 909 N. Michigan Ave., 943-9625
Selected Restaurants:
Biggs Restaurant, 1150 N. Dearborn Pkwy.,
  787-0900
Cape Cod Room, Drake Hotel, 787-2200
Gordon Restaurant, 500 N. Clark, 467-9780
House of Hunan, 535 N. Michigan Ave., 329-9494
Lawry's The Prime Rib, 100 E. Ontario St.,
  787-5000
Nick's Fishmarket, 1 First National Plaza, Monroe
  at Dearborn, 621-0200
Pizzeria Uno, 29 E. Ohio St., 321-1000
The Pump Room, Omni Ambassador East Hotel,
  1301 State Pkwy., 266-0360
Signature Room at the Ninety-Fifth, John Hancock
  Center, 172 E. Chestnut, 787-9596
Su Casa, 49 E. Ontario St., 943-4041
Information Sources:
Chicago Convention & Tourism Bureau, Inc.
McCormick Place
2301 S. Lake Shore Dr.
Chicago, Illinois 60616
312-567-8500

Dallas-Fort Worth, Texas
Population: 3,885,415
Altitude: 450 to 750 feet
Average Temp.: Jan., 44°F (7°C); July, 86°F (30°C)
Telephone Area Code: (Dallas) 214, (Fort Worth)
817
Time Zone: Central
Selected Hotels: DALLAS
The Adolphus Hotel, 1321 Commerce St., 742-8200
Fairmont Hotel, 1717 N. Akard St., 720-2020
Hyatt Regency–Dallas-Fort Worth Airport,
  International Pkwy., 453-1234
Loews Anatole Hotel, 2201 Stemmons Frwy.,
  748-1200
The Mansion on Turtle Creek, 2821 Turtle Creek
  Blvd., 559-2100
Plaza of the Americas Hotel, 650 N. Pearl St.,
  979-9000
Stouffer Dallas Hotel, 2222 N. Stemmons Frwy.,
  631-2222
Westin Galleria, 13340 Dallas Pkwy., 934-9494
Selected Restaurants: DALLAS
Butcher Shop, 808 Munger Ave., 720-1032
Il Sorrento, 8616 Turtle Creek Blvd., 352-8759
Old Warsaw, 2610 Maple Ave., 528-0032

The Pyramid Room, Fairmont Hotel, 720-2020
650 North, Plaza of the Americas Hotel, 979-9000
Information Sources: DALLAS
Dallas Convention & Visitors Bureau
1201 Elm St., Suite 2000
Dallas, Texas 75270
214-746-6677
Selected Hotels: FORT WORTH
Green Oaks Inn, 6901 W. Freeway, 738-7311
Hampton Inn West, 2700 Cherry Lane, 560-4180
Holiday Inn South, 100 Alta Mesa Blvd., 293-3088
Radisson Plaza, 815 Main St., 870-2100
Ramada Hotel, 1701 Commerce St., 335-7000
Worthington Hotel, 200 Main St., 870-1000
Selected Restaurants: FORT WORTH
The Balcony, 6100 Camp Bowie Blvd., 731-3719
Cactus Bar and Grill, Radisson Plaza, 870- 2100
The Cattle Drive, 1900 Ben Ave., 534-4908
Mac's House, 4255 Camp Bowie Blvd., 377-3744
Information Sources: FORT WORTH
Fort Worth Convention & Visitors Bureau
415 Throckmorton St.
Fort Worth, Texas 76102
817-336-8791

Denver, Colorado

Population: 1,848,319
Altitude: 5,130 to 5,470 feet
Average Temp.: Jan., 31°F (-1°C); July, 74°F (23°C)
Telephone Area Code: 303
Time Zone: Mountain
Selected Hotels:
The Brown Palace Hotel, 321 17th St., 297-3111
The Burnsley Hotel, 1000 Grant St., 830-1000
Holiday Inn Denver Downtown, 1450 Glenarm Pl.,
  573-1450
Hyatt Regency Denver, 1750 Welton St., 295-1200
Radisson Hotel Denver, 1550 Court Pl., 893-3333
Stapleton Plaza Hotel, 3333 Quebec St., 321-3500
Selected Restaurants:
Ellyngton's, Brown Palace Hotel, 297-3111
Marlowe's, Glenarm and 16th St., 595-3700
Normandy French Restaurant, 1515 Madison St.,
  321-3311
Palace Arms, Brown Palace Hotel, 297-3111
Tante Louise, 4900 E. Colfax Ave., 355-4488
Information Sources:
Denver Metro Convention and Visitors Bureau
225 W. Colfax Avenue
Denver, Colorado 80202
303-892-1112

Detroit, Michigan

Population: 4,665,236
Altitude: 573 to 672 feet
Average Temp.: Jan., 26°F (-3°C); July, 73°F (28°C)
Telephone Area Code: 313
Time Zone: Eastern
Selected Hotels:
Clarion Inn–Metro Airport, 31200 Industrial
  Expwy., 728-2260
Hotel St. Regis, 3071 W. Grand Blvd., 873-3000
Hyatt Regency Dearborn, Fairlane Town Center
  Dr., Dearborn, 593-1234
Northfield Hilton, 5500 Crooks Rd., Troy,
  (810) 879-2100

The Plaza, 16400 J.L. Hudson Dr., Southfield,
  559-6500
The Westin Hotel Renaissance, Renaissance Center,
  568-8000
Selected Restaurants:
Carl's Chop House, 3020 Grand River Ave.,
  833-0700
Caucus Club, 150 W. Congress St., 965-4970
Charley's Crab, 5498 Crooks Rd., Troy,
  (810) 879-2060
The Golden Mushroom, 18100 W. 10 Mile Rd.,
  Southfield, (810) 559-4230
Joe Muer's Sea Food, 2000 Gratiot Ave., 567-1088
London Chop House, 155 W. Congress St.,
  963-7778
Mario's Restaurant, 4222 2nd Ave., 833-9425
St. Regis Restaurant, Hotel St. Regis, 3071 W.
  Grand Blvd., 873-3000
Van Dyke Place, 649 Van Dyke Ave., 821-2620
Information Sources:
Metropolitan Detroit Convention & Visitors Bureau
100 Renaissance Center, Suite 1900
Detroit, Michigan 48243
313-259-4333

Frankfurt Am Main, Germany

Population: 1,855,000
Altitude: 325 ft. (99m.)
Average Temp.: Jan., 34°F (1°C); July, 67°F (19°C)
Selected Hotels:
An der Messe, Westend Str. 104
Arabella Grand, Konrad Adenauer Str. 7
Gravenruch Kempinski, Neu Isenberg
Hessiche Hof, Fredrich Ebert Anlage 40
Liebig, Liebig Str. 45
Park, Wiesenhutten Pl. 28-38
Schwille, Grosse Bockenheimer Str. 50
Steigenberger Frankfurter Hof, Kaiserplatz
Selected Restaurants:
Altes Zollhaus, Avocado, Erno's Bistro, Bistro 77,
  Börsenkeller, Charlot, Gildestuben, Papillon,
  Restaurant Français, Weinhaus Brückenkeller
Banking: Hours are 9 A.M. to 4 P.M., Monday
  through Friday; except for Thursday, when most
  banks remain open until 5:30 or 6 P.M.
Information Sources:
German National Tourist Offices
122 E. 42nd Street, 52nd Floor
New York, New York 10168
212-661-7200

Hong Kong (Xianggang)

Population: 4,770,000
Altitude: 50 ft., (15m.)
Average Temp.: Jan., 59°F (15°C); July, 84°F (29°C)
Selected Hotels:
Excelsior, 281 Gloucester Rd., Causeway
Hilton, 2 Queen's Rd., Central
Holiday Inn Harbour View, 70 Mody Rd., Kowloon
Hyatt Regency, 67 Nathan Rd., Kowloon
Mandarin Oriental, 5 Connaught Rd., Central
Miramar, 130 Nathan Rd., Kowloon
Omni Marco Polo, Harbour City, Kowloon
Peninsula, Salisbury Rd., Kowloon
Regent, 185 Salisbury Rd., Kowloon
Ritz-Carlton, Connaught Rd., Central
Shangri-La, 64 Mody Rd., Kowloon

74   Guide to Selected Cities

Selected Restaurants:
Bodhi Vegetarian, Chesa, Gaddi's, Jimmy's
  Kitchen, Lai Ching Heen, Mah Wah, Mandarin
  Grill, Papillon, Peking Garden, Star Seafood,
  Tandoor, The Chinese Restaurant, Yung Kee
Banking: Hours are 9 A.M. to 4 P.M., Monday
  through Friday; 9 A.M. to 12:30 P.M. Saturday.
Information Sources:
Hong Kong Tourist Association
590 5th Avenue, 5th Floor
New York, New York 10036
212-869-5008

Honolulu, Hawaii

Population: 836,231
Altitude: Sea level to 4,020 feet
Average Temp.: Jan., 72°F (22°C); July, 80°F (27°C)
Telephone Area Code: 808
Time Zone: Hawaiian (Two hours earlier than
  Pacific standard time)
Selected Hotels:
Halekulani, 2199 Kalia Rd., 923-2311
Hawaiian Regent, 2552 Kalakaua Ave., 922-6611
Hilton Hawaiian Village, 2005 Kalia Rd., 949-4321
Hyatt Regency Waikiki, 2424 Kalakaua Ave.,
  923-1234
Ilikai Hotel Nikko Waikiki, 1777 Ala Moana Blvd.,
  949-3811
Queen Kapiolani, 150 Kapahulu Ave., 922-1941
Royal Hawaiian, 2259 Kalakaua Ave., 923-7311
Sheraton Moana Surfrider, 2365 Kalakaua Ave.,
  922-3111
Selected Restaurants:
Furusato, 2500 Kalakaua Ave., 922-5502
Golden Dragon Room (Chinese), Hilton Hawaiian
  Village, 949-4321
The Hanohano Room, Sheraton Hilton, 922-4422
Michel's, Colony Surf Hotel, 2895 Kalakaua Ave.,
  923-6552
Pikake Terrace, Sheraton Princess Kaiulani Hotel,
  120 Kaiulani Ave., 922-5811
The Plantation Cafe, Ala Moana Hotel, 410
  Atkinson Dr., 955-4811
Information Sources:
Hawaii Visitors Bureau
2270 Kalakaua Ave., 8th Floor
Honolulu, Hawaii 96815
808-923-1811

Istanbul, Turkey

Population: 7,550,000
Altitude: 30 ft. (9m.)
Average Temp.: Jan., 42°F (6°C); July, 74°F (23°C)
Selected Hotels:
Aya Sofia Pansiyons, Sogukcesme Sok.
Buyuk Tarabya, Kefelikoy Cad.
Curagan Palace, Curagan Cad. 84
Divan, Cumhuriyet Cad. 2
Hilton, Cumhuriyet Cad.
Hyatt Regency, Abdi Ipekri Cad. 34-12
Merit Antique, Ordu Cad. 226
Swissotel, Bayildim Cad. 2
Yesilev, Kabasakal Sok. 5
Selected Restaurants:
Balik, Borsa Lok Antasi, Cemal, Club 29, Divan,
  Gelik, Korfez, Sarnic, Tugra, Urcan, Ziya

Banking: Hours are 8:30 A.M. to noon and 1:30
  P.M. to 5:30 P.M., Monday through Friday.
Information Sources:
Turkish Govt. Tourism and Information Office
821 United Nations Plaza
New York, New York 10017
212-687-2194

Johannesburg, South Africa

Population: 3,650,000
Altitude: 5,750 ft. (1,753m.)
Average Temp.: Jan., 67°F, (19°C); July, 51°F (11°C)
Selected Hotels:
Balalaika Hotel & Crown Court, Maude St.
Carlton, Main St.
Holiday Inn Johannesburg Int'l., Rte 24, Kempton
  Park
Karos Indaba, Hartebeespoort Dam Rd.
Parktonian, 120 De Korte St.
Rosebank, Tyrwhitt & Sturdee Aves.
Sandton Sun & Towers, Fifth & Alice Sts.
Sunnyside Park, 2 York Rd.
Selected Restaurants:
Armadillo, Ciro at the Ritz, Daruma, Gramadoelas,
  Ile de France, Leipoldt's, Linger Longer, Ma
  Cuisine, O Fado, Osteria Tre Nonni, Paros
  Taverna, Pescador, Turtle Creek Winery
Banking: Hours are 9 A.M. to 4 P.M., Monday
  through Friday, 8:30 A.M. to 11 A.M. Saturday.
Information Sources:
South African Tourist Board
500 5th Avenue, 20th Floor
New York, New York 10110
212-822-5368

Kuala Lumpur, Malaysia

Population: 1,800,000
Altitude: 112 ft. (34 m.)
Average Temp.: Jan., 79°F (26°C); July, 81°F (27°C)
Selected Hotels:
Carcosa Seri Negara, Taman Tasik Perdana
Crown Princess, Jln. Tun Razak
Equatorial, Jln. Sultan Ismail
Holiday Inn City Centre, 12 Jln. Raja Laut
Kuala Lumpur Hilton, Jln. Sultan Ismail
Legend, 100 Jln. Putra
Nikko Kuala Lumpur, 165 Jln. Ampang
Pan Pacific, Putra World Trade Center
Park Royal of Kuala Lumpur, Jln. Sultan Ismail
Petaling Jaya Hilton, 2 Jln. Barat
Regent, 126 Jln. Bukit Bintang
Shangri-La, 11 Jln. Sultan Ismail
Selected Restaurants:
Bon Ton, Coliseum Cafe, Eden at Petalung Jaya,
  Happy Hour Seafood Restaurant, Melaka Grill,
  Nonya Heritage, Regent Grill, Seri Melayu,
  Taman Titiwangsa, Terrace Garden
Banking: Hours are 10 A.M. to 3 P.M., Monday
  through Friday; 9:30 A.M. to 11:30 A.M.
  Saturday.
Information Sources:
Malaysian Tourism Promotion Board
595 Madison Avenue, Suite 1800
New York, New York 10022
212-754-1113

London, England

Population: 11,100,000
Altitude: 20 ft. (6m.)
Average Temp.: Jan., 40°F (4°C); July, 64°F (18°C)
Selected Hotels:
Beaufort, 33 Beaufort Gardens
Berkeley, Wilton Pl., Knightsbridge
Capital, 22-24 Basil St., Knightsbridge
Claridge's, Brook St.
Dorchester, Park Lane
Grosvenor House, Park Lane
Halkin, Halkin St.
Lanesborough, 1 Lanesborough Pl.
Le Meridien, Piccadilly
Pelham, 15 Cromwell Place
Ritz, Piccadilly
Savoy, The Strand
Selected Restaurants:
Alastair Little, Bibendum, Cafe Fish, Chez Nico at
  Ninety Park Lane, Clarke's, La Gavroche, La
  Tante Claire, Mulligan's, Quaglino's, Rules,
  Savoy Grill, The Capitol, The Ritz, Walton's
Banking: Hours are 9:30 A.M. to 4:30 P.M.,
  Monday through Friday. Some major banks are
  open on Saturday morning.
Information Sources:
British Tourist Authority
551 5th Avenue, Suite 701
New York, New York 10019
212-986-2200

Los Angeles, California

Population: 14,531,529
Altitude: Sea level to 5,074 feet
Average Temp.: Jan., 55°F (13°C); July, 73°F (23°C)
Telephone Area Code: 213
Time Zone: Pacific
Selected Hotels:
Beverly Hills Hotel, 9641 Sunset Blvd.,
  (310) 276-2251
Biltmore Hotel, 506 S. Grand Ave., 624-1011
Century Plaza, 2025 Avenue of the Stars,
  (310) 277-2000
Crowne Plaza Los Angeles Downtown, 3540 S.
  Figueroa St., 748-4141
Holiday Inn-Hollywood, 1755 N. Highland Ave.,
  462-7181
Hyatt Los Angeles Airport, 6225 W. Century Blvd.
  (310) 672-1234
Le Parc, 733 N. West Knoll Dr., (310) 855-8888
Los Angeles Airport Marriott, 5855 W. Century
  Blvd., (310) 641-5700
Los Angeles Hilton and Towers, 930 Wilshire Blvd.,
  629-4321
The New Otani Hotel and Garden, 120 S. Los
  Angeles St., 629-4321
Sheraton Universal Hotel, 333 Universal Terrace
  Pkwy., Universal City, (818) 980-1212
The Westin Bonaventure Hotel, 404 S. Figueroa St.,
  624-1000
Selected Restaurants:
Bernard's, Biltmore Hotel, 612-1580
Lawry's Prime Rib, 55 N. La Cienega Blvd.,
  652-2827

L'Orangerie, 903 N. La Cienega Blvd.,
  (310) 652-9770
Madame Wu's Garden, 2201 Wilshire Blvd.,
  828-5656
Pacific Dining Car, 1310 W. 6th St., 483-6000
Stepps, 330 S. Hope St., 277-1840
The Tower, 1150 S. Olive St., 626-0900
Information Sources:
Los Angeles Convention & Visitors Bureau
633 W. 5th St., Suite 6000
Los Angeles, California 90071
213-624-7300

Madrid, Spain

Population: 4,650,000
Altitude: 2,100 ft. (640m.)
Average Temp.: Jan., 41°F (5°C); July, 76°F (24°C)
Selected Hotels:
El Prado, Calle Prado 11
Lagasca, Lagasca 64
Palace, Plaza de las Cortes 7
Plaza, Gran Via 84
Reina Victoria, Plaza del Angel 7
Ritz, Plaza de Lealtad 5
Santo Mauro, Zurbano 36
Tryp Ambassador, Cuesta Santo Domingo 5-7
Villa Magna, Plaza de la Castellana 22
Zurbano, Zurbano 79-81
Selected Restaurants:
Brasserie de Lista, Casa Botin, Casa Paco, El
  Cenadordel Prado, El Pescador, Gure-Etxea,
  Horcher, La Bola, La Trainera, Lhardy,
  Mentidero de la Villa, Viridiana, Zalacain
Banking: Hours are 8:30 A.M. to 2 P.M., Monday
  through Friday; 8:30 A.M. to 1 P.M. Saturday.
Information Sources:
Spanish National Tourist Office
665 5th Avenue
New York, New York 10022
212-759-8822

Manila, Philippines

Population: 6,800,000
Altitude: 10 ft. (3m.)
Average Temp.: Jan, 78°F (26°C); July, 82°F (28°C)
Selected Hotels:
Admiral, 2138 Roxas Blvd.
Century Park Sheraton, Vito Cruz at Adriatico St.
Hyatt Regency, 2702 Roxas Blvd.
Mandarin Oriental, Makati Ave. at Paseo de
  Roxas St.
Manila Hotel, Rizal Park
Nikko Manila Garden, Makati Commercial Center
Peninsula, Ayala and Makati Aves.
Philippine Plaza, Cultural Center Complex, Roxas
  Blvd.
Shangri-La, Ayala and Makati Aves.
Selected Restaurants:
Aristocrat, Ben Kay, Bistro Remedios, Cafe
  Intermezzo, Champagne Room at Manila Hotel,
  Flavours & Spices, Gene's Bistro, Kamayan, La
  Tasca, Sea Food Market, Tim Hau, Via Mare
  Seafood Specialty Restaurant
Banking: Usual hours are 9 A.M. to 3 P.M.,
  Monday through Friday.

Information Sources:
Philippine Department of Tourism
Philippine Center
556 5th Avenue
New York, New York 10036
212-575-7915

Mexico City (Ciudad de México), Mexico
Population: 14,100,000
Altitude: 7,300 ft. (2,225m.)
Average Temp.: Jan., 54°F (12°C); July, 64°F (18°C)
Selected Hotels:
Aristos, Paseo de la Reforma 276
Camino Real, Mariano Escobedo 700
Century, Liverpool 152
Continental Plaza Aeropuerto, Benito Juarez
 Internacional Airport
El Presidenté Inter-Continental Chapultepec,
 Campos Eliseos 218
Four Seasons, Paseo de la Reforma 500
Hotel de Cortes, Av. Hidalgo 85
Marco Polo, Amberes 27
Maria Isabel Sheraton, Paseo de la Reforma 325
Marquis Reforma, Paseo de la Reforma 465
Selected Restaurants:
El Arroyo, El Centenario, El Parador de Manolo,
 Estoril, Focolare, Fonda El Refugio, Hacienda de
 los Morales, Isadora, La Jolla, Les Celebrites,
 Lincoln, Los Irabien, Prendes, San Angel Inn
Banking: Hours are 9:30 A.M. to 1:30 P.M.,
 Monday through Friday. Most large banks open
 weekdays, 4 P.M. to 6 P.M.; and 10 A.M. to 1:30
 P.M. Saturday.
Information Sources:
Mexican Government Tourism Office
405 Park Avenue, Suite 1401
New York, New York 10022

Miami, Florida
Population: 3,192,582
Altitude: Sea level to 30 feet
Average Temp.: Jan., 69°F (21°C); July, 82°F (28°C)
Telephone Area Code: 305
Time Zone: Eastern
Selected Hotels:
Don Shula's Hotel & Golf Club, 15255 Bull Run
 Rd., Miami Lakes, 821-1150
Doubletree Hotel at Coconut Grove, 2649 S.
 Bayshore Dr., 858-2500
Inn at the Civic Center, 1170 NW. 11th St.,
 324-0800
Miami Airport Hilton & Towers, 5101 Blue Lagoon
 Dr., 262-1000
Miami Airport Marriott, 1201 NW. LeJeune Rd.,
 649-5000
The Omni Colonnade, 180 Aragon Ave., Coral
 Gables, 441-2600
Ramada Hotel-Miami International Airport, 3941
 NW. 22nd St., 871-1700
Selected Restaurants:
Bay 61, 9561 E. Bay Harbor Dr., 866-8779
Centro Vasco, 2235 SW. 8th St., 643-9606
The Chart House, 51 Charthouse Dr., Coconut
 Grove, 856-9741
La Paloma, 10999 Biscayne Blvd., 891-0505

Renato's, 9561 E. Bay Harbor Dr., 866-8779
Information Sources:
Greater Miami Convention and Visitors Bureau
701 Brickell Ave., Suite 2700
Miami, Florida 33131
305-539-3000; (800) 933-8448

Milan (Milano), Italy
Population: 3,750,000
Altitude: 400 ft. (122m.)
Average Temp.: Jan., 34°F (1°C); July, 73°F (23°C)
Selected Hotels:
Canada, Via Santa Sofia 16
Carlton-Senato, Via Senato 5
Casa Svizzera, Via San Raffaele 3
Duomo, Via San Raffaele 1
Four Seasons, Via Gesu 8
Hotel de la Ville, Via Hoepli
London, Via Rovello 3
Pierre, Via de Amicis
Principe Di Savoia, Piazza della Repubblica 17
Selected Restaurants:
Al Cantinone, Antica Trattoria della Pesa, Bistro di
 Gualtiero Marchese (brunch only), La Capanna,
 La Libera, Nabucco, Savini, Trattoria Milanese
Banking: Hours are 8:30 A.M. to 1 P.M., 3:45 P.M.
 to 4:45 P.M., Monday through Friday.
Information Sources:
Italian Government Travel Office
630 5th Avenue, Suite 1565
New York, New York 10111
212-245-4822

Montréal, Canada
Population: 2,921,357
Altitude: 50 ft. (15m.)
Average Temp.: Jan., 16°F (-9°C); July, 71°F (22°C)
Telephone Area Code: 514
Selected Hotels:
Grand Hotel, University St. & St. James
Hotel le Westin Mont-Royal, 1050 Sherbrooke
 St. W.
Le Centre Sheraton, 1201 René-Lévesque Blvd. W.
Le Chateau Champlain, 1 Pl. du Canada
Le Meridien Montréal, 4 Complexe Desjardins
Montréal Hilton Bonaventure, 1 Pl. Bonaventure
Queen Elizabeth Hotel, 900 René-Lévesque
 Blvd. W.
The Ritz-Carlton Kempinski Hotel, 1228
 Sherebrooke St. W.
Selected Restaurants:
Beaver Club, Bocca d'Oro, Café de Paris, Chez
 Chine, Chez Plume, Guy and Dodo Morali,
 L'Express, Le Castillon, Le Passe-Partout, Les
 Halles, Milos, Moishe's, Nuances, Toque
Banking: Hours are generally from 10 A.M. to 3
 P.M., Monday through Thursday; and from 10
 A.M. to 6 P.M. on Friday. If Friday is a holiday,
 Friday hours are observed on Thursday. Many
 larger banks are open on Saturday.
Information Sources:
Greater Montréal Convention & Tourism Bureau
1555 Peel St., Suite 600
Montréal, Québec H3A 1X6
514-844-5400

Moscow (Moskva), Russia

Population: 13,100,000
Altitude: 395 ft. (120m.)
Average Temp.: Jan., 14°F (-10°C); July, 66°F (19°C)
Selected Hotels:
Aerostar, 37 Leningradsky Prospekt
Baltschug Kempinski, 1 Balchug St.
Intourist, 3-5 Gorky St.
Marco Polo, 9 Spiridonyevsky Per.
Metropole, 1 Marx Ave.
Olympic Penta, 18-1 Olympysky Prospekt
Palace Pervaya, 19 Tverskaya-Yamskaya
Radisson Slavyanskya, 2 Berezhkovskaya Emb.
Rossiya, 6 Razin St.
Savoy, 3 Ul. Rozhdestvenka
Ukraina, 2-1 Kutuzovsky Ave.
Selected Restaurants:
Baku, Exchange, Glazur, Grand Imperial,
  Kropotkinskaya 36, Le Romanoff, Metropole,
  Panda, Praga, Savoy, Strastnoy Bulvar 7,
  Tren-Mos
Banking: Hours are 9 A.M. to 6 P.M., Monday
  through Friday. Banks close at noon on days
  before holidays.
Information Sources:
Russia National Tourist Office
800 3rd Avenue, Suite 3101
New York, New York 10022
212-758-1162

New Orleans, Louisiana

Population: 1,238,816
Altitude: 5 to 25 feet
Average Temp.: Jan., 55°F (13°C); July, 82°F (28°C)
Telephone Area Code: 504
Time Zone: Central
Selected Hotels:
Fairmont Hotel, 123 Baronne St., 529-7111
Hyatt Regency New Orleans, 500 Poydras Plaza,
  561-1234
The Monteleone Hotel, 214 Royal St., 523-3341
New Orleans Hilton Riverside, 2 Poydras St. at the
  Mississippi River, 561-0500
New Orleans Marriott Hotel, 555 Canal St.,
  581-1000
Omni Royal Orleans, 621 St. Louis St., 529-5333
The Pontchartrain Hotel, 2031 St. Charles Ave.,
  524-0581
Royal Sonesta Hotel, 300 Bourbon St., 586-0300
Selected Restaurants:
Brennan's, 417 Royal St., 525-9711
Broussard's, 819 Conti St., 581-3866
Caribbean Room, Pontchartrain Hotel, 524-0581
Commander's Palace Restaurant, 1403 Washington
  Ave., 899-8221
Galatoire's Restaurant, 209 Bourbon St., 525-2021
Louis XVI French Restaurant, 730 Bienville,
  581-7000
Sazerac Restaurant, Fairmont Hotel, 529-7111
Information Sources:
New Orleans Metropolitan Convention & Visitors
  Bureau
1520 Sugar Bowl Dr.
New Orleans, Louisiana 70112
504-566-5011

New York, New York

Population: 18,087,251
Altitude: Sea level to 410 feet
Average Temp.: Jan., 33°F (-1°C); July, 75°F (24°C)
Telephone Area Code: 212
Time Zone: Eastern
Selected Hotels:
The Carlyle, 35 E. 76th St. at Madison Ave,
  744-1600
The Hotel Pierre, 2 E. 61st St. at 5th Ave.,
  838-8000
Marriott Marquis, 1535 Broadway at 46th St.,
  398-1900
The New York Hilton and Towers at Rockefeller
  Center, 1335 Avenue of the Americas, 586-7000
The Plaza, 768 5th Ave., 759-3000
The Regency Hotel, 540 Park Ave., 759-4100
Sherry-Netherland, 781 5th Ave., 355-2800
United Nations Plaza-Park Hyatt, 1 U.N. Plaza,
  758-1234
Selected Restaurants:
The Four Seasons, 99 E. 52nd St., 754-9494
La Côte Basque, 5 E. 55th St., 688-6525
Lutèce, 249 E. 50th St., 752-2225
Mitsukoshi, 461 Park Ave., 935-6444
"21" Club, 21 W. 52nd St., 582-7200
Information Sources:
New York Convention and Visitors Bureau, Inc.
Two Columbus Circle
New York, New York 10019
212-397-8222; (800) 692-8474

Osaka, Japan

Population: 16,450,000
Altitude: 16 ft. (5m.)
Average Temp.: Jan., 40°F (4°C); July, 80°F (27°C)
Selected Hotels:
Grand, 2-3-18 Nakanoshima, Kita-ku
Hilton, 8-8 Umeda 1-chome, Kita-ku
Holiday Inn Nankai, 5-15 Shin-Saibashi-suji
  2-chome, Chuo-ku
Hyatt Regency, 1-13 Nanko-Kita, Suminoe-ku
International, 2-33 Honmachibashi, Chuo-ku
Miyako, 6-1-55 Ue-Honmachi, Tennoji-ku
New Otani, 4-1 Shiromi 1-chome, Chuo-ku
Nikko, 1-3-3 Nishi-Shin-Saibashi, Chuo-ku
Royal, 5-3-68 Nakanoshima, Kita-ku
Sheraton, 1-3-1- Dojimahama, Kita-ku
Selected Restaurants:
Benkay, Chambord, Fughisa, Kani Doraku, Kanki,
  Kobe Misono, Kushitaru, Little Carnival, Mimiu,
  Osaka Joe's, Ron, Tako-ume, The Seasons
Banking: Hours are 9 A.M. to 3 P.M., Monday
  through Friday.
Information Sources:
Japan National Tourist Organization
1 Rockefeller Plaza, Suite 1250
New York, New York 10020
212-757-5640

Paris, France

Population: 9,775,000
Altitude: 140 ft. (43m.)
Average Temp.: Jan., 44°F (7°C); July, 76°F (24°C)

Selected Hotels:
Crillon, Place de la Concorde 10
Duc de Saint-Simon, Rue St-Simon 14
Grand Hotel Inter-Continental, Rue Scribe 2
Hilton, Ave. de Suffren 18
L'Abbaye Saint-Germain, Rue Cassette 10
L'Hotel, Rue des Beaux-arts 13
Plaza Athenée, Ave. Montaigne 25
Ritz, Place Vendome 15
Selected Restaurants:
Au Trou Gascon, Chez Pauline, Guy Savoy, Joel Robuchon, L'Arpege, Ledoyen, La Butte Chaillot, Le Cap Vernet, Le Bistro d'a Cote, Le Bistro de l'Etoile, Le Grand Vefour, Le Rotisserie d'en Face, Les Bookinistes, Maxim's, Michael Rosta
Banking: Hours are 9 A.M. to 4:30 P.M., Monday through Friday; 9 A.M. to noon day before holidays.
Information Sources:
French Government Tourist Office
444 Madison Avenue
New York, New York 10022
212-838-7800

Rio De Janeiro, Brazil

Population: 10,150,000
Altitude: 30 ft. (9m.)
Average Temp.: Jan., 79°F (26°C); July, 69°F (21°C)
Selected Hotels:
Caesar Park, Av. Antionio Carlos Jobim 460, Ipanema
Copacabana Palace, Av. Atlantica 1702, Copacabana
Inter-Continental, Av. Prefeito Mendes de Morais 222, Sao Conrado Beach
Internacional Rio, Av. Atlantica 1500, Copacabana
Leme Palace, Av. Atlantica 656, Leme
Meridien, Av. Atlantica 1020, Copacabana
Miramar Palace, Av. Atlantica 3668, Copacabana
Rio Othon Palace, Av. Atlantica 3264, Copacabana
Rio Palace, Av. Atlantica 4240, Copacabana
Sheraton, Av. Niemeyer 121, Vidigal Beach
Selected Restaurants:
Baby Beef Paes Mendonca, Cafe do Teatro, Casa de Feijoada, Club Gourmet, Le Bec Fin, Le Pre Catelan, Le Saint Honoré, Monseigneur, Petronius, Rodeio, Troisgros, Valentino's
Banking: Hours are 10 A.M. to 4:30 P.M., Monday through Friday.
Information Sources:
Brazilian Tourism Office
551 5th Avenue
New York, New York 10176
212-286-9600

Rome (Roma), Italy

Population: 3,175,000
Altitude: 80 ft. (24m.)
Average Temp.: Jan., 46°F (8°C); July, 75°F (24°C)
Selected Hotels:
Ambasciatori Palace, Via Veneto 70
Bernini Bristol, Piazza Barberini 23
Cavalieri Hilton, Via Cadlolo 101
Excelsior, Via Vittorio Veneto 125
Flora, Via Vittorio Veneto 191
Grand, Via V.E. Orlando 3
Mediterraneo, Via Cavour 15

Parco dei Principi, Via G. Frescobaldi 5
Quirinale, Via Nazionale 7
Sheraton Roma, Viale del Pattinaggio
Selected Restaurants:
Albert Ciarla, Checchino dal 1887, La Rosetta, Le Restaurant, Passetto, Patrizia e Roberto del Pianeta Terra, Quinzi Gabrieli, Ranieri, Relais le Jardin, San Souci
Banking: Hours are 8:30 A.M. to 1:30 P.M., Monday through Friday.
Information Sources:
Italian Government Travel Office
630 5th Avenue, Suite 1565
New York, New York 10111
212-245-4822

San Francisco, California

Population: 6,253,311
Altitude: Sea level to 934 feet
Average Temp.: Jan., 50°F (10°C); July, 59°F (15°C)
Telephone Area Code: 415
Time Zone: Pacific
Selected Hotels:
Fairmont Hotel and Tower, 950 Mason St. on Nob Hill, 772-5000
Four Seasons Clift Hotel, 495 Geary St., 775-4700
Grand Hyatt on Union Square, 345 Stockton St., 398-1234
The Holiday Inn Union Square, 480 Sutter St., 398-8900
Hotel Nikko, 222 Mason St., 394-1111
Huntington Hotel-Nob Hill, 1075 California St., 474-5400
Hyatt Regency San Francisco, 5 Embarcardero Center, 788-1234
Mark Hopkins Inter-Continental, One Nob Hill, 392-3434
Miyako Hotel, 1625 Post St., 922-3200
The Phoenix, 601 Eddy St., 776-1380
The Queen Anne, 1590 Sutter St., 441-2828
The Westin St. Francis, 335 Powell St., 397-7000
Selected Restaurants:
Amelio's, 1630 Powell St., North Beach, 397-4339
Empress of China, 838 Grant Ave., 434-1345
Ernie's Restaurant, 847 Montgomery St., 397-5969
Fleur de Lys, 777 Sutter St., 673-7779
Fournou's Ovens, in The Stouffer Stanford Court Hotel, 989-1910
The Waterfront Restaurant, Pier 7, The Embarcadero, 391-2696
Information Sources:
San Francisco Convention & Visitors Bureau
201 3rd St., Suite 900
San Francisco, California 94103
415-974-6900

São Paulo, Brazil

Population: 15,175,000
Altitude: 2,375 ft. (724m.)
Average Temp.: Jan., 71°F (22°C); July, 58°F (14°C)
Selected Hotels:
Brasilton, Rua Martins Fontes 330
Caesar Park Hotel, Rua Augusta 1508
Eldorado, Ave. São Luis 234
Grande Hotel Ca D'Oro, Rua Augusta 129
Jaraguá, Viaduto Major Quedinho 40
Maksoud Plaza, Al. Campinas 150

Othon Palace, Rua Libero Badaró 190
São Paulo Center, Lgo. Sta. Ifigenia 40
São Paulo Hilton, Ave. Ipiranga 165
Selected Restaurants:
Abril em Portugal, Andrade, Baiúa, Bolinha, Chalet
   Suisse, La Casserole, Manhattan, Os Vikings,
   Presidente, Tarraço Italia, Via Veneto
Banking: Hours are 8 A.M. to 6:30 P.M., Monday
   through Friday.
Information Sources:
Brazilian Tourism Office
551 Fifth Avenue
New York, New York 10176
212-286-9600

Singapore, Singapore

Population: 3,000,000
Altitude: 35 ft. (11m.)
Average Temp.: Jan., 79°F (26°C); July, 81°F (27°C)
Selected Hotels:
Boulevard, 200 Orchard Rd.
Carlton, 76 Bras Basah Rd.
Dynasty, 320 Orchard Rd.
Goodwood Park, 22 Scotts Rd.
Hilton, 581 Orchard Rd.
Omni Marco Polo, Tanglin Oriental, 6 Raffles
   Blvd.
Shangri-La, 22 Orange Grove Rd.
Sheraton Towers, 39 Scotts Rd.
Selected Restaurants:
Alkaff Mansion, Aziza's, Bintang Timur, Cherry
   Garden, Dragon City, Gordon's Grill, Latour,
   Min Jiang, Pine Court, Sukmaindra, Xin Cuisine
Banking: Hours are 10 A.M. to 3 P.M., Monday
   through Friday; 9:30 A.M. to 11:30 A.M.
   Saturday.
Information Sources:
Singapore Tourist Promotion Board
590 5th Avenue, 12th Floor
New York, New York 10036
212-302-4861

Stockholm, Sweden

Population: 1,449,972
Altitude: 55 ft. (17m.)
Average Temp.: Jan., 27°F (-3°C); July, 64°F (18°C)
Selected Hotels:
Berns, Nackstromsgatan 8
Birger Jarl, Tulegatan 8
Diplomat, Strandvagen 7C
Grand Sodra Blasieholmshamnen 8, opposite the
   Royal Palace
Lady Hamilton, Storkyrkobrinken 5
Reisen, Skeppsbron 12-14
Royal Viking, Vasagatan 1
Scandic Crown, Guldgrand 8
Sergel Plaza, Brunkebergstorg 9
Sheraton, Tegelbacken 6
Selected Restaurants:
Clas pa Hornet, De Fryas Krog, Den Glydene
   Freden, Edsbacka Krog, Franska Matsalen,
   Gasen, Hannas Krog, Kallaren Aurora,
   Operakällaren, Paul and Norbert, Stallmästare
   Garden
Banking: Hours are 9:30 A.M. to 3 P.M. on
   weekdays, but many larger banks stay open later.

Information Sources:
Scandinavian Tourist Board
655 3rd Avenue, Suite 1810
New York, New York 10017
212-949-2333

Sydney, Australia

Population: 3,623,550
Altitude: 75 ft. (23m.)
Average Temp.: Jan., 71°F (22°C); July, 53°F (12°C)
Selected Hotels:
Ana, 176 Cumberland St.
Holiday Inn, 242 Arden St., Coogee Beach
Hyatt Kingsgate, Kings Cross Road, Kings Cross
Inter-Continental, 117 Macquarie St.
Manly Pacific Park Royal, 55 N. Steyne, Manly
Nikko Potts Point, 81 Macleay St., Potts Point
Observatory, 89-113 Kent St., The Rocks
Ramada Renaissance, 30 Pitt St.
Regent, 199 George St.
Ritz-Carlton, 93 Macquarie St.
Selected Restaurants:
Bennelong, Berowra Waters Inn, Bilson's, Bourbon
   and Beefsteak, Claude's, Danny's Seafood,
   Darling Mills, Doyle's on the Beach, Forty-One,
   Kable's, Le Trianon, Oasis Seros, Oyster Bar,
   Paramount, Rockpool, Tet Suya's
Banking: Hours are 9:30 A.M. to 4 P.M., Monday
   through Thursday; 9:30 A.M. to 5 P.M. Friday.
   Major branches are open for extended hours.
Information Sources:
Australian Tourist Commission
100 Park Avenue, 25th Floor
New York, New York 10017
212-687-6300

Tel Aviv (Tel Aviv-Yafo), Israel

Population: 1,735,000
Altitude: 35 ft. (11m.)
Average Temp.: Jan., 57°F (14°C); July, 77°F (25°C)
Selected Hotels:
Carlton, 10 Hayarkon St.
Dan Panorama, 10 Y. Kaufman St.
Dan Tel Aviv, 99 Hayarkon St.
Grand Beach, 50 Haya
Moriah Plaza, 155 Hayarkon St.
Ramada Continental, 121 Hayarkon St.
Regency Suites, 80 Hayarkon St.
Sheraton Tel Aviv, 115 Hayarkon St.
Yamit Towers, 79 Hayarkon St.
Selected Restaurants:
Alexander's, Casba, Dixie, Keren, King Solomon
   Grill, Le Relais Jaffa, Little Tel Aviv/Mandy's,
   Loft, Prego, Succa Levana, Taboon, Twelve
   Tribes, Turquoise
Banking: Hours are 8:30 A.M. to 12:30 P.M. and 4
   P.M. to 6 P.M., Sunday through Friday; 4 P.M.
   to 6 P.M. on Tuesday and Thursday.
Information Sources:
Israel Tourist Office
800 Second Avenue, 16th Floor
New York, New York 10017
212-499-5600

Tōkyō, Japan
Population: 27,700,000
Altitude: 20 ft. (6m.)
Average Temp.: Jan., 39°F (4°C); July, 77°F (25°C)
Selected Hotels:
Capital, 10-3 Nagatacho 2-chome, Chiyoda-ku
Century Hyatt, 2-7-2 Nishi-Shinjuku, Shinjuku-ku
Hilton, 6-2 Nishi-Shinjuku 6-chome, Shinjuku-ku
Imperial, 1-1-1- Uchisaiwaicho, Chiyoda-ku
New Otani, 4-1 Kioicho, Chiyoda-ku
Okura, 10-4 Torahomon 2-chome, Minato-ku
Palace, 1-1-1 Marunouchi, Chiyoda-ku
Park Hyatt, 3-7-1-2 Nishi-Shinjuku, Shinjuku-ku
Seiyo Ginza, 1-11-2 Ginza, Chuo-ku
Westin, 2-18-9 Nishi-Asakusa, Taito-ku
Selected Restaurants:
Edo-Gin, Hakkaku, Heichinrou, Higo Batten,
  L'Orangerie, Robata, Sasashin, Sasashu, Takeno,
  Tatsumiya, Tokyo Joe's
Banking: Hours are 9 A.M. to 3 P.M., Monday
  through Friday.
Information Sources:
Japan National Tourist Organization
1 Rockefeller Plaza, Suite 1250
New York, New York 10020
212-757-5640

Toronto, Canada
Population: 3,427,168
Altitude: 275 ft. (84m.)
Average Temp.: Jan., 23°F (-5°C); July, 69°F (21°C)
Telephone Area Code: 416
Selected Hotels:
Best Western Chestnut Park, 108 Chestnut St.
Delta Chelsea Inn, 33 Gerrard St. W.
Four Seasons Hotel, 21 Avenue Rd.
The King Edward Hotel, 37 King St. E.
Novotel, 45 The Esplanade
Park Plaza, 4 Avenue Rd.
Royal York, 100 Front St. W.
Sheraton Centre Hotel & Towers, 123 Queen St. W.
Toronto Hilton, 145 Richmond St.
Westin Harbour Castle, 1 Harbour Sq.
Selected Restaurants:
Auberge du Pommier, Bistro Nine-Ninety, Boba,
  Cafe Victoria, Centro, Il Posto, Joso's, La Serre,
  Movenpick, North Forty-Four, Prego, Prince
  Arthur Room, Pronto, Royal Tea Room
Banking: Hours generally are 10 A.M. to 3 P.M.,
  Monday through Thursday, and 10 A.M. to 5
  P.M. or 6 P.M. on Friday. If Friday is a holiday,
  Friday hours are observed on Thursday. Many
  larger banks are open on Saturday.
Information Sources:
Tourism Toronto
207 Queens Quay West, Suite 590
Toronto, Ontario M5J 1A7
416-203-2600

Vienna (Wien), Austria
Population: 1,875,000
Altitude: 560 ft. (171m.)
Average Temp.: Jan., 30°F (-1°C); July, 68°F (20°C)
Selected Hotels:
Alt Stadt, Kirchengasse 41

Ambassador, Neuer Markt 5
Bristol Karntner Ring 1
Europa, Neuer Markt 3
Hilton, Am Stadtpark
Imperial, Karntner Ring 16
Konig Von Ungarn, Schulerstrasse 10
Marriott, Park Ring 12A
Opern Ring, Opern Ring 11
Palais Schwarzenberg, Schwarzenbergplatz 9
Sacher, Philharmonikstrasse 28
Selected Restaurants:
Hedrich, Imperial Cafe, Kaiserwalzer, Korso, Palais
  Schwarzenberg, Plachutta, Sirk, Schnattl, Steirer
  Eck, Vier Jahrenzeiten, Zu den Drei Husaren
Banking: Hours are 8:00 A.M. to 3 P.M., Monday
  through Friday. On Thursday, most banks remain
  open until 5:30 P.M.
Information Sources:
Austrian National Tourist Office
500 5th Avenue, 20th Floor
New York, New York 10110
212-944-6880

Zurich, Switzerland
Population: 870,000
Altitude: 1,339 ft. (408m.)
Average Temp.: Jan., 31°F (0°C); July, 63°F (17°C)
Selected Hotels:
Baur au Lac, Talstrasse 1
Central-Plaza, Central 1
City, Lowenstrasse 34
Dolder Grand, Kurhaustrasse 65
Glockenhof, Rossligasse 7
Neues Schloss, Stockerstrasse 17
Savoy Bauer en Ville, Am Paradeplatz
Schweizerhof, Bahnhofplatz 7
Splugenschloss, Splugenstrasse 2
Zum Storchen, Weinplatz 2
Selected Restaurants:
Grill Room, Haus zum Ruden, Hummer und
  Austern, Kronenhalle, La Rotonde, Petermann's
  Kunststuben, Piccoli Accademia, Tubli, Veltliner
  Keller, Zunfthaus zur Waag
Banking: Hours are 8:15 A.M. to 4:30 P.M.,
  Monday through Friday; most banks stay open
  until 6 P.M. on Thursday.
Information Sources:
Swiss National Tourist Office
608 5th Avenue
New York, New York 10020
212-757-5944

World Travel Maps

Inhabited Localities
The symbol represents the number of inhabitants within the locality

At scales 1:6,000,000 to 1:12,000,000

•	0–10,000
○	10,000–25,000
◉	25,000–100,000
▣	100,000–250,000
▣	250,000–1,000,000
■	>1,000,000

At 1:24,000,000 scale

•	0–50,000
◉	50,000–100,000
▣	100,000–250,000
▣	250,000–1,000,000
■	>1,000,000

 Urban Area (area of continuous industrial, commercial, and residential development)

The size of type indicates the relative economic and political importance of the locality

Écommoy	Lisieux	**Rouen**
Trouville	Orléans	**PARIS**

Capitals of Political Units

BUDAPEST — Independent Nation

Cayenne — Dependency (Colony, protectorate, etc.)

Lasa — State, Province, etc.

Alternate Names

MOSKVA / MOSCOW — English or second official language names are shown in reduced size lettering

Volgograd (Stalingrad) — Historical or other alternates in the local language are shown in parentheses

Political Boundaries

International (First-order political unit)

— Demarcated and Undemarcated

— Indefinite or Undefined

— Demarcation Line (used in Korea)

Internal

State, Province, etc. (Second-order political unit)

MURCIA — **Historical Region** (No boundaries indicated)

Transportation

— Primary Road
— Secondary Road
Canal du Midi — Navigable Canal
—]------[— Tunnel
— Ferry

Hydrographic Features

Intermittent Stream

Rapids, Falls

Irrigation or Drainage Canal

Reef

The Everglades — Swamp

VATNAJÖKULL — Glacier

L. Victoria — Lake, Reservoir

Tuz Gölü — Salt Lake

Intermittent Lake, Reservoir

Dry Lake Bed

Topographic Features

Matterhorn 4478	△	Elevation Above Sea Level
76	▽	Elevation Below Sea Level
Mount Cook 3764	▲	Highest Elevation in Country
Khyber Pass 1067	✕	Mountain Pass
133	▼	Lowest Elevation in Country

Elevations are given in meters, the Highest and Lowest Elevation in a continent are underlined

 Sand Area

 Lava

 Salt Flat

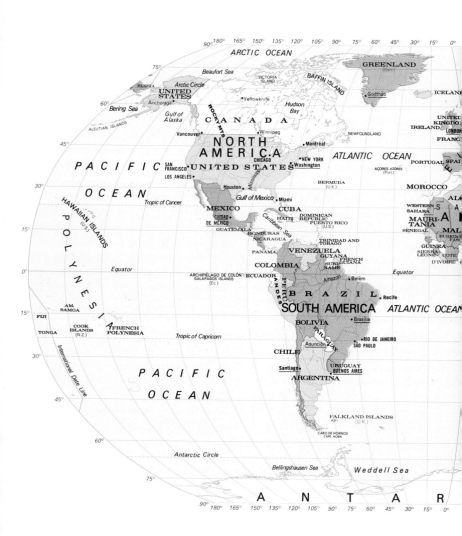

ARCTIC OCEAN

90° 180° 165° 150° 135° 120° 105° 90° 75° 60° 45° 30° 15°

75°

Beaufort Sea

GREENLAND
(Den.)

VICTORIA
ISLAND

BAFFIN ISLAND

ICELAND

RUSSIA

Arctic Circle

60°

•Yellowknife

Godthåb

UNITED
STATES

Hudson
Bay

UNITED
KINGDOM

Bering Sea

•Anchorage

C A N A D A

IRELAND

LONDON

NEWFOUNDLAND

FRANCE

Gulf of
Alaska

ROCKY MTS.

45°

ALEUTIAN ISLANDS

Vancouver•

•Winnipeg

NORTH
AMERICA

•Montréal

ATLANTIC   OCEAN

P A C I F I C

SAN
FRANCISCO•

CHICAGO
•

UNITED STATES

•NEW YORK
Washington

PORTUGAL SPAIN

LOS ANGELES •

AÇORES AZORES
(Port.)

30°

O C E A N

Houston
•

Gulf of Mexico

•Miami

BERMUDA
(U.K.)

MOROCCO

HAWAIIAN ISLANDS

Tropic of Cancer

AL

(U.S.)

MEXICO

CUBA

WESTERN
SAHARA

S   A

CIUDAD
DE MEXICO

HAITI

DOMINICAN
REPUBLIC
PUERTO RICO
(U.S.)

MAURI-
TANIA

A

15°

P

GUATEMALA

MAL

O

HONDURAS

Caribbean Sea

SENEGAL

BURKINA
FASO

L

NICARAGUA

GUINEA

Y

TRINIDAD AND
TOBAGO

SIERRA
LEONE

CÔTE
D'IVOIRE

0°

Equator

N

PANAMA

VENEZUELA

GUYANA
FRENCH

Equator

E

ARCHIPIÉLAGO DE COLÓN
GALÁPAGOS ISLANDS
(Ec.)

COLOMBIA

ECUADOR

SURI-
NAME

GUIANA

S

PERU

Amazon

•Belém

I

B R A Z I L

A

•Recife

15°

FIJI

AM.
SAMOA

A

SOUTH AMERICA

ATLANTIC OCEAN

ANDES

COOK
ISLANDS
(N.Z.)

FRENCH
POLYNESIA

BOLIVIA

•Brasília

TONGA

PARAGUAY

•RIO DE JANEIRO

Tropic of Capricorn

Asunción•

SÃO PAULO

30°

International Date Line

CHILE

Santiago•

URUGUAY
BUENOS AIRES

P A C I F I C

ARGENTINA

45°

O C E A N

FALKLAND ISLANDS
(U.K.)

60°

CABO DE HORNOS
CAPE HORN

Antarctic Circle

75°

Bellingshausen Sea

W e d d e l l   S e a

A N T A R   R

90° 180° 165° 150° 135° 120° 105° 90° 75° 60° 45° 30° 15° 0°

ARCTIC OCEAN

NOVOSIBIRSKIJE
OSTROVA

75°

Barents Sea   NOVAJA
               ZEML'A

Archangel'sk

RUSSIA   Arctic Circle

Jenisej   Lena

SANKT-PETERBURG   60°

FINLAND
Stockholm
NORWAY
SWEDEN

MOSKVA

BELA.

Sea of   Bering Sea
Okhotsk

DEN.
NETH.
GER.
POL.
UKRAINE

Novosibirsk

60°
OSTROV
SACHALIN

E U R O P E

ALPS
ITALY
ROM.
BUL.   Black Sea

KAZAKH.

MONGOLIA

GOBI

Harbin

Sea
of
Japan

45°

A S I A

KYRG.

BEIJING
PEKING

KOREA   JAPAN

Mediterranean
Sea
GREECE   TURKEY

UZBEK.
TURK.
Taškent
TAJIK.

TŌKYŌ

30°

SYRIA
ISRAEL
AL-QÁHIRAH
CAIRO   IRAQ
JORDAN
IRAN

AFGHANISTAN

C H I N A

HIMALAYAS

International Date Line

NEPAL   Chongqing   SHANGHAI

ERIA LIBYA   EGYPT   KUWAIT   PAKISTAN
QATAR   Tropic of Cancer

PACIFIC

H A R A
R I C A   SAUDI
ARABIA   OMAN

BNGL.
CALCUTTA

HONG
KONG   TAIWAN

OCEAN

15°

NIGER   CHAD
Red Sea
Nile   YEMEN   MUMBAI   INDIA
MYANMAR   LAOS
THAILAND   VIETNAM

South
China   Philippine
Sea   MANILA

MICRONESIA

SUDAN   Arabian
Sea   Bay of
Bengal   CAMB.   Sea   PHILIPPINES

KIRIBATI

NIGERIA
CAMEROON
CEN.
AFR. REP.
ETHIOPIA
SOMALIA
SRI
Colombo   LANKA

GABON   CONGO   DEM.   UGANDA
REP.   Lake   KENYA
Victoria
CONGO   TANZANIA

MALAYSIA

Equator   Equator   0°

SEYCHELLES   JAKARTA   INDONESIA   PAPUA
NEW GUINEA

MELANESIA

SOLOMON
ISLANDS

ANGOLA
ZAMBIA   I N D I A N   Port Moresby   15°

ZIMBABWE
MOZAMBIQUE
NAMIBIA
BOTSWANA   O C E A N   Coral
Sea   FIJI

Johannesburg   MADAGASCAR   Tropic of Capricorn

SWAZILAND   AUSTRALIA   Brisbane   30°

SOUTH
AFRICA   Perth   Sydney

Cape Town
CAPE OF GOOD HOPE   Melbourne   NEW
ZEALAND

TASMANIA   Wellington   45°

Antarctic Circle   60°

75°

C   T   I   C   A

Copyright © 1980
by Rand McNally & Co.
C-510000-064-9ᵛ-11ᵛ-11ᵛ-18ᵛ³

15°   30°   45°   60°   75°   90°   105°   120°   135°   150°   165°   180°   90°

Kilometres   0   1000   2000   3000 Km.
Miles   0   1000   2000   3000   Mi.
Robinson Projection

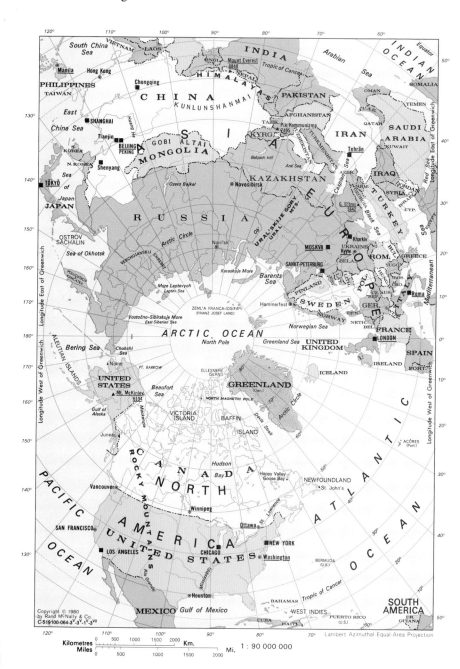

Kilometres 0 500 1000 1500 2000 Km.
Miles 0 500 1000 1500 2000 Mi.

1 : 90 000 000

Lambert Azimuthal Equal-Area Projection

Copyright © 1980
by Rand McNally & Co.
C-519100-064-3³-3³-1³-3V2

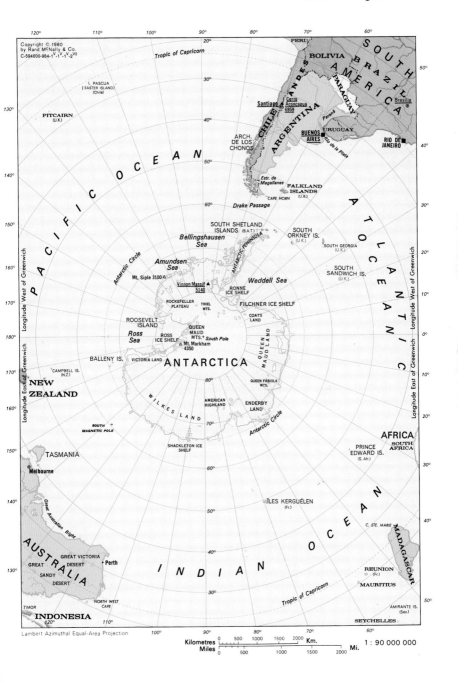

Copyright © 1980
by Rand McNally & Co.
C-594000-964-1ᵛ-1ᵛ-1ᵛ-2ᵛ²

Tropic of Capricorn

PERU
BOLIVIA
SOUTH AMERICA
BRAZIL

I. PASCUA
(EASTER ISLAND)
(Chile)

PITCAIRN
(U.K.)

Santiago
Cerro
Aconcagua
6959
CHILE
ARGENTINA
PARAGUAY
Brasilia

Paraná

ARCH.
DE LOS
CHONOS

BUENOS
AIRES
URUGUAY
Río de la Plata

RIO DE
JANEIRO

P A C I F I C   O C E A N

Estr. de
Magallanes
FALKLAND
ISLANDS
(U.K.)
CAPE HORN

Drake Passage

Antarctic Circle

SOUTH SHETLAND
ISLANDS (B.A.T.)
Bellingshausen
Sea
ANTARCTIC PENINSULA

SOUTH
ORKNEY IS.
(U.K.)

SOUTH GEORGIA
(U.K.)

A T L A N T I C

Amundsen
Sea

Mt. Siple 3100

Vinson Massif
5140

ROCKEFELLER
PLATEAU
THIEL
MTS.

RONNE
ICE SHELF

Weddell Sea

FILCHNER ICE SHELF

SOUTH
SANDWICH IS.
(U.K.)

O C E A N

Longitude West of Greenwich

ROOSEVELT
ISLAND

Ross
Sea
ROSS
ICE SHELF

QUEEN
MAUD
MTS.† South Pole
△ Mt. Markham
4350

COATS
LAND

Q
U
E
E
N

M
A
U
D

L
A
N
D

Longitude West of Greenwich

BALLENY IS.
VICTORIA LAND
A N T A R C T I C A

QUEEN FÁBIOLA
MTS.

Longitude East of Greenwich

CAMPBELL IS.
(N.Z.)

NEW
ZEALAND

W I L K E S   L A N D

AMERICAN
HIGHLAND
ENDERBY
LAND

Antarctic Circle

Longitude East of Greenwich

SOUTH
MAGNETIC POLE

SHACKLETON ICE
SHELF

AFRICA
SOUTH
AFRICA

PRINCE
EDWARD IS.
(S. Afr.)

TASMANIA

Melbourne

ÎLES KERGUÉLEN
(Fr.)

C. STE. MARIE

I N D I A N   O C E A N

Great Australian Bight

A U S T R A L I A

GREAT VICTORIA
DESERT

GREAT
SANDY
DESERT

Perth

REUNION
(Fr.)

MADAGASCAR

MAURITIUS

TIMOR

NORTH WEST
CAPE

INDONESIA

Tropic of Capricorn

AMIRANTE IS.
(Sey.)

SEYCHELLES

Lambert Azimuthal Equal-Area Projection

Kilometres 0 500 1000 1500 2000 Km.
Miles 0 500 1000 1500 2000

1 : 90 000 000

Kilometres 0 200 400 600 Km.
Miles 0 200 400 600 Mi.

1 : 24 000 000

Miller Oblated Stereographic Projection

ATLANTIC OCEAN

NORTH SEA

ATLANTIC OCEAN

Conic Projection, Two Standard Parallels

Kilometres 0 50 100 150 Km.
Miles 0 50 100 150 Mi.

1 : 7 500 000

Scale at bottom:

Kilometres 0 100 200 300 Km.

Miles 0 100 200 300 Mi.

1 : 13 000 000

Lambert Conformal Conic Projection

90

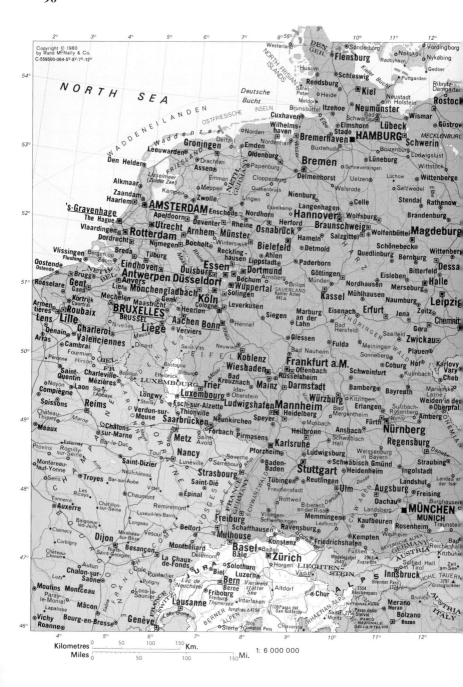

NORTH SEA

Kilometres 0 50 100 150 Km.
Miles 0 50 100 150 Mi.
1 : 6 000 000

BALTIC SEA

JGEN
Sassnitz
Stralsund
eifswald   Pomeranian
            Bay
emmin
eubrandenburg
eustrelitz
Prenzlau
Angermunde
erswalde
ERLIN
    Fürsten-
    walde
Potsdam
BRANDENBURG
ucken-
alde
Finster
walde
Cottbus
orgau   Lauch-
            hammer
Riesa
eiberg Dresden
Meissen
        Bautzen
Döbeln
sti nad Labem
Most
romutov Krupky nad
         Vltavou
Ostrov Kladno
        Beroun
Plzeň
Příbram
Strakonice
Pisek   Tábor
Vodňany

AP ARKONA

SŁOWIŃSKI
PARK NARODOWY
Władysławowo
Wejherowo   Hel
Darłowo   Słupsk
(Stolp)
Koszalin   Sławno N
(Köslin)
Kołobrzeg   Biały Bór
Karlino
Goleniów
Świnoujście
(Swinemünde)
WOLIŃSKI PARK
NARODOWY
Dobiegniew
Świdwin
Szczecinek
(Neustettin)
Chojnice
Szczecin (Stettin)
Stargard
Szczeciński
(Stargard in
Pommern)
Wałcz   Piła
(Schneidemühl)
Kcynia
Gorzów
Wielkopolski
(Landsberg) Oborniki
Chodzież
Szamotuły
Kostrzyn   Międzyrzecz
Frankfurt
an der Oder
Eisenhüttenstadt
Zielona   Sulechów Kościan
Góra
Guben   Lubsko Nowa Sól
(Grünberg) (Neusalz) Leszno
Żary   Szprotawa Rawicz
(Sorau)
Weisswasser Żmigród
Bolesławiec Legnica Wrocław
(Liegnitz) (Breslau)
Jelenia Góra Świdnica
(Hirschberg) (Schweidnitz)
Zittau   Liberec
Jablonec Trutnov
nad Nisou
Dvůr Králové
Mladá   Hradec
Boleslav Králové
Brandýs   Pardubice
Čáslav   Česko
Kolín   Třebová Svitavy
Hořovice
Kutná Hora
Havlíčkův
Brod
Čechtice Žďár nad
          Sázavou
Jihlava   Blansko
Jindřichův Třebíč
Hradec
Brno

Wisła
Gdynia
Gdańsk
(Danzig)
Starogard
Gdański
Tczew
Malbork
(Marienburg)
Elbląg
(Elbing)
Grudziądz
Świecie
Bydgoszcz
Toruń
Inowrocław
Włocławek
Gniezno
Poznań
WIELKOPOLSKI
PARK
NARODOWY
Września
Warta
Konin
WIELKOPOLSKA
Jarocin
Poddębice
Ostrów
Wielkopolski
Grabów
nad Prosną
Kluczbork
Oleśnica
Brzeg
Namysłów
Oława
Kłodzko
Nysa (Neisse)
Kłobuck
Opole
(Oppeln)
Kędzierzyn
Racibórz
(Ratibor)
Krnov
Opava
Ostrava

Gulf of
Danzig
Braniewo
Frombork
Ostróda
Morąg
Olsztyn
(Allenstein)
Nidzica
Działdowo
Mława
Wąbrzeźno
Nowe
Miasto
Lubawskie
Sierpc
Płock
Nowy Dwór
Mazowiecki
Łódź
Zduńska
Wola
Piotrków
Trybunalski
Radomsko
Częstochowa
Zawiercie
Bytom (Beuthen)
Zabrze
Katowice
Kraków
Bielsko-Biała
Żywiec

OWŚWIĘCIM
BABIÓ-GÓRSKI
PARK
NARODOWY
Zakopane

Baltijsk
Kaliningrad
(Königsberg)
RUSSIA
Lidzbark
Warmiński
Szczytno
Ostrołęka
Przasnysz
Ciechanów
Narew
Ostrów
Mazowiecka
Wyszków
Radziejów
Żyrardów
Grójec
Pruszków
WARSZAWA
WARSAW
KAMPINOSKI
PARK NARODOWY
Zgierz
Tomaszów
Mazowiecki
Radom
Pilica
Końskie
Skarżysko-
Kamienna
Kielce
Jędrzejów
Mielec
Tarnów
Nowy
Sącz
Jasło
Myślenice

Czerniachovsk
(Insterburg)
Bartoszyce
Gizycko
Mrągowo
Kolno
Łomża
POLAND
Ełk
Jezioro
Śniardwy
Grajewo
Nowy Dwór
Mazowiecki
Ostrów
Mazowiecka
Siedlce
Łuków
Dęblin
Puławy
Wieprz
Kock
Lublin
Skarżysko
Starachowice
Ostrowiec
Świętokrzyski
Stalowa
Wola
Nisko
Sokołów
Rzeszów
Krosno
Sanok
Ustrzyki
Dolne

Marijampole
Alytus
Suwałki
LITHUANIA
Nemunas
Augustów
Grodno
BELARUS
Białystok
BIAŁOWIESKI PARK
NARODOWY
Bug
Biała
Podlaska
POLAND
Brest
Minsk
Mazowiecki
Krasnystaw
Chełm
Włodawa
Krasnystaw
Zamość
Biłgoraj
Tomaszów
Lubelski
Jarosław
Przemyśl
Sambir
Turka

CZECH
REP.
POL.
Frýdek-Místek
Rožnov pod
Radhoštem
Žilina
Ružomberok
Poprad
Prešov
Košice
Michalovce
Uzhhorod
Muka-
cheve

GALICIA
BESKID MTS.
CARPATHIAN MOUNTAINS
TRANSKARPATSKA
Gerlachovský Štít
2655
Giraltovce
BIESZCZADZKI
PARK
Sanok
Turka

Cínovec
Teplice
Děčín
Česká Lípa

Praha
PRAGUE

CZECHOSLOVAKIA
Olomouc
Prostějov
Hranice
Vyškov
Slavkov u
Brna
Kyjov
Uherské
Hradiště
Zlín
Uherský
Brod
Trenčín
Nové Město
nad Váhom
Piešťany
Trnava
Nitra
Levice

SLOVAKIA
Martin
Prievidza
Banská
Bystrica
Zvolen
Žiar nad
Hronom
Rimavská
Sobota
Hron
Lučenec
Salgótarján
Vác
Eger
Miskolc
Ózd
Nyíregyháza
Satu Mare
Carei

HUNGARY
SLOVAKIA
Sárospatak
Polgár
Gyöngyös
Hajdúszoboszló
Debrecen
Berettyóújfalu
Oradea
Beiuş

Pribram
Strakonice
Pisek
Tábor
Vodňany
České
Budějov
Vyšší
Brod
Jindřichův
Hradec
Znojmo
Hodonín
Senica
ERMANY
FOREST
Schärding
Riedi
Innkreis
ickelarcbrucko
Linz
Wels
Steyr
MÜHLVIERTEL
Allentsteig
Hollabrunn
nad Váhom
Krems an
der Donau
Stockerau
Sankt
Pölten
Ybbs
an der
Donau
Baden
WIEN
VIENNA
Eisenstadt
Wiener
Neustadt
Neusiedler
See
Bratislava
Nové Zámky
Komárno
Győr
Sopron
Tatabánya
Komló
Budapest
BUDAPEST
Vecsés
Nagykáta
Karcag
Szolnok
Cegléd
Kecskemét
Szarvas
Békéscsaba
Gyula
Orosháza
Hódmezővásárhely
Szeged
Makó
Arad
Lipova
Mures
Nucet
Zerind

Salzburg
Bad Ischl
rchtesgaden
Sankt Johann
im Pongau
Radstadt
Spittal an der Drau
tsbach
Villach
KARAWANKEN
Klagenfurt
Wolfsberg
SLOVENIA
Maribor
Graz
Leoben
Oberwart
Mürzzuschlag
Kapfenberg
Frohnleiten
Hochschwab
2277
Hochgolling
2863
Ötscher
1893
Kirchdorf
an der
Krems
Hochschwab
Pfarrkirchen
Szombathely
Fürstenfeld
Zalaegerszeg
Nagykanizsa
Kaposvár
Szekszárd
Pécs
Mohács
Baja
Subotica
Kikinda
YUGO.
BANAT
Mura
HUNGARY
Keszthely
Ajka
Pápa
Veszprém
Székesfehérvár
Dunaújváros
Balaton
Tamási
Kiskunfélegyháza
Kiskunhalas
Kalocsa
Sombor
Bačko
Drava
Dráva
Varaždin
Koprivnica
Bjelovar
CROATIA
Tisza
1015
Kékes
víztároló

14° 15° 16° 17° 18° 19° 20° 21° 22° 23° 24°
54° 53° 52° 51° 50° 49° 48° 47° 46°

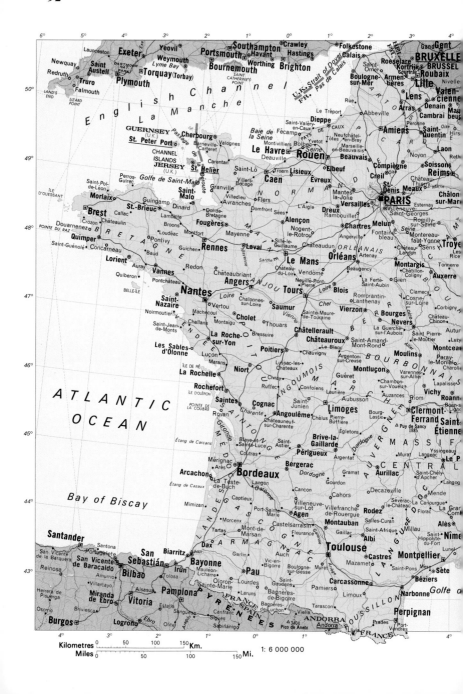

Lambert Conformal Conic Projection

Bay of Biscay

El Ferrol
del Caudillo
La Coruña
Cedeira
Vivero
Ribadeo
Mondoñedo
Luarca
Avilés
Gijón
Santander
San
Sebastián
Irún

Betanzos
Cangas
de Onis
San Vicente
de la Barquera
Portugalete
Santoña

Vimianzo
G A L I C I A
A S T U R I A S
C A N T Á B R I C A
San Vicente
de Baracaldo
Bilbao
Tolosa

Ordenes
Lugo
Grandas
C O R D I L L E R A
Reinosa
Villarcayo
Amurrio
Assua

Santiago de
Compostela
La Robla
Guardo
Herrera de
Pisuerga
Miranda
de Ebro
Vitoria
Estella

Padrón
Monforte
de Lemos
Ponferrada
León
Astorga
Sedano
Haro
Briviesca
Torrecilla en
Cameros
Logroño
Calahorra

Santa Eugenia
La Estrada
S P A I N
La Cañiza
Orense
Puebla
de Trives
Teleño
2188
La Bañeza
Valencia de
Don Juan
Osorno
Astudillo
Burgos
S I S T E M A

Vigo
Pontevedra
La Guardia
Miño
Minho
Valença
Montalegre
Benavente
Villalpando
Medina de
Rioseco
Banos
de Cerrato
Palencia
Lerma
Aranda
de Duero
Soria
Agreda

Viana do Castelo
P O R T U G A L
Chaves
Bragança
Alcañices
T I E R R A D E C A M P O S
Valladolid
Peñafiel
El Burgo
de Osma
Duero
Almazán
I B É R I C O

Vila do Conde
Braga
Mirandela
Duero
Toro
Tordesillas
Medina
del Campo
Arévalo
Riaza
Atienza
Molina de
Aragón

Porto
Vila Nova de Gaia
Vila Real
Douro
Torre de
Moncorvo
Zamora
Fuentesaúco
C A S T I L L A   L A   V I E J A
Ateca

São João
da Madeira
Vila Nova
de Foz Côa
La Fregeneda
Salamanca
Peñaranda de
Bracamonte
Segovia
Lozoyuela
Jadraque

Aveiro
Albergaria-
a-Velha
Viseu
Pinhel
Ciudad
Rodrigo
La Fuente de
San Esteban
Béjar
Guijuelo
Ávila
Colmenar
Viejo
Guadalajara
Sacedón

Figueira
da Foz
Estrela
1993
Belmonte
Guarda
S I S T E M A S
Peñaranda de
Navalcarnero
MADRID
Alcalá
de Henares
Huete
N U E V A
Cuenca

Mealhada
Covilhã
Hoyos
Pico de
Almanzor
2592
Getafe
Tarancón

Coimbra
Pombal
Plasencia
C A S T I L L A
Talavera
de la Reina
Maqueda
Aranjuez
Corral de
Almaguer

Leiria
Sertã
Castelo Branco
Tagus Tajo
Navalmoral
de la Mata
Torrijos
Toledo
Mora
Villacañas
Quintanar
de la Orden
Motilla d
Palancar

Alcobaça
Torres
Novas
Vila Velha
de Ródão
Garrovillas
Cáceres
Trujillo
Belvis de
la Jara
Tagus Tajo
Consuegra
Alcázar
de San Juan
La Roda

Caldas
da Rainha
Tagus Tejo
Portalegre
Valencia de
Alcántara
Montánchez
Navalvillar
de Pela
Herrera
del Duque
Socuéllamos
A

Vilafranca
de Xira
Azambuja
Santarém
Monforte
Estremoz
Elvas
Mérida
Guadiana
Daimiel
Tomelloso

Cascais
LISBOA
LISBON
Montemor-o-Novo
Badajoz
Don
Benito
Piedrabuena
C A S T I L L A
L A   M A N C H A
Albacete

Barreiro
Setúbal
Torrão
Évora
Alconchel
Almendralejo
Zafra
Cabeza
del Buey
Almadén
Ciudad
Real
Manzanares
Valdepeñas
Alcaraz

Alcácer do Sal
Viana do
Alentejo
Villafranca
de los Barros
S I E R R A
M O R E N A
Puertollano

Santiago do Cacém
A L E N T E J O
Barrancos
Fregenal
de la Sierra
Peñarroya-
Pueblonuevo
Azuaga
La Carolina
Linares
Villacarrillo
Caravaca

Odemira
Castro
Verde
Beja
Aracena
Constantina
Andújar
Bailén
Úbeda
La Sagra
2381
Lorc

Aljezur
Almodóvar
Calañas
Valverde
del Camino
Palma
del Río
Córdoba
Torredonjimeno
Fernán-Núñez
Jaén
Mancha Real
Baza
Vélez
Rubio
Huércal-
Overa

Portimão
Ayamonte
Lepe
Bollullos par
del Condado
Huelva
Carmona
Guadalquivir
Écija
Baena
Aguilar
Lucena
Granada
Guadix
Sorbas
Vera

CABO DE
SÃO VICENTE
Albufeira
Sagres
Faro
Golfo de
Los Palacios
y Villafranca
Sevilla
Alcalá de
Guadaira
Osuna
Estepa
A N D A L U C Í A
Mulhacén
3478
Almería

Cádiz
Sanlúcar de
Barrameda
Lebrija
Morón de
la Frontera
Ronda
Antequera
Loja
Motril
CABO DE GA

El Puerto de Santa María
Cádiz
Jerez de
la Frontera
S I S T E M A S
Málaga
Adra

San Fernando
Jimena de
la Frontera
Alhaurín
el Grande
Torremolinos

A T L A N T I C
Vejer de
la Frontera
Estepona

Algeciras
Gibraltar (U.K.)
Strait of Gibraltar
Estrecho de Gibraltar

O C E A N
Tanger
Tangier
Ceuta (Sp.)
Restinga
ISLA DE ALBORÁN
(Sp.)

Asilah
Tétouan
Souk-el-Arba-
de-Beni-Hassan
Melilla
(Sp.)

Larache
Ksar-el-
Kebir
Jbel
Bouhalla
2170
R I F
Al-Hoceima
M O R O C C O
Aït Youssef
ou Ali
Selouane
Ghazaouet

Conic Projection, Two Standard Parallels

Morcenx · Mont-de-Marsan · Tartas · Dax Garlin

Bayonne · Biarritz Mauléon-Licharre · Pau · Vic-en-Bigorre · Boulogne-sur-Gesse

GASCOGNE ARMAGNAC Castelsarrasin · Montauban · Albi · Gaillac Saint-Affrique

Fleurance · Auch Toulouse · Castres · Mazamet G. Saint-Pons

Saint-Hippolyte-du-Fort · Nîmes · Avignon · Manosque · Cavaillon · Beaucaire · Aix-en-Provence · Castellane MONACO · Nice Grasse · Cannes · Fréjus CÔTE D'AZUR

Muret · Ariège · Pamiers Montpellier · Sète · Béziers · Narbonne Mezo Lunel · Arles · Miramas · Martigues Marseille · Toulon · Hyères · La Seyne

LANGUEDOC

Oloron-Sainte-Marie · Lourdes · Saint-Gaudens · Bagnères-de-Bigorre Limoux · Carcassonne

amplona · iguesa · Pic d'Anie △2504 · Cónfranc · Sigüés Bagnères-de-Luchon · Viella · Pont de Suert · Seo de Urgel FRANCE SPAIN PYRENEES ANDORRA Llívia · Prades Perpignan · Port-Vendres

Golfe du Lion

Sabiñánigo dela · Huesca Jaca Barbastro · Monzón Solsona · Ripoll · Figueras · La Bisbal Gerona ROUSSILLON

Zuera Zaragoza · Lérida Balaguer · Cervera · Vich · Manresa · Granollers San Felíu de Guixols

lagón · Almunia · Doña Godina Pina · Fraga Borjas Blancas · Valls · Tarrasa Badalona BARCELONA

latayud · Daroca Caspe · Gandesa Hospitalet Reus · Villanueva y Geltrú Tarragona

Alcañiz onreal el Campo · Montalbán DELTA DEL EBRO

Santa Eulalia · Teruel Morella · Amposta San Carlos de la Rápita

orre aja Javalambre △2020 Benicarló

Landete · Viver Castellón de la Plana

VALENCIA Vall de Uxó · Sagunto

equenà Torrente · Golfo de Valencia

Ayora · Sueca Valencia Alcira · Gandía IBIZA

imansa Játiva · Albaida · Denia San Antonio Abad Ibiza

Villena · Alcoy Villajoyosa ISLAS BALEARES BALEARIC ISLANDS

Elda Alicante

Crevillente · Elche Torrevieja

Murcia Totana MEDITERRANEAN SEA

aza · Cartagena

MENORCA MINORCA

Puerto de Pollensa · Ciudadela · Mahón

Sóller · Palma · Manacor · Artá MALLORCA MAJORCA

ALGER ALGIERS Dellys · Tizi-Ouzou Bejaïa (Bougie) · Djidjelli · El Milia

Bordj Menaiel KABYLIE El Kseur · Kherrata Oued Athmenia

Cherchell · Koléa Lakhdaria · Bouira Tamgout de Lalla Khedidja △2308 Sétif Chergoum el Aïd

Ténès · Djebel bou Maad △1415 Blida · Médéa Bir Ghbalou MOUNTAINS TELLIEN Bordj Bou Arreridj El Eulma · Batna

DAHRA Khemis Miliana Col de Ben-Chicao 1230 ATLAS MONTS DU HODNA

Mostaganem El Asnam (Orléansville) Sidi Aïssa M'Sila

Ighil Izane Oued Chelif · Oued Rhiou Djebel Ouarsenis △1985 Ksar el Boukhari ALGERIA PLAINE DU HODNA Aïn Touta

Oran (Ouahran) ATLAS TELLIEN ATLAS Bougzoul · Aïn Oussera Bou Saâda Chott el Hodna

Sig · Mohammadia Tissemsilt

Hassi el Ghella Sebkha d'Oran Aïn mouchent Sidi bel Abbès Remchi

Kilometres 0   50   100   150 Km.
Miles 0   50   100   150 Mi.
1: 6 000 000

Kilometres
Miles

1: 6 000 000

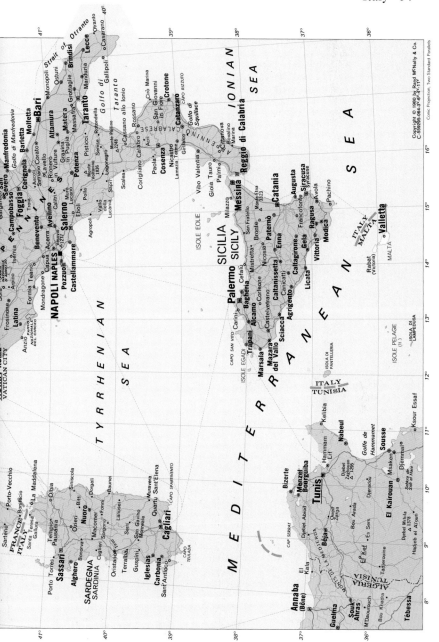

Strait of Otranto

Otranto

Casarano 40°

Lecce

Brindisi

Monopoli · Ostuni

Manduria

Grottaglie

Bari

Molfetta

Barletta

Golfo di Manfredonia

Mantredonia

San Severo

Gargano

Cerignola

Foggia

Troia

Molise

Campobasso

Isernia

Altamura

Matera

Massafra

Taranto

Golfo di Taranto

Taranto

Ciro Marina

Crotone

CAPO RIZZUTO

Catanzaro

Golfo di Squillace

IONIAN SEA

Ascoli Satriano

Corato

Lavello

Gravina in Puglia

Pisticci

Senise

Rotondella

San Giovanni in Fiore

APPENNINO

CALABRESE

Rionero in Vulture

Potenza

Muro Lucano

Monte Vulture 1326

Laghi

Monte Pollino 2248

Cassano allo Ionio

Corigliano Calabro

Rossano

Acri

Cosenza

Catania

Benevento

Avellino

Salerno

Acerra

Eboli

Battipaglia

Agropoli

Valle della Lucania

Sapri

Scalea

Paola

Nicastro

Lamezia Terme

Gioiaco

Vibo Valentia

Reggio di Calabria

Messina

Milazzo

Augusta

Siracusa

Syracuse

Avola

Pachino

E N N I N O

ROME

VATICAN CITY

NAPOLI NAPLES

Pozzuoli

Castellammare

Sorrento

Capua

Acerra

Mondragone

Formia

Teano

Arpino

Latina

Anzio

PARCO NAZIONALE DEL CIRCEO

Frosinone

Gaeta

Golfo di Napoli

ISCHIA

CAPRI

San Fratello

Mistretta

Bronte

Nicosia

Monte Etna 3323

Patern

SICILIA

SICILY

Palermo

Bagheria

Cefalù

Caltanissetta

Enna

Caltagirone

Gela

Ragusa

Modica

Vittoria

Licata

Agrigento

Canicattì

Castelvetrano

Sciacca

Mazara del Vallo

Marsala

Trapani

Alcamo

Carini

CAPO SAN VITO

ISOLE EGADI

ISOLA DI PANTELLERIA

ISOLE EOLIE

ITALY

MALTA

Valletta

MALTA

Rabat (Victoria)

ISOLA DI LAMPEDUSA

ISOLE PELAGE (It.)

T Y R R H E N I A N

S E A

M E D I T E R R A N E A N

S E A

ITALY

TUNISIA

Kelibia

Nabeul

Golfe de Hammamet

Sousse

Msaken

Djemmal

Ksour Essaf

Hammam Lif

Menzel Bourguiba

Bizerte

Tunis

El Kairouan

Djebel Zaghouan 1295

Sahra el Haïrl

Djebel Mdila 1378

Sfax

SARDEGNA

SARDINIA

Sartène

Porto-Vecchio

Bonifacio

FRANCE

ITALY

Santa Teresa Gallura

La Maddalena

Tempio-Pausania

Olbia

Siniscola

Bitti

Dorgali

Nuoro

Oliena

Baunei

Ozieri

Macomer

Sorgono

Lanusei

Seui

Porto Torres

Sassari

Alghero

Bonorva

Cagliari

Oristano

Terralba

Guspini

San Giovanni Suergiu

Montevecchio

Iglesias

Carbonia

Sant'Antioco

Quartu Sant'Elena

Cagliari

CAPO SPARTIVENTO

CAPO TEULADA

CAP SERRAT

CAP DE FER

Annaba (Bône)

Guelma

Souk Ahras

M'Daourouch

Bou Khadra

Tébessa

ALGERIA

TUNISIA

El Kala

Djebel Abiod

Oued Zarga

Béja

Tadjerouine

Bou Arada

Chaïl Zarga

Es Sers

M O N T S   D E   L A   M E D J E R D A

38°

39°

37°

36°

38°

39°

40°

41°

37°

36°

8°

9°

10°

11°

12°

13°

14°

15°

16°

Conic Projection, Two Standard Parallels

Copyright © 1980 by Rand McNally & Co.

C-559295-064-3°-6°-4°-11°

1 : 6 500 000

Kilometres 0 50 100 150 Km.

Miles 0 50 100 150 Mi.

1: 6 000 000

33° 34° 35° 36° 37° 38° 39° 40° 41° 42° 43° 44° 45°

Ustje
zero
doga Lodejnoe Polje Annenskij Most Isakovo Ogibalovo Velikodvorskaja Volockaja Sergijevskaja Suchoj Pavolvo 60°
virica Pavšozero Levino Ostrov Kadnikovskij Michajlovskij
Alechovščina M'agozero Kovžinski Lipin Bor Krutec S'amža Gora Tot'ma Zelencovo
S'as'stroj Krasnaja Gora Zavod Ozero Popovka Žitjevo Starina
Kost'kovo Bol'šaja Chundala Pustin' Beloje Beloz'orsk Fominskoje Kn'azovo Nikol'skoje
Volchov Radogošča Sofronovo Bičevinka Ustje Cekšino Golubj Jurenino Pankratovo
Tichvin Čuny Leonicha Sokol Sujskoje Soligalič Kologriv
lazevo Podborovje Velikoje Voskresenskoje Moločnoje Vologda Vosja kotrema Bol'šaja 59°
Boksitogorsko Babajevo Šeksna Korcevo Cuchloma Pas'ma
Budogošč Somino Kaduj Fominskoje Gr'azovec Manturovo
Nebolči Sazonovo Čerepovec Baklanka Nikolo-Berezovec Neja
ol'šaja Anciferovo Chvojnaja Imeni Vanskoje M'aksa Buj Lopar'ovo 58°
šera Zarubino Žel'abova Vesjegonsk DARVINSKIJ Pošechonje L'ubim Galič Kommunar
Malaja Ustreka Pestovo ZAPOVEDNIK Volodarsk Danilov Severnoje Voronjo Makarjev
Visera Verb'jo Rybinskoje Vodochranilišče Ostrovskoje Gorcucha
Okulovka Vel'gija Bol'šoje Ovinišče Danilov Severnoje Voronjo
Krestcy Borovici Lesnoje Ramenje Krasnyj Cholm Rybinsk Kostroma Makarjev Gorcucha
Uglovka Karel'skij Gorodok Volga Volga Tutajev Zavolžsk
Lyčkovo Berezajka Udoml'a Sonkovo Jaroslavl' Nekrasovskoje 57°
Valdaj Bologoje Bežeck Uglič Kinešma Jurjevec Gorkovskoje Vodochranilišče
Polnovo- Trud Morkiny Nerechta Furmanov Vičuga Sokol'skoje
Seliger Firovo Vyšnij Voloček Gory Gavrilov-Jam Okt'abr'skij Pučez
ALDAJSKAJA Spirovo Kašin Kal'azino Rostov Ivanovo Myt Gorodec
arevo Kalašnikovo Goricy Gora Tarchov Petrovskoje Tejkovo Šuja Pučez
Ostaškov Kuvšinovo Toržok Vasiljevskij Cholm 294 Archipovka NIŽNIJ 56°
Peno Selizarovo Moch Belyj Gorodok Kimry Pereslavl'-Zalesskij Juža NOVGOROD
teklino Babino Tver' Dubna Jurjev- Gavrilov Posad (GORKY)
VO ZVYŠENNOST' Suchoverkovo Zaprudn'a Pol'skij Kovrov V'azniki Dzeržinsk
CENTRAL'NOLESNOJ Turginovo Krasnozavodsk Aleksandrov Vladimir Orgtrud Stepancevo Bogorodsk
ZAPOVEDNIK Bachmutovo Vysokovsk Dmitrov Sergijev Posad Pavlovo
Nelidovo Ržev Stepurino Volokolamsk Solnečnogorsk Krasnoarmejsk Krasa Oka Vaca
Obuchova Novos'olki Sachovskaja Istra Mytišči Balašicha Sobinka Krasnoje Černucha
Žarkovskij Tatarinka Syčovka Ruza Moskva Orechovo- Echo Murom 55°
Vladimirskij Tupik Novodugino Tučkovo MOSKVA L'ubercy Zujevo Rošal' Gus'-Chrustal'nyj Kulebaki
Cholm- Gagarin MOSCOW Čerusti Melenki Vyksa Ardatov
Zirkovskij Kasn'a Možajsk Aprelevka Jegorjevsk Velikodvorskij Koselicha
ulgakovo V'az'ma Peredel Naro- Podol'sk Domodedovo Voskresensk Spas-Klepiki Semilovo MORDOVSKIJ
arcevo Safonovo Fominsk Čechov Kolomna Kasimov Jelat'ma ZAPOVEDNIK Jermiš
Koloďn'a Mytišino Obninsk PRIOKSKO Ozery Solotca OKSKIJ ZAPOVEDNIK Poltevy Javas 54°
Ozerišče Dejln'a Ugra Klimov Kondrovo Serpuchov TERRASNYJ Kašira Beloomut Pen'ki At'urjevo
SKO L'udovo Zavod Polotn'anyj ZAPOVEDNIK R'azan' Murmino Cučkovo Torbejevo
Spas-Demensk Peremyšl Aleksin Jasnogorsk Serebr'anyje Spassk-R'azanskij Zubova Vysa
Chislaviči Jekimoviči Meščovsk Dugna Venev Prudy Mosolovo Pol'ana
Kirov Voloje Leninskij Tula Novomoskovsk Skopin Ucholovo Sapožok Šack Zemetčino
Roslavl' Suchiniči Čerepet' Ščokino Donskoj Kimovsk Sarai Algasovo 53°
Šum'aci Dubrovka Kozel'sk Odojev Bogorodick Gorn'ak Moršansk
Miloslaviči Duchovščij Bel'ovo Chot'kovo Meščerino Tovarkovskij Aleksandro-Nevskij Starojurjevo Otjassy Rudovka
Kletn'a D'at'kovo Jelenskij Bolchov Turdej Dankov Caplygino Pervomajskij Basmakovo
Belynkoviči Fokino Mcensk Korsakovo Lebed'an' Gorelo je 52°
Mglin Br'ansk Belyje Berega Or'ol Novosil' Lamskoje Kujman' Mičurinsk Rasskazovo Tambov
Suraž Počep Sven' Somovo Rizmalkovo Lipeck Belomestnaja Um'ot
Klincy Ramasucha Navl'a Altuchovo Kromy Zmijovki Syrskij Gr'azi Kotovsk Inža vino
Starodub Trubč'ovsk Dmitrovsk Maloarchangel'sk Livny Verchn' Nižnaja Sampur R'aksa Vyselki
Klimovo Belaja Ber'ozka Orlovski Železnogorsk Kolpny Oki'abr'skoje Matrenka Taličkij Čamlyk Uvarovo
Sem'onovka Znob-Novgorodskoje Sevsk Fat'oz Dolgoje Usman' VORONEŽSKIJ Žerdevka Šapkino
Urickoje ZAPOVEDNIK

33° 34° 35° 36° 37° 38° 39° 40°

Kilometres 0 200 400 600 **Km.**
Miles 0 200 400 600 **Mi.**

1 : 24 000 000

80° 125° 130° 135° 140° 145° 150° 155° 160° 165° 170° 175° 180° 175° 170°

70°

80°

75°

60°

55°

50°

45°

40°

175°

180°

175°

170°

165°

160°

155°

150°

145°

Chukchi Sea

OSTROV VRANGELA

Arctic Circle

Bering Strait

Providenija

MYS SEUKKO

EKVATAPSKIJ CHREBET

MYS SMIDTA

Egvekinot

Provideniji

Beringovskij

MORE LAPTEVYCH

NOVOSIBIRSKIJE OSTROVA

VOSTOČNO-SIBIRSKOJE MORE

EAST SIBERIAN SEA

OSTROV NOVAJA SIBIR

OSTROV BOLSOJ LACHOVSKIJ

LAPTEV SEA

OSTROV KOTEL'NYJ

Ust-Čaun

Gora Gvozd 1853

Ust-Belaja

Anadyr'

Anadyr

MYS SV'ATOJ NOS

Ust-Bel'aja

Bering

180°

175°

Tabor

Ambarčik

Belaja

Anuj

Jeropol

Chatyrka

170°

60°

Buolkalach

Sklad

Sokol

Lena

Čcholodach

Indigirka

Kazačje

Severnaja

Omolon

Nizkovo

Oloj

Penžina

Manily

Sugoj

KORAKSKOJE NAGORJE

Bering Sea

170°

Udza

Sikt'ach

Kjusjur

Žardzan

Suchana

SIBERIA

VERCHOJANSKIJ

Verchojansk

Adiča

CHREBET ČERSKOGO

Choniu

Gora Pobeda 3147

Zyr'anka

Balygyčan

Omsukčan

Sejmčan

Kedon

Gižiga

Zaliv Šelichova

Palana

165°

60°

Sologoncy

Syalach

JE

N'urba

Suordach

Oj'mjakon

Chandyga

Gora Mus-Chaja 2959

Kadykčan

Inia

Onča

Spornoje

Tumany

Jamsk

Kirovskij

Ključevskaja Sopka 4750

55°

Tuobuja

Jakutsk

Amga

Ust-Maja

CHREBET

Lena

Ynykčanskij

Magadan

Ochotsk

Morošečnoje

Skapino

Kirovskij

Petropavlovsk Kamčatskij

160°

O'okminsk

Aldan

Lena

Ulu

Cagda

Gonam

Ajan

Ner'kan

ŠANTARSKIJE OSTROVA

SEA OF OKHOTSK

OCHOTSKOJE MORE

POLUOSTROV KAMČATKA

Maka

Žertovskij

Severo-Kuril'sk

50°

Kropotkin

Bodajbo

NAGORJE

STANOVOJE

Čumikan

Ocha

Nikolajevsk-na-Amure

OSTROV SACHALIN SAKHALIN

KURIL'SKIJE OSTROVA

KURIL ISLANDS

155°

STANOVOJ

MOUNTAINS

Kalakan

Tyndinskij

Zeja

Selemdža

Guga

Aleksandrovsk-Sachalinskij

Aleutka

Kuril'sk

45°

Bagdarin

Vitim

Mogoča

Never

Zeja

Amur

Poronajsk

Kuril'sk

Simanovsk

Cegdomyn

Sovetskaja Gavan

Južno-Sachalinsk

150°

Bukacaca

Stretensk

Svobodnyj

Komsomol'sk-na-Amure

Čita

Nerčinskij Zavod

Rajčichinsk

Blagoveščensk

Chabarovsk

La Perouse Strait

Wakkanai

Borz'a

Birobidžan

Nayoro

145°

Chapčeranga

Manzhouli

Cojbalsan

Hailar

Butehaqi

NEI MONGGOL ZIZHIQU

INNER MONGOLIA

Beian

HEILONGJIANG

Hegang

Shuangyashan

Bikin

Lesozavodsk

SICHOTE-ALIN'

Terney

Asahikawa

Obihiro

Kushiro

PACIFIC

Qiqihar

Hurao

Jixi

Spassk-Dal'nij

Kavalerovo

Sapporo

Muroran

HOKKAIDO

OCEAN

Tailai

Harbin

Mudanjiang

JILIN

Ussurijsk

Vladivostok

Nachodka

SEA OF JAPAN

Hakodate

Aomori

JAPAN

Hachinohe

HONSHU

Akita

Morioka

CHINA

115°

120°

Lambert Conformal Conic Projection

45°

135°

40°

145°

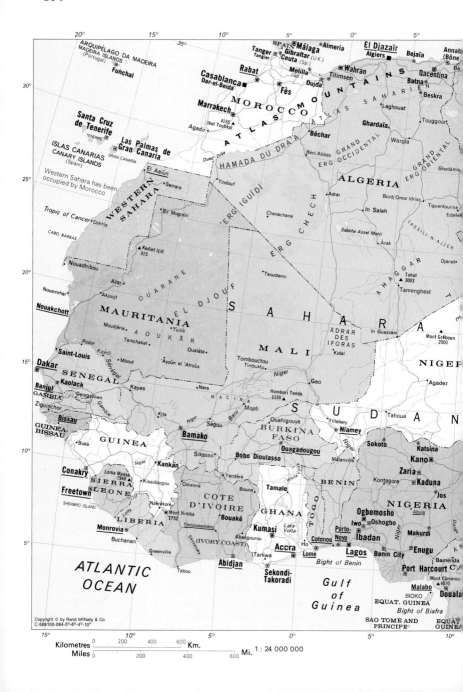

ARQUIPÉLAGO DA MADEIRA
MADEIRA ISLANDS
(Portugal)
Funchal

SPAIN
Tanger ■Málaga ●Almería
Tanger Gibraltar (U.K.) El Djazaïr Bejaïa Annab
Tangier Ceuta (Sp.) Algiers (Bône
Melilla Be
Rabat (Sp.) ■Wahran Qacentina
Casablanca ●Oujda Tilimsen Batna● ●Beskra
Dar-el-Beida■ Fès Laghouat Touggoúrt
Marrakech MOROCCO Ghardaïa● Wargla

Santa Cruz
de Tenerife 4165▲ Jbel Toubkal Ghardaïa● GRAND Ghudámis
TENERIFE Agadir ATLAS MOUNTAINS ERG OCCIDENTAL
ISLAS CANARIAS ATLAS SAHARIEN ERG
CANARY ISLANDS Oued Drâa Béchar ORIENTAL
GRAN CANARIA HAMADA DU DRÂA Béni Abbas
Las Palmas de
Gran Canaria

Western Sahara has been
occupied by Morocco El Aaiún ALGERIA
Tropic of Cancer Semara Adrar TASSILI-N-AJJER
CABO BARBAS Dakhla Tindouf Chenachane In Salah Tiguentourine
Bir Mogrein Bordj Omar Idriss Edjelei
WESTERN ERG IGUIDĪ Sebkha Azzel Matti Djanet
SAHARA Árak
Kediet Ijill ERG CHECH AHAGGAR Tahat
915▲ Taoudenni ▲3003
Nouadhibou Tamenghest
Nouamrhar● Atar● OUARANE In Guezzam Mont Grébou
Akjoujt SAHARA 2000▲
Nouakchott EL DJOUF
MAURITANIA ADRAR NIGER
Moudjéria● A O U K Â R DES
Saint-Louis Tamchakt IFORAS
Kaédi Ouâlâta MALI Kidal ●Agadez
Podor Mbout
Dakar ●Ayoûn el 'Atroûs Tombouctou
SENEGAL Nara Timbouctou Gao
Kaolack Kayes Niger
Banjul Georgetown Hombori Tondo SUDAN Tahoua
GAMBIA Gambie M A C I N A 1155▲
Ziguinchor Kita Mopti Tillabery
BISSAU Niger Ségou Bani Niamey Sokoto Katsina
GUINEA- Ouahigouya
BISSAU Boké BURKINA Kano
GUINEA Bamako FASO Malanville Zaria
Sikasso Bobo Dioulasso Ouagadougou Kontagora Kaduna
Kankan ●Jos
Conakry Loma Mansa Kissidougou Odienné Yendéré Bouna BENIN NIGERIA
1948▲ White Abuja
Freetown SIERRA Tamale TOGO Ogbomosho
LEONE Nzérékoré Mont Nimba Iwo● ●Oshogbo
SHERBRO ISLAND 1752▲ COTE Bouaké GHANA Ibadan Makurdi
LIBERIA D'IVOIRE Kumasi Lake Porto- Benin City Enugu
Monrovia Yamoussoukro Abengourou Volta Novo Lagos
Buchanan (IVORY COAST) Ho Cotonou Port Harcourt C.
Greenville Accra Bamend
Tarkwa Lomé Malabo Mont Cameroun
ATLANTIC Tabou Abidjan Bight of Benin BIOKO 4070▲ Douala
OCEAN Sekondi- Gulf EQUAT. GUINEA Bight of Biafra
Takoradi of SAO TOME AND EQUAT
Copyright © by Rand McNally & Co. Guinea PRINCIPE GUINEA
C-589100-064-5ᵛ-6ᵛ-4ᵛ-10ᵛ

15° 10° 5° 0° 5° 10°
Kilometres 0 200 400 600 Km.
Miles 0 200 400 600 Mi. 1 : 24 000 000

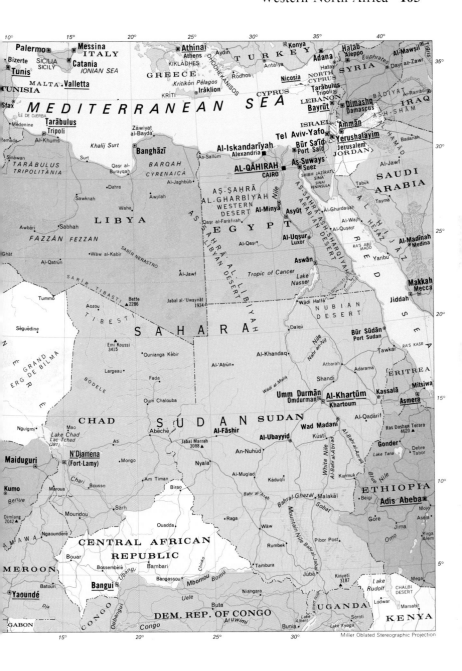

10° 15° 20° 25° 30° 35° 40°

Palermo Messina **ITALY**
Bizerte SICILIA Catania 35°
Tunis SICILY IONIAN SEA
MALTA **Valletta**
TUNISIA
Sfax
Ṭarābulus
Médenine Tripoli
Temada Al-Khums

Athínai Aydin **TURKEY** Konya **Halab** Al-Mawṣil
Athens KIKLADHES Antalya Adana Aleppo Euphrates Dayr az-Zawr
GREECE DODEKANISOS Hatay **SYRIA** IRAQ
Kritikón Pélagos Rhodos NORTH **Nicosia** **Ṭarābulus** BĀDIYAT
KRITI Iráklion CYPRUS Tripoli AŞ ŞĀM Ar-Ramādī
MEDITERRANEAN SEA LEBANON **Dimashq** HAMAD
Bayrūt **Damascus** ASH SHĀM

ÎLE DE DJERBA
Sināwan TARĀBULUS
Ṣawknah

Zāwiyat al-Bayḍā' Khalīj Surt
Banghāzī BARQAH
Surt Qaṣr al-Burayqah CYRENAICA
Al-Jaghbūb
As-Sallūm
Al-Iskandarīyah
Alexandria **Būr Saʿīd**
Port Said
Al-Qāhirah
CAIRO
As-Suways
Suez

ISRAEL
Tel Aviv-Yafo
'Ammān
Yerushalayim
Jerusalem
JORDAN

BADIYAT
HAMAD Badanah
Al-Jawf
SAUDI
Tabūk ARABIA

Dahra
AŞ-ṢAḤRĀ AL-GHARBĪYAH
WESTERN DESERT
Al-Minyā
SHIBH JAZĪRAT SĪNĀ
SINAI PENINSULA
Al-Ghurdaqah
Tayma

LIBYA
Awbārī •Sabhah
FAZZĀN FEZZAN
Ghāt Al-Qatrūn

Āwjilah
Waha
Qaṣr al-Farāfirah
Al-Minyā **Asyūṭ**
EGYPT
Al-Qaṣr
Al-Uqṣur
Luxor
Aswān

AL MADINAH
Medina

Al-Wajh
Al-Quṣayr
RAʾS ABŪ MADD

AL HEJAZ
Yanbu

Al-Madīnah
Medina

Tummo
Awbari
SARĪR TIBESTĪ
Bette 2286
Aozou
TIBESTI
Séguédine
Emi Koussi 3415

GRAND ERG DE BILMA
Largeau
BODÉLÉ

SARĪR NERASTRO
Āl-Jawf
Tropic of Cancer
Jabal al-'Uwaynāt 1934▲
SAHARA

Lake Nasser
NUBIAN DESERT
Wādī Ḥalfā

Dalqū

Bûr Sûdân
Port Sudan
RAʾS KASR

Makkah
Mecca
Jiddah

Nguigmi
Mao
Lake Chad
Lac Tchad (281)
N'Djamena
(Fort-Lamy)
Maiduguri
Kumo
Benue
Dimlang 2042▲

CHAD
Ati •Mongo
Chari
•Bousso
•Maroua
Moundou
Ngaoundéré

Abéché•
Jabal Marrah 3088▲
•Am Timan
SUDAN
Al-Fāshir
Nyala•
Al-Muglad
KĀduqli
•Birao
•Sarh

Ouanga Kébir
Fada•
•Oum Chalouba
Al-'Atrūn
Al-Khandaq•

Largeau
SARĪR TIBESTĪ
Al-Khandaq•
Atbarah
Shandi

Abéché•
Jabal Marrah 3088▲
Al-Ubayyiḍ
An-Nuhūd•
Bahr al-'Arab

SUDAN
Wad Madani
Al-Kharṭūm
Khartoum
Umm Durmān
Omdurman

Nahr an Nīl
Nile
Tawkar

Kassalā
Asmera
ERITREA
Mitsiwa

Ras Dashen Terara 4620▲
Gonder
Lake Tana
Debre Tabor

Kûstī
Al-Qaḍārif

CENTRAL AFRICAN REPUBLIC
Bouar
Bossembélé•
Bambari•
Bangui
Batouri•
Dja•

•Raga
Wāw•
Ouadda•
Rumbek•
Bangassou•
Mbomou
Bomu
Niangara•
Uele
Buta•

Mountain Nile
Baḥr al-Ghazal
Sobat
Malakāl•
Pibor Post•

White Nile
Baḥr al-Jabal

Adis Abeba
ETHIOPIA
•Beigi
Gore•
Jima•
Mojo•
Asela•
Yirga Alem•
Omo

Kinyeti 3187
Jûba
Tambura•
CAMEROON
Yaoundé
GABON

CONGO
Congo
Oubangui
Chinko
Aruwimi
DEM. REP. OF CONGO
Bunia•
Lake Albert

UGANDA
Soroti•
Lake Kyoga

•Mega
CHALBI DESERT
Lake Rudolf
Lowdar•
Marsabit•
KENYA

15° 20° 25° 30°

Miller Oblated Stereographic Projection

35°
30°
25°
20°
15°
10°
5°

SAO TOME AND PRINCIPE
•São Tomé
Libreville
Port-Gentil
Iguéla•
Mouila•
Tchibanga•

EQUATORIAL GUINEA
Mekambo•
Boouê
GABON
Franceville•
Lambaréné•
Lac Mai-Ndombe
Kibangou
Dolisie•

CAMEROON
•Ouesso
Oubangui
•Befale
Basankusu
Congo
Basoko•
Bokungu
Ikela•
Ubundi•
Lokoloma•
Lomela•
Bena-Dibele•

Aruwimi
Bunia•
Lake Albert
Lake Kyoga
Kisangani (Stanleyville)
5109
Margherita Pk.
STANLEY FALLS
Kampala
Entebbe
UGA

Fort-Rousset•
Mossaka•
Bikoro•
Mbandaka (Coquilhatville)
DEM. REP.

Brazzaville
Pointe-Noire
CABINDA (Angola)
Boma
Matadi
Kinshasa (Léopoldville)
Kikwit•
Bandundu•
Kutu•

OF THE
CONGO
Kindu•
Bukavu•
RWANDA
BURUNDI
Kigali
Bujumbura
Lake Tanganyika

N'zeto•
Ambriz•
Luanda
Caxito•
Dondo•
Porto Amboim•
M'Banza Congo
Negage•
Sanza Pombo•
Feshi•
Popokabaka•
Cuango•
Kahemba•
Chitato•
Camissombo•
Kapanga•
Tshikapa•
Kananga (Luluabourg)
Mbuji-Mayi (Bakwanga)
Kaniama•
Kamina•
Kongolo•
Tshota•
Manono•
Kalémie (Albertville)
Mpanda•
Lake Rukwa
Kasanga•
Mbala•

ANGOLA
Malange•
Caúngula•
Saurimo•
Kasaji•
Lubudi•
Kolwezi•
Likasi (Jadotville)
Lubumbashi (Elisabethville)
Mufulira
Kitwe
Ndola
Luanshya
Kawambwa•
Kasenga•
Kasama•
Lake Mweru
MUCHINGA MTS.
Mpika•

ATLANTIC
Lobito
Serra do Môco 2620▲
Huambo (Nova Lisboa)
Caconda•
Kuito•
Munhango•
Luena•
Balovale•
Solwezi•
Mumbwa•
ZAMBIA
Kabwe (Broken Hill)
Lusaka

OCEAN
Namibe
Lubango•
Kassinga•
Caiundo•
Menongue•
N'Riquinha•
Mussuma•
Mongu•
Senanga•
Mankoya•
Choma•
Zambezi
Zumbo•

Foz do Cunene
CAPE FRIA
Xangongo•
Ondangua•
Cuangar•
Okavango
CAPRIVI STRIP
Shakawe•
Livingstone
Lake Kariba
Hwange•
Chinhoyi•
Harare

CABO DE SANTA MARIA
Kuvango•
Cunene
OVAMBOLAND
Sesfontein•
•Tsumeb
Okavango Swamp
Toteng•
ZIMBABWE
Gweru•
Kwekwe•

NAMIBIA
Brandberg 2579▲
Okahandja•
NAMIB
Makgadikgadi Pans
Gwanda•
Bulawayo
Masvingo•
Mwenezi•

Tropic of Capricorn
Walvis Bay
Windhoek
Ghanzi•
BOTSWANA
Serowe•
Francistown•
Shashi
Messina•
Pafuri•

Mariental•
Gibeon•
DESERT
KALAHARI DESERT
Kakia•
Mochudi•
Thabazimbi•
Potgietersrus•
Louis Trichardt•

Keetmanshoop•
Aus•
Koes•
Kanye•
Gaborone
Pietersburg•
Zeerust•
Pretoria (Lourenço Marques)
Maputo

Bogenfels•
Karasburg•
Upington•
Askham•
Kuruman•
Vryburg•
JOHANNESBURG
Springs
Mbabane
SWAZILAND

Alexander Bay
Port Nolloth•
Pofadder•
Kenhardt•
Kimberley•
Klerksdorp•
Welkom•
Vereeniging
Kroonstad•
Virginia•
Bethlehem•
Ladysmith•
Injasuti 3408
Pietermaritzburg
Durban

Garies•
Springbok•
De Aar•
Bloemfontein
Springfontein•
LESOTHO
DRAKENSBERG
TRANSKEI
ZULULAND

Lambert's Bay•
Vanrhynsdorp•
Clanwilliam•
Beaufort West•
Murraysburg•
Middelburg•
SOUTH AFRICA
Graaff-Reinet•
Queenstown•
Port Shepstone•

Saldanha•
GREAT KARROO
Laingsburg•
East London
Paarl
Cape Town
Swellendam•
Uitenhage
Mosselbaai•
Port Elizabeth
CAPE OF GOOD HOPE
CAPE AGULHAS

Miller Oblated Stereographic Projection

ATLANTIC OCEAN

CONGO
Orange
Limpopo
Zambezi
Kasai

35°   40°   45°   50°   55°   60°

INDIAN OCEAN

Equator   0°

Seroti
Mbale
Eldoret
NDA
Lake
Lietofia
Nakuru
KENYA
Kirinyaga
5199
Mado
Gashi
SOMALIA
Baraawe
Afmadow
Kismaayo
Nairobi
Bura
RIFT VALLEY
Lamu

5°

SEYCHELLES
Victoria

SERENGETI
Mwanza
PLAIN
Shinyanga
MASAI
Arusha
STEPPE
Kilimanjaro
5895
Voi
YATTA PLATEAU
Mombasa
PEMBA ISLAND

AMIRANTE ISLANDS
(Sey.)
PLATTE ISLAND (Sey.)

Tabora
Singida
Kipembawe
TANZANIA
Dodoma
Morogoro
Mikumi
Tanga
Zanzibar
ZANZIBAR
Dar es Salaam

ALPHONSE ISLAND (Sey.)

Iringa
Utete
Mahenge
Njombe
Lindi
Mtwara

ALDABRA ISLANDS
(Sey.)

10°

ASTOVE ISLAND
(Sey.)
PROVIDENCE ISLAND
(Sey.)
FARQUHAR GROUP
(Sey.)
AGALEGA ISLANDS
(Mauritius)

Manda
Mzuzu
Songea
Masasi
Ruvuma
Lindazi
Lake
Nyasa
MALAWI
Lilongwe
Lichinga
Mandimba
Maúa
Montepuez
Pemba
NJAZIDJA
Moroni
COMOROS
MAYOTTE
(Fr.)
Dzaoudzi
ILES GLORIEUSES
(Fr.)
CAP D'AMBRE
Antsiranana

NOSY BE
Andoany
iharana
Maromokotro
2876
Analalava
Antalaha
Maroantsetra

Vila
Coutinho
Malema
Nampula
Moçambique
Mahajanga
Marovoay
Port-Bergé
Mananara
TROMELIN
(Fr.)

15°

NOSY BARAHA

Blantyre
Zomba
Sapitwa 3002
Tete
MOZAMBIQUE
Angoche
Pebane
Quelimane
Chinde
Besalampy
Maevatanana
Tambohorano
Betsiboka
Ankavandra
Antananarivo
Toamasina

Mozambique
Channel

Mutare
Monte Binga
2436
Inyangani 2592
Beira
MADAGASCAR
Belo
Antsirabe
Mahanoro
Ambositra

Nova Mambone
BASSAS DA INDIA
(Fr.)
Morondava
Malaimbandy
Fianarantsoa
Pic Boby
2658
Manakara

20°

MAURITIUS
Port Louis
Saint-Denis
REUNION
(Fr.)
MASCARENE
ISLANDS

Massangena
PONTA SÃO SEBASTIÃO
ILE EUROPA
(Fr.)
Morombe
Beroroha
Ankazobe
PONTA DA BARRA FALSA
Inhambane
Toliara
Betroka
Vangaindrano

Tropic of Capricorn

Inharrime
Androka
Bekily
Midongy
Atsimo
Xai-Xai
Faradofay
CAP SAINTE-MARIE

25°

INDIAN OCEAN

Copyright © 1980,1987
by Rand McNally & Co.
C-589200-064   -6ᵛ¹ -9ᵛ¹ -6ᵛ -17ᵛ

Kilometres 0   200   400   600 Km.
Miles   0   200   400   600 Mi.

1 : 24 000 000

35°   40°   45°   50°   55°   60°

Kilometres 0 200 400 600 Km.
Miles 0 200 400 600 Mi. 1 : 25 300 000

Miller Oblated Stereographic Projection

Copyright © 1980,1987
by Rand McNally & Co.
C-589391-064-6⁴-6⁵-6⁶-16ᵛ¹

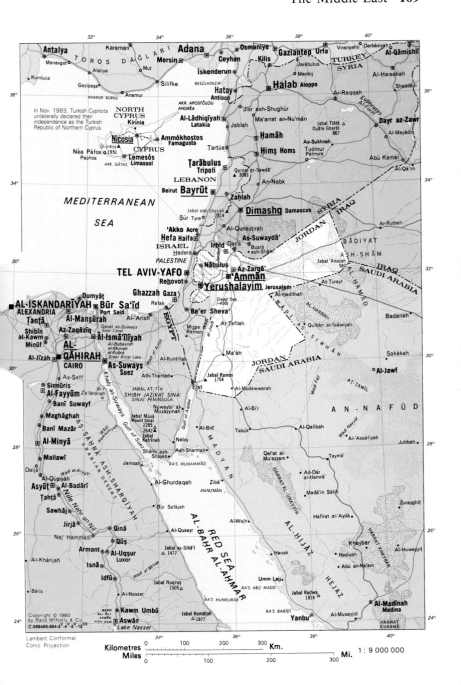

Copyright © 1980
by Rand McNally & Co.
C-569495-964-3'-4'-5'-12¹/₃

Lambert Conformal
Conic Projection

Kilometres 0   100   200   300 Km.
Miles   0   100   200   300 Mi.

1 : 9 000 000

The boundary between India and Pakistan through the disputed state of Jammu and Kashmir follows the "line of control" agreed upon by both countries in 1972.

Copyright © 1980,1987
by Rand McNally & Co.
C-569400-964-7ᵛ-7ᵛ-5ᵛ-15ᵛ¹

Lambert Conformal
Conic Projection

1 : 24 000 000

Kilometres 0   200   400   600 Km.
Miles 0   200   400   600 Mi.

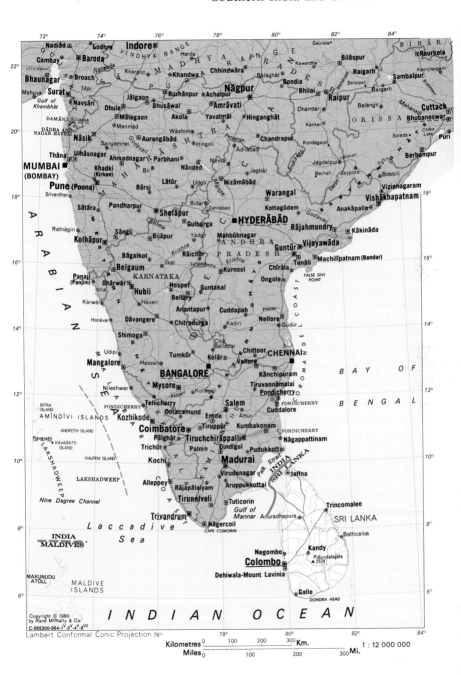

112

The boundary between India and Pakistan through the disputed state of Jammu and Kashmir follows the "line of control" agreed to by both countries in 1972.

Kilometres 0 100 200 300 Km.

Miles 0 100 200 300 Mi.

1 : 12 000 000

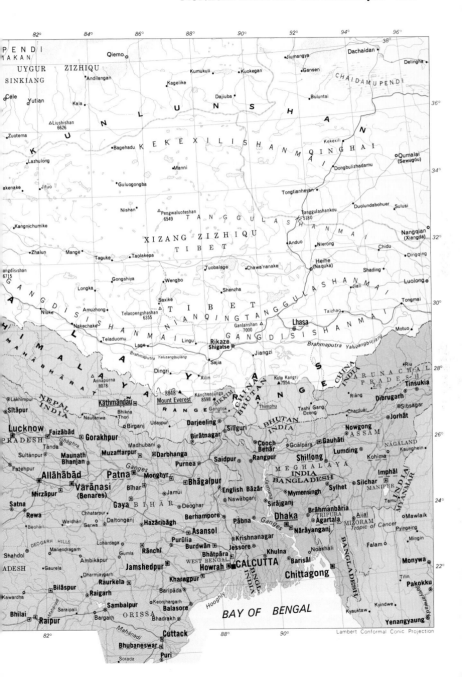

PENDI
IAKAN
UYGUR   ZIZHIQU
SINKIANG

Qiemo
Jiumangya   Dachaidan   Delingha
Kumukuli   •Kuokegan   •Gansen   CHAIDAMU PENDI
•Andilangan   Kagelike   Dajiuba   •Buluntai

•Cele
•Yutian   Kala
△Liushishan   6626

•Zuotema

K
U
N
L
U
N   S
H
A   N   MQINGHAI

KEKEXILI SHAN
Kekexili
•Bagehadu   •Qumalai (Sewugou)
•Lazhulong   Dongbulizhadamu   •Duolundabohuer   Sulusi
akenake   •Jituo   •Manni
•Guluogongba   Tongtianheyan

•Kangnichumike

•Zhalun   Mange   Taguke   Taolakepa
angdisishan   6715
G   NISHAN   •Pengwaluoteshan   6549   T A N G G U L A S H A N   Tanggulashankou   5180
Nangqian (Xiangda)
•Nierong   Chidu   •Dingqing
XIZANG   ZIZHIQU   Anduo   •Nierong   Shading•   Luolong•
T   I   B   E   T
Gongshiya   •Wengbo   Tuobalage   •Chawa'nanake   Heihe (Naquka)   Jiali   Taizhao
Longka   △Saxike   6355   N I A N Q I N G T A N G G U L A S H A N   Motuo•
Amuzhong   Teladuomu   Lingu   Lhasa   G A N G D I S I S H A N   Tongmai•
Niuke   Telaopengshashan   Lage   Rikaze   Shenzha   Taizhao
Nakechake   Shigatse   Jiangzi   Brahmaputra   Yaluzangbujiang
Teladuomu   Brahmaputra Yaluzangbujiang
Dingri   Xilin

H
I
M
A
L
A
Y
A
Annapurna   8078   •8848 Mount Everest   Kanchenjunga 8598   SIKKIM   Kula Kangri △7554   CHINA INDIA   ARUNACHAL PRADESH   •Riu   Tinsukia
M A H A B H A R A T   R A N G E   Gangtok   Riang   Zirb   Charduar•   •Dibrugarh
Bhikna   Thori   Darjeeling•   Thimphu   Tashi Gang Dzong   •Sibsagar
NEPAL INDIA   Nautanwa•   •Birganj   Udaypur   Siliguri   BHUTAN   BHUTAN INDIA   •Jorhat
•Lakhimpur   •Sitapur   Faizabad   •Gorakhpur   Birātnagar   Cooch Behar   Nowgong   •Gauhati   ASSAM   NAGALAND
Lucknow   Madhubani   Saidpur   •Goalpara   Lumding   •Kaunghein
PRADESH   Tānda   Muzaffarpur   Darbhanga   Purnea   Rangpur   SHILLONG   Kohima
Sultanpur   Maunath Bhanjan   Monghyr   Bhāgalpur   MEGHALAYA   INDIA   Silchar   Imphal
•Fatehpur   Allahābād   Patna   Bihar   English Bazar   Nawābganj   Sirājganj   Sylhet   MANIPUR
Mirzāpur   Vārānasi (Benares)   •Jamui   Mymensingh   BANGLADESH   Brāhmanbāria   Ajial   Mawlaik
•Satna   Gaya   BIHAR   Deoghar   Pābna   Dhaka   TRIPURA   Agartala   MIZORAM   Tropic of Cancer   •Pyingaing
•Rewa   •Chhatarpur   Daltonganj   Garwa   Hazaribāgh   Berhampore   Krishnanagar   Nārāyanganj   Noakhali   Falam   •Mingin
•Beohari   Waidhan   Asansol   Jessore   •Barisal   Monywa
DEOGARH HILLS   Lohardaga   Purūlia   Burdwan   Khulna   •Tilin
Shahdol   Manendragarh   Gumla   Rānchi   Bhātpāra   WEST BENGAL   CALCUTTA   Chittagong   Pakokku
ADESH   •Gaurela   Ambikāpur   Dharmjaygarh   Jamshedpur   Howrah   BANGLADESH   Kyaukse
•Bilāspur   Raurkela   Kharagpur   BENGAL INDIA   •Kyindwe
•Bhilai   Raigarh   Baripada   Hooghly   Kyauktaw   Yenangyaung
Saraipali   Sambalpur   Keonjhargarh   Balasore   BAY OF BENGAL
Bhilai   Raipur   Bargarh   ORISSA   Bhadrakh
•Kawardha   Mahānadi   Cuttack   Lambert Conformal Conic Projection
Bhubaneswar
Sorada   Puri

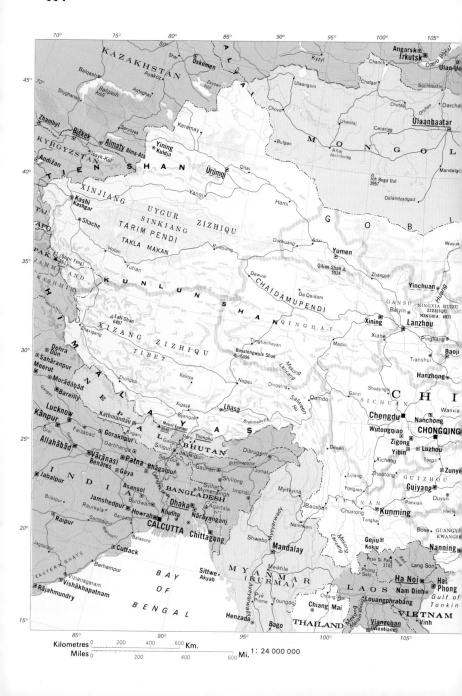

Kilometres 0 200 400 600 Km.
Miles 0 200 400 600 Mi.   1: 24 000 000

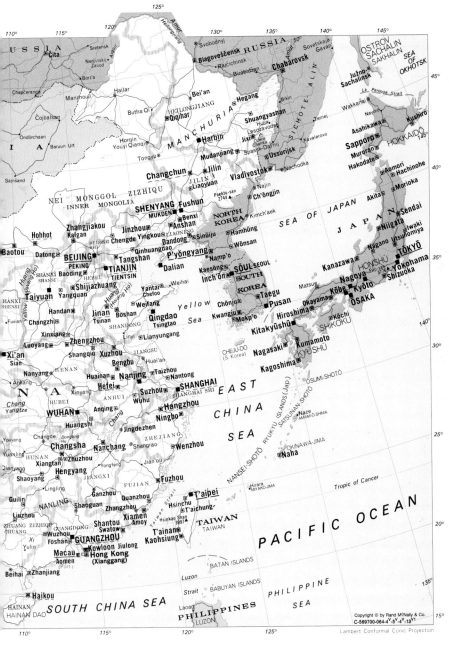

Lambert Conformal Conic Projection

116

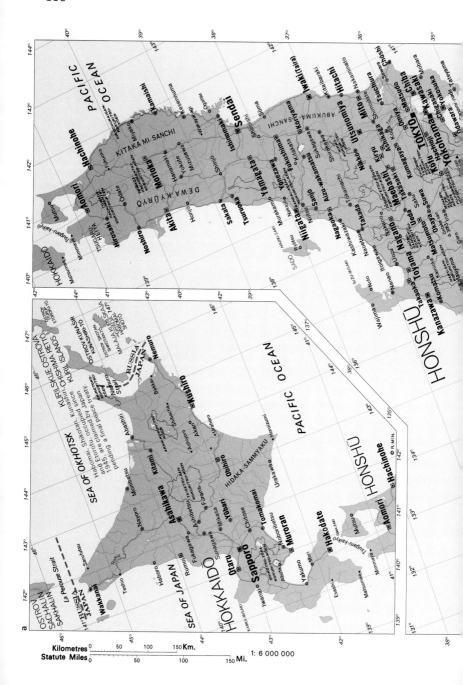

Kilometres 0 50 100 150 Km.

Statute Miles 0 50 100 150 Mi.

1: 6 000 000

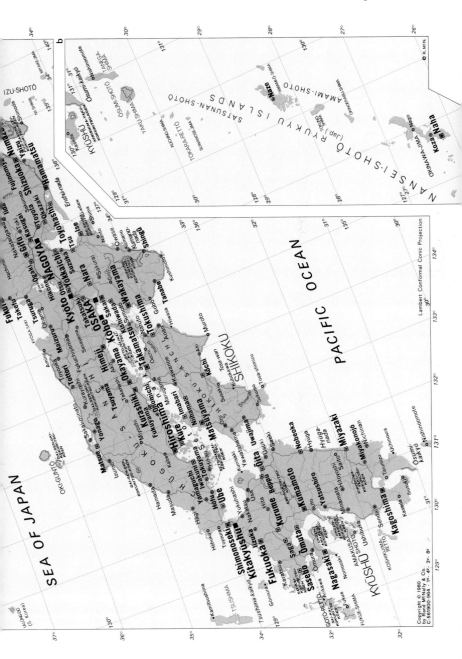

Lambert Conformal Conic Projection

SEA OF JAPAN

PACIFIC OCEAN

KYUSHU

SHIKOKU

NANSEI-SHOTŌ RYUKYU ISLANDS (Jap.)

SATSUNAN-SHOTŌ

AMAMI-SHOTŌ

OSUMI-SHOTŌ

IZU-SHOTŌ

Naha
Koza
OKINAWA-JIMA

Naze

NAGOYA
OSAKA
Kyōto
Kōbe
Hiroshima
Kitakyūshū
Fukuoka
Nagasaki
Kumamoto
Kagoshima
Miyazaki
Matsuyama
Takamatsu
Kōchi
Tokushima
Wakayama
Okayama
Himeji
Tottori
Matsue
Yamaguchi
Ube
Hōfu
Ōita
Beppu
Kurume
Saga
Sasebo
Ōmuta
Shimonoseki
Fukui
Tsuruga
Maizuru
Hikone
Ōtsu
Nara
Tsu
Ise
Shingū
Tanabe
Toyohashi
Hamamatsu
Shizuoka
Numazu
Fujinomiya
Gifu
Ōgaki
Kasugai
Yokkaichi
Suzuka
Okazaki
Toyota
Iida

Copyright © 1980
by Rand McNally & Co.
C-561900-964 IV- 4V- 3V- 8V

© R. MN.

95°   100°   105°   110°   115°

INDIA Shwebo
Chittagong   CHINA GUANGXI GUANGDONG GUANGZHOU Shantou
BANGLA-   Mandalay   YUNNAN Gejiu Kokiu ZHUANGZU CANTON   Swatow
DESH   Phan Si Pang 3143 Nanning ZIZHIQU Yulin Foshan Kowloon (Jiulong) Hong Kong
Sittwe   Myingyan   Phongsali   Ha Noi Beihai Macau Aomen (Port.) (Xianggang)
(Akyab)   Prome   MYANMAR Keng Tung LAOS Nam Dinh Gulf of Haikou Taiwan Str.
          (Pye)   (BURMA)   Chiang Rai Louangphrabang Hai Phong
Henzada   Chiang   Mai   Vinh Tonkin HAINAN
RANGOON Bago   Mai   Viangchan Udon   Dong Hoi
YANGON   (Vientiane) Thani
Mawlamyine   THAILAND   Khon Kaen Mekong Hue
                  Nakhon   Nakhon   Da Nang
BAY OF   Sawan   Ratchasima Pakxé
BENGAL   Dawei   VIETNAM SOUTH CHINA
ANDAMAN   KRUNG THEP Stœng Trêng Qui Nhon
ISLANDS   Mergui   BANGKOK CAMBODIA
(India) ANDAMAN MERGUI   Gulf of Phnum Pénh Nha Trang SEA
         SEA   ARCHIPELAGO   Thailand Bien Hoa
Port Blair   Chumphon Kâmpóng Saôm Phan Thiet
                  ISTHMUS   Rach Gia THANH PHO HO CHI MINH
NICOBAR   OF   Can Tho (SAIGON)
ISLANDS   KRA   Nakhon Si   Puerto Princesa
(India) Great   Phuket   Thammarat   PALAWAN
         Channel   Songkhla
Banda Aceh   Alor Setar   Kota Baharu   Kudat
                  MALAY   KEPULAUAN   Kota Kinabalu Gunung Kinabalu Sandakan
                  PENINSULA   BUNGURAN   4101
         Medan   George Town   UTARA   Bandar Seri Begawan Bukit
                  (Pinang) MALAYSIA   BRUNEI Pagon Tarakan
Pematangsiantar   MALAYA   1850
         Sibolga Kuala Lumpur   MALAYSIA
                  Melaka   2053 Kong Kemul Talo
         PULAU   SINGAPORE SINGAPORE TANDJUNG   Sibu Rajang
         NIAS   DATU Kuching   BORNEO Kayan
Equator Pakanbaru KEPULAUAN LINGGA   KALIMANTAN
         SUMATERA   Pontianak   Samarinda
         Padang   SUMATRA   Balikpapan
KEPULAUAN Gunung Jambi   BELITUNG Sampit
MENTAWAI Kerinci   Banjarmasin
         3800   Pangkalpinang   GREATER   SU
         Palembang
Bengkulu Lahat   INDONESIA   ISLAND
         Telukbetung   LAUT JAWA JAVA SEA
                                     JAKARTA   Laut
INDIAN   OCEAN   Bogor Cirebon Semarang MADURA
                                     BANDUNG Tasikmalaya SURABAYA
                                     Surakarta Madiun Malang
                                     Yogyakarta   BALI LOMBOK Laut
                                     JAWA   Denpasar SUMBAWA
                                     JAVA   LESSER
                         CHRISTMAS ISLAND
                         (Austl.)

Copyright © 1980,1987
by Rand McNally & Co.
C-569800-064-5-9-8-12

Kilometres 0   200   400   600 Km.
Miles 0   200   400   600 Mi.
                         1 : 24 000 000

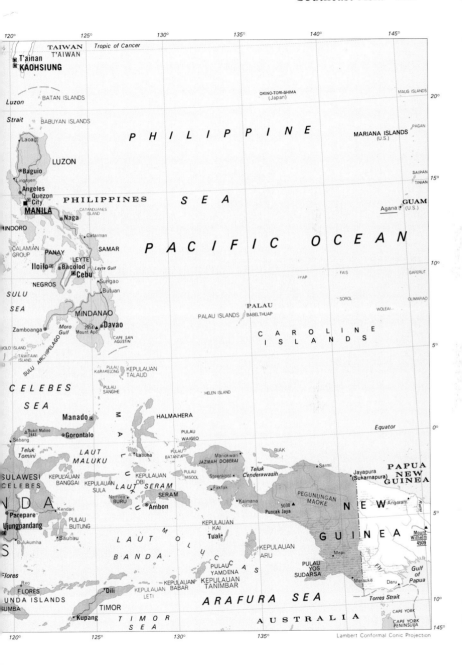

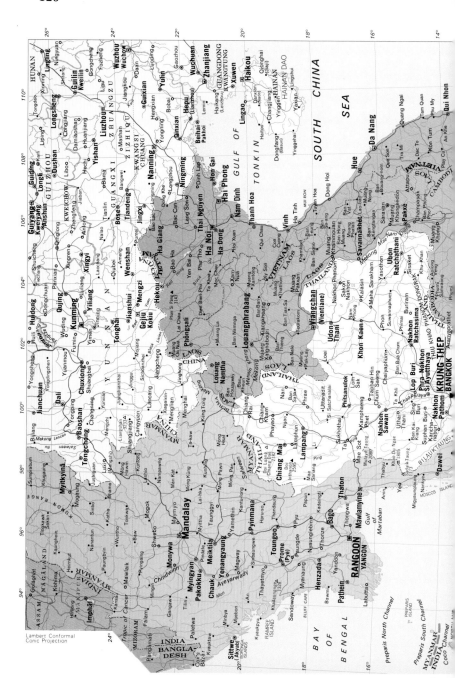

Kilometres 0 100 200 300 Km.
Miles 0   100   200 Mi.
1: 12 000 000

Surakarta Malang
Yogyakarta Blitar Jember BALI SUMBAWA SUNDA ISLANDS TIMOR
JAWA JAVA LOMBOK LESSER SUMBA Laut Sawu
INDONESIA PULAU ROTI Kupang Timor
PULAU SAWU

MELVILLE
ISLAND
BATHURST Van Diemen
ISLAND Gulf
Darwin
CARTIER ISLAND CAPE ARNHEM
LONDONDERRY Joseph LAND
Bonaparte Rum Jungle
Gulf Katherine
BONAPARTE Wyndham Victoria Birdum
ARCHIPELAGO
CAPE LEVEQUE KIMBERLEY PLATEAU
ROWLEY △ Mount Ord NORTHER
SHOALS 936
Broome Fitzroy Halls
Creek
BEACH

I N D I A N

O C E A N

DAMPIER Port EIGHTY MILE GREAT SANDY DESERT TERRITOR
ARCHIPELAGO Hedland
Roebourne Barrow Cree
Fortescue Nullagine Lake Mackay
Onslow (Dry Salt Lake)
NORTH WEST CAPE HAMERSLEY RANGE Lake Mount Zeil
1235 Disappointment 1511
Mount Bruce (Dry Salt Lake) Mount Leisler Ali
WESTERN 901 Sprin
GIBSON DESERT MACDONNEL
Lake Macleod △ Mount Augustus A U S T R
1105 Mount
Carnarvon Essendon Lake Carnegie Mount Aloysius Mount Woodro
BERNIER ISLAND 906 (Dry) 1085 1439
Wooramel
DIRK HARTOG Meekatharra Wiluna
ISLAND GREAT VICTORIA DESER
Mount A U S T R A L I A
Magnet Lake Carey SOUTH
Geraldton Lake Leonora (Dry Salt Lake)
Barlee
Dongara Forrest Ooldea
Dalwallinu
Kalgoorlie Eucla
Southern CAPE ADIEU
Perth Northam Cross Norseman
Bunbury DARLING RANGE
Ravensthorpe Esperance
CAPE NATURALISTE Augusta CAPE Great Australian Bigh
CAPE LEEUWIN Albany ARID
CAPE VANCOUVER

Tropic of Capricorn

I N D I A N   O C E A

Kilometres 0 200 400 600 Km.
Statute Miles 0 200 400 600 Mi.
1 : 24 000 000

Sea

135° 140° 145° 150° 155°

Daru

Gulf of
Papua

Torres   Strait

CAPE
YORK

**Port
Moresby**

OWEN STANLEY RANGE

**PAPUA
NEW GUINEA**

NEW GUINEA

D'ENTRECASTEAUX ISLANDS

TROBRIAND
ISLANDS

WOODLARK
ISLAND

LOUISIADE ARCHIPELAGO

TAGULA
ISLAND

ROSSEL
ISLAND

VELLA
LAVELLA Gizo NEW
GEORGIA

**SOLOMON
ISLANDS**

Honiara 160°

Mt. Popomanaseu
2331

SANTA
ISABEL

Solomon Sea

10°

RENNELL

WESSEL ISLANDS

CAPE ARNHEM

CAPE

CAPE

Gulf

GROOTE
EYLANDT

of

Limmen Bight   Carpentaria PENINSULA

YORK

MORNINGTON
ISLAND

Mitchell

Cooktown

GREAT

BARRIER

REEF

C o r a l   S e a

15°

WILLIS GROUP
(Austl.)

BARKLY TABLELAND

Normanton Ravenshoe

CAPE GRAFTON

Cairns

HINCHINBROOK
ISLAND

GREAT BARRIER REEF

TREGOSSE ISLETS
(Austl.)

ÎLES
CHESTERFIELD
(N. Cal.)

ILE DE SABLE
(N. Cal.)

ennant
reek

Mount
Isa

Cloncurry Hughenden

Townsville

CUMBERLAND
ISLAND

•Mackay

SWAIN
REEFS

SAUMAREZ
REEF

CAYE DE
L'OBSERVATOIRE
(N. Cal.)

20°

RANGES

SIMPSON

DESERT

A
L
I
A

Winton

QUEENSLAND

GREAT   ARTESIAN

Emerald

Blackall

Rockhampton

CURTIS I.

CATO
ISLAND

Tropic of Capricorn

Lake Eyre
North
(Dry Salt Lake)

Lake Eyre
South

AUSTRALIA

Lake
Torrens

Woomera

Lake
Gairdner

GAWLER RANGES

EYRE PENINSULA

Port Pirie

Peterborough

Port
Augusta

Saint Mary
Peak
1165

FLINDERS RANGE

B A S I N

RANGE

GREY
RANGE

STURT   DESERT

Quilpie

Milparinka

Charleville

•Bourke

Theodore

Saint George

Paroo

Warrego

Walgett

Darling

Bundaberg

FRASER ISLAND

Maryborough

Mount Kiangarow
1135

Toowoomba

Tenterfield

Brisbane

Ipswich

Lismore

PACIFIC

OCEAN

25°

MIDDLETON REEF

Nyngan

Round Mountain
1608

Tamworth

Dubbo

Grafton

LORD HOWE ISLAND
(N.S.W.)

Port
Macquarie

165°

30°

SPENCER
GULF

Port
Lincoln

Gulf
Saint Vincent

CAPE
CATASTROPHE

KANGAROO
ISLAND

Adelaide

Murray

Mildura

Hay

Macquarie

NEW SOUTH WALES

Orange

Wagga
Wagga

GREAT

DIVIDING

RANGE

Newcastle

SYDNEY

Wollongong

Encounter
Bay

Bordertown

V I C T O R I A

Murray

Bendigo

Albury

Canberra

A.C.T.

T a s m a n

165°

Mount Gambier

Geelong

Portland

Warrnambool

CAPE OTWAY

SOUTH POINT

NINETY MILE BEACH

MELBOURNE

Mount
Kosciusko
2228

CAPE HOWE

S e a

35°

KING ISLAND

Bass Strait

FLINDERS ISLAND

Smithton

Burnie

Banks Strait

Mount Ossa ▲
1617

Launceston

TASMANIA

Hobart

40°

SOUTH
WEST
CAPE

SOUTH
EAST
CAPE

35°   140°   145°   150°   155°   160° Lambert Conformal Conic Projection

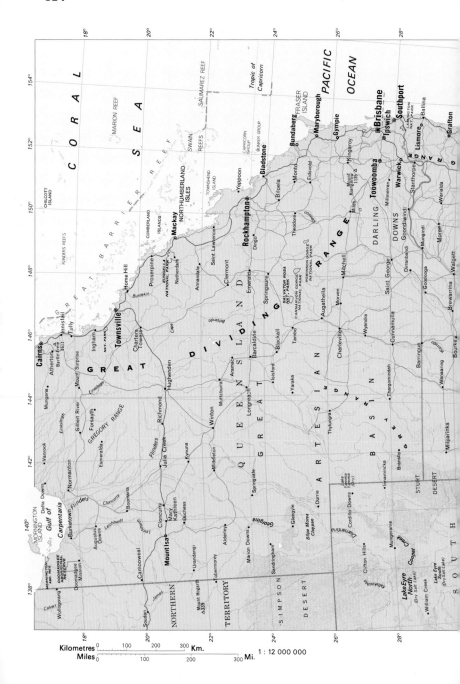

Kilometres 0   100   200   300 Km.

Miles 0   100   200   300 Mi.

1 : 12 000 000

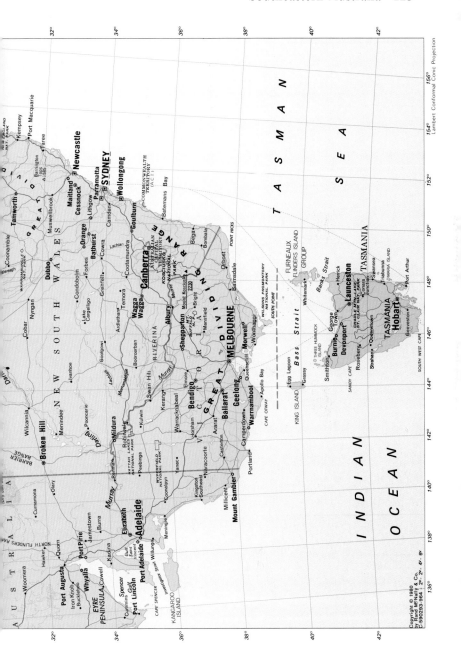

Lambert Conformal Conic Projection

168°   170°   172°   174°   176°   178°

NORTH CAPE

PACIFIC

Doubtless Bay

OCEAN

TAUROA POINT

Okaihau

Whangarei

Dargaville

36°   36°

Wellsford   GREAT
BARRIER
ISLAND

Kaipara
Harbour   **Takapuna**   COROMANDEL
PENINSULA

Devonport

Auckland   Thames

Waihi

Hamilton   Morrinsville   Bay of
Plenty

NORTH   Te Kuiti   **Tauranga**   EAST
CAPE

38°   ISLAND   **Rotorua**   38°

Waikato   Murupara   Opotiki

Taupo

Taumarunui

New Plymouth   Lake
Taupo   Wairoa   **Gisborne**

Opunake   Ruapehu   **Napier**   Hawke   MAHIA
PENINSULA

Raethi   2797   Bay

Hawera   Taihape

Wanganui   **Hastings**

Waipukurau

40°   CAPE FAREWELL   **Palmerston North**   40°

D'URVILLE
ISLAND   Levin   Woodville

Takaka   Tasman
Bay   **Masterton**

Karamea   **Nelson**   Cook   **Lower Hutt**

Bight   **Wellington**

Westport   **Blenheim**   CAPE PALLISER

Tapuaenuku
2885

42°   Reefton   42°

Greymouth   Kaikoura

Hokitika   Weiau

Waipara

SOUTH   Whataroa   Pegasus Bay

Sheffield

Mount Cook   **Christchurch**

ISLAND   3764   **Ashburton**   Southbridge   BANKS
PENINSULA

CASCADE   Haast   Fairlie   Canterbury
POINT   Bight

44°   Mount   Omarama   **Timaru**   44°
Aspiring
3039   Wanaka

Queenstown   **Oamaru**

Lake   Kingston   PACIFIC

SOUTH   Te Anau   Alexandra   Palmerston

ISLAND   Te Anau   Beaumont   OCEAN

Mossburn   **Dunedin**

46°   Winton   Gore   46°

Invercargill   Kaitangata

Foveaux

STEWART   Bluff

ISLAND   Strait

TASMAN

SEA

Copyright © 1980
by Rand McNally & Co.
C-591600-964 · 2° · 2° · 4° · 7°

168°   170°   172°   174°   176°   Conic Projection

Kilometres   0   100   200   300 Km.

Miles   0   100   200   300 Mi.   1 : 9 000 000

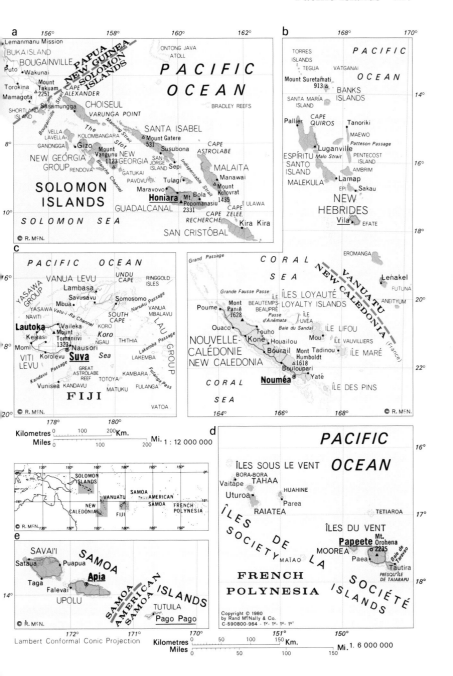

a

156° 158° 160° 162°

Lemanmanu Mission
BUKA ISLAND
BOUGAINVILLE
PAPUA NEW GUINEA SOLOMON ISLANDS
Puto · Wakunai
ONTONG JAVA ATOLL

PACIFIC OCEAN

Torokina Mount Takuam △2251
Mamagota
CAPE ALEXANDER
BRADLEY REEFS

SHORTLAND ISLAND
Sasamungga
CHOISEUL
VARUNGA POINT

Bougainville Strait
The Slot
Manning Strait

VELLA LAVELLA
KOLOMBANGARA
SANTA ISABEL
△Mount Gatere 531

GANONGGA · Gizo
NEW GEÓRGIA GROUP
Vangunu NEW GEORGIA 1123
RENDOVA
GATUKAI
SAN JORGE ISLAND
Susubona
CAPE ASTROLABE

Blanche Channel
Sepi
Indispensable Strait

PAVÚVU
Maravovo
Tulagi
MALAITA
Manawai
△Mount Kolovrat

SOLOMON ISLANDS
Honiara
Mt. Bola Popomanasiu 2331
1435
ULAWA
CAPE ZELEE
RECHERCHE
Kira Kira

SOLOMON SEA
GUADALCANAL
SAN CRISTÓBAL

© R. McN.

8°
10°

b

168° 170°

TORRES ISLANDS
· TEGUA VATGANAI
PACIFIC OCEAN

Mount Suretamati 913△
BANKS ISLANDS
14°

SANTA MARÍA ISLAND

Pallier
CAPE QUIROS
Tanoriki
MAEWO
Patteson Passage

ESPÍRITU SANTO ISLAND
Luganville
Malo Strait
PENTECOST ISLAND
16°

MALEKULA
AMBRIM
Lamap
EPI · Sakau

NEW HEBRIDES
Vila · EFATE
18°

c

PACIFIC OCEAN

VANUA LEVU
UNDU CAPE
RINGGOLD ISLES

YASAWA GROUP
Lambasa
Savusavu
Somosomo
Nanuku passage
6°

YASAWA
Vatu-i-Ra Channel
SOUTH CAPE
VANJA MBALAVU

NAVITI
KORO
THITHIA
LAU GROUP

Lautoka
· Waileka
△Mount Tomanivi 1323
Koro Sea
NGAU

Momi
Keiyasi
Nausori
Korolevu
Suva
Lakemba Passage
LAKEMBA
KAMBARA

VITI LEVU
Kandavu Passage
GREAT ASTROLABE REEF
TOTOYA
FULANGA
Fulanga Pass

Vunisea KANDAVU
MATUKU

FIJI
VATOA

© R. McN.

8°
20°

178° 180°

Grand Passage
CORAL SEA
EROMANGA

Grande Fausse Passe
ÎLES LOYAUTÉ
LOYALTY ISLANDS
VANUATU NEW CALEDONIA
Lenakel
FUTUNA
20°

Poume
Mont Panié 1628
BEAUTEMPS-BEAUPRÉ
Passe d'Anémata
ÎLE UVÉA
ANEITYUM

Ouaco
Kone
Houailou
Baie du Sandal
ÎLE LIFOU
Mou
LE VAUVILLIERS

NOUVELLE-CALÉDONIE NEW CALEDONIA
Bourail
Mont Tadinou △1618
Humboldt
Bouloupari
ÎLE MARÉ
22°

CORAL SEA
Nouméa
Yaté
ÎLE DES PINS

(France)

164° 166° 168°
© R. McN.

Kilometres 0 100 200 Km.
Miles 0 100 200 Mi. 1 : 12 000 000

SOLOMON ISLANDS
VANUATU
SAMOA
AMERICAN SAMOA
NEW CALEDONIA
FIJI
FRENCH POLYNESIA
© R. McN.

d

PACIFIC OCEAN
16°

ÎLES SOUS LE VENT
BORA-BORA
Vaitape
TAHAA
Uturoa
HUAHINE
Parea
RAIATEA
TETIAROA
17°

ÎLES DE LA SOCIETY
ÎLES DU VENT
Papeete Mt. Orohena 2235
MOOREA
MAÏAO
Paea
Tautira
PRESQU'ÎLE DE TAIARAPU
Baie de Taravao

FRENCH POLYNESIA
SOCIÉTÉ ISLANDS
18°

e

SAVAI'I
Sataua · Puapua
SAMOA
Taga
Falevai
UPOLU
Apia
SAMOA AMERICAN SAMOA ISLANDS

TUTUILA
Pago Pago

© R. McN.

172° 171° 170° 151° 150°
Lambert Conformal Conic Projection
Kilometres 0 50 100 150 Km.
Miles 0 50 100 150 Mi. 1 : 6 000 000

128

PACIFIC

OCEAN

Tropic of Cancer

ISLAS
REVILLAGIGEDO
(Mex.)
ISLA
SOCORRO

Copyright © 1980
by Rand McNally & Co.
C-531600-964 - 3⁵· 3⁴· 4⁵· 8⁵

Kilometres 0   100   200   300 Km.
Miles 0   100   200   300 Mi.   1 : 13 300 000

100°   98°   96°   94°   92°   90°   88°

Lamesa • Snyder • Stamford **Fort Worth** • Minden • Bastrop • Yazoo City

Big Spring • Abilene • Weatherford **Dallas** Longview• Marshall • Shreveport • Monroe • Vicksburg • **Jackson** • Meridian • Selma   32°

T E X A S • Corsicana • Tyler • Winnfield • MISSISSIPPI • Laurel • ALABAMA

Midland • Ballinger • Brownwood • Palestine • Jacksonville • Natchitoches • Natchez • Hattiesburg

DWARDS • San Angelo • Colorado San • Eden • Saba • **Killeen** • **Waco** • Nacogdoches • Toledo Bend Reservoir • Alexandria • Natchez • McComb • Bogalusa • **Mobile** FLA.

LATEAU • Barnhart • Junction • Fredericksburg • Georgetown • **Temple** • Lufkin • Sam Rayburn Reservoir • LOUISIANA • **Baton Rouge** • Hammond • Biloxi • Pensacola

Sonora • New • San • **Austin** • Bryan • Huntsville • Woodville • Opelousas • Lafayette • Pontchartrain • Gulfport • CHANDELEUR ISLANDS   30°

Del Rio • Braunfels • Marcos Seguin • **Houston** • Beaumont • Orange • Charles • Jennings • **New Orleans** • Chalmette

Ciudad Acuña • Uvalde • El Campo • Galveston Bay • Port Arthur • MISSISSIPPI DELTA

Jiménez • Eagle Pass • Crystal City • **San Antonio** • Victoria • **Texas City** • **Galveston** GALVESTON ISLAND • MARSH ISLAND

Piedras Negras • Carrizo Springs • Beeville • Bay City • Porto Lavaca • Freeport

Nueva Rosita • Allende • Villa • Freer • Alice • **Corpus Christi** • MATAGORDA ISLAND

Ciudad Melchor Múzquiz • Sabinas • Union • **Nuevo Laredo** • Kingsville • SAN JOSE ISLAND

Ciudad Anáhuac • Lampazos de Naranjo • Falfurrias • PADRE ISLAND

Ila Frontera • **Monclova** • Ciudad Mier • Edinburg • Laguna Madre   26°

Ciudad de Villaldama • Sabinas Hidalgo • Ciudad McAllen • **Harlingen** • **Brownsville**

ARQUE NACIONAL CUMBRES DE MONTERREY • **Guadalupe** • **Reynosa** • General Bravo • **Matamoros** • Díaz Ordaz de Marzo

Saltillo • **Monterrey** • Montemorelos • German • Laguna Madre • GULF

San Rafael • San José de Raíces • Linares • San Carlos • San Fernando

nceptión del Oro • Hidalgo • Santander Jiménez   OF

Matehuala • **Ciudad Victoria** • Llera • Santa Cruz • Villa González • MEXICO   24°

lescas • Charcas • Huizache • **Ciudad Mante** • Tropic of Cancer

Salinas de Hidalgo • Cerritos • Ebano • Ciudad Madero • CABO CATOCHE

Loreto • **San Luis Potosí** • **Ciudad de Valles** • **Tampico** • ISLA DEL IDOLO • Río Lagartos • Motul de Felipe Carrillo Puerto • Tizimín • Puerto Juárez

León • **Guanajuato** • San Luis de la Paz • Tantoyuca • Progreso • Celestún • **Mérida** • Chichén Itzá • ISLA DE COZUMEL   20°

apuato • **Querétaro** • San Juan del Río • Tamazunchale • Tuxpan de Rodríguez Cano • Halachó • Ticul • Peto • Tulum

La Valle de Santiago • **Celaya** • **Pachuca** • Poza Rica de Hidalgo • Zacualtipán • Tenabo • **Campeche** • YUCATÁN • Felipe Carrillo Puerto

edad • **Acámbaro** • **Morelia** • **Tulancingo** • Martínez de la Torre • Bahía de Campeche • Hopelchén • PENINSULA

PARQUE NACIONAL COFRE DE PEROTE • **Jalapa** Enríquez • Champotón • Escárcega de Matamoros • Ciudad Chetumal

CIUDAD DE MÉXICO MEXICO CITY • PARQUES NACIONALES • Volcán Citlaltépetl (Pico de Orizaba) 5700 • Córdoba • **Veracruz** • Frontera • **Ciudad del Carmen** • Orange Walk   18°

Uruapan • **Cuernavaca** • Taxco de Alarcón • **Puebla** • **Córdoba** • Alvarado • San Andrés Tuxtla • **Coatzacoalcos** • **Villahermosa** • BELIZE

lueva Italia de Ruíz • Popocatépetl 5452 • **Tehuacán** • PARQUE NACIONAL CAÑON DE RIO BLANCO • Tierra Blanca • **Minatitlán** • Las Choapas • Teapa • Palenque • Piedras Negras • San Benito • Victoria Peak 1122 • **Belize**

SIERRA • Taxco de Alarcón • Presa Miguel Alemán • Tuxtepec • ISTMO • Jesús Carranza • Pichucalco • Presa Nezahualcóyotl • San Cristóbal de las Casas • Ocozocoautla • **Belmopan**

Zihuatanejo • **Chilpancingo** • Metlatonoc • **Oaxaca** • Tlacolula • DE • Matías Romero • Tuxtla Gutiérrez • Comitán • Guadalupe • San Luis • Gulf of Honduras   16°

Tecpan de Galeana • San Marcos • Ejutla de Crespo • **TEHUANTEPEC** • Venustiano Carranza • Puerto Cortés • San Pedro Sula

Acapulco • Cuajinicuilapa • Jamiltepec • Miahuatlán de Porfirio Díaz • Santa María Tehuantepec • Salina Cruz • **Tuxtla Gutiérrez** • Tonalá • SIERRA • GUATEMALA • El Estor • El Progreso

SUR • Puerto Escondido • Golfo de Tehuantepec • Pijijiapan • Volcán Tajumulco 4220 • Huehuetenango • Zacapa • HONDURAS

02° Lambert Conformal Conic Projection   98° • Puerto Ángel • 96° • Escuintla • Huixtla • MADRE • **Tapachula** • 94° • **Guatemala** • 88°

GULF OF MEXICO

Fort Myers · UNITED STATES · West Palm Beach
FLORIDA · GRAND BAHAMA
The Everglades · Fort Lauderdale · GREAT ABACO
EVERGLADES NATIONAL PARK · Miami Beach · ELEUTHE
MIAMI
Key West · FLORIDA KEYS · ANDROS ISLAND · Nassau
NEW PROVIDENCE

Yucatan Channel

LA HABANA · Straits of Florida
HAVANA · Nicholas Channel · GREAT BAHAMA BANK
Mariano · Cárdenas · Sagua · Old Bahama Channel · W E S
Artemisa · Matanzas · la Grande · Santa Clara · Placetas · Ciego de Avila
Pinar del Río · Güines · Golfo de Batabanó · Cienfuegos · Sancti Spíritus · Florida · Nuevitas
Santa Fe · Camagüey · Bane
ISLA DE LA JUVENTUD (ISLA DE PINOS) · C U B A · Holguín
Manzanillo · Bayan

Río Lagartos · CABO CATOCHE · CABO SAN ANTONIO · CABO CORRIENTES
Progreso · Tizimin · Puerto Juárez
Mérida · Pico Turquino 1994 · Santia de Cu
Celestún · Halachó · Ticul · Chichen Itzá · Cozumel
Tenabo · Peto · ISLA DE COZUMEL · CAYMAN ISLANDS · G R E A T E R
Campeche · YUCATAN · Tulum · George-Town · (U.K.)
Hopelchén · Felipe Carrillo Puerto
Champotón · PENINSULA · Montego Bay · Kingston
Ciudad del Carmen · MEXICO · JAMAICA · Spanish Town
Frontera · Escárcega de Matamoros · Ciudad Chetumal
Usumacinta · Tiradero · Orange Walk · Chetumal Bay
Palenque · BELIZE
Ocozingo · Piedras Negras · Belize
Comitán · San Benito · Belmopan
Sayaxché · 1122 Victoria Peak · Gulf of Honduras · ISLAS DE LA BAHÍA
San Luis · GUATEMALA · Puerto Barrios · La Ceiba · Limón · Brus Laguna
4220 Volcán Tajumulco · El Estor · Puerto Cortes · Yoro · Patuca
Huehuetenango · San Pedro Sula · CARI
SIERRA DE LAS MINAS · El Progreso
Tapachula · Cerro Las Minas 2865 · CORDILLERA DE AGALTA · CABO GRACIAS A DIOS
Guatemala · Juticalpa · Coco · Waspán
Tiquisate · HONDURAS · San Ramón
Escuintla · Tegucigalpa · Puerto Cabezas
Santa Ana · Nueva · San Salvador · Cerro Mogotón 2107
San Salvador · San Vicente · San Miguel · Cerro Pija 1800 · Prinzapolca
EL SALVADOR · La Union · Estelí · La Cruz
Chinandega · El Sauce · Matagalpa · Río Grande · ISLA DE SAN ANDRES (COL.)
León · NICARAGUA · San Andrés
Managua · Granada · Rama · CORN ISLANDS (NIC.)
Diriamba · Lago de Nicaragua · Punta Gorda
Rivas · ISLA DE SAN CARLOS
ISLA DE OMETEPE · San Juan del Norte
Volcán Miravalles 2028
Liberia · COSTA RICA
PACIFIC OCEAN · PENINSULA DE NICOYA · Limón
Puntarenas · Cartago
CABO BLANCO · San José · Cerro Chirripó 3819 · Bocas del Toro · Colón · ISTMO DE PANAMÁ
Puerto Cortes · Volcán Baru 3475 · Golfo de los Mosquitos · Portobelo · Lori
PEN. DE OSA · La Chorrera · Chepo · Mulatupo · Cerr
Puerto Armuelles · David · Aguadulce · Río Hato · PANAMÁ · Monteri
PUNTA BURICA · Golfo de Gulf · ISLA DEL REY · La Palma · Acandi
Chiriqui · PENINSULA DE AZUERO · Panama · Yaviza · Turbo
ISLA DE COIBA · Jaqué

Copyright © 1980 by Rand McNally & Co.
C-530100-964 · 2ᵛ· 6ᵛ· 5ᵛ· 12ᵛ²

Kilometres 0 100 200 300 Km.
Miles 0 100 200 300 Mi.   1 : 12 000 000

92° 90° 88° 86° 84° 82° 80° 78°
26° 24° 22° 20° 18° 16° 14° 12° 10° 8°

74° 72° 70° 68° 66° 64° 62° 60°

26°
24°
22°
20°
18°
16°
14°
12°

60°
60°

BAHAMAS

CAT ISLAND

Tropic of Cancer

LONG ISLAND
CROOKED ISLAND
Sound Island
Crooked Passage
MAYAGUANA

ATLANTIC

OCEAN

TURKS AND CAICOS ISLANDS (U.K.)

LITTLE INAGUA
CAICOS ISLANDS
TURKS ISLANDS
Grand Turk

Matthew Town
GREAT INAGUA
Sagua de Tánamo
HAITI

I N D I E S

VIRGIN ISLANDS (U.S.)(U.K.)
ANGUILLA (U.K.)

Guantánamo
Cap-Haitien
Montecristi
San Francisco de Macoris
PUERTO RICO (U.S.)
San Juan
Charlotte Amalie
LEEWARD ISLANDS

POINTE DU CHEVAL BLANC
Gonaives
Santiago
Concepcion de la Vega
Arecibo
Caguas

Golfe de la Gonave
Pico Duarte 3175
Higüey
BARBUDA
SAINT CHRISTOPHER (SAINT KITTS)

Jérémie
ÎLE DE LA GONAVE
HISPANIOLA
Azua
San Pedro de Macoris
Mayagüez
Ponce
SAINT CROIX
Basseterre
ANTIGUA

Port-au-Prince
Chaîne de la Selle 2674
Santo Domingo
ST. KITTS AND NEVIS (U.K.)
MONTSERRAT (U.K.)
GRANDE-TERRE

Les Cayes
DOMINICAN REPUBLIC
Basse-Terre
GUADELOUPE (Fr.)

A N T I L L E S
DOMINICA
Roseau

Montagne Pelée 1397
Fort-de-France
MARTINIQUE (Fr.)
Castries

B E A N   S E A
L E S S E R   A N T I L L E S
SAINT LUCIA
SAINT VINCENT

Kingstown
Bridgetown
BARBADOS

ARUBA (Neth.)
NETHERLANDS ANTILLES
Oranjestad
CURAÇAO
Willemstad
BONAIRE
LA BLANQUILLA (Ven.)
GRENADA
Saint George's

CABO DE LA VELA
PENÍNSULA DE LA GUAJIRA
PENÍNSULA DE PARAGUANÁ
ISLAS LOS ROQUES (Ven.)
ISLA DE MARGARITA
WINDWARD ISLANDS
TOBAGO

Barran-quilla
Santa Marta
Riohacha
Golfo de Venezuela
Punto Fijo
Coro
Puerto Cumarebo
San Juan de los Cayos
ISLA LA TORTUGA (Ven.)
Porlamar
Carúpano
Port of Spain

Cartagena
Ciénaga
Pico Cristóbal 5775
Pedregal
San Luis
Puerto Cabello
PARQ. NAC. HENRY PITTIER
Cumaná
Puerto la Cruz
Caripito
San TOBAGO
TRINIDAD AND

Arjona
Valledupar
Villa del Rosario
Maracaibo
San Felipe
Maiquetía
CARACAS
Barcelona
Maturin
Fernando

San Jacinto
San Onofre
Augustin Codazzi
Cabimas
Ciudad Ojeda
Barqui-simeto
Valencia
PARQ. NAC. GUATOPO
Maracay
Altagracia de Orituco
DELTA

Sincelejo
Magangué
El Banco
Rio Arauisa
Lago de Maracaibo
Tinaco
San Juan de los Morros
Zaraza
Cantaura
El Tigre
San José de Guanipa
Barrancas
ORINOCO
Tucupita
60°

Planeta Rica
Nechí
Encontrados
Trujillo
Acarigua
Calabozo
Valle de la Pascua
Ciudad Guayana

San Carlos del Zulia
Valera
Villa Bruzual
Arismendi
Ciudad Bolívar
Upata
El Palmar

Ocaña
Mérida
Pico Bolívar 5002
Bárinas
Libertad
Puerto de Nutrias
San Fernando de Apure
San Fernando
Mapire
802
Cerro Bolívar
El Manteco

Cúcuta
San Cristóbal
Apure
Achaguas
Orinoco
Maripa
Caroní

Cáceres

CORDILLERA DE PERIJÁ
SIERRA DE PERIJÁ
COLOMBIA
VENEZUELA
CORDILLERA DE MÉRIDA
L L A N O S

Magdalena

74° 72° 70° 68° 66° 64°

Lambert Conformal Conic Projection

CARIBBEAN SEA

NETH. ANTILLES

LESSER ANTILLES

SAINT VINCENT GRENAD

ISLA DE SAN ANDRÉS (Col.)

CORN ISLANDS (Nic)

ARUBA

PENÍNSULA DE LA GUAJIRA

CURAÇÃO (Neth)

Willemstad

TRINIDA

Granada
Managua
NICARAGUA
Lago de Nicaragua

Punto Fijo
Golfo de Venezuela
Coro
Maracaibo

Port of Spain

Puntarenas
San José
Liberia
COSTA RICA
Cerro Chirripó 3819
PENÍNSULA DE NICOYA
Volcán Barú 3475
Golfo de los Mosquitos
Colón
PANAMÁ
Panamá
Golfo de Chiriquí
PENÍNSULA DE AZUERO
Golfo de Panamá
ISTMO DE PANAMÁ
Colón

Santa Marta
Ríohacha
Barranquilla
Cartagena
Montería
Turbo
Magangué
Cabimas
Valencia
CARACAS
Cúmana
Maracay
Puerto la Cruz
Maturín
El Tigre
Ciudad Bolívar
Ciudad Guayana
La Paragua
Tumere
Barquisimeto
Acarigua
Calabozo
Valera
Pico Bolívar 5007
VENEZUELA
SALTO ÁNGEL ANGEL FALLS
LA GRAN SABANA
PAKARAIM

Cúcuta
San Cristóbal
Bucaramanga
Puerto Berrío
Medellín
Tunja
Manizales
SANTA FE DE BOGOTÁ
Pereira
Ibagué
Villavicencio
Cali
Neiva
Popayán
Florencia
Puerto Nutrias
San Fernando de Apure
Puerto Carreño
San Fernando de Atabapo
Maroa
San Carlos de Río Negro
Caracarai
Boa
Quibdó
CABO CORRIENTES
Buenaventura
San José del Guaviare
Mitú
Içana
Tapurucuara
Barcelos
Moura

ISLA DEL COCO (Costa Rica)
ISLA DE MALPELO (Col.)

COLOMBIA

Tumaco
Esmeraldas
Pasto
Tulcán
Puerto Asís
Puerto Leguízamo
El Encanto
Putumayo
Arica
Içá
Santo António do Içá
Solimões
Tefé
Codajás
Manaus

Equator

Quito
Manta
ECUADOR
Chimborazo 6310
Riobamba
Guayaquil
Golfo de Guayaquil
Cuenca
Azogues
Tumbes
Loja
Talara
Sullana
Piura
PUNTA NEGRA
Olmos
Jaén
Bellavista
Chiclayo
Cajamarca
Pacasmayo
Trujillo
Huallanca
Nevado Huascarán 6768
Chimbote
Huaraz
Amazon
Napo
Tigre
Iquitos
Leticia
Esperanza
Carauari
Marañón
Yurimaguas
Ucayali
Cruzeiro do Sul
Feijó
Eirunepé
Humaitá
Purus
Manicoré
Prainha
Madeira

SELVA

Sena Madureira
Boca do Acre
Pôrto Velho
Rondônia
CHAPADA DO

Huánuco
Cerro de Pasco
PERU
Huancayo
Callao
LIMA
Machupicchu
Cuzco
Pisco
PUNTA CARRETAS
Ica
Nazca
Pucallpa
Puerto Maldonado
Quincemil
Sandia
Sicuani
Juliaca
Puno
Lago Titicaca
Santa Ana
Reyes
Riberalta
Guajará Mirim
Cobija
Villa Bella
Rio Branco
Príncipe da Beira
Magdalena
Trinidad
Santa Ana
Beni
Concepción
BOLIVIA
La Paz
Nevado Illimani 6402
Cochabamba
Buena Vista
Santa Cruz
San José de Chiquitos
Oruro
Sucre
Zudáñez
Potosí
Lagunillas
General Eugenio A Garai
Mariscal Estigarri

Arequipa
Mollendo
Ilo
Tacna
Arica
Nevado Sajama 6542
ALTIPLANO
Lago Poopó
DESIERTO DE ATACAMA
Iquique
Uyuni
CHILE
Tarija
Villazón
La Quiaca
Cerro Sairecabur 5970
ARGENTINA
CORDILLERA REAL
PAR

PACIFIC OCEAN

CORDILLERA OCCIDENTAL
CORDILLERA CENTRAL
CORDILLERA ORIENTAL

Kilometres 0 200 400 600 Km.
Miles 0 200 400 600
Mi. 1 : 24 000 000

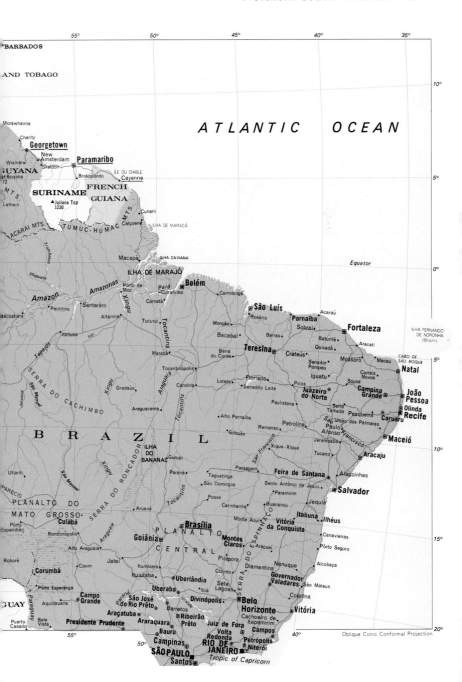

55°   50°   45°   40°   35°

BARBADOS

AND TOBAGO

10°

Morawhanna

Charity   **ATLANTIC   OCEAN**
Georgetown
New
Amsterdam **Paramaribo**
Wismar   *Skeldon*
GUYANA   *Brokopondo*   ÎLE DU DIABLE
at Roraima   **Cayenne**
72   **FRENCH**   5°
SURINAME GUIANA
Lethem   ▲Juliana Top
1230

Cunani

ACARAI MTS.   TUMUC-HUMAC MTS.   *Calçoene*

Mepuera   ILHA DE MARACÁ

Macapá   *Equator*   0°

ILHA CAVIANA

ILHA DE MARAJÓ

Amazon **Amazonas** Porto de *Pará* **Belém**
Parintins *Santarém* Moz *Curralinho* *Camiranga*
acoatiara   *Cametá*

Altamira *Tucuruí* *Monção* **São Luís**
ll.   *Rosário* **Parnaíba** *Acaraú*
Itaituba   *Bacabal* *Barras* *Sobral* **Fortaleza**
Tapajós   *Baturité* ILHA FERNANDO
Marabá Barra **Teresina** *Quixadá* *Aracati* DE NORONHA
SERRA DO CACHIMBO *Tocantinópolis* do Corda *Crateús* *Senador* *Mossoró* *Macau* CABO DE (Brazil)
Carolina *Loreto* *Floriano* Pompeu *Currais* SÃO ROQUE 5°
Gradaús *Benedito Leite* *Picos* *Iguatu* Novos **Natal**
B R A Z I L *Araguacema* *Paulistana* **Juàzeiro** *Sousa* **Campina**
Alto Parnaíba *do Norte* Serra *Pesqueira* **Grande**
Remanso *Petrolina* União dos Palmares **João**
ILHA *Gilbués* *Xique-Xique* Paulo **Pessoa**
DO *Gurupi* *Jeremoabo* Afonso **Olinda**
BANANAL *Paraná* *Passagem* *Tucano* **Caruaru Recife**
Utiariti *Taguatinga* **Feira de Santana** **Maceió**
PARECIS *São Domingos* Santo Antônio de Jesus *Alagoinhas* 10°
PLANALTO DO *Paramirim* **Aracaju**
MATO GROSSO **Cuiabá** *Posse* *Guanambi* **Salvador**
Porto *Rondonópolis* *Carinhanha* *Jequié* **Itabuna**
Esperidiào *Aruana* Monte Azul **Vitória** **Ilhéus**
Roboré **Brasília** *da Conquista*
Alto Araguaia PLANALTO **Montes** *Araçuaí* *Canavieiras*
Goiânia C E N T R A L **Claros** *Pôrto Seguro* 15°
Jataí *Itumbiara* *Pirapora* *Diamantina* *Alcobaça*
Corumbá *Coxim* *Ituiutaba* *Colinto* **Governador**
Pôrto Esperança *Itumbiara* *Sete* **Valadares** *São Mateus*
GUAY *Aquiduana* **Campo** *Ibiá* Lagoas *Colatina*
Bela **Grande** **Uberlândia** **Belo** **Vitória**
Puerto *Vista* *São José* *Divinópolis* **Horizonte** *Cachoeiro de*
Casado *do Rio Prêto* *Barretos* *Itapemirim*
Aragatuba **Ribeirão** *Juiz de Fora* **Campos**
55° **Presidente Prudente** *Araraquara* *Prêto* *Volta* *Petrópolis* 20°
50° *Bauru* **RIO DE** *Redonda* *Niterói* 40° Oblique Conic Conformal Projection
Campinas **JANEIRO**
SÃO PAULO *Tropic of Capricorn*
Santos

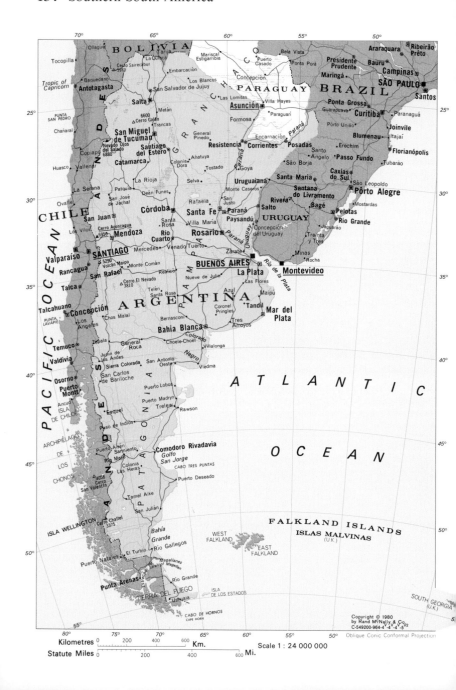

Oblique Conic Conformal Projection

Kilometres 0   200   400   600 Km.

Statute Miles 0   200   400   600 Mi.

Scale 1 : 24 000 000

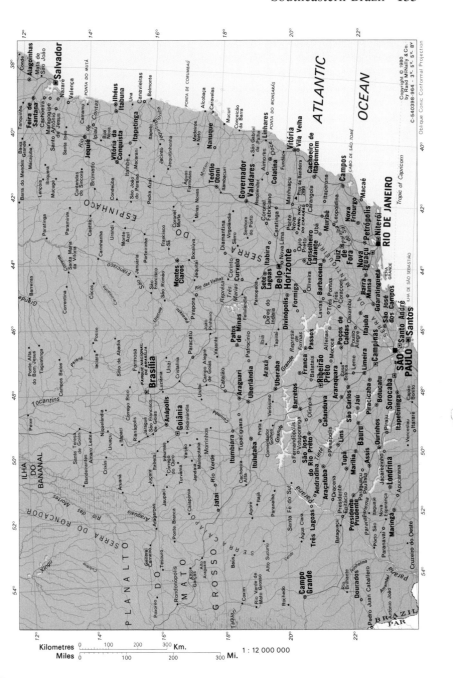

Kilometres
Miles

1 : 12 000 000

ATLANTIC

OCEAN

Copyright © 1980
by Rand McNally & Co.
C-540398-964 - 3Y. 6Y. 5Y. 8Y
Oblique Conic Conformal Projection

Tropic of Capricorn

CABO DE SÃO TOMÉ

Salvador
Feira de Santana
Ilhéus
Itabuna
Vitória da Conquista
Itapetinga
Jequié
Nanuque
Teófilo Otoni
Governador Valadares
Linhares
Vitória
Vila Velha
Cachoeiro de Itapemirim
Campos
Macaé
RIO DE JANEIRO
Niterói
Nova Friburgo
Petrópolis
Nova Iguaçu
Juiz de Fora
Belo Horizonte
Sete Lagoas
Montes Claros
Divinópolis
Brasília
Anápolis
Goiânia
Barbacena
Conselheiro Lafaiete
Itaúna
Formiga
Passos
Poços de Caldas
Franca
Ribeirão Prêto
Barretos
Araraquara
São Carlos
Campinas
Limeira
Piracicaba
São José dos Campos
Guaratinguetá
Santo André
Santos
SÃO PAULO
Sorocaba
Itapetininga
Botucatu
Jaú
Bauru
Marília
Assis
Londrina
Maringá
Presidente Prudente
Três Lagoas
Campo Grande
Dourados

SERRA DO ESPINHAÇO
SERRA DO MAR
PLANALTO DO MATO GROSSO
SERRA DO RONCADOR
ILHA DO BANANAL

Tocantins
Paraná
Paranaíba
Grande
Rio das Mortes
Xingu

BRAZIL
PAR

BROOKS RANGE

Beaufort Sea

BANKS ISLAND

MELVILLE ISLAND

BATHURST ISLAND

Yukon
Fort Yukon

Mt. McKINLEY

Anchorage

Fairbanks

ALASKA RANGE

Cook Inlet

Seward

Valdez

Old Crow

Aklavik

Mackenzie Bay

Tuktoyaktuk

Amundsen Gulf

CAPE LAMBTON

PEEL POINT

Viscount Melville Sound

Holman Island

VICTORIA ISLAND

PRINCE OF WALES ISLAND

SOME

Dawson

YUKON

KLONDIKE

Kluane

Carmacks

Whitehorse

PELLY MOUNTAINS

SELWYN MOUNTAINS

Fort Good Hope

Fort Norman

Fort Franklin

Great Bear L.

Hottah

N   O   R   T   H   W   E   S   T

Coronation Gulf

WOLLASTON PENINSULA

Cambridge Bay

Queen Maud Gulf

Bathurst Inlet

Gjoa Haven

CAPE SWINBURNE

BOOTH

PENINSU

Gulf of Alaska

CAPE ST. ELIAS

Mt. Fairweather 4663

Mt. Logan 5951

Juneau

Sitka

Petersburg

CHICHAGOF ISLAND

PACIFIC

Ketchikan

Prince Rupert

PRINCE OF WALES ISLAND

QUEEN CHARLOTTE ISLANDS

Hecate Strait

Queen Charlotte Sound

CAPE ST. JAMES

SCOTT ISLANDS

Stewart

Bronlund Pk. 2851

Summit Lake

Fort Nelson

2987 Mt. Smythe

Watson Lake

Fort Simpson

MACKENZIE MOUNTAINS

ROCKY

Great Slave Lake

Fort Resolution

Hay River

Yellowknife

Fort Reliance

Dubawnt

Baker Lake

Kaminuriak L.

Rankin Inl

Eskir Poin

OCEAN

CAPE DISAPPOINTMENT

VANCOUVER ISLAND

Campbell River

Bella Coola

Burns Lake

Williams

BRITISH COLUMBIA

Prince George

Fraser

Good Hope Mtn. 3233

Meander River

Keg River

Fort St. John

Peace River

Fort McMurray

Athabasca

La Loche

Fort Fitzgerald

Fort Chipewyan

Lake Athabasca

Fond du Lac

Brochet

Churchill Lake

La Ronge

Wholdaia L.

Ennadai L.

Tadoule L.

Lynn Lake

South Indian Lake

Churchill

Churchill

You Facto

MOUNTAINS

Vancouver

Victoria

Bellingham

Mt. Olympus 2423

Tacoma

Seattle

Olympia

WASHINGTON

Yakima

Columbia

Portland

Salem

Eugene

Mt. Hood 3424

OREGON

Kamloops

Kelowna

Revelstoke

Mt. Columbia 3747

Wetaskiwin

Edmonton

Red Deer

Biggar

Lloydminster

Prince Albert

SASKATCHEWAN

Saskatoon

Flin Flon

Hudson

Grand Rapids

MANITOBA

Berens River

Sani

Rock

Mt. Assiniboine 3619

Calgary

Medicine Hat

Kindersley

Moose Jaw

Watrous

Swan River

Yorkton

Dauphin

L. Manitoba

Gimli

Lake Winnipeg

Red Lake

Kenora

Lake of the Woods

Jasper

Hinton

Edson

2700 Roberts Pk.

Columbia

ALBERTA

Lac la Biche

Revelstoke

Mt. Nelson

Banff

Fort Macleod

Lethbridge

Regina

Melita

Virden

Neepawa

Morden

Winnipeg

International Falls

Bemidji

Hibbi

Duluth

Fort

Kaslo

Spokane

Lewiston

Walla Walla

BLUE MOUNTAINS

SALMON RIVER MOUNTAINS

Nampa

Boise

IDAHO

Idaho Falls

El Capitan 3043

Butte

Helena

Missoula

Great Falls

M O N T A N A

Miles City

Yellowstone

Yellowstone

Fort Peck Lake

Williston

Missouri

Minot

N O R T H   D A K O T A

Bismarck

Grand Forks

Fargo

M I N N E S O T

Aberdeen

Watertown

Minneapolis

St. Pa

CANADA

UNITED STATES

CASCADE

Mount Shasta 4316

Klamath Falls

Eugene

COAST RANGES

SIERRA NEVADA

CALIFORNIA

Sacramento

Oakland

SAN FRANCISCO

San Jose

Fresno

Salinas

Reno

Humboldt

Carson City

GREAT

NEVADA

BASIN

Elko

Great Salt L.

Ogden

Salt Lake City

Provo

UTAH

Twin Falls

Pocatello

Grand Teton 4197

BIGHORN MTS.

Sheridan

W Y O M I N G

Casper

Rock Springs

Laramie

Cheyenne

COLORADO

Scottsbluff

N E B R A S K A

Lake Oahe

S O U T H   D A K O T A

Pierre

Rapid City

BLACK HILLS

Brookings

Sioux Falls

Mankato

Rochester

IOWA

Sioux City

Waterlo

Mass

City

Kilometres   0   200   400   600   Km.
Miles   0   200   400   600   Mi.

1 : 24 000 000

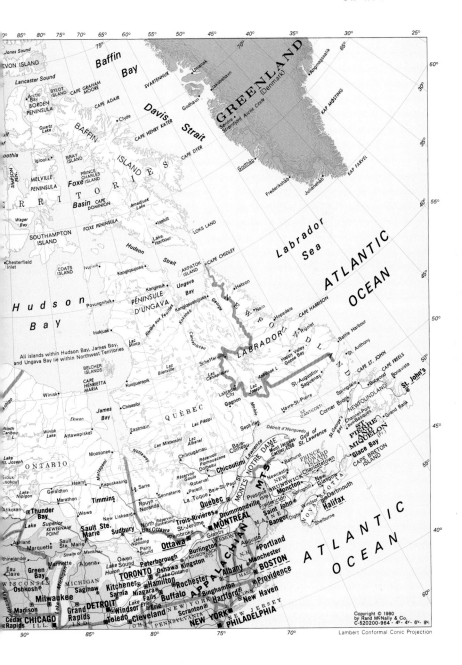

Jones Sound
DEVON ISLAND
Lancaster Sound
Arctic Bay
BYLOT ISLAND
BORDEN PENINSULA
CAPE GRAHAM MOORE
Baffin Bay
75°
Gulf
Quartz Lake
CAPE ADAIR
BAFFIN
ISLAND
Clyde
Davis
Strait
SVARTENHUK
Umanak
Jakobshavn
Godthavn
GREENLAND
(Denmark)
Sandre Stromfjord Arctic Circle
Angmagssalik
KAP MÖSTING
SIMPSON PEN.
MELVILLE PENINSULA
Igloolik
BRAY ISLAND
PRINCE CHARLES ISLAND
CAPE DOMINION
Foxe
Basin
Amadjuak Lake
CAPE HENRY KATER
T E R R I T O R I E S
CAPE DYER
Goothåb
KAP FARVEL
Boothia
Wager Bay
SOUTHAMPTON ISLAND
FOXE PENINSULA
Ipujik
LOKS LAND
Lake Harbour
Frederikshåb
Julianehåb
Chesterfield Inlet
COATS ISLAND
Ivujivik
Hudson
Strait
AKPATOK ISLAND
CAPE CHIDLEY
Labrador Sea
ATLANTIC
H u d s o n
Kangiqsujuaq
Kangirsuk
PÉNINSULE D'UNGAVA
Ungava Bay
Hebron
OCEAN
B a y
Povungnituk
Kangiqsualujjuaq
George
Nain
Hopedale
CAPE HARRISON
All islands within Hudson Bay, James Bay, and Ungava Bay lie within Northwest Territories
Inukjuak
Lac Minto
Rivière aux Feuilles
Kuujjuaq
Kaniapiscau
Rigolet
Battle Harbour
St. Anthony
BELCHER ISLANDS
CAPE HENRIETTA MARIA
Kuujjuarapik
Lac Bienville
Schefferville
Happy Valley-Goose Bay
Springdale
CAPE ST. JOHN
CAPE FREELS
Winisk
James
Bay
Chisasibi
L A B R A D O R
Labrador City
St-Augustin-Saguenay
Botwood
Bonavista
St. John's
North Caribou Lake
Winisk Lake
Ekwan
Gagnon
Corner Brook
Channel-Port aux Basques
NEWFOUNDLAND
Grand Bank
Eastmain
Attawapiskat
Lac Plétipi
ÎLE D'ANTICOSTI
Lake St. Joseph
Moosonee
Nottaway
Lac Mistassini
Lac Albanel
Sept-Îles
Détroit d'Honguedo
Gulf of St. Lawrence
ST. PIERRE AND MIQUELON
Sioux Lookout
O N T A R I O
Geraldton
Hearst
Kapuskasing
La Sarre
Chibougamau
Réservoir Gouin
Doucet
Baie-Comeau
Havre-St-Pierre
Bathurst
Glace Bay
CAPE BRETON ISLAND
Lake Nipigon
Marathon
Wawa
Timmins
Rouyn-Noranda
Senneterre
Parent
Réservoir Pipmuacan
Doibeau
Réservoir Outardes
Baie-St-Paul
Chicoutimi
CHICOUTIMI
MONTS NOTRE DAME
Newcastle
NEW BRUNSWICK
Moncton
PRINCE EDWARD ISLAND
Charlottetown
New Glasgow
Atikokan
Thunder Bay
Lake Superior
Sault Ste. Marie
KEWEENAW POINT
Sudbury
New Liskeard
Réservoir Gouin
La Tuque
Québec
QUÉBEC
Trois-Rivières
Drummondville
Fredericton
Mont Jacques Cartier
St. Lawrence
MAINE
Windsor
NOVA SCOTIA
Dartmouth
Halifax
Ashland
Marquette
Sault Ste. Marie
Straits of Mackinac
Owen Sound
North Bay
St-Jérôme
MONTRÉAL
Granby
Saint John
Digby
Shelburne
Rhinelander
Eau Claire
WISCONSIN
Green Bay
Oshkosh
MICHIGAN
Alpena
Parry Sound
Peterborough
Lake Nipissing
Ottawa
OTTAWA
Burlington
VERMONT
ADIRONDACK MTS.
Montpelier
N.H.
Augusta
Portland
Manchester
APPALACHIAN
ATLANTIC
OCEAN
Cedar Rapids
Madison
Milwaukee
CHICAGO
ILL.
Saginaw
Grand Rapids
DETROIT
Windsor
Sarnia
TORONTO
Hamilton
Kitchener
Niagara Falls
Oshawa
Lake Ontario
Rochester
Peterborough
Kingston
Lake Erie
Buffalo
Binghamton
Albany
MASS.
BOSTON
Providence
Hartford
New Haven
INDIANA
Toledo
Cleveland
OHIO
PENNSYLVANIA
Scranton
NEW YORK
NEW YORK
NEW JERSEY
PHILADELPHIA

Copyright © 1980
by Rand McNally & Co.
C-520200-964 - 4V- 4V- 6V- 9V-

Lambert Conformal Conic Projection

90° 85° 80° 75° 70° 65° 60° 55° 50° 45° 40° 35° 30° 25°

Copyright © 1980
by Rand McNally & Co.
C-520500-964 - 6ᵛ- 6ᵛ- 7ᵛ- 10ᵛ

Kilometres 0 200 400 600 Km.
Miles 0   200   400   600 Mi.

1 : 24 000 000

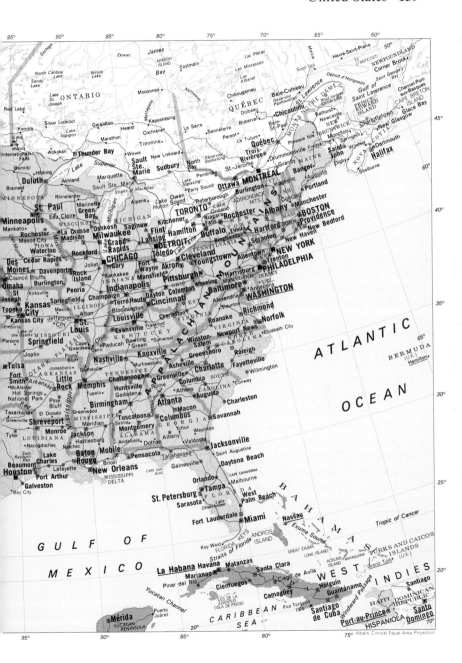

Kilometres 0 50 100 150 Km.
Miles 0 50 100 150 Mi.
1:6 000 000

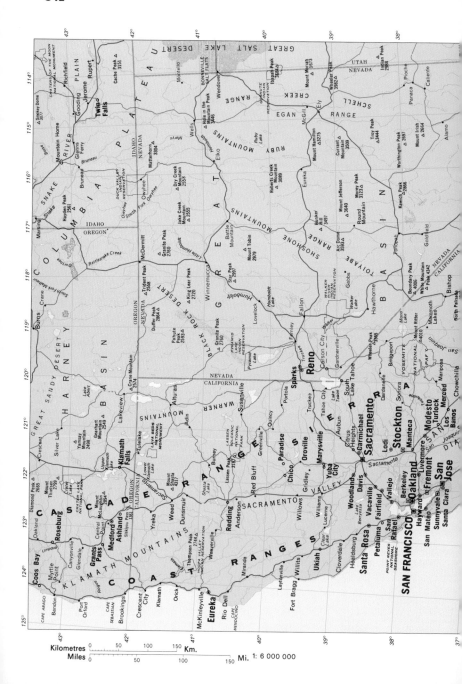

Kilometres 0   50   100   150 Km.
Miles 0   50   100   150 Mi.   1: 6 000 000

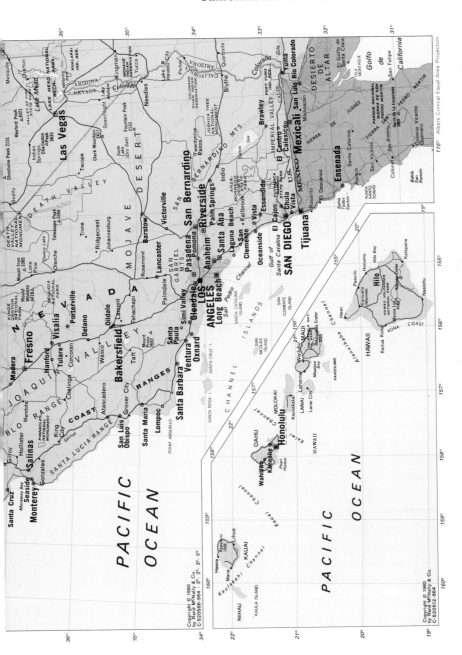

Albers Conical Equal-Area Projection

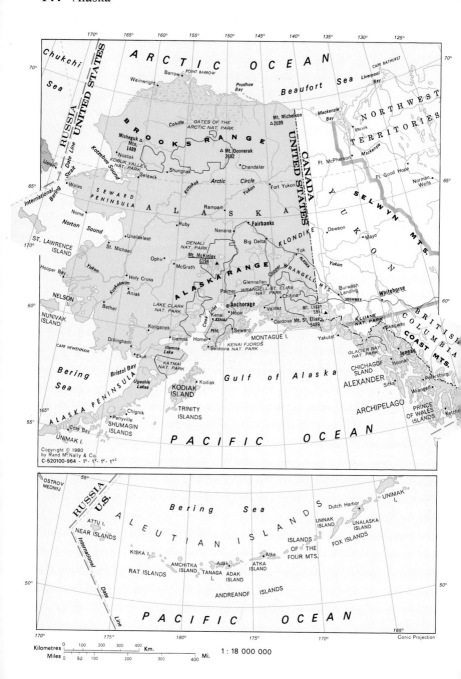

Kilometres 0 100 200 300 400 Km.

Miles 0 50 100 200 300 400 Mi.

1 : 18 000 000

Conic Projection

THE CONTINENTS

Continent	Area	Estimated Population	Population Density	Mean Elevation	Highest Elevation	Lowest Elevation
Africa	11,700,000 sq. mi. (30,300,000 sq. km.)	722,200,000	62/sq. mi. (24/sq. km.)	1,900 ft. (600 m.)	Kilimanjaro, Tanzania, 19,341 ft. (5,895 m.)	Lac Assal, Djibouti, -502 ft. (-153 m.)
Antarctica	5,400,000 sq. mi. (14,000,000 sq. km.)	No permanent population		6,000 ft. (1,800 m.)	Vinson Massif, 16,864 ft. (5,140 m.)	Deep Lake, -184 ft. (-56 m.)
Asia	17,300,000 sq. mi. (44,900,000 sq. km.)	3,509,800,000	203/sq. mi. (78/sq. km.)	3,000 ft. (900 m.)	Mt. Everest, China (Tibet)-Nepal, 29,028 ft. (8,848 m.)	Dead Sea, Israel-Jordan, -1,399 ft. (-408 m.)
Australia	2,966,155 sq. mi. (7,682,300 sq. km.)	18,430,000	6.2/sq. mi. (2.4/sq. km.)	1,000 ft. (300 m.)	Mt. Kosciusko, New South Wales, 7,310 ft. (2,228 m.)	Lake Eyre, South Australia, -52 ft. (-16 m.)
Europe	3,800,000 sq. mi. (9,900,000 sq. km.)	712,900,000	188/sq. mi. (72/sq. km.)	1,000 ft. (300 m.)	Gora El'brus, Russia, 18,510 ft. (5,642 m.)	Caspian Sea, -92 ft. (-28 m.)
North America	9,500,000 sq. mi. (24,700,000 sq. km.)	459,600,000	48/sq. mi. (19/sq. km.)	2,000 ft. (600 m.)	Mt. McKinley, U.S. (Alaska), 20,320 ft. (6,194 m.)	Death Valley, U.S. (Calif.), -282 ft. (-86 m.)
Oceania, incl. Australia	3,300,000 sq. mi. (8,500,000 sq. km.)	29,000,000	8.8/sq. mi. (3.4/sq. km.)	. . .	Mt. Wilhelm, Papua New Guinea, 14,793 ft. (4,509 m.)	Lake Eyre, South Australia, -52 ft. (-16 m.)
South America	6,900,000 sq. mi. (17,800,000 sq. km.)	319,500,000	46/sq. mi. (18/sq. km.)	1,800 ft. (550 m.)	Cerro Aconcagua, Argentina, 22,831 ft. (6,959 m.)	Salinas Chicas, Argentina, -138 ft. (-42 m.)
WORLD	57,900,000 sq. mi. (150,100,000 sq. km.)	5,753,000,000	99/sq. mi. (38/sq. km.)	. . .	Mt. Everest, China (Tibet)-Nepal, 29,028 ft. (8,848 m.)	Dead Sea, Israel-Jordan, -1,399 ft. (-408 m.)

Principal Mountains

Mountains	Location	Feet	Meters
Aconcagua, Cerro	Argentina	22,831	6,959
Adams, Mt.	U.S.	12,276	3,742
Ağrı Dağı (Mt. Ararat)	Turkey	16,804	5,122
Annapurna	Nepal	26,503	8,078
Apo, Mt.	Philippines	9,692	2,954
Barú, Volcán	Panama	11,401	3,475
Blanc, Mont	France-Italy	15,771	4,807
Bolívar, Pico	Venezuela	16,411	5,002
Boundary Pk.	U.S.	13,143	4,006
Cameroun, Mont	Cameroon	13,353	4,070
Chimborazo	Ecuador	20,702	6,310
Chirripó, Cerro	Costa Rica	12,530	3,819
Citlaltépetl, Volcán	Mexico	18,701	5,700
Columbia, Mt.	Canada	12,293	3,747
Cook, Mt.	New Zealand	12,349	3,764
Cristóbal Colón, Pico	Colombia	18,947	5,775
Dhawalāgiri	Nepal	26,810	8,172
Dimlang	Nigeria	6,699	2,042
Duarte, Pico	Dominican Republic	10,417	3,175
Dufour Spitze	Italy-Switzerland	15,203	4,634
Elbert, Mt.	U.S.	14,433	4,399
El'brus, Gora	Russia	18,510	5,642
Etna, Monte	Italy	10,902	3,323
Everest, Mt.	China-Nepal	29,028	8,848
Fuji-san	Japan	12,388	3,776
Gannett Pk.	U.S.	13,804	4,207
Glittertinden	Norway	8,110	2,472
Grand Teton	U.S.	13,770	4,197
Grossglockner	Austria	12,457	3,797
Guadalupe Pk.	U.S.	8,749	2,667
Hood, Mt.	U.S.	11,234	3,424
Huascarán, Nevado	Peru	22,205	6,768
Humphreys Pk.	U.S.	12,633	3,851
Hvannadalshnúkur	Iceland	6,952	2,119
Illimani, Nevado	Bolivia	21,004	6,402
Inthanon, Doi	Thailand	8,513	2,595
Inyangani	Zimbabwe	8,504	2,592
Jaya, Puncak	Indonesia	16,503	5,030
Jungfrau	Switzerland	13,642	4,158
K2 (Qogir Feng)	China-Pakistan	28,251	8,611
Kānchenjunga	Nepal-India	28,209	8,598
Kāmet	China-India	25,446	7,756
Katrīnah, Jabal	Egypt	8,668	2,642
Kebnekaise	Sweden	6,926	2,111
Kerinci, Gunung	Indonesia	12,467	3,800
Kilimanjaro	Tanzania	19,341	5,895
Kinabalu, Gunong	Malaysia	13,455	4,101
Kirinyaga (Mt. Kenya)	Kenya	17,057	5,199
Kommunizma, Pik	Tajikistan	24,590	7,495
Kosciusko, Mt.	Australia	7,310	2,228
Koussi, Emi	Chad	11,204	3,415
Kula Kangri	Bhutan	24,783	7,554
Las Minas, Cerro	Honduras	9,400	2,865
Lassen Pk.	U.S.	10,457	3,187
Logan, Mt.	Canada	19,524	5,951
Makālu	China-Nepal	27,825	8,481
Marcy, Mt.	U.S.	5,344	1,629
Margherita Pk.	Uganda-D.R. Congo	16,763	5,109
Maromokotro	Madagascar	9,436	2,876
Matterhorn	Italy-Switzerland	14,692	4,478
Mauna Loa	U.S.	13,679	4,169
McKinley, Mt.	U.S.	20,320	6,194
Mitchell, Mt.	U.S.	6,684	2,037
Mogotón, Cerro	Nicaragua	6,913	2,107
Mulhacén	Spain	11,411	3,478
Nanda Devi	India	25,646	7,817
Nānga Parbat	Pakistan	26,660	8,126
Narodnaja, Gora	Russia	6,214	1,894
Nevis, Ben	U.K.	4,406	1,343
Ojos del Salado, Nevado	Argentina-Chile	22,572	6,880
Ólimbos (Mt. Olympus)	Greece	9,570	2,917
Olympus, Mt.	U.S.	7,965	2,428
Orohena, Mt.	French Polynesia	7,333	2,235
Ossa, Mt.	Australia	5,305	1,617
Pelée, Montagne	Martinique	4,583	1,397
Pidurutalagala	Sri Lanka	8,281	2,524
Pikes Pk.	U.S.	14,110	4,301
Pobedy, pik	China-Kyrgyzstan	24,406	7,439
Popocatépetl, Volcán	Mexico	17,887	5,452
Rainier, Mt.	U.S.	14,410	4,392
Ras Dashen Terara	Ethiopia	15,157	4,620
Sajama, Nevado	Bolivia	21,463	6,542
Selle, Châine de la	Haiti	8,773	2,674
Shasta, Mt.	U.S.	14,162	4,317
Tahat	Algeria	9,852	3,003
Tajumulco, Volcán	Guatemala	13,845	4,220
Toubkal, Jbel	Morocco	13,665	4,165
Triglav	Yugoslavia	9,393	2,863
Uncompahgre Pk.	U.S.	14,309	4,361
Vesuvio	Italy	4,190	1,277
Vinson Massif	Antarctica	16,864	5,140
Wilhelm, Mount	Papua New Guinea	14,793	4,509

Oceans, Seas, and Gulfs

Name	Location	Sq. Mi.	Sq. Km.
Arabian Sea	Asia-Africa	1,492,000	3,864,000
Arctic Ocean		5,400,000	14,000,000
Atlantic Ocean		31,800,000	82,400,000
Baltic Sea	Eur.	163,000	422,000
Bengal, Bay of	Asia	839,000	2,173,000
Bering Sea	Asia-N.A.	876,000	2,269,000
Black Sea	Eur.-Asia	178,000	461,000
Caribbean Sea	N.A.-S.A.	1,063,000	2,753,000
East China Sea	Asia	482,000	1,248,000
Greenland Sea	Eur.-N.A.	465,000	1,204,000
Hudson Bay	Canada	475,000	1,230,000
Indian Ocean		28,900,000	74,900,000
Japan, Sea of	Asia	389,000	1,008,000
Mediterranean Sea		967,000	2,505,000
Mexico, Gulf of	N.A.	596,000	1,544,000
North Sea	Eur.	222,000	575,000
Norwegian Sea	Eur.-N.A.	597,000	1,546,000
Okhotsk, Sea of	Asia	619,000	1,603,000
Pacific Ocean		63,800,000	165,200,000
Red Sea	Africa-Asia	169,000	438,000
South China Sea	Asia	1,331,000	3,447,000
Yellow Sea	China-Korea	480,000	1,200,000

Principal Islands

Name	Location	Sq. Mi.	Sq. Km.
Baffin I.	Canada	195,928	507,451
Banks I.	Canada	27,038	70,028
Borneo	Asia	287,300	744,100
Bougainville	Papua New Guinea	3,600	9,300
Cape Breton I.	Canada	3,981	10,311
Corse (Corsica)	France	3,367	8,720
Cuba	N.A.	42,800	110,800
Cyprus	Asia	3,572	9,251
Devon I.	Canada	21,331	55,247
Ellesmere I.	Canada	75,767	196,236
Great Britain	United Kingdom	88,795	229,978
Greenland	N.A.	840,000	2,175,600
Hainan Dao	China	13,100	34,000
Hawaii	U.S.	4,034	10,448
Hispaniola	N.A.	29,300	76,200
Hokkaidō	Japan	32,245	83,515
Honshū	Japan	89,176	230,966
Iceland	Europe	39,800	103,000
Ireland	Europe	32,600	84,400
Jamaica	N.A.	4,200	11,000
Jawa (Java)	Indonesia	51,038	132,187
Kodiak I.	U.S.	3,670	9,505
Kríti (Crete)	Greece	3,189	8,259
Kyūshū	Japan	17,129	44,363
Long I.	U.S.	1,377	3,566
Luzon	Philippines	40,420	104,688
Madagascar	Africa	227,000	587,000
Melville I.	Canada	16,274	42,149
Mindanao	Philippines	36,537	94,630
Mindoro	Philippines	3,759	9,735
Negros	Philippines	4,907	12,710
New Britain	Papua New Guinea	14,093	36,500
New Caledonia	Oceania	6,252	16,192
Newfoundland	Canada	42,031	108,860
New Guinea	Oceania	309,000	800,000
North I.	New Zealand	44,333	114,821
Novaja Zeml'a	Russia	31,900	82,600
Palawan	Philippines	4,550	11,785
Prince of Wales I.	Canada	12,872	33,339
Puerto Rico	N.A.	3,500	9,100
Sachalin, Ostrov	Russia	29,500	76,400
Samar	Philippines	5,100	13,080
Sardegna (Sardinia)	Italy	9,301	24,090
Seram (Ceram)	Indonesia	7,191	18,625
Shikoku	Japan	7,258	18,799
Sicilia (Sicily)	Italy	9,926	25,709
Somerset I.	Canada	9,570	24,786
Southampton I.	Canada	15,913	41,214
South I.	New Zealand	57,708	149,463
Spitsbergen	Norway	15,260	39,523
Sri Lanka	Asia	24,900	64,600
Sulawesi (Celebes)	Indonesia	73,057	189,216
Sumatera (Sumatra)	Indonesia	182,860	473,606
T'aiwan	Asia	13,900	36,000
Tasmania	Austl.	26,200	67,800
Tierra del Fuego	S.A.	18,600	48,200
Timor	Indonesia	5,743	14,874
Vancouver I.	Canada	12,049	31,285

Principal Lakes

Name	Location	Sq. Mi.	Sq. Km.
Albert, L.	Uganda-D.R. Congo	2,160	5,594
Aral Sea	Kazakhstan-Uzbekistan	24,700	64,100
Athabasca, L.	Canada	3,064	7,935
Bajkal, Ozero (L. Baikal)	Russia	12,200	31,500
Balqash kölï (L. Balkhash)	Kazakhstan	7,100	18,300
Caspian Sea	Asia-Europe	143,240	370,990
Chad, L.	Cameroon-Chad-Nigeria	6,300	16,300
Erie, L.	Canada-U.S.	9,910	25,667
Eyre, L.	Australia	3,700	9,500
Great Bear L.	Canada	12,095	31,326
Great Salt L.	U.S.	1,680	4,351
Great Slave L.	Canada	11,030	28,568
Huron, L.	Canada-U.S.	23,000	60,000
Ladožskoje Ozero	Russia	6,833	17,700
Mai-Ndombe, Lac	D.R. Congo	3,100	8,000
Michigan, L.	U.S.	22,300	57,800
Nicaragua, Lago de	Nicaragua	3,150	8,158
Nyasa, L.	Malawi-Mozambique-Tanzania	11,150	28,878
Ontario, L.	Canada-U.S.	7,540	19,529
Rudolf, L.	Ethiopia-Kenya	2,473	6,405
Superior, L.	Canada-U.S.	31,700	82,100
Tanganyika. L.	Africa	12,350	31,986
Titicaca, Lago	Bolivia-Peru	3,200	8,300
Tônlé Sab	Cambodia	2,500	6,500
Torrens, Lake	Australia	2,300	5,900
Vänern	Sweden	2,156	5,584
Victoria, L.	Kenya-Tanzania-Uganda	26,820	69,463
Winnipeg, L.	Canada	9,416	24,387
Woods, Lake of the	Canada-U.S.	1,727	4,472

Principal Rivers

Name	Location	Mi.	Km.
Amazon	S.A.	4,000	6,400
Amur (Heilong)	Asia	2,744	4,416
Angara	Asia	1,105	1,779
Arkansas	N.A.	1,459	2,348
Ayeyarwady (Irrawaddy)	Asia	1,300	2,100
Brahmaputra	Asia	1,770	2,849
Chang (Yangtze)	Asia	3,900	6,300
Churchill	N.A.	1,000	1,600
Colorado	N.A.	1,450	2,334
Columbia	N.A.	1,243	2,000
Congo (Zaïre)	Africa	2,880	4,700
Danube	Europe	1,776	2,858
Darling	Australia	864	1,390
Dnieper	Europe	1,367	2,200
Dniester	Europe	840	1,352
Don	Europe	1,162	1,870
Euphrates	Asia	1,510	2,430
Ganges	Asia	1,560	2,511
Grande, Rio	N.A.	1,885	3,034
Huang (Yellow)	Asia	3,395	5,464
Indus	Asia	1,800	2,900
Jenisej (Yenisey)	Asia	2,543	4,092
Kasai	Africa	1,338	2,153
Lena	Asia	2,734	4,400
Limpopo	Africa	1,100	1,770
Mackenzie	N.A.	2,635	4,241
Madeira	S.A.	2,013	3,240
Mekong	Asia	2,600	4,200
Mississippi	N.A.	2,348	3,779
Mississippi-Missouri	N.A.	3,740	6,019
Murray	Australia	1,566	2,520
Negro	S.A.	1,300	2,100
Niger	Africa	2,600	4,200
Nile	Africa	4,145	6,671
Ob'-Irtyš	Asia	3,362	5,410
Ohio	N.A.	981	1,579
Orange	Africa	1,300	2,100
Orinoco	S.A.	1,600	2,600
Paraguay	S.A.	1,610	2,591
Peace	N.A.	1,195	1,923
Pečora	Europe	1,124	1,809
Purus	S.A.	1,860	2,993
Red	N.A.	1,270	2,044
Rhine	Europe	820	1,320
Rio de la Plata--Paraná	S.A.	3,030	4,876
St. Lawrence	N.A.	800	1,300
Salween (Nu)	Asia	1,750	2,816
São Francisco	S.A.	1,988	3,199
Saskatchewan--Bow	N.A.	1,205	1,939
Snake	N.A.	1,038	1,670
Tennessee	N.A.	652	1,049
Tigris	Asia	1,180	1,899
Ural	Asia	1,509	2,428
Uruguay	S.A.	1,025	1,650
Volga	Europe	2,194	3,531
Yukon	N.A.	1,770	2,849
Zambezi	Africa	1,700	2,700

Largest Countries: Area

	Country	Sq. Mi.	Sq. Km.
1	Russia	6,592,849	17,075,400
2	Canada	3,849,674	9,970,610
3	United States	3,787,425	9,809,431
4	China	3,689,631	9,556,100
5	Brazil	3,300,171	8,547,404
6	Australia	2,966,155	7,682,300
7	India	1,237,062	3,203,975
8	Argentina	1,073,519	2,780,400
9	Kazakhstan	1,049,156	2,717,300
10	Sudan	967,500	2,505,813
11	Algeria	919,595	2,381,741
12	Dem. Rep. of the Congo	905,446	2,345,095
13	Greenland	840,004	2,175,600
14	Saudi Arabia	830,000	2,149,690
15	Mexico	759,534	1,967,183
16	Indonesia	752,410	1,948,732
17	Libya	679,362	1,759,540
18	Iran	630,578	1,633,189
19	Mongolia	604,829	1,566,500
20	Peru	496,225	1,285,216
21	Chad	495,755	1,284,000
22	Niger	489,191	1,267,000
23	Mali	482,077	1,248,574
24	Angola	481,354	1,246,700
25	South Africa	471,010	1,219,909
26	Ethiopia	446,953	1,157,603
27	Colombia	440,831	1,141,748
28	Bolivia	424,165	1,098,581
29	Mauritania	397,956	1,030,700
30	Egypt	386,662	1,001,449
31	Tanzania	364,900	945,087
32	Nigeria	356,669	923,768
33	Venezuela	352,145	912,050
34	Pakistan	339,732	879,902
35	Namibia	317,818	823,144
36	Mozambique	308,642	799,380
37	Turkey	300,948	779,452
38	Chile	292,135	756,626
39	Zambia	290,586	752,614
40	Myanmar	261,228	676,577
41	Afghanistan	251,826	652,225
42	Somalia	246,201	637,657
43	Central African Republic	240,535	622,984
44	Ukraine	233,090	603,700
45	Madagascar	226,658	587,041
46	Kenya	224,961	582,646
47	Botswana	224,711	582,000
48	France	211,208	547,026
49	Yemen	203,850	527,968
50	Thailand	198,115	513,115
51	Spain	194,885	504,750
52	Turkmenistan	188,456	488,100
53	Cameroon	183,568	475,440
54	Papua New Guinea	178,704	462,840

Smallest Countries: Area

	Country	Sq. Mi.	Sq. Km.
1	Vatican City	0.2	0.4
2	Monaco	0.7	1.9
3	Nauru	8.1	21
4	Tuvalu	10	26
5	San Marino	24	61
6	Guernsey	30	78
7	Anguilla	35	91
8	Jersey	45	116
9	Liechtenstein	62	160
10	Marshall Islands	70	181
11	Aruba	75	193
12	Cook Islands	91	236
13	Niue	100	259
14	St. Kitts and Nevis	104	269
15	Maldives	115	298
16	Malta	122	316
17	Grenada	133	344
18	St. Vincent and the Grenadines	150	388
19	Barbados	166	430
20	Antigua and Barbuda	171	442
21	Andorra	175	453
	Seychelles	175	453
22	Northern Mariana Islands	184	477
23	Palau	196	508
24	Isle of Man	221	572
25	St. Lucia	238	616
26	Singapore	246	636
27	Bahrain	267	691
28	Federated States of Micronesia	271	702
29	Tonga	288	747
30	Dominica	305	790
31	Netherlands Antilles	309	800
32	Kiribati	313	811
33	Sao Tome and Principe	372	964
34	Faeroe Islands	540	1,399
35	Mauritius	788	2,040
36	Comoros	863	2,235
37	Luxembourg	998	2,586
38	Samoa	1,093	2,831
39	North Cyprus	1,295	3,355
40	Cape Verde	1,557	4,033
41	Trinidad and Tobago	1,980	5,128
42	Brunei	2,226	5,765
43	Cyprus	2,276	5,896
44	Puerto Rico	3,515	9,104
45	Lebanon	4,015	10,400
46	Gambia	4,127	10,689
47	Jamaica	4,244	10,991
48	Qatar	4,412	11,427
49	Vanuatu	4,707	12,190
50	Bahamas	5,382	13,939
51	Swaziland	6,704	17,364

Largest Countries: Population

	Country	Population
1	China	1,209,110,000
2	India	944,980,000
3	United States	265,130,000
4	Indonesia	196,830,000
5	Brazil	161,700,000
6	Russia	150,500,000
7	Pakistan	132,330,000
8	Bangladesh	129,500,000
9	Japan	125,760,000
10	Nigeria	102,850,000
11	Mexico	94,830,000
12	Germany	81,800,000
13	Vietnam	74,360,000
14	Philippines	74,070,000
15	Iran	65,340,000
16	Turkey	63,020,000
17	Thailand	60,630,000
18	Egypt	60,080,000
19	United Kingdom	58,410,000
20	Italy	58,320,000
21	France	58,280,000
22	Ethiopia	56,820,000
23	Ukraine	51,940,000
24	Myanmar	45,510,000
25	South Korea	45,040,000
26	Dem. Rep. of the Congo	44,765,000
27	South Africa	42,235,000
28	Spain	39,485,000
29	Poland	38,870,000
30	Colombia	35,400,000
31	Argentina	34,465,000
32	Sudan	30,480,000
33	Canada	29,725,000
34	Tanzania	29,075,000
35	Kenya	28,960,000
36	Algeria	28,855,000
37	Morocco	27,430,000
38	Peru	24,305,000
39	North Korea	23,700,000
40	Uzbekistan	23,345,000
41	Afghanistan	22,780,000
42	Romania	22,715,000
43	Venezuela	21,845,000
44	Nepal	21,820,000
45	Taiwan	21,585,000
46	Iraq	21,015,000
47	Malaysia	19,940,000
48	Uganda	19,790,000
49	Saudi Arabia	19,065,000
50	Australia	18,430,000
51	Sri Lanka	18,185,000
52	Ghana	18,030,000
53	Kazakhstan	17,180,000
54	Mozambique	16,200,000
55	Netherlands	15,500,000

Smallest Countries: Population

	Country	Population
1	Vatican City	1,000
2	Niue	1,800
3	Anguilla	7,000
4	Nauru	10,000
	Tuvalu	10,000
5	Palau	17,000
6	Cook Islands	19,000
7	San Marino	25,000
8	Liechtenstein	31,000
9	Monaco	32,000
10	St. Kitts and Nevis	41,000
11	Faeroe Islands	49,000
12	Northern Mariana Islands	52,000
13	Marshall Islands	57,000
14	Greenland	58,000
15	Guernsey	64,000
16	Aruba	66,000
17	Andorra	67,000
	Antigua and Barbuda	67,000
18	Isle of Man	73,000
19	Seychelles	75,000
20	Kiribati	80,000
21	Dominica	83,000
22	Jersey	87,000
23	Grenada	94,000
24	Federated States of Micronesia	110,000
	Tonga	110,000
25	St. Vincent and the Grenadines	117,000
26	North Cyprus	135,000
	Sao Tome and Principe	135,000
27	St. Lucia	157,000
28	Samoa	170,000
29	Vanuatu	175,000
30	Netherlands Antilles	205,000
31	Belize	217,000
32	Barbados	256,000
33	Bahamas	258,000
34	Maldives	259,000
35	Iceland	267,000
36	Brunei	296,000
37	Malta	371,000
38	Luxembourg	406,000
	Solomon Islands	406,000
39	Equatorial Guinea	425,000
40	Suriname	433,000
41	Cape Verde	443,000
42	Comoros	559,000
43	Qatar	562,000
44	Djibouti	579,000
45	Bahrain	583,000
46	Cyprus	605,000
47	Guyana	721,000
48	Fiji	778,000
49	Swaziland	982,000

Highest Urban Population

Country	Percent Urban
1 Monaco	100%
Nauru	100%
Singapore	100%
Vatican City	100%
2 Belgium	97%
Kuwait	97%
3 San Marino	94%
4 Venezuela	93%
5 Iceland	92%
6 Israel	91%
Qatar	91%
7 Bahrain	90%
Malta	90%
United Kingdom	90%
Uruguay	90%
8 Luxembourg	89%
Netherlands	89%
9 Argentina	88%
10 Bahamas	87%
Germany	87%
Lebanon	87%
11 Libya	86%
New Zealand	86%
12 Australia	85%
Denmark	85%

Lowest Urban Population

Country	Percent Urban
1 Bhutan	6%
Rwanda	6%
2 Burundi	8%
3 Ethiopia	13%
Oman	13%
Uganda	13%
4 Malawi	14%
Nepal	14%
5 Grenada	15%
6 Papua New Guinea	16%
7 Eritrea	17%
Niger	17%
Solomon Islands	17%
8 Bangladesh	18%
9 Vanuatu	19%
10 Afghanistan	20%
Thailand	20%
11 Chad	21%
Cambodia	21%
Liechtenstein	21%
Vietnam	21%
Samoa	21%
12 Guinea-Bissau	22%
Laos	22%
Sri Lanka	22%

Highest Life Expectancy

Country	Years M	F
1 San Marino	77	85
2 Japan	77	83
3 Andorra	76	82
Sweden	76	82
4 Greece	76	81
Guernsey	76	81
Iceland	76	81
5 Cyprus	76	80
6 Faeroe Islands	75	82
Switzerland	75	82
7 Australia	75	81
Canada	75	81
Netherlands	75	81
Spain	75	81
8 Israel	75	79
Italy	75	79
Malta	75	79
United Kingdom	75	79
9 Barbados	74	79
10 Monaco	74	82
11 Belgium	74	81
France	74	81
Liechtenstein	74	81
Norway	74	81
12 Austria	74	80
Dominica	74	80

Lowest Life Expectancy

Country	Years M	F
1 Sierra Leone	39	43
2 Uganda	42	44
3 Malawi	44	45
4 Guinea-Bissau	44	47
5 Afghanistan	45	46
6 Zambia	45	47
7 Burkina Faso	45	48
Mozambique	45	48
Rwanda	45	48
8 Gambia	45	49
9 Guinea	46	47
10 Mali	46	50
11 Niger	47	50
12 Angola	47	51
Benin	47	51
Somalia	47	51
13 Chad	48	51
14 Congo	48	52
Equatorial Guinea	48	52
Ethiopia	48	52
15 Central African Republic	48	53
16 Cote d'Ivoire	49	51
17 Djibouti	49	52
18 Burundi	49	53
19 Senegal	50	52
Zimbabwe	50	52

Highest Literacy

Country	Percent Literate
1 Australia	100%
Estonia	100%
Finland	100%
Iceland	100%
Latvia	100%
Liechtenstein	100%
Luxembourg	100%
Tonga	100%
Vatican City	100%
2 Armenia	99%
Austria	99%
Barbados	99%
Belgium	99%
North Cyprus	99%
Czech Republic	99%
Denmark	99%
France	99%
Georgia	99%
Germany	99%
Hungary	99%
Japan	99%
North Korea	99%
Netherlands	99%
New Zealand	99%
Norway	99%
Poland	99%
Slovenia	99%
Sweden	99%
Switzerland	99%
United Kingdom	99%

Lowest Literacy

Country	Percent Literate
1 Burkina Faso	18%
2 Oman	20%
3 Sierra Leone	21%
4 Benin	23%
5 Ethiopia	24%
Guinea	24%
Somalia	24%
6 Nepal	26%
7 Gambia	27%
Sudan	27%
8 Niger	28%
9 Afghanistan	29%
10 Chad	30%
11 Mali	32%
12 Mozambique	33%
13 Bangladesh	35%
Haiti	35%
Cambodia	35%
Mauritania	35%
Pakistan	35%
14 Guinea-Bissau	36%
15 Central African Republic	38%
Namibia	38%
Senegal	38%
Yemen	38%
16 Liberia	40%
17 Angola	42%
18 Togo	43%

Highest GDP U.S. $ / Capita

Country	GDP/ Capita
1 United States	25,978
2 United Arab Emirates	23,291
3 Luxembourg	22,943
4 Canada	22,891
5 Liechtenstein	22,500
6 Norway	22,251
7 Qatar	21,315
8 Switzerland	21,197
9 Australia	20,869
10 Japan	20,245
11 Singapore	20,113
12 Denmark	19,880
13 France	18,726
14 Sweden	18,646
15 Belgium	18,060
16 United Kingdom	18,033
17 Netherlands	18,003
18 Monaco	18,000
19 Kuwait	17,705
20 Italy	17,627
21 Austria	17,604
22 Iceland	17,176
23 Aruba	16,923
24 Germany	16,614
25 Bahamas	16,296

Lowest GDP U.S. $ / Capita

Country	GDP/ Capita
1 Ethiopia	393
2 Dem. Rep. of the Congo	451
3 Somalia	505
4 Eritrea	508
5 Chad	529
6 Angola	553
7 Niger	561
8 Mali	605
9 Burundi	615
10 Cambodia	639
Mozambique	639
11 Burkina Faso	663
12 Bhutan	703
13 Equatorial Guinea	711
14 Central African Republic	712
15 Tuvalu	722
16 Comoros	728
17 Tanzania	765
18 Liberia	796
19 Madagascar	809
20 Kiribati	816
Malawi	816
21 Togo	819
22 Sudan	820
23 Guinea-Bissau	849

Index

Introduction to the Index

This universal index includes in a single alphabetical list more than 7,000 names of features that appear on the world travel maps on pages 81 through 144. Each name is followed by latitude and longitude coordinates and a page reference.

Names: Local official names are used on the maps and in the index. The names are shown in full, including diacritical marks. Features that extend beyond the boundaries of one country and have no single official name are usually named in English. Many conventional English names and former names are cross-referenced to the official names. Names that appear in shortened versions on the maps due to space limitiations are spelled out in full in the index. The portions of these names omitted from the maps are enclosed in brackets—for example, Acapulco [de Juárez].

Transliteration: For names in languages not written in the Roman alphabet, the locally official transliteration system has been used where one exists. Thus, names in Russia and Bulgaria have been transliterated according to the systems adopted by the academies of science of these countries. Similarly, the transliteration of mainland Chinese names follows the Pinyin system, which has been officially adopted in mainland China. For languages with no one locally accepted system, notably Arabic, transliteration closely follows a system adopted by the United States Board on Geographic Names.

Abbreviation and Capitalization: Abbreviations of names on the maps have been standardized as much as possible. Names that are abbreviated on the maps are generally spelled out in full in the index. Periods are used after all abbreviations regardless of local practice. The abbreviation "St." is used only for "Saint". "Sankt" and other forms of this term are spelled out.

Most initial letters of names are capitalized, except for a few Dutch names, such as "'s-Gravenhage". Capitalization of noninitial words in a name generally follows local practice.

Alphabetization: Names are alphabetized in the order of the letters of the English alphabet. Spanish *ll* and *ch,* for example, are not treated as distinct letters. Furthermore, diacritical marks are disregarded in alphabetization—German or Scandinavian *ä* or *ö* are treated as *a* or *o.*

The names of physical features may appear inverted, since they are always alphabetized under the proper,

not the generic, part of the name, thus: "Gibraltar, Strait of ᴚ". Otherwise every entry, whether consisting of one word or more, is alphabetized as a single continuous entity. "La Habana," for example, appears after "Lagunillas" and before "Lahaina." Names beginning with articles (Le Havre, Den Helder, Al-Qāhirah, As-Suways) are not inverted. Names beginning "St.", "Ste." and "Sainte" are alphabetized as though spelled "Saint."

In the case of identical names, towns are listed first, then political divisions, then physical features. Entries that are completely identical (including symbols, discussed below) are distinguished by abbreviations of their country names. The country abbreviations used for places in the United States, Canada and United Kingdom indicate the state, province or political division in which the feature is located. (See List of Abbreviations on page 154).

Symbols: City names are not followed by symbols. The names of all other features are followed by symbols that graphically represent broad categories of features, for example, ᴧ for mountain (Everest, Mount ᴧ). Superior numbers indicate finer distinctions, for example, ᴧ¹ for volcano (Fuji-san ᴧ¹). A complete list of symbols, including those with superior numbers, follows the List of Abbreviations.

All cross-references are indicated by the symbol →.

Page References and Geographical Coordinates: The page references and geographical coordinates are found in the last three columns of each entry.

The page number generally refers to the map that shows the feature at the best scale. Countries, mountain ranges and other extensive features are usually indexed to maps that both show the features completely and also show them in their relationship to broad areas. Page references to two-page maps always refer to the left-hand page. If a page contains several maps or insets, a lowercase letter may identify the specific map or inset.

Latitude and longitude coordinates for point features, such as cities and mountain peaks, indicate the locations of the symbols. For extensive areal features, such as countries or mountain ranges, locations are given for the approximate center of the feature. Those for linear features, such as canals and rivers, are given to the mouth or terminal point.

List of Abbreviations

	English	Local Name		English	Local Name
Ab., Can.	Alberta, Can.	Alberta	Cam.	Cameroon	Cameroun (French) / Cameroon (English)
Afg.	Afghanistan	Afghānestān			
Afr.	Africa	—			
Ak., U.S.	Alaska, U.S.	Alaska			
Al., U.S.	Alabama, U.S.	Alabama	Camb.	Cambodia	Kâmpŭchéa
Alb.	Albania	Shqipëri	Can.	Canada	Canada
Alg.	Algeria	Algérie (French) / Djazaïr (Arabic)	C.A.R.	Central African Republic	République centrafricaine
			Cay. Is.	Cayman Islands	Cayman Islands
Am. Sam.	American Samoa	American Samoa (English) / Amerika Samoa (Samoan)	Chad	Chad	Tchad
			Chile	Chile	Chile
			China	China	Zhongguo
			Christ. I.	Christmas Island	Christmas Island
And.	Andorra	Andorra	C. Iv.	Cote d'Ivoire	Côte d'Ivoire
Ang.	Angola	Angola	Co., U.S.	Colorado, U.S.	Colorado
Anguilla	Anguilla	Anguilla	Cocos Is.	Cocos (Keeling) Islands	Cocos (Keeling) Islands
Ant.	Antarctica	—			
Antig.	Antigua and Barbuda	Antigua and Barbuda	Col.	Colombia	Colombia
			Com.	Comoros	Comores (French) / Al-Qumur (Arabic)
Ar., U.S.	Arkansas, U.S.	Arkansas			
Arg.	Argentina	Argentina			
Arm.	Armenia	Hayastan	Congo	Congo	Congo
Aruba	Aruba	Aruba	Cook Is.	Cook Islands	Cook Islands
Asia	Asia	—	C.R.	Costa Rica	Costa Rica
Aus.	Austria	Österreich	Cro.	Croatia	Hrvatska
Austl.	Australia	Australia	Ct., U.S.	Connecticut, U.S.	Connecticut
Az., U.S.	Arizona, U.S.	Arizona			
Azer.	Azerbaijan	Azerbaijan	Cuba	Cuba	Cuba
Bah.	Bahamas	Bahamas	C.V.	Cape Verde	Cabo Verde
Bahr.	Bahrain	Al-Baḥrayn	Cyp.	Cyprus	Kípros (Greek) / Kıbrıs (Turkish)
Barb.	Barbados	Barbados			
B.C., Can.	British Columbia, Can.	British Columbia (English) / Colombie-Britannique (French)	Czech Rep.	Czech Republic	Česká Republika
			D.C., U.S.	District of Columbia, U.S.	District of Columbia
Bdi.	Burundi	Burundi			
Bel.	Belgium	Belgique (French) / België (Flemish)	De., U.S.	Delaware, U.S.	Delaware
			Den.	Denmark	Danmark
			Dji.	Djibouti	Djibouti
			Dom.	Dominica	Dominica
Bela.	Belarus	Belarus	Dom. Rep.	Dominican Republic	República Dominicana
Belize	Belize	Belize			
Benin	Benin	Bénin	D.R.C.	Democratic Republic of the Congo	République démocratique du Congo
Ber.	Bermuda	Bermuda			
Bhu.	Bhutan	Druk-Yul			
B.I.O.T.	British Indian Ocean Territory	British Indian Ocean Territory	Ec.	Ecuador	Ecuador
			Egypt	Egypt	Miṣr
			El Sal.	El Salvador	El Salvador
Bngl.	Bangladesh	Bangladesh	Eng., U.K.	England, U.K.	England
Bol.	Bolivia	Bolivia	Eq. Gui.	Equatorial Guinea	Guinea Ecuatorial
Bos.	Bosnia and Herzegovina	Bosna i Hercegovina			
			Erit.	Eritrea	Eritrea
Bots.	Botswana	Botswana	Est.	Estonia	Eesti
Braz.	Brazil	Brasil	Eth.	Ethiopia	Ityopiya
Br. Vir. Is.	British Virgin Islands	British Virgin Islands	Eur.	Europe	—
			Faer. Is.	Faeroe Islands	Føroyar
Bru.	Brunei	Brunei			
Bul.	Bulgaria	Bâlgarija	Falk. Is.	Falkland Islands	Falkland Islands
Burkina	Burkina Faso	Burkina Faso			
Ca., U.S.	California, U.S.	California	Fiji	Fiji	Fiji

	English	Local Name		English	Local Name
Fin.	Finland	Suomi (Finnish) / Finland (Swedish)	**Kor., N.**	North Korea	Chosŏn-minjujuŭi-inmīn-konghwaguk
Fl., U.S.	Florida, U.S.	Florida	**Kor., S.**	South Korea	Taehan-min'guk
Fr.	France	France			
Fr. Gu.	French Guiana	Guyane française	**Ks., U.S.**	Kansas, U.S.	Kansas
			Kuw.	Kuwait	Al-Kuwayt
Fr. Poly.	French Polynesia	Polynésie française	**Ky., U.S.**	Kentucky, U.S.	Kentucky
			Kyrg.	Kyrgyzstan	Kyrgyzstan
Ga., U.S.	Georgia, U.S.	Georgia	**La., U.S.**	Louisiana, U.S.	Louisiana
Gabon	Gabon	Gabon	**Laos**	Laos	Lao
Gam.	Gambia	Gambia	**Lat.**	Latvia	Latvija
Geor.	Georgia	Sakartvelo	**Leb.**	Lebanon	Lubnān
Ger.	Germany	Deutschland	**Leso.**	Lesotho	Lesotho
Ghana	Ghana	Ghana	**Lib.**	Liberia	Liberia
Gib.	Gibraltar	Gibraltar	**Libya**	Libya	Lībiyā
Grc.	Greece	Ellás	**Liech.**	Liechtenstein	Liechtenstein
Gren.	Grenada	Grenada	**Lith.**	Lithuania	Lietuva
Grnld.	Greenland	Kalaallit Nunaat (Eskimo) / Grønland (Danish)	**Lux.**	Luxembourg	Luxembourg
			Ma., U.S.	Massachusetts, U.S.	Massachusetts
			Macao	Macao	Macau
			Mac.	Macedonia	Makedonija
Guad.	Guadeloupe	Guadeloupe	**Madag.**	Madagascar	Madagasikara (Malagasy) / Madagascar (French)
Guam	Guam	Guam			
Guat.	Guatemala	Guatemala			
Guernsey	Guernsey	Guernsey	**Malay.**	Malaysia	Malaysia
Gui.	Guinea	Guinée	**Mald.**	Maldives	Maldives
Gui.-B.	Guinea-Bissau	Guiné-Bissau	**Mali**	Mali	Mali
Guy.	Guyana	Guyana	**Malta**	Malta	Malta
Haiti	Haiti	Haïti	**Marsh. Is.**	Marshall Islands	Marshall Islands
Hi., U.S.	Hawaii, U.S.	Hawaii			
Hond.	Honduras	Honduras	**Mart.**	Martinique	Martinique
Hung.	Hungary	Magyarország	**Maur.**	Mauritania	Mauritanie (French) / Mūrītāniyā (Arabic)
Ia., U.S.	Iowa, U.S.	Iowa			
Ice.	Iceland	Ísland			
Id., U.S.	Idaho, U.S.	Idaho			
Il., U.S.	Illinois, U.S.	Illinois	**May.**	Mayotte	Mayotte
In., U.S.	Indiana, U.S.	Indiana	**Mb., Can.**	Manitoba, Can.	Manitoba
India	India	India (English) / Bharat (Hindi)	**Md., U.S.**	Maryland, U.S.	Maryland
			Me., U.S.	Maine, U.S.	Maine
			Mex.	Mexico	México
Indon.	Indonesia	Indonesia	**Mi., U.S.**	Michigan, U.S.	Michigan
I. of Man	Isle of Man	Isle of Man	**Micron.**	Federated States of Micronesia	Federated States of Micronesia
Iran	Iran	Īrān			
Iraq	Iraq	Al-'Irāq			
Ire.	Ireland	Ireland (English) / Éire (Gaelic)	**Mid. Is.**	Midway Islands	Midway Islands
			Mn., U.S.	Minnesota, U.S.	Minnesota
Isr.	Israel	Yisra'el (Hebrew) / Isrā'īl (Arabic)	**Mo., U.S.**	Missouri, U.S.	Missouri
			Mol.	Moldova	Moldova
			Mon.	Monaco	Monaco
			Mong.	Mongolia	Mongol Ard Uls
Isr. Occ.	Israeli Occupied Areas	—	**Monts.**	Montserrat	Montserrat
			Mor.	Morocco	Al-Magreb
Italy	Italy	Italia	**Moz.**	Mozambique	Moçambique
Jam.	Jamaica	Jamaica	**Mrts.**	Mauritius	Mauritius
Japan	Japan	Nihon	**Ms., U.S.**	Mississippi, U.S.	Mississippi
Jersey	Jersey	Jersey			
Jord.	Jordan	Al-Urdun	**Mt., U.S.**	Montana, U.S.	Montana
Kaz.	Kazakhstan	Kazachstan	**Mwi.**	Malawi	Malaŵi
Kenya	Kenya	Kenya	**Mya.**	Myanmar	Myanmar
Kir.	Kiribati	Kiribati	**N.A.**	North America	—

	English	Local Name		English	Local Name
Nauru	Nauru	Nauru (English) / Naoero (Nauruan)	**Or., U.S.**	Oregon, U.S.	Oregon
			Pa., U.S.	Pennsylvania, U.S.	Pennsylvania
N.B., Can.	New Brunswick, Can.	New Brunswick (English) / Nouveau-Brunswick (French)	**Pak.**	Pakistan	Pākistān
			Palau	Palau	Palau (English) / Belau (Palauan)
N.C., U.S.	North Carolina, U.S.	North Carolina	**Pan.**	Panama	Panamá
			Pap. N. Gui.	Papua New Guinea	Papua New Guinea
N. Cal.	New Caledonia	Nouvelle-Calédonie	**Para.**	Paraguay	Paraguay
			P.E., Can.	Prince Edward Island, Can.	Prince Edward Island (English) / Île-du-Prince-Édouard (French)
N. Cyp.	North Cyprus	Kuzey Kıbrıs			
N.D., U.S.	North Dakota, U.S.	North Dakota			
Ne., U.S.	Nebraska, U.S.	Nebraska	**Peru**	Peru	Perú
Nepal	Nepal	Nepāl	**Phil.**	Philippines	Pilipinas / Philippines
Neth.	Netherlands	Nederland			
Neth. Ant.	Netherlands Antilles	Nederlandse Antillen	**Pit.**	Pitcairn	Pitcairn
			Pol.	Poland	Polska
Nf., Can.	Newfoundland, Can.	Newfoundland (English) / Terre-Neuve (French)	**Port.**	Portugal	Portugal
			P.Q., Can.	Quebec, Can.	Québec
			P.R.	Puerto Rico	Puerto Rico
			Qatar	Qatar	Qaṭar
N.H., U.S.	New Hampshire, U.S.	New Hampshire	**Reu.**	Reunion	Réunion
			R.I., U.S.	Rhode Island, U.S.	Rhode Island
Nic.	Nicaragua	Nicaragua	**Rom.**	Romania	România
Nig.	Nigeria	Nigeria	**Russia**	Russia	Rossija
Niger	Niger	Niger	**Rw.**	Rwanda	Rwanda
N. Ire., U.K.	Northern Ireland, U.K.	Northern Ireland	**S.A.**	South America	—
			S. Afr.	South Africa	South Africa (English) / Suid-Afrika (Afrikaans)
Niue	Niue	Niue			
N.J., U.S.	New Jersey, U.S.	New Jersey			
N.M., U.S.	New Mexico, U.S.	New Mexico	**Samoa**	Samoa	Samoa
			Sau. Ar.	Saudi Arabia	Al-'Arabīyah as-Su'ūdīyah
N. Mar. Is.	Northern Mariana Islands	Northern Mariana Islands	**S.C., U.S.**	South Carolina, U.S.	South Carolina
Nmb.	Namibia	Namibia	**Scot., U.K.**	Scotland, U.K.	Scotland
Nor.	Norway	Norge	**S.D., U.S.**	South Dakota, U.S.	South Dakota
Norf. I.	Norfolk Island	Norfolk Island			
N.S., Can.	Nova Scotia, Can.	Nova Scotia (English) / Nouvelle-Écosse (French)	**Sen.**	Senegal	Sénégal
			Sey.	Seychelles	Seychelles
			Sing.	Singapore	Singapore
			Sk., Can.	Saskatchewan, Can.	Saskatchewan
N.T., Can.	Northwest Territories, Can.	Northwest Territories (English) / Territoires du Nord-Ouest (French)	**S.L.**	Sierra Leone	Sierra Leone
			Slo.	Slovenia	Slovenija
			Slov.	Slovakia	Slovensko
			S. Mar.	San Marino	San Marino
			Sol. Is.	Solomon Islands	Solomon Islands
			Som.	Somalia	Somaliya
Nv., U.S.	Nevada, U.S.	Nevada	**Spain**	Spain	España
N.Y., U.S.	New York, U.S.	New York	**Sp. N. Afr.**	Spanish North Africa	Plazas de Soberanía en el Norte de África
N.Z.	New Zealand	New Zealand			
Oc.	Oceania	—			
Oh., U.S.	Ohio, U.S.	Ohio	**Sri L.**	Sri Lanka	Sri Lanka
Ok., U.S.	Oklahoma, U.S.	Oklahoma	**St. Hel.**	St. Helena	St. Helena
			St. K./N.	St. Kitts and Nevis	St. Kitts and Nevis
Oman	Oman	'Umān			
On., Can.	Ontario, Can.	Ontario	**St. Luc.**	St. Lucia	St. Lucia

	English	Local Name		English	Local Name
St. P./M.	St. Pierre and Miquelon	Saint-Pierre-et-Miquelon	**U.A.E.**	United Arab Emirates	Al-Imārāt al-'Arabīyah al-Muttaḥidah
S. Tom./P.	Sao Tome and Principe	São Tomé e Príncipe	**Ug.**	Uganda	Uganda
St. Vin.	St. Vincent and the Grenadines	St. Vincent and the Grenadines	**U.K.**	United Kingdom	United Kingdom
Sudan	Sudan	As-Sūdān	**Ukr.**	Ukraine	Ukraina
Sur.	Suriname	Suriname	**Ur.**	Uruguay	Uruguay
Swaz.	Swaziland	Swaziland	**U.S.**	United States	United States
Swe.	Sweden	Sverige	**Ut., U.S.**	Utah, U.S.	Utah
Switz.	Switzerland	Schweiz (German) / Suisse (French) / Svizzera (Italian)	**Uzb.**	Uzbekistan	Uzbekistan
			Va., U.S.	Virginia, U.S.	Virginia
			Vanuatu	Vanuatu	Vanuatu
			Vat.	Vatican City	Cittá del Vaticano
Syria	Syria	Sūrīyah	**Ven.**	Venezuela	Venezuela
Tai.	Taiwan	T'aiwan	**Viet**	Vietnam	Viet Nam
Taj.	Tajikistan	Tajikistan	**V.I.U.S.**	Virgin Islands (U.S.)	Virgin Islands (U.S.)
Tan.	Tanzania	Tanzania			
T./C. Is.	Turks and Caicos Islands	Turks and Caicos Islands	**Vt., U.S.**	Vermont, U.S.	Vermont
			Wa., U.S.	Washington, U.S.	Washington
Thai.	Thailand	Prathet Thai	**Wake I.**	Wake Island	Wake Island
Tn., U.S.	Tennessee, U.S.	Tennessee	**Wales, U.K.**	Wales, U.K.	Wales
Togo	Togo	Togo	**Wal./F.**	Wallis and Futuna	Wallis et Futuna
Tok.	Tokelau	Tokelau			
Tonga	Tonga	Tonga	**Wi., U.S.**	Wisconsin, U.S.	Wisconsin
Trin.	Trinidad and Tobago	Trinidad and Tobago	**W. Sah.**	Western Sahara	—
Tun.	Tunisia	Tunisie (French) / Tunis (Arabic)	**W.V., U.S.**	West Virginia, U.S.	West Virginia
			Wy., U.S.	Wyoming, U.S.	Wyoming
			Yemen	Yemen	Al-Yaman
Tur.	Turkey	Türkiye	**Yk., Can.**	Yukon Territory, Can.	Yukon Territory
Turk.	Turkmenistan	Turkmenistan			
Tuvalu	Tuvalu	Tuvalu	**Yugo.**	Yugoslavia	Jugoslavija
Tx., U.S.	Texas, U.S.	Texas	**Zam.**	Zambia	Zambia
			Zimb.	Zimbabwe	Zimbabwe

Key to Symbols

ʌ	**Mountain**	ıı	**Islands**	c¹	Estuary	□³	State, Canton,
ʌ¹	Volcano			c²	Fjord		Republic
ʌ²	Hill	⬤	**Other Topographic**	c³	Bight	□⁴	Province, Region,
			Features				Oblast
⩗	**Mountains**	⬤¹	Continent	⊜	**Lake, Lakes**	□⁵	Department, District,
⩗¹	Plateau	⬤²	Coast, Beach	⊜¹	Reservoir		Prefecture
⩗²	Hills	⬤³	Isthmus			□⁸	Miscellaneous
)(	**Pass**	⬤⁴	Cliff	⇞	**Swamp**	□⁹	Historical
		⬤⁶	Crater	⊠	**Ice Features, Glacier**		
⩔	**Valley, Canyon**	⬤⁸	Dunes			✦	**Recreational Site**
⪰	**Plain**	⬤⁹	Lava Flow	⊤	**Other Hydrographic**		
⪰¹	Basin				**Features**	✦	**Miscellaneous**
⪰²	Delta	⪦	**River**	⊤¹	Ocean	✦¹	Region
		⪵	**Canal**	⊤²	Sea	✦²	Desert
⪢	**Cape**			⊤⁴	Oasis, Well, Spring	✦³	Forest, Moor
⪢¹	Peninsula	ʟ	**Waterfall, Rapids**			✦⁴	Reserve, Reservation
		⪣	**Strait**	□	**Political Unit**	✦⁶	Dam
ı	**Island**			□¹	Independent Nation	✦⁸	Neighborhood
ı¹	Atoll	c	**Bay, Gulf**	□²	Dependency		

Index to the Maps

Name	Page No.	Lat.	Long.	Name	Page No.	Lat.	Long.
				Adriatic Sea ⊤²	86	42.30N	16.00 E
A				Aegean Sea ⊤²	98	38.30N	25.00 E
Aachen	90	50.47N	6.05 E	Afghanistan □¹	110	33.00N	65.00 E
Ābādān	108	30.20N	48.16 E	Afjord	89	63.58N	10.12 E
Abakan	102	53.43N	91.26 E	Afmadow	106	0.32N	42.10 E
'Abd al-Kūrī ı	108	12.12N	52.15 E	Africa ⬤¹	82	10.00N	22.00 E
Abéché	104	13.49N	20.49 E	Afton	140	42.13N	75.31W
Abengourou	104	6.44N	3.29W	Agadez	104	16.58N	7.59 E
Abenrå	89	55.02N	9.26 E	Agadir	104	30.26N	9.36W
Aberdeen, Scot., U.K.	88	57.10N	2.04W	Agalega Islands ıı	106	10.24S	56.37 E
Aberdeen, Md., U.S.	140	39.30N	76.09W	Agana	118	13.28N	144.45 E
Aberdeen, S.D., U.S.	138	45.27N	98.29W	Āgra	112	27.11N	78.01 E
Abert, Lake ⊜	142	42.38N	120.13W	Ağrı Dağı (Mount			
Aberystwyth	88	52.25N	4.05W	Ararat) ʌ	86	39.42N	44.18 E
Abidjan	104	5.19N	4.02W	Agrigento	96	37.18N	13.35 E
Abilene	138	32.26N	99.43W	Agrínion	98	38.37N	21.24 E
Abuja	104	9.21N	7.11 E	Agua Caliente	128	23.20N	105.20W
Abū Kamāl	109	34.27N	40.55 E	Aguadulce	130	8.15N	80.33W
Abū Madd, Ra's ⪢	108	24.50N	37.07 E	Aguascalientes	128	21.53N	102.18W
Abū Ẓaby	108	24.28N	54.22 E	Agulhas, Cape ⪢	106	34.52S	20.00 E
Acacio	128	24.50N	102.44W	Ahaggar ⩗	104	23.00N	6.30 E
Acadia National Park ✦	140	44.18N	68.15W	Ahlen	90	51.46N	7.53 E
Acámbaro	128	20.02N	100.44W	Ahmadābād	112	23.02N	72.37 E
Acandí	130	8.32N	77.14W	Ahmadnagar	111	19.05N	74.44 E
Acapulco [de Juárez]	128	16.51N	99.55W	Ahuacatlán	128	21.03N	104.29W
Acarai Mountains ʌ	132	1.50N	57.40W	Ahvāz	108	31.19N	48.42 E
Acarigua	132	9.33N	69.12W	Ahvenanmaa (Åland) ıı	89	60.15N	20.00 E
Acayucan	128	17.57N	94.55W	Aimorés	135	19.30S	41.04W
Accra	104	5.33N	0.13W	Aix-en-Provence	92	43.32N	5.26 E
Acklins Island ı	138	22.26N	73.58W	Aizu-wakamatsu	116	37.30N	139.56 E
Aconcagua, Cerro ʌ	134	32.39S	70.01W	Ajaccio	96	41.55N	8.44 E
Açores (Azores) ıı	82	38.30N	28.00W	Ajjer, Tassili-n- ⩗¹	104	25.10N	8.00 E
Adak Island ı	144	51.45N	176.40W	Ajmer	112	26.27N	74.38 E
Adamawa ⩗	104	7.00N	12.00 E	Ajtos	98	42.42N	27.15 E
'Adan	108	12.45N	45.12 E	Akimiski Island ı	138	53.00N	81.20W
Adana	109	37.01N	35.18 E	Akita	116	39.43N	140.07 E
Ad-Dahnā' ✦²	108	24.30N	48.10 E	'Akko (Acre)	109	32.55N	35.05 E
Ad-Dawḩah (Doha)	108	25.17N	51.32 E	Aklavik	136	68.12N	135.00W
Addison	140	41.59N	84.21W	Akola	111	20.44N	77.00 E
Adelaide	122	34.55S	138.35 E	Akron	140	41.04N	81.31W
Aden, Gulf of c	108	12.30N	48.00 E	Akureyri	86	65.44N	18.08W
Adige ⪦	96	45.10N	12.20 E	Alagoinhas	132	12.07S	38.26W
Adirondack Mountains				Al-'Amārah	108	31.50N	47.09 E
⩗	140	44.00N	74.00W	Alamogordo	138	32.53N	105.57W
Adis Abeba	108	9.00N	38.50 E	Alamosa	138	37.28N	105.52W
Adrar	104	27.54N	0.17W	Al-'Arīsh	109	31.08N	33.48 E
Adrian	140	41.53N	84.02W				

Name	Page No.	Lat.	Long.
Alaska □³	144	65.00N	153.00W
Alaska, Gulf of ᴄ	144	58.00N	146.00W
Alaska Peninsula ≻¹	144	57.00N	158.00W
Alaska Range ⋏	144	62.30N	150.00W
Albacete	94	38.59N	1.51W
Albanel, Lac ⊜	136	50.55N	73.12W
Albania □¹	86	41.00N	20.00E
Albany, Austl.	122	35.02S	117.53E
Albany, Ga., U.S.	138	31.34N	84.09W
Albany, N.Y., U.S.	140	42.39N	73.45W
Al-Baṣrah	108	30.30N	47.47E
Albert, Lake ⊜	106	1.40N	31.00E
Alberta □⁴	136	54.00N	113.00W
Albert Nile ≏	108	3.36N	32.02E
Ålborg	89	57.03N	9.56E
Albuquerque	138	35.05N	106.39W
Albury	122	36.05S	146.55E
Alcalá de Guadaira	94	37.20N	5.50W
Alcalá de Henares	94	40.29N	3.22W
Alcira	94	39.09N	0.26W
Alcoy	94	38.42N	0.28W
Aldabra Islands I¹	106	9.25S	46.22E
Aldama	128	28.51N	105.54W
Aldan	102	58.37N	125.24E
Aleksandrovsk-Sachalinskij	102	50.54N	142.10E
Alentejo □⁹	94	38.00N	8.00W
Alenuihaha Channel ⋓	143	20.26N	156.00W
Alessandria	96	44.54N	8.37E
Aleutian Islands II	144	52.00N	176.00W
Alexander, Cape ≻	127a	6.35S	156.30E
Alexander Archipelago II	144	56.30N	134.00W
Alexander Bay	106	28.40S	16.30E
Alexandra	126	45.15S	169.24E
Alexandria → Al-Iskandarīyah, Egypt	104	31.12N	29.54E
Alexandria, Rom.	98	43.58N	25.20E
Alexandria, La., U.S.	128	31.18N	92.26W
Alexandria, Va., U.S.	140	38.48N	77.02W
Alexandria Bay	140	44.20N	75.55W
Alexandroúpolis	98	40.50N	25.52E
Al-Fāshir	104	13.38N	25.21E
Al-Fayyūm	104	29.19N	30.50E
Alfenas	135	21.25S	45.57W
Alfred	140	45.34N	74.53W
Algeciras	94	36.08N	5.30W
Algeria □¹	104	28.00N	3.00E
Alghero	96	40.34N	8.19E
Algiers → El Djazaïr	104	36.47N	3.03E
Al-Harrah ♨⁹	109	31.00N	38.30E
Al-Hijāz ♦¹	109	24.30N	38.30E
Al-Hudaydah	108	14.48N	42.57E
Al-Hufūf	108	25.22N	49.34E
Alicante	94	38.21N	0.29W
Alice	128	27.45N	98.04W
Alice Springs	122	23.42S	133.53E
Alīgarh	112	27.54N	78.05E
Al-Iskandarīyah (Alexandria)	104	31.12N	29.54E
Al-Ismāʿīlīyah	109	30.35N	32.16E
Al-Jawf	108	29.50N	39.52E
Al-Jīzah	104	30.01N	31.13E
Al-Khandaq	104	18.36N	30.34E
Al-Kharṭūm (Khartoum)	104	15.36N	32.32E
Alkmaar	90	52.37N	4.44E
Al-Kuwayt	108	29.20N	47.59E
Al-Lādhiqīyah (Latakia)	109	35.31N	35.47E
Allāhābād	112	25.27N	81.51E
Allegheny Mountains ⋏	140	38.30N	80.00W
Allentown	140	40.36N	75.28W
Al-Madīnah (Medina)	108	24.28N	39.36E
Al-Manāmah	108	26.13N	50.35E
Al-Manṣūrah	109	31.03N	31.23E
Almaty (Alma-Ata)	102	43.15N	76.57E
Al-Mawṣil	108	36.20N	43.08E
Almendralejo	94	38.41N	6.24W
Almería	94	36.50N	2.27W
Al-Minyā	104	28.06N	30.45E
Al-Mukallā	108	14.32N	49.08E
Al-Mukhā	108	13.19N	43.15E
Alor Setar	120	6.07N	100.22E
Alpena	140	45.03N	83.25W
Alpine	128	30.21N	103.39W
Alps ⋏	92	46.25N	10.00E
Al-Qaḍārif	104	14.02N	35.24E
Al-Qāhirah (Cairo)	104	30.03N	31.15E
Al-Qāmishlī	109	37.02N	41.14E
Al-Qaṭrūn	104	24.56N	14.38E
Alsace □⁹	92	48.30N	7.30E
Alta	89	69.55N	23.12E
Altagracia de Orituco	130	9.52N	66.23W
Altamura	96	40.50N	16.33E
Altiplano ⋏¹	132	18.00S	68.00W
Alton	138	38.53N	90.11W
Altoona	140	40.31N	78.23W
Al-Ubayyiḍ	104	13.11N	30.13E
Al-Uqṣur (Luxor)	104	25.41N	32.39E
Alva	138	36.48N	98.39W
Alvarado	128	18.46N	95.46W
Amami-shotō II	117b	28.16N	129.21E
Amarillo	138	35.13N	101.49W
Amazon (Solimões) (Amazonas) ≏	132	0.05S	50.00W
Amberg	90	49.27N	11.52E
Ambon	118	3.43S	128.12E
Ambositra	106	20.31S	47.15E
Ambre, Cap d' ≻	106	11.57S	49.17E
Amecameca [de Juárez]	128	19.07N	98.46W
American Highland ⋏¹	85	72.30S	78.00E
American Samoa □²	127e	14.20S	170.00W
Amherstburg	140	42.06N	83.06W
Amiens	92	49.54N	2.18E
Amīndīvi Islands II	111	11.23N	72.23E
Amirante Islands II	106	6.00S	53.10E
ʿAmmān	109	31.57N	35.56E
Ammókhostos (Famagusta)	109	35.07N	33.57E
Åmot	89	59.35N	8.07E
Amoy → Xiamen	114	24.28N	118.07E
Amrāvati	112	20.56N	77.45E
Amritsar	112	31.35N	74.53E
Amsterdam, Neth.	90	52.22N	4.54E
Amsterdam, N.Y., U.S.	140	42.56N	74.11W
Amu Darya (Amudarja) ≏	110	42.30N	59.15E
Amundsen Gulf ᴄ	136	71.00N	124.00W
Amundsen Sea ▼²	85	72.30S	112.00W
Amur (Heilongjiang) ≏	102	52.56N	141.10E
Anaheim	142	33.50N	117.54W
Anakāpalle	111	17.41N	83.01E
Anápolis	135	16.20S	48.58W
Añatuya	134	28.28S	62.50W
Anchorage	144	61.13N	149.54W
Ancona	96	43.38N	13.30E
Ancud	134	41.52S	73.50W
Andalucía □⁹	94	37.36N	4.30W
Andaman Islands II	120	12.00N	92.45E
Andaman Sea ▼²	120	10.00N	95.00E
Andes ⋏	82	20.00S	68.00W
Andfjorden ⋓	89	69.10N	16.20E
Andhra Pradesh □³	111	16.00N	79.00E
Andkhvoy	112	36.56N	65.08E
Andoany	106	13.25S	48.16E
Andorra	94	42.30N	1.31E
Andorra □¹	86	42.30N	1.30E
Andradina	135	20.54S	51.23W

Name	Page No.	Lat.	Long.
Andreanof Islands II	144	52.00N	176.00W
Andrews	128	32.19N	102.32W
Ándros I	98	37.45N	24.42 E
Andros Island I	130	24.26N	77.57W
Andújar	94	38.03N	4.04W
Anegada Passage ʮ	130	18.30N	63.40W
Aneto, Pico de ʌ	94	42.38N	0.40 E
Angarsk	102	52.34N	103.54 E
Ángel, Salto (Angel Falls) ʟ	132	5.57N	62.30W
Ángel de la Guarda, Isla I	128	29.20N	113.25W
Angeles	118	15.09N	120.35 E
Angel Falls → Ángel, Salto ʟ	132	5.57N	62.30W
Ångermanälven ≃	89	62.48N	17.56 E
Angermünde	90	53.01N	14.00 E
Angers	92	47.28N	0.33W
Angmagssalik	136	65.36N	37.41W
Angola	140	42.38N	79.01W
Angola □ [1]	106	12.30S	18.30 E
Angoram	118	4.04S	144.04 E
Angoulême	92	45.39N	0.09 E
Anguilla □ [2]	130	18.15N	63.05W
Aniak	144	61.35N	159.33W
Anina	98	45.05N	21.51 E
Ankara	86	39.56N	32.52 E
Annaba (Bône)	104	36.54N	7.46 E
An-Nafūd ◂ [2]	109	28.30N	41.00 E
An-Najaf	108	31.59N	44.20 E
Annapolis	140	38.58N	76.29W
Annapurna ʌ	112	28.34N	83.50 E
Ann Arbor	140	42.16N	83.43W
Annecy	92	45.54N	6.07 E
An-Nuhūd	104	12.42N	28.26 E
Anqing	114	30.31N	117.02 E
Ansbach	90	49.17N	10.34 E
Anshan	114	41.08N	122.59 E
Antalaha	106	14.53S	50.16 E
Antalya	86	36.53N	30.42 E
Antananarivo	106	18.55S	47.31 E
Antarctica ♁ [1]	85	90.00S	0.00
Antarctic Peninsula ⩥ [1]	85	69.30S	65.00W
Antequera	94	37.01N	4.33W
Anticosti, Île d' I	138	49.30N	63.00W
Antigua and Barbuda □ [1]	130	17.03N	61.48W
Antofagasta	134	23.39S	70.24W
António Enes	106	16.14S	39.54 E
Antsirabe	106	19.51S	47.02 E
Antsiranana	106	12.16S	49.17 E
Antwerp → Antwerpen	90	51.13N	4.25 E
Antwerpen (Anvers)	90	51.13N	4.25 E
Anvers → Antwerpen	90	51.13N	4.25 E
Aomori	116	40.49N	140.45 E
Aôral, Phnum ʌ	120	12.02N	104.10 E
Aosta	96	45.44N	7.20 E
Aoukâr ◂ [1]	104	18.00N	9.30W
Apatzingán [de la Constitución]	128	19.05N	102.21W
Apeldoorn	90	52.13N	5.58 E
Apia	127e	13.50S	171.44W
Apo, Mount ʌ	118	6.59N	125.16 E
Apostólou Andréa, Akrotírion ⩥	109	35.42N	34.35 E
Appalachian Mountains ⩥	138	41.00N	77.00W
Appennino (Apennines) ⩥	96	43.00N	13.00 E
Appennino Abruzzese ⩥	96	42.00N	14.00 E
Appennino Calabrese ⩥	96	39.00N	16.30 E
Appennino Ligure ⩥	96	44.30N	9.00 E
Appennino Tosco-Emiliano ⩥	96	44.00N	11.30 E
Appennino Umbro-Marchigiano ⩥	96	43.00N	13.00 E
Apure ≃	130	7.37N	66.25W
Aqaba, Gulf of c	109	29.00N	34.40 E
Aqmola	102	51.10N	71.30 E
Aqtöbe	86	50.17N	57.10 E
'Arab, Baḥr al- ≃	104	9.02N	29.28 E
Arabian Sea ⊤ [2]	82	15.00N	65.00 E
Aracaju	132	10.55S	37.04W
Araçatuba	132	21.12S	50.25W
Arad	98	46.11N	21.20 E
Arafura Sea ⊤ [2]	118	11.00S	135.00 E
Arago, Cape ⩥	142	43.18N	124.25W
Aragón □ [9]	94	41.00N	1.00W
Aragón ≃	94	42.13N	1.44W
Araguaia ≃	132	5.21S	48.41W
Araguari	135	18.38S	48.11W
Árakhthos ≃	98	39.01N	21.03 E
Aral Sea ⊤ [2]	86	45.00N	59.00 E
Aran Islands II	88	53.07N	9.43W
Aranjuez	94	40.02N	3.36W
Aranyaprathet	120	13.41N	102.30 E
Araraquara	132	21.47S	48.10W
Ararat, Mount → Ağrı Dağı ʌ [1]	86	39.42N	44.18 E
Araxá	135	19.35S	46.55W
Arbroath	88	56.34N	2.35W
Arc Dome ʌ	142	38.51N	117.22W
Archangel'sk (Archangel)	86	64.34N	40.32 E
Arctic Bay	136	73.02N	85.11W
Arctic Ocean ⊤ [1]	84	85.00N	170.00 E
Ardennes ◂ [1]	92	50.10N	5.45 E
Arecibo	130	18.28N	66.43W
Arendal	89	58.27N	8.48 E
Arequipa	132	16.24S	71.33W
Arezzo	96	43.25N	11.53 E
Argentina □ [1]	134	34.00S	64.00W
Argonne ◂ [1]	92	49.30N	5.00 E
Árgos	98	37.39N	22.44 E
Arguello, Point ⩥	142	34.35N	120.39W
Argun (Eergu'nahe) ≃	114	53.20N	121.28 E
Århus	89	56.09N	10.13 E
Arica, Chile	132	18.29S	70.20W
Arica, Col.	132	2.08S	71.47W
'Arīsh, Wādī al- V	109	31.09N	33.49 E
Arismendi	130	8.29N	68.22W
Arizona □ [3]	138	34.00N	112.00W
Arjona	130	10.15N	75.21W
Arkansas □ [3]	138	34.50N	93.40W
Arkansas ≃	138	33.48N	91.04W
Armant	109	25.37N	32.32 E
Armavir	86	45.00N	41.08 E
Armenia □ [1]	86	40.00N	45.00 E
Armentières	92	50.41N	2.53 E
Arnhem	90	51.59N	5.55 E
Arnhem Land ◂ [1]	122	13.10S	134.30 E
Arran, Island of I	88	55.35N	5.15W
Arras	92	50.17N	2.47 E
Ar-Riyāḍ (Riyadh)	108	24.38N	46.43 E
Ar-Rub' al-Khālī ◂ [2]	108	20.00N	51.00 E
Artemisa	130	22.49N	82.46W
Artesia	128	32.50N	104.24W
Aru, Kepulauan II	118	6.00S	134.30 E
Aruba □ [2]	130	12.30N	69.58W
Arunachal Pradesh □ [8]	112	28.30N	95.00 E
Arusha	106	3.22S	36.41 E
Aruwimi ≃	106	1.13N	23.36 E
Asahikawa	116a	43.46N	142.22 E
Asansol	112	23.41N	86.59 E
Asbestos	140	45.46N	71.57W
Ascensión	128	31.06N	107.59W
Aseb	108	13.00N	42.45 E

Name	Page No.	Lat.	Long.
Asenovgrad	98	42.01 N	24.52 E
Ashburton	126	43.55 S	171.45 E
Asheville	138	35.36 N	82.33 W
Ashikaga	116	36.20 N	139.27 E
Ashland, Ky., U.S.	140	38.28 N	82.38 W
Ashland, N.H., U.S.	140	43.41 N	71.37 W
Ashland, Or., U.S.	142	42.11 N	122.42 W
Ashland, Wi., U.S.	138	46.35 N	90.53 W
Ashtabula	140	41.51 N	80.47 W
Ashville	140	39.42 N	82.57 W
Asia ≛¹	82	50.00 N	100.00 E
Asia Minor ◆¹	86	39.00 N	32.00 E
Askham	106	26.59 S	20.47 E
Asmera	108	15.20 N	38.53 E
Aspiring, Mount ʌ	126	44.23 S	168.44 E
Assam ◻³	112	26.00 N	92.00 E
Assen	90	52.59 N	6.34 E
Assiniboine, Mount ʌ	136	50.52 N	115.39 W
As-Sulaymānīyah	86	35.33 N	45.26 E
As-Suwaydā'	109	32.42 N	36.34 E
As-Suways (Suez)	104	29.58 N	32.33 E
Asti	96	44.54 N	8.12 E
Astrachan'	86	46.21 N	48.03 E
Astrolabe, Cape ⊁	127a	8.20 S	160.34 E
Asunción	134	25.16 S	57.40 W
Aswān	104	24.05 N	32.53 E
Aswān High Dam ◆⁶	108	24.05 N	32.53 E
Asyūṭ	104	27.11 N	31.11 E
Atacama, Desierto de ◆²	132	20.00 S	69.15 W
Atar	104	20.31 N	13.03 W
Atbarah	104	17.42 N	33.59 E
Atbasar	102	51.48 N	68.20 E
Athabasca	136	54.43 N	113.17 W
Athabasca, Lake ⊜	136	59.07 N	110.00 W
Athens → Athínai, Grc.	98	37.58 N	23.43 E
Athens, Ga., U.S.	138	33.57 N	83.22 W
Athens, Oh., U.S.	140	39.19 N	82.06 W
Athens, Pa., U.S.	140	41.57 N	76.31 W
Athínai (Athens)	98	37.58 N	23.43 E
Athlone	88	53.25 N	7.56 W
Atikokan	136	48.45 N	91.37 W
Atikonak Lake ⊜	136	52.40 N	64.30 W
Atka Island I	144	52.15 N	174.30 W
Atlanta	138	33.44 N	84.23 W
Atlantic City	140	39.21 N	74.25 W
Atlantic Ocean ▼¹	82	0.00	25.00 W
Atlas Mountains ⋌	104	33.00 N	2.00 W
Atlas Saharien ⋌	104	33.25 N	1.20 E
Atotonilco el Alto	128	20.33 N	102.31 W
Atrato ≃	130	8.17 N	76.58 W
Attawapiskat	136	52.55 N	82.26 W
Attu Island I	144	52.55 N	173.00 E
Atyraŭ	86	47.07 N	51.56 E
Auburn	140	42.55 N	76.33 W
Auckland	126	36.52 S	174.46 E
Augsburg	90	48.23 N	10.53 E
Augusta, Austl.	122	34.19 S	115.10 E
Augusta, Italy	96	37.13 N	15.13 E
Augusta, Ga., U.S.	138	33.28 N	82.01 W
Augusta, Ky., U.S.	140	38.46 N	84.00 W
Augusta, Me., U.S.	140	44.18 N	69.46 W
Augustus, Mount ʌ	122	24.20 S	116.50 E
Aurillac	92	44.56 N	2.26 E
Aurora	140	44.00 N	79.28 W
Aus	106	26.40 S	16.15 E
Austin	138	30.16 N	97.44 W
Australia ◻¹	122	25.00 S	135.00 E
Australian Capital Territory ◻⁸	124	35.30 S	149.00 E
Austria ◻¹	86	47.20 N	13.20 E
Autlán de Navarro	128	19.46 N	104.22 W
Auvergne ◻⁹	92	45.25 N	2.30 E
Auxerre	92	47.48 N	3.34 E
Aveiro	94	40.38 N	8.39 W
Avellino	96	40.54 N	14.47 E
Avesta	89	60.09 N	16.12 E
Avezzano	96	42.02 N	13.25 E
Avignon	92	43.57 N	4.49 E
Ávila	94	40.39 N	4.42 W
Avilés	94	43.33 N	5.55 W
Avon	140	42.54 N	77.44 W
Axiós (Vardar) ≃	98	40.31 N	22.43 E
Aydın	98	37.51 N	27.51 E
Ayeyarwady ≃	120	15.50 N	95.06 E
Aylmer West	140	42.46 N	80.59 W
Ayr	88	55.28 N	4.38 W
Azerbaijan ◻¹	86	40.30 N	47.30 E
Azogues	132	2.44 S	78.50 W
Azores → Açores II	82	38.30 N	28.00 W
Azov, Sea of ▼²	86	46.00 N	36.00 E
Azraq, Al-Bahr al- (Blue Nile) ≃	104	15.38 N	32.31 E
Azua	130	18.27 N	70.44 W
Azuaga	94	38.16 N	5.41 W
Azuero, Península de ⊁¹	130	7.40 N	80.35 W
Azul	134	36.47 S	59.51 W
Az-Zaqāzīq	104	30.35 N	31.31 E
Az-Zarqā'	109	32.05 N	36.06 E

B

Babaeski	98	41.26 N	27.06 E
Babelthuap I	118	7.30 N	134.36 E
Babuyan Islands II	118	19.10 N	121.40 E
Bacău	98	46.34 N	26.55 E
Bac Lieu	120	9.17 N	105.44 E
Bacolod	118	10.40 N	122.57 E
Badajoz	94	38.53 N	6.58 W
Badalona	94	41.27 N	2.15 E
Baden, Aus.	90	48.00 N	16.14 E
Baden, Switz.	92	47.29 N	8.18 E
Baden-Baden	90	48.46 N	8.14 E
Bad Ischl	90	47.43 N	13.37 E
Bad Kreuznach	90	49.52 N	7.51 E
Baffin Bay �c	136	73.00 N	66.00 W
Baffin Island I	136	68.00 N	70.00 W
Bāgalkot	111	16.11 N	75.42 E
Bagdad → Baghdād	108	33.21 N	44.25 E
Bagé	134	31.20 S	54.06 W
Baghdād	108	33.21 N	44.25 E
Bagheria	96	38.05 N	13.30 E
Baghlān	112	36.13 N	68.46 E
Bago	120	17.20 N	96.29 E
Baguio	118	16.25 N	120.36 E
Bahamas ◻¹	130	24.15 N	76.00 W
Bahāwalnagar	112	29.59 N	73.16 E
Bahāwalpur	110	29.24 N	71.41 E
Bahía, Islas de la II	130	16.20 N	86.30 W
Bahía Blanca	134	38.43 S	62.17 W
Bahrain ◻¹	108	26.00 N	50.30 E
Baia-Mare	98	47.40 N	23.35 E
Baie-Comeau	136	49.13 N	68.10 W
Baie-Saint-Paul	136	47.27 N	70.30 W
Băilești	98	44.02 N	23.21 E
Baja	90	46.11 N	18.57 E
Baja California ⊁¹	128	28.00 N	113.30 W
Bajkal, Ozero (Lake Baikal) ⊜	102	53.00 N	107.40 E
Baker, Mt., U.S.	138	46.22 N	104.17 W
Baker, Or., U.S.	138	44.46 N	117.49 W
Baker Lake	136	64.15 N	96.00 W
Bakersfield	142	35.22 N	119.01 W
Bakhtaran	108	34.19 N	47.04 E
Baku	86	40.23 N	49.51 E
Balakovo	86	52.02 N	47.47 E
Balaton ⊜	90	46.50 N	17.45 E

Name	Page No.	Lat.	Long.
Bâle			
→ Basel	92	47.33N	7.35 E
Baleares, Islas (Balearic			
Islands) II	94	39.30N	3.00 E
Bali I	118	8.20S	115.00 E
Balikesir	98	39.39N	27.53 E
Balikpapan	118	1.17S	116.50 E
Balkan Mountains			
→ Stara Planina ⚹	98	43.15N	25.00 E
Ballina	88	54.07N	9.09W
Ballinger	128	31.44N	99.56W
Balmoral Castle	88	57.02N	3.15W
Balqash	102	46.49N	74.59 E
Balqash köli ⊜	102	46.00N	74.00 E
Balsas ≃	128	17.55N	102.10W
Baltic Sea ▼²	89	57.00N	19.00 E
Baltimore	140	39.17N	76.36W
Baluchistan □⁹	110	28.00N	63.00 E
Bamako	104	12.39N	8.00W
Bambari	104	5.45N	20.40 E
Bamenda	104	5.56N	10.10 E
Banbury	88	52.04N	1.20W
Banda, Laut (Banda			
Sea) ▼²	118	5.00S	128.00 E
Banda Aceh	118	5.34N	95.20 E
Bandar-e 'Abbās	108	27.11N	56.17 E
Bandar Seri Begawan	118	4.56N	114.55 E
Bandırma	98	40.20N	27.58 E
Bandon	142	43.07N	124.24W
Bandundu	106	3.18S	17.20 E
Bandung	118	6.54S	107.36 E
Banes	130	20.58N	75.43W
Bangalore	111	12.59N	77.35 E
Bangassou	104	4.50N	23.07 E
Banggai, Kepulauan II	118	1.30S	123.15 E
Banghāzī	104	32.07N	20.04 E
Bangkok			
→ Krung Thep	120	13.45N	100.31 E
Bangladesh □¹	110	24.00N	90.00 E
Bangor, N. Ire., U.K.	88	54.40N	5.40W
Bangor, Wales, U.K.	88	53.13N	4.08W
Bangor, Me., U.S.	140	44.48N	68.46W
Bangui	104	4.22N	18.35 E
Bani ≃	104	14.30N	4.12W
Banī Mazār	104	28.30N	30.48 E
Banī Suwayf	104	29.05N	31.05 E
Banja Luka	96	44.46N	17.11 E
Banjarmasin	118	3.20S	114.35 E
Banjul	104	13.28N	16.39W
Banks Island I	136	73.15N	121.30W
Banks Islands II	127b	13.50S	167.30 E
Banks Peninsula ≻¹	126	43.45S	173.00 E
Bannu	112	32.59N	70.36 E
Ban Pak Phraek	120	8.13N	100.12 E
Banská Bystrica	90	48.44N	19.07 E
Baoding	114	38.52N	115.29 E
Baoji	114	34.22N	107.14 E
Baotou	114	40.40N	109.59 E
Baquedano	134	23.20S	69.51W
Baraawe	108	1.05N	44.02 E
Barbacena	135	21.14S	43.46W
Barbados □¹	130	13.10N	59.32W
Barbaros	98	40.54N	27.27 E
Barbas, Cabo ≻	104	22.18N	16.41W
Barbuda I	130	17.38N	61.48W
Barcelona, Mex.	128	26.12N	103.25W
Barcelona, Spain	94	41.23N	2.11 E
Barcelona, Ven.	130	10.08N	64.42W
Bardufoss	89	69.04N	18.30 E
Bareilly	112	28.21N	79.25 E
Barents Sea ▼²	84	74.00N	36.00 E
Bar Harbor	140	44.23N	68.12W
Bari	96	41.07N	16.52 E
Barinas	130	8.38N	70.12W
Barisāl	112	22.42N	90.22 E
Barlee, Lake ⊜	122	29.10S	119.30 E

Name	Page No.	Lat.	Long.
Barletta	96	41.19N	16.17 E
Barmouth	88	52.43N	4.03W
Barnaul	102	53.22N	83.45 E
Barnegat	140	39.45N	74.13W
Baroda	112	22.18N	73.12 E
Barqah (Cyrenaica) ◂ ¹	104	31.00N	22.30 E
Barquisimeto	132	10.04N	69.19W
Barra Falsa, Ponta da ≻	106	22.55S	35.37 E
Barranquilla	132	10.59N	74.48W
Barre	140	44.11N	72.30W
Barreiro	94	38.40N	9.04W
Barretos	132	20.33S	48.33W
Barrie	140	44.24N	79.40W
Barrow, Point ≻	144	71.23N	156.30W
Barrow Creek	122	21.33S	133.53 E
Barrow-in-Furness	88	54.07N	3.14W
Barstow	142	34.53N	117.01W
Barú, Volcán ⋀¹	130	8.48N	82.33W
Basatongwula Shan ⋀	114	33.05N	91.30 E
Basel (Bâle)	92	47.33N	7.35 E
Baskatong, Réservoir			
⊜¹	136	46.48N	75.50W
Basseterre	130	17.18N	62.43W
Basse-Terre I	130	16.10N	61.40W
Bass Harbor	140	44.14N	68.20W
Bass Strait ⥾	124	39.20S	145.30 E
Bastia	92	42.42N	9.27 E
Bastogne	90	50.00N	5.43 E
Bastrop	128	32.46N	91.54W
Batabanó, Golfo de ᴄ	130	22.15N	82.30W
Batamaj	102	63.31N	129.27 E
Batan Islands II	118	20.30N	121.50 E
Batatais	135	20.53S	47.37W
Batavia	140	42.59N	78.11W
Bātdâmbâng	120	13.06N	103.12 E
Bath, Eng., U.K.	88	51.23N	2.22W
Bath, Me., U.S.	140	43.54N	69.49W
Bath, N.Y., U.S.	140	42.20N	77.19W
Bathurst	136	47.36N	65.39W
Bathurst Island I,			
Austl.	122	11.37S	130.27 E
Bathurst Island I, N.T.,			
Can.	136	76.00N	100.30W
Batna	104	35.34N	6.11 E
Baton Rouge	138	30.27N	91.09W
Batouri	104	4.26N	14.22 E
Battle Creek	140	42.19N	85.10W
Battle Harbour	136	52.16N	55.35W
Battle Mountain	142	40.38N	116.56W
Batumi	86	41.38N	41.38 E
Bauru	132	22.19S	49.04W
Bautzen	90	51.11N	14.26 E
Bayamo	130	20.23N	76.39W
Bay City, Mi., U.S.	140	43.35N	83.53W
Bay City, Tx., U.S.	138	28.58N	95.58W
Baydhabo (Baidoa)	108	3.04N	43.48 E
Bayerische Alpen ⚹	90	47.30N	11.00 E
Bayonne	92	43.29N	1.29W
Bayreuth	90	49.57N	11.35 E
Bayrūt (Beirut)	109	33.53N	35.30 E
Bay Shore	140	40.43N	73.14W
Be, Nosy I	106	13.20S	48.15 E
Beatrice	138	40.16N	96.44W
Beatty	142	36.54N	116.45W
Beaufort Sea ▼²	84	73.00N	140.00W
Beaufort West	106	32.18S	22.36 E
Beaumont, N.Z.	126	45.49S	169.32 E
Beaumont, Tx., U.S.	138	30.05N	94.06W
Beautemps-Beaupré,			
Île I	127b	20.24S	166.09 E
Beaver Falls	140	40.45N	80.19W
Bečej	98	45.37N	20.03 E
Béchar	104	31.37N	2.13W
Beckley	140	37.46N	81.11W
Be'er Sheva'	109	31.14N	34.47 E
Beeville	128	28.24N	97.44W

Name	Page No.	Lat.	Long.	Name	Page No.	Lat.	Long.
Beian	114	48.15N	126.30 E	Bermuda □²	138	32.20N	64.45 W
Beihai	114	21.29N	109.05 E	Bern (Berne)	92	46.57N	7.26 E
Beijing (Peking)	114	39.55N	116.25 E	Bernasconi	134	37.54S	63.43 W
Beira	106	19.49S	34.52 E	Bernburg	90	51.48N	11.44 E
Beirut				Berne			
→ Bayrūt	109	33.53N	35.30 E	→ Bern	92	46.57N	7.26 E
Beja, Port.	94	38.01N	7.52 W	Berner Alpen ⋩	92	46.30N	7.30 E
Béja, Tun.	104	36.44N	9.11 E	Berryessa, Lake ⊜¹	142	38.35N	122.14 W
Bejaïa	104	36.45N	5.05 E	Besançon	92	47.15N	6.02 E
Békéscsaba	90	46.41N	21.06 E	Beskid Mountains ⋩	90	49.40N	20.00 E
Belarus □¹	86	53.00N	28.00 E	Beskra	104	34.51N	5.44 E
Belcher Islands II	136	56.20N	79.30 W	Bethel	144	60.48N	161.46 W
Beled Weyne	108	4.47N	45.12 E	Bethlehem, S. Afr.	106	28.15S	28.15 E
Belém	132	1.27S	48.29 W	Bethlehem, Pa., U.S.	140	40.37N	75.22 W
Belfast	88	54.35N	5.55 W	Beticos, Sistemas ⋩	94	37.00N	4.00 W
Belfort	92	47.38N	6.52 E	Betsiboka ≏	106	16.03S	46.36 E
Belgaum	111	15.52N	74.30 E	Bette ⋀	104	22.00N	19.12 E
Belgium □¹	86	50.50N	4.00 E	Béziers	92	43.21N	3.15 E
Belgorod	86	50.36N	36.35 E	Bhāgalpur	112	25.15N	87.00 E
Belgrade				Bhaunagar	112	21.46N	72.09 E
→ Beograd	98	44.50N	20.30 E	Bhopāl	112	23.16N	77.24 E
Belitung I	118	2.50S	107.55 E	Bhutan □¹	110	27.30N	90.30 E
Belize □¹	130	17.15N	88.45 W	Biafra, Bight of c³	104	4.00N	8.00 E
Belize City	130	17.30N	88.12 W	Białystok	90	53.09N	23.09 E
Bella Coola	136	52.22N	126.46 W	Biarritz	92	43.29N	1.34 W
Bellaire	140	44.58N	85.12 W	Bicaz	98	46.54N	26.05 E
Bellavista	132	7.04S	76.35 W	Biddeford	140	43.29N	70.27 W
Belle-Île I	92	47.20N	3.10 W	Biel (Bienne)	92	47.10N	7.12 E
Belleville	140	44.10N	77.23 W	Bielefeld	90	52.01N	8.31 E
Bellingham	138	48.45N	122.29 W	Bielsko-Biała	90	49.49N	19.02 E
Bellingshausen Sea ▼²	85	71.00S	85.00 W	Bien Hoa	120	10.57N	106.49 E
Bellinzona	92	46.11N	9.02 E	Bienville, Lac ⊜	136	55.05N	72.40 W
Bellows Falls	140	43.08N	72.26 W	Big Bend National			
Belmont	140	42.13N	78.02 W	Park ✦	128	29.12N	103.12 W
Belmopan	130	17.15N	88.46 W	Biggar	136	52.04N	108.00 W
Belo Horizonte	132	19.55S	43.56 W	Bighorn Mountains ⋩	138	44.00N	107.30 W
Beloje More (White				Big Spring	128	32.15N	101.28 W
Sea) ▼²	102	65.30N	38.00 E	Bihār	112	25.11N	85.31 E
Belovo	102	54.25N	86.18 E	Bijsk	102	52.34N	85.15 E
Bemidji	138	47.28N	94.52 W	Bīkaner	112	28.01N	73.18 E
Benares				Bilauktaung Range ⋩	120	13.00N	99.00 E
→ Vārānasi	112	25.20N	83.00 E	Bilbao	94	43.15N	2.58 W
Bendigo	122	36.46S	144.17 E	Billings	138	45.46N	108.30 W
Benevento	96	41.08N	14.45 E	Biloxi	138	30.23N	88.53 W
Bengal, Bay of c	82	15.00N	90.00 E	Binga, Monte ⋀	106	19.45S	33.04 E
Bengbu	114	32.58N	117.24 E	Binghamton	140	42.05N	75.55 W
Benghazi				Bioko I	104	3.30N	8.40 E
→ Banghāzī	104	32.07N	20.04 E	Birao	104	10.17N	22.47 E
Bengkulu	118	3.48S	102.16 E	Birātnagar	112	26.29N	87.17 E
Beni ≏	132	10.23S	65.24 W	Birch Run	140	43.15N	83.47 W
Béni Abbas	104	30.08N	2.10 W	Birdum	122	15.39S	133.13 E
Benin □¹	104	9.30N	2.15 E	Bīrganj	112	27.00N	84.52 E
Benin, Bight of c³	104	5.30N	3.00 E	Bîrlad	98	46.14N	27.40 E
Benin City	104	6.19N	5.41 E	Birmingham, Eng.,			
Bennington	140	42.52N	73.11 W	U.K.	88	52.30N	1.50 W
Bénoué (Benue) ≏	104	7.48N	6.46 E	Birmingham, Al., U.S.	138	33.31N	86.48 W
Benue (Bénoué) ≏	104	7.48N	6.46 E	Birobidžan	102	48.48N	132.57 E
Benxi	114	41.18N	123.45 E	Bisbee	128	31.26N	109.55 W
Beograd (Belgrade)	98	44.50N	20.30 E	Biscay, Bay of c	86	44.00N	4.00 W
Beppu	116	33.17N	131.30 E	Biškek	114	42.54N	74.36 E
Berati	98	40.42N	19.57 E	Bismarck	138	46.48N	100.47 W
Berbera	108	10.25N	45.02 E	Bissau	104	11.51N	15.35 W
Berens River	136	52.22N	97.02 W	Bistriţa	98	47.08N	24.30 E
Berg	89	69.26N	17.15 E	Bitola	98	41.01N	21.20 E
Bergama	98	39.07N	27.11 E	Bitterfeld	90	51.37N	12.20 E
Bergamo	96	45.41N	9.43 E	Biwa-ko ⊜	116	35.15N	136.05 E
Bergen	89	60.23N	5.20 E	Bizerte	104	37.17N	9.52 E
Bergen op Zoom	90	51.30N	4.17 E	Black (Lixian) (Da) ≏	120	21.15N	105.20 E
Bergerac	92	44.51N	0.29 E	Blackall	122	24.25S	145.28 E
Bering Sea ▼²	82	59.00N	174.00 W	Blackburn	88	53.45N	2.29 W
Bering Strait ⌣	144	65.30N	169.00 W	Black Hills ⋩	138	44.00N	104.00 W
Berkåk	89	62.50N	10.00 E	Blackpool	88	53.50N	3.03 W
Berkeley	142	37.52N	122.16 W	Black Rock Desert ➝²	142	41.10N	119.00 W
Berlevåg	89	70.51N	29.06 E	Black Sea ▼²	86	43.00N	35.00 E
Berlin, Ger.	90	52.31N	13.24 E	Blagoevgrad	98	42.01N	23.06 E
Berlin, N.H., U.S.	140	44.28N	71.11 W	Blagoveščensk	102	50.17N	127.32 E

Name	Page No.	Lat.	Long.
Blanc, Mont (Monte			
Bianco) ▲	92	45.50N	6.52 E
Blanco, Cabo ⊁	130	9.34N	85.07W
Blantyre	106	15.47S	35.00 E
Blenheim	126	41.31S	173.57 E
Blida	94	36.28N	2.50 E
Blind River	140	46.10N	82.58W
Bloemfontein	106	29.12S	26.07 E
Bloomington	138	39.10N	86.32W
Blue Mountains ⋌	138	45.30N	118.15W
Blue Nile (Al-Bahr			
al-Azraq) ≃	108	15.38N	32.31 E
Blue Ridge ⋌	140	38.40N	78.15W
Bluff	126	46.36S	168.20 E
Bluffton	140	40.44N	85.10W
Blumenau	134	26.56S	49.03W
Blyth	88	55.07N	1.30W
Blythe	142	33.36N	114.35W
Blytheville	138	35.55N	89.55W
Boa Vista	132	2.49N	60.40W
Bobcaygeon	140	44.33N	78.33W
Bobo Dioulasso	104	11.12N	4.18W
Bobrujsk	100	53.09N	29.14 E
Boby, Pic ▲	106	22.12S	46.55 E
Bocas del Toro	130	9.20N	82.15W
Bocholt	90	51.50N	6.36 E
Bochum	90	51.28N	7.13 E
Bodele ⬦¹	104	16.30N	16.30 E
Boden	89	65.50N	21.42 E
Bodensee ⊜	90	47.35N	9.25 E
Bodø	89	67.17N	14.23 E
Bogalusa	128	30.47N	89.50W
Bogenfels	106	27.23S	15.22 E
Bogor	118	6.35S	106.47 E
Bogotá			
→ Santa Fe de			
Bogotá	132	4.36N	74.05W
Bohemian Forest ⋌	90	49.15N	12.45 E
Boise	138	43.36N	116.12W
Boise, South Fork ≃	142	43.36N	115.51W
Bola	127a	9.37S	160.39 E
Bolesławiec	90	51.16N	15.34 E
Bolívar, Cerro ▲	130	7.28N	63.25W
Bolívar, Pico ▲	132	8.30N	71.02W
Bolivia □¹	132	17.00S	65.00W
Bollnäs	89	61.21N	16.25 E
Bologna	96	44.29N	11.20 E
Bol'ševik, Ostrov I	102	78.40N	102.30 E
Bol'šoj L'achovskij,			
Ostrov I	102	73.35N	142.00 E
Bolzano (Bozen)	96	46.31N	11.22 E
Boma	106	5.51S	13.03 E
Bombay			
→ Mumbai	111	18.58N	72.50 E
Bomu (Mbomou) ≃	104	4.08N	22.26 E
Bonaire I	130	12.10N	68.15W
Bonarbridge	88	57.53N	4.21W
Bonavista	136	48.39N	53.07W
Bône			
→ Annaba	104	36.54N	7.46 E
Bonn	90	50.44N	7.05 E
Boonville	140	43.29N	75.20W
Boothia, Gulf of ⊂	136	71.00N	91.00W
Bora-Bora I	127d	16.30S	151.45W
Boraha, Nosy I	106	16.50S	49.55 E
Borås	89	57.43N	12.55 E
Bordeaux	92	44.50N	0.34W
Bordertown	122	36.19S	140.47 E
Bordj Bou Arreridj	94	36.04N	4.46 E
Bordj Omar Idriss	104	28.09N	6.43 E
Borisoglebsk	86	51.23N	42.06 E
Borlänge	89	60.29N	15.25 E
Borneo (Kalimantan) I	118	0.30N	114.00 E
Bornholm I	89	55.10N	15.00 E
Boronga Islands II	120	19.58N	93.06 E
Boroviči	100	58.24N	33.55 E

Name	Page No.	Lat.	Long.
Borz'a	102	50.38N	115.38 E
Boshan	114	36.29N	117.50 E
Bosnia and			
Herzegovina □¹	96	44.15N	17.50 E
Bosporus			
→ İstanbul Boğazı ⋃	98	41.06N	29.04 E
Boston	140	42.21N	71.03W
Botev ▲	98	42.43N	24.55 E
Bothnia, Gulf of ⊂	89	63.00N	20.00 E
Botoşani	98	47.45N	26.40 E
Botswana □¹	106	22.00S	24.00 E
Bottenhavet			
(Selkämeri) ⊂	89	62.00N	20.00 E
Botwood	136	49.09N	55.21W
Bouaké	104	7.41N	5.02W
Bouar	104	5.57N	15.36 E
Bougainville I	127a	6.00S	155.00 E
Bougainville Strait ⋃	127a	6.40S	156.10 E
Bouillon	90	49.48N	5.04 E
Boulder	138	40.00N	105.16W
Boulogne-sur-Mer	92	50.43N	1.37 E
Bouloupari	127b	21.52S	166.04 E
Boundary Peak ▲	142	37.51N	118.21W
Bourail	127b	21.34S	165.30 E
Bourges	92	47.05N	2.24 E
Bourgogne □⁹	92	47.00N	4.30 E
Bourke	122	30.05S	145.56 E
Bournemouth	88	50.43N	1.54W
Bøvågen	89	60.40N	4.58 E
Bøverdal	89	61.43N	8.21 E
Bowie	140	39.00N	76.46W
Bowling Green, Ky.,			
U.S.	138	36.59N	86.26W
Bowling Green, Oh.,			
U.S.	140	41.22N	83.39W
Bowling Green, Va.,			
U.S.	140	38.02N	77.20W
Boyoma Falls (Stanley			
Falls) ⌣	106	0.15N	25.30 E
Brač, Otok I	96	43.20N	16.40 E
Brad	98	46.08N	22.47 E
Bradford, On., Can.	140	44.07N	79.34W
Bradford, Pa., U.S.	140	41.57N	78.38W
Braga	94	41.33N	8.26W
Bragança	94	41.49N	6.45W
Brāhmanbāria	112	23.59N	91.07 E
Brahmaputra			
(Yaluzangbujiang) ≃	112	24.02N	90.59 E
Brăila	98	45.16N	27.58 E
Brainerd	138	46.21N	94.12W
Branco ≃	132	1.24S	61.51W
Brandberg ▲	106	21.10S	14.33 E
Brandenburg	90	52.24N	12.32 E
Brandenburg □⁹	90	52.00N	13.30 E
Br'ansk	100	53.15N	34.22 E
Brantford	140	43.08N	80.16W
Brasília	132	15.47S	47.55W
Braşov	98	45.39N	25.37 E
Brateş, Lacul ⊜	98	45.30N	28.05 E
Bratislava	90	48.09N	17.07 E
Bratsk	102	56.05N	101.48 E
Brattleboro	140	42.51N	72.33W
Braunschweig	90	52.16N	10.31 E
Bravo del Norte (Rio			
Grande) ≃	138	25.55N	97.09W
Brawley	142	32.58N	115.31W
Brazil □¹	132	10.00S	55.00W
Brazzaville	106	4.16S	15.17 E
Breda	90	51.35N	4.46 E
Bremen	90	53.04N	8.49 E
Bremerhaven	90	53.33N	8.34 E
Brenner Pass ⋋	92	47.00N	11.30 E
Brescia	96	45.33N	13.15 E
Brest, Bela.	100	52.06N	23.42 E
Brest, Fr.	92	48.24N	4.29W
Bretagne □⁹	92	48.00N	3.00W

Name	Page No.	Lat.	Long.
Bridgeport	140	41.10N	73.12W
Bridgeton	140	39.25N	75.14W
Bridgetown	130	13.06N	59.37W
Bridgeville	140	38.44N	75.36W
Brighton	88	50.50N	0.08W
Brindisi	96	40.38N	17.56 E
Brisbane	122	27.28S	153.02 E
Bristol, Eng., U.K.	88	51.27N	2.35W
Bristol, Ct., U.S.	140	41.41N	72.57W
Bristol Bay c	144	58.00N	159.00W
British Columbia □⁴	136	54.00N	125.00W
Brno	90	49.12N	16.37 E
Brochet	136	57.53N	101.40W
Brockton	140	42.05N	71.01W
Brockville	140	44.35N	75.41W
Broken Hill, Austl.	122	31.57S	141.27 E
Broken Hill → Kabwe, Zam.	106	14.27S	28.27 E
Brokopondo	132	5.04N	54.58W
Bronlund Peak ʌ	136	57.26N	126.38W
Brookings, Or., U.S.	142	42.03N	124.16W
Brookings, S.D., U.S.	138	44.18N	96.47W
Brooks Range ⋌	144	68.00N	154.00W
Broome	122	17.58S	122.14 E
Brown City	140	43.12N	82.59W
Brownsville	138	25.54N	97.29W
Brownville Junction	140	45.21N	69.03W
Brownwood	128	31.42N	98.59W
Bruce, Mount ʌ	122	22.36S	118.08 E
Bruce Peninsula ⋋¹	140	44.50N	81.20W
Brugge	90	51.13N	3.14 E
Bruneau	142	42.52N	115.47W
Bruneau ≈	142	42.57N	115.58W
Brunei □¹	118	4.30N	114.40 E
Brus Laguna	130	15.47N	84.35W
Brussels → Bruxelles	90	50.50N	4.20 E
Bruxelles (Brussel)	90	50.50N	4.20 E
Bryan	140	41.28N	84.33W
Brzeg	90	50.52N	17.27 E
Bucaramanga	132	7.08N	73.09W
Buchanan	104	5.57N	10.02W
Bucharest → București	98	44.26N	26.06 E
Buckhannon	140	38.59N	80.13W
Buckingham	140	45.35N	75.25W
București (Bucharest)	98	44.26N	26.06 E
Budapest	90	47.30N	19.05 E
Buenaventura	132	3.53N	77.04W
Buena Vista	132	17.27S	63.40W
Buenos Aires	134	34.36S	58.27W
Buffalo	140	42.53N	78.52W
Bug ≈	86	52.31N	21.05 E
Buhuși	98	46.43N	26.41 E
Bujumbura	106	3.23S	29.22 E
Buka Island I	127a	5.15S	154.35 E
Bukavu	106	2.30S	28.52 E
Bukovina □⁹	98	48.00N	25.30 E
Bulawayo	106	20.09S	28.36 E
Bulgan	114	48.45N	103.34 E
Bulgaria □¹	86	43.00N	25.00 E
Bunbury	122	33.19S	115.38 E
Bundaberg	122	24.52S	152.21 E
Bunguran Utara, Kepulauan II	118	4.40N	108.00 E
Bunia	106	1.34N	30.15 E
Buon Me Thuot	120	12.40N	108.03 E
Burgas	98	42.30N	27.28 E
Burgos	94	42.21N	3.42W
Buriram	120	15.00N	103.07 E
Burkina Faso □¹	104	13.00N	2.00W
Burlington, Ia., U.S.	138	40.48N	91.06W
Burlington, Vt., U.S.	140	44.28N	73.12W
Burma → Myanmar □¹	118	22.00N	98.00 E
Burnie	122	41.04S	145.54 E
Burns	142	43.35N	119.03W
Burns Lake	136	54.14N	125.46W
Bursa	98	40.11N	29.04 E
Būr Saʿīd (Port Said)	104	31.16N	32.18 E
Būr Sūdān (Port Sudan)	104	19.37N	37.14 E
Burton	140	43.02N	83.36W
Buru I	118	3.24S	126.40 E
Burundi □¹	106	3.15S	30.00 E
Burwick	88	58.44N	2.57W
Buta	104	2.48N	24.44 E
Butler, Oh., U.S.	140	40.35N	82.25W
Butler, Pa., U.S.	140	40.51N	79.53W
Butte	138	46.00N	112.32W
Butterworth	120	5.25N	100.24 E
Butung, Pulau I	118	5.00S	122.55 E
Büyükmenderes ≈	98	37.27N	27.11 E
Buzău	98	45.09N	26.49 E
Buzuluk	86	52.47N	52.15 E
Bydgoszcz	90	53.08N	18.00 E
Bytom (Beuthen)	90	50.22N	18.54 E

C

Name	Page No.	Lat.	Long.
Cabimas	132	10.23N	71.28W
Cabinda □⁵	106	5.00S	12.30 E
Cáceres, Col.	130	7.35N	75.20W
Cáceres, Spain	94	39.29N	6.22W
Cache Peak ʌ	142	42.11N	113.40W
Cachoeira	135	12.36S	38.58W
Cachoeiro de Itapemirim	132	20.51S	41.06W
Cadillac	140	44.15N	85.24W
Cádiz	94	36.32N	6.18W
Cádiz, Golfo de c	94	36.50N	7.10W
Caen	92	49.11N	0.21W
Caenarvon	88	53.08N	4.16W
Cagliari	96	39.20N	9.00 E
Caguas	130	18.14N	66.02W
Caiapó, Serra ⋌	135	17.00S	52.00W
Caicos Islands II	130	21.56N	71.58W
Cairns	122	16.55S	145.46 E
Cairo → Al-Qāhirah, Egypt	104	30.03N	31.15 E
Cairo, Il., U.S.	138	37.00N	89.10W
Cajamarca	132	7.10S	78.31W
Calabozo	132	8.56N	67.26W
Calais, Fr.	92	50.57N	1.50 E
Calais, Me., U.S.	140	45.11N	67.16W
Calais, Pas de (Strait of Dover) ∪	92	51.00N	1.30 E
Calamian Group II	118	12.00N	120.00 E
Călărași	98	44.11N	27.20 E
Calcutta	112	22.32N	88.22 E
Caldas da Rainha	94	39.24N	9.08W
Calexico	142	32.40N	115.29W
Calgary	136	51.03N	114.05W
Cali	132	3.27N	76.31W
Caliente	142	37.36N	114.30W
California □³	138	37.30N	119.30W
California, Golfo de c	128	28.00N	112.00W
Callao	132	12.04S	77.09W
Caltagirone	96	37.14N	14.31 E
Caltanissetta	96	37.29N	14.04 E
Camacho	128	24.25N	102.18W
Camagüey	130	21.23N	77.55W
Ca Mau, Mui ⋋	120	8.38N	104.44 E
Cambodia □¹	118	13.00N	105.00 E
Cambrian Mountains ⋌	88	52.35N	3.35W
Cambridge, On., Can.	140	43.22N	80.19W
Cambridge, Eng., U.K.	88	52.13N	0.08 E
Cambridge, Md., U.S.	140	38.33N	76.04W
Cambridge, Oh., U.S.	140	40.02N	81.35W
Cambridge Bay	136	69.03N	105.05W
Camden, Me., U.S.	140	44.12N	69.03W

Name	Page No.	Lat.	Long.
Camden, N.J., U.S.	140	39.55 N	75.07 W
Cameroon □¹	104	6.00 N	12.00 E
Cameroun, Mont ʌ	104	4.12 N	9.11 E
Campbell Island I	85	52.30 S	169.05 E
Campbell River	136	50.01 N	125.15 W
Campbells Bay	140	45.44 N	76.36 W
Campbeltown	88	55.26 N	5.36 W
Campeche	128	19.51 N	90.32 W
Campeche, Bahía de c	128	20.00 N	94.00 W
Campina Grande	132	7.13 S	35.53 W
Campinas	132	22.54 S	47.05 W
Campobasso	96	41.34 N	14.39 E
Campo Grande	132	20.27 S	54.37 W
Campos	132	21.45 S	41.18 W
Cam Ranh	120	11.54 N	109.09 E
Cam Ranh, Vinh c	120	11.53 N	109.10 E
Canada □¹	136	60.00 N	95.00 W
Çanakkale	98	40.09 N	26.24 E
Çanakkale Boğazı (Dardanelles) ʉ	98	40.15 N	26.25 E
Cananea	128	30.57 N	110.18 W
Canarias, Islas (Canary Islands) II	104	28.00 N	15.30 W
Canaveral, Cape ⸙	138	28.27 N	80.32 W
Canavieiras	135	15.39 S	38.57 W
Canberra	122	35.17 S	149.08 E
Caniapiscau ≏	136	57.40 N	69.30 W
Caniapiscau, Lac ⊜	136	54.10 N	69.55 W
Cannes	92	43.33 N	7.01 E
Cantábrica, Cordillera ⸙	94	43.00 N	5.00 W
Cantaura	130	9.19 N	64.21 W
Canterbury	88	51.17 N	1.05 E
Canterbury Bight c³	126	44.15 S	171.38 E
Canton → Guangzhou, China	114	23.06 N	113.16 E
Canton, Oh., U.S.	140	40.47 N	81.22 W
Canyonville	142	42.55 N	123.16 W
Cape Breton Island I	136	46.00 N	60.30 W
Cape Cod National Seashore ✦	140	41.56 N	70.06 W
Cape Girardeau	138	37.18 N	89.31 W
Cape May	140	38.56 N	74.54 W
Cape Town (Kaapstad)	106	33.55 S	18.22 E
Cape York Peninsula ⸙¹	122	14.00 S	142.30 E
Cap-Haïtien	130	19.45 N	72.12 W
Caprivi Strip □⁹	106	17.59 S	23.00 E
Caracal	98	44.07 N	24.21 E
Caracas	132	10.30 N	66.56 W
Carangola	135	20.44 S	42.02 W
Caratinga	135	19.47 S	42.08 W
Carbó	128	29.42 N	110.58 W
Carbondale	140	41.34 N	75.30 W
Carcans, Étang de c	92	45.08 N	1.08 W
Carcassonne	92	43.13 N	2.21 E
Cárdenas	130	23.02 N	81.12 W
Cardiff	88	51.29 N	3.13 W
Cardigan	88	52.06 N	4.40 W
Caribbean Sea ⊤²	130	15.00 N	73.00 W
Caripito	130	10.08 N	63.06 W
Carleton Place	140	45.08 N	76.09 W
Carlisle, Eng., U.K.	88	54.54 N	2.55 W
Carlisle, Pa., U.S.	140	40.12 N	77.11 W
Carlsbad	128	32.25 N	104.13 W
Carlsbad Caverns National Park ✦	128	32.08 N	104.35 W
Carmacks	136	62.05 N	136.18 W
Carmarthen	88	51.52 N	4.19 W
Carmona	94	37.28 N	5.38 W
Caroline Islands II	118	8.00 N	140.00 E
Caroní ≏	130	8.21 N	62.43 W
Carpathian Mountains ⸙	86	48.00 N	24.00 E
Carpaţii Meridionali ⸙	98	45.30 N	24.15 E
Carpentaria, Gulf of c	122	14.00 S	139.00 E
Carrara	96	44.05 N	10.06 E
Carrauntoohill ʌ	88	52.00 N	9.45 W
Carrizo Springs	128	28.31 N	99.51 W
Carson City	142	39.10 N	119.46 W
Cartagena, Col.	132	10.25 N	75.32 W
Cartagena, Spain	94	37.36 N	0.59 W
Cartago	130	9.52 N	83.55 W
Caruaru	132	8.17 S	35.58 W
Carúpano	130	10.40 N	63.14 W
Casablanca (Dar-el-Beida)	104	33.39 N	7.35 W
Casa Grande	128	32.52 N	111.45 W
Casale Monferrato	96	45.08 N	8.27 E
Cascade Point ⸙	126	44.00 S	168.22 E
Cascade Range ⸙	138	49.00 N	120.00 W
Cascais	94	38.42 N	9.25 W
Casper	138	42.52 N	106.18 W
Caspian Sea ⊤²	86	42.00 N	50.30 E
Cassai (Kasai) ≏	106	3.06 S	16.57 E
Castelo Branco	94	39.49 N	7.30 W
Castile	140	42.37 N	78.03 W
Castletown	88	54.04 N	4.40 W
Castres	92	43.36 N	2.15 E
Castries	130	14.01 N	61.00 W
Catalão	135	18.10 S	47.57 W
Cataluña □⁹	94	42.00 N	2.00 E
Catamarca	134	28.28 S	65.47 W
Catanduanes Island I	118	13.45 N	124.15 E
Catanduva	135	21.08 S	48.58 W
Catania	96	37.30 N	15.06 E
Catanzaro	96	38.54 N	16.36 E
Cat Island I	130	24.27 N	75.30 W
Catoche, Cabo ⸙	128	21.35 N	87.05 W
Catskill Mountains ⸙	140	42.10 N	74.30 W
Caucasus ⸙	86	42.30 N	45.00 E
Caxambu	135	21.59 S	44.56 W
Caxias do Sul	134	29.10 S	51.11 W
Cayenne	132	4.56 N	52.20 W
Cayman Islands □²	130	19.30 N	80.40 W
Cayuga Lake ⊜	140	42.45 N	76.45 W
Cazaux, Étang de c	92	44.30 N	1.10 W
Čeboksary	86	56.09 N	47.15 E
Çebu	118	10.18 N	123.54 E
Čechy □⁹	90	49.50 N	14.00 E
Cedar City	138	37.40 N	113.03 W
Cedar Rapids	138	42.00 N	91.38 W
Çegléd	90	47.10 N	19.48 E
Čel'abinsk	86	55.10 N	61.24 E
Celaya	128	20.31 N	100.49 W
Celebes → Sulawesi I	118	2.00 S	121.00 E
Celebes Sea ⊤²	118	3.00 N	122.00 E
Celestún	128	20.52 N	90.24 W
Celle	90	52.37 N	10.05 E
Çel'uskin, Mys ⸙	102	77.45 N	104.20 E
Cenderawasih, Teluk c	118	2.30 S	135.20 E
Central, Cordillera ⸙	132	8.00 S	77.00 W
Central, Massif ⸙	92	45.00 N	3.10 E
Central, Planalto ⸙¹	132	18.00 S	47.00 W
Central, Sistema ⸙	94	40.30 N	5.00 W
Central African Republic □¹	104	7.00 N	21.00 E
Čeremchovo	102	53.09 N	103.05 E
Čerepovec	100	59.08 N	37.54 E
Cereté	130	8.53 N	75.48 W
Černogorsk	102	53.49 N	91.18 E
Cerritos	128	22.26 N	100.17 W
Cerro de Pasco	132	10.41 S	76.16 W
Čerskogo, Chrebet ⸙	102	65.00 N	144.00 E
Cesena	96	44.08 N	12.15 E
České Budějovice	90	48.59 N	14.28 E
Ceuta	104	35.53 N	5.19 W
Chabarovsk	102	48.27 N	135.06 E
Chad □¹	104	15.00 N	19.00 E

Name	Page No.	Lat.	Long.
Chad, Lake (Lac Tchad) ⬙	104	13.20N	14.00 E
Chadron	138	42.49N	103.00W
Chalbi Desert ⬥²	108	3.00N	37.20 E
Chalmette	128	29.56N	89.57W
Châlons-sur-Marne	92	48.57N	4.22 E
Chalon-sur-Saône	92	46.47N	4.51 E
Chaltel, Cerro (Monte Fitzroy) ▲	134	49.17S	73.05W
Chambal ≏	110	26.30N	79.15 E
Chamberlain	138	43.48N	99.19W
Chambéry	92	45.34N	5.56 E
Champagne □⁹	92	49.00N	4.30 E
Champaign	138	40.06N	88.14W
Champasak	120	14.53N	105.52 E
Champlain	140	44.42N	73.24W
Champlain, Lake ⬙	140	44.45N	73.15W
Chañaral	134	26.21S	70.37W
Chandeleur Islands II	128	29.48N	88.51W
Chang (Yangtze) ≏	114	31.48N	121.10 E
Changchun	114	43.53N	125.19 E
Changsha	114	28.11N	113.01 E
Changzhi	114	36.11N	113.08 E
Chanka, Ozero ⬙	114	45.00N	132.24 E
Channel Islands II, Eur.	92	49.20N	2.20W
Channel Islands II, Ca., U.S.	142	34.00N	120.00W
Channel-Port-aux-Basques	136	47.34N	59.09W
Chanthaburi	120	12.36N	102.09 E
Chao Phraya ≏	120	13.32N	100.36 E
Chapala, Lago de ⬙	128	20.15N	103.00W
Chapmanville	140	37.58N	82.01W
Charcas	128	23.08N	101.07W
Charente ≏	92	45.57N	1.05W
Chari ≏	104	12.58N	14.31 E
Charity	132	7.24N	58.36W
Char'kov → Kharkiv	86	50.00N	36.15 E
Charleroi	90	50.25N	4.26 E
Charleston, S.C., U.S.	138	32.46N	79.55W
Charleston, W.V., U.S.	140	38.20N	81.37W
Charleston Peak ▲	142	36.16N	115.42W
Charleville	122	26.24S	146.15 E
Charlotte	138	35.13N	80.50W
Charlotte Amalie	130	18.21N	64.56W
Charlottesville	140	38.01N	78.28W
Charlottetown	136	46.14N	63.08W
Chārsadda	112	34.09N	71.44 E
Chartres	92	48.27N	1.30 E
Chatanga	102	71.58N	102.30 E
Châtellerault	92	46.49N	0.33 E
Chatham	140	42.24N	82.11W
Chattahoochee ≏	138	30.52N	84.57W
Chattanooga	138	35.02N	85.18W
Chau Doc	120	10.42N	105.07 E
Chauk	120	20.54N	94.50 E
Chaves	94	41.44N	7.28W
Cheb	90	50.01N	12.25 E
Cheboygan	140	45.38N	84.28W
Chech, Erg ⬥²	104	25.00N	2.15W
Cheju-do I	114	33.20N	126.30 E
Chełm	90	51.10N	23.28 E
Chelmsford	88	51.44N	0.28 E
Chelyabinsk → Čel'abinsk	86	55.10N	61.24 E
Chemnitz	90	50.50N	12.55 E
Chénéville	140	45.53N	75.03W
Chengde	114	40.58N	117.53 E
Chengdu	114	30.39N	104.04 E
Chennai	111	13.05N	80.17 E
Chepo	130	9.10N	79.06W
Cher ≏	92	47.21N	0.29 E
Cherbourg	92	49.39N	1.39W
Cherkasy	86	49.26N	32.04 E
Chernihov	86	51.30N	31.18 E
Chernivtsy	86	48.18N	25.56 E
Chesapeake Bay c	140	38.40N	76.25W
Chesapeake Beach	140	38.41N	76.32W
Chester	140	39.50N	75.21W
Chesterfield, Îles II	122	19.30S	158.00 E
Chesterfield Inlet	136	63.21N	90.42W
Chesuncook Lake ⬙	140	46.00N	69.20W
Cheyenne	138	41.08N	104.49W
Chiang Mai	120	18.47N	98.59 E
Chiang Rai	120	19.54N	99.50 E
Chiautla de Tapia	128	18.17N	98.36W
Chiba	116	35.36N	140.07 E
Chibougamau	136	49.55N	74.22W
Chicago	138	41.51N	87.39W
Chichagof Island I	144	57.30N	135.30W
Chichén Itzá	128	20.40N	88.34W
Chiclayo	132	6.46S	79.51W
Chico	142	39.43N	121.50W
Chicoutimi	136	48.26N	71.04W
Chidley, Cape ⊁	136	60.23N	64.26W
Chieti	96	42.21N	14.10 E
Chigasaki	116	35.19N	139.24 E
Chihuahua	128	28.38N	106.05W
Chile □¹	134	30.00S	71.00W
Chillicothe	140	39.19N	82.58W
Chiloé, Isla de I	134	42.30S	73.55W
Chilpancingo [de los Bravos]	128	17.33N	99.30W
Chimborazo ▲¹	132	1.28S	78.48W
Chimbote	132	9.05S	78.36W
China □¹	114	35.00N	105.00 E
Chinandega	130	12.37N	87.09W
Chindwinn ≏	120	21.26N	95.15 E
Chinhoyi	106	17.22S	30.12 E
Chinko ≏	104	4.50N	23.53 E
Chioggia	96	45.13N	12.17 E
Chīrāla	111	15.49N	80.21 E
Chiricahua National Monument ✦	128	32.02N	109.19W
Chiriquí, Golfo c	130	8.00N	82.20W
Chirripó, Cerro ▲	130	9.29N	83.30W
Chisasibi	136	53.50N	79.00W
Chişinău	98	47.00N	28.50 E
Chittagong	112	22.20N	91.50 E
Choapan	128	17.20N	95.57W
Choele-Choel	134	39.16S	65.41W
Choiseul I	127a	7.05S	157.00 E
Chomutov	90	50.28N	13.26 E
Chon Buri	120	13.22N	100.59 E
Ch'ŏngjin	114	41.47N	129.50 E
Chongqing	114	29.39N	106.34 E
Chŏnju	114	35.49N	127.08 E
Chonos, Archipiélago de los II	134	45.00S	74.00W
Chōshi	116	35.44N	140.50 E
Chos Malal	134	37.23S	70.16W
Chovd	114	48.01N	91.38 E
Christchurch	126	43.32S	172.38 E
Christmas Island □²	118	10.30S	105.40 E
Chukchi Sea ⊤²	84	69.00N	171.00W
Chula Vista	142	32.38N	117.05W
Chum Saeng	120	15.54N	100.19 E
Chungking → Chongqing	114	29.39N	106.34 E
Chur	92	46.51N	9.32 E
Churchill	136	58.46N	94.10W
Churchill ≏	136	58.47N	94.12W
Churchill Lake ⬙	136	55.55N	108.20W
Ciego de Avila	130	21.51N	78.46W
Ciénaga	130	11.01N	74.15W
Cienfuegos	130	22.09N	80.27W
Cieza	94	38.14N	1.25W
Çimkent	110	42.18N	69.36 E
Cincinnati	140	39.09N	84.27W
Cirebon	118	6.44S	108.34 E
Čita	102	52.03N	113.30 E
Citrus Heights	142	38.42N	121.16W

Name	Page No.	Lat.	Long.
Ciudad Acuña	128	29.18N	100.55W
Ciudad Anáhuac	128	27.14N	100.09W
Ciudad Bolívar	132	8.08N	63.33W
Ciudad Camargo	128	26.19N	98.50W
Ciudad Chetumal	128	18.30N	88.18W
Ciudad del Carmen	128	18.38N	91.50W
Ciudad de México (Mexico City)	128	19.24N	99.09W
Ciudad de Valles	128	21.59N	99.01W
Ciudad de Villaldama	128	26.30N	100.26W
Ciudad Guayana	132	8.22N	62.40W
Ciudad Guerrero	128	28.33N	107.30W
Ciudad Ixtepec	128	16.34N	95.06W
Ciudad Jiménez	128	27.08N	104.55W
Ciudad Juárez	128	31.44N	106.29W
Ciudad Madero	128	22.16N	97.50W
Ciudad Mante	128	22.44N	98.57W
Ciudad Melchor Múzquiz	128	27.53N	101.31W
Ciudad Obregón	128	27.29N	109.56W
Ciudad Ojeda	130	10.12N	71.19W
Ciudad Real	94	38.59N	3.56W
Ciudad Victoria	128	23.44N	99.08W
Clanwilliam	106	32.11S	18.54 E
Claremont	140	43.22N	72.20W
Clarksburg	140	39.16N	80.20W
Clearfield	140	41.01N	78.26W
Clear Lake ◎ ¹	142	39.02N	122.50W
Clermont-Ferrand	92	45.47N	3.05 E
Cleveland, Oh., U.S.	140	41.29N	81.41W
Cleveland, Tx., U.S.	128	30.20N	95.05W
Clifton Forge	140	37.48N	79.49W
Clinton, Mi., U.S.	140	42.04N	83.58W
Clinton, Ok., U.S.	138	35.30N	98.58W
Clio	138	31.42N	85.36W
Cloncurry	122	20.42S	140.30 E
Clonmel	88	52.21N	7.42W
Clovis	138	34.24N	103.12W
Cluj-Napoca	98	46.47N	23.36 E
Clyde	136	70.25N	68.30W
Clyde, Firth of ᴄ¹	88	55.42N	5.00W
Coalinga	142	36.08N	120.21W
Coast Mountains ✗	136	55.00N	129.00W
Coast Ranges ✗	138	41.00N	123.30W
Coaticook	140	45.08N	71.48W
Coatzacoalcos	128	18.09N	94.25W
Cobija	132	11.02S	68.44W
Cobourg	140	43.58N	78.10W
Coburg	90	50.15N	10.58 E
Cochabamba	132	17.24S	66.09W
Coco ≃	130	15.00N	83.10W
Coco Channel ᴜ	120	13.45N	93.00 E
Cod, Cape ➤	140	41.42N	70.15W
Cognac	92	45.42N	0.20W
Coiba, Isla de ɪ	130	7.27N	81.45W
Coimbatore	111	11.00N	76.58 E
Coimbra	94	40.12N	8.25W
Čojbalsan	114	48.34N	114.50 E
Colatina	132	19.32S	40.37W
Coldwater	140	40.28N	84.37W
Coleman	140	43.45N	84.35W
Coleraine	88	55.08N	6.40W
Colima	128	19.14N	103.43W
Cologne → Köln	90	50.56N	6.59 E
Colombia ◻¹	132	4.00N	72.00W
Colombo	111	6.56N	79.51 E
Colón	130	9.22N	79.54W
Colón, Archipiélago de (Galapagos Islands) ɪɪ	82	0.30S	90.30W
Colonia Dora	134	28.36S	62.57W
Colonia Las Heras	134	46.33S	68.57W
Colorado ◻³	138	39.30N	105.30W
Colorado ≃, Arg.	134	39.50S	62.08W
Colorado ≃, N.A.	138	31.54N	114.57W
Colorado ≃, Tx., U.S.	128	28.36N	95.58W
Colorado Springs	138	38.50N	104.49W
Columbia, Md., U.S.	140	39.14N	76.50W
Columbia, S.C., U.S.	138	34.00N	81.02W
Columbia ≃	136	46.15N	124.05W
Columbia, Mount ʌ	136	52.09N	117.25W
Columbia Plateau ✗¹	142	44.00N	117.30W
Columbus, Ga., U.S.	138	32.29N	84.59W
Columbus, Ne., U.S.	138	41.25N	97.22W
Columbus, Oh., U.S.	140	39.57N	82.59W
Colville ≃	144	70.25N	150.30W
Comitán	128	16.15N	92.08W
Communism Peak → Kommunizma, Pik ʌ	110	38.57N	72.01 E
Como	96	45.47N	9.05 E
Como, Lago di ◎	96	46.00N	9.20 E
Comodoro Rivadavia	134	45.52S	67.30W
Comorin, Cape ➤	111	8.04N	77.34 E
Comoros ◻¹	106	12.10S	44.10 E
Compiègne	92	49.25N	2.50 E
Conakry	104	9.31N	13.43W
Concepción, Bol.	132	16.15S	62.04W
Concepción, Chile	134	36.50S	73.03W
Concepción, Para.	134	23.25S	57.17W
Concepción de la Vega	130	19.13N	70.31W
Concepción del Uruguay	134	32.29S	58.14W
Conchos ≃	128	29.35N	104.25W
Concord	140	43.12N	71.32W
Congo ◻¹	106	1.00S	15.00 E
Congo, Democratic Republic of the ◻¹	106	4.00S	25.00 E
Congo (Zaïre) ≃	106	6.04S	12.24 E
Connaught ◻⁹	88	53.45N	9.00W
Connecticut ◻³	138	41.45N	72.45W
Connemara ◆¹	88	53.25N	9.45W
Connersville	140	39.38N	85.15W
Constanţa	98	44.11N	28.39 E
Contas, Rio de ≃	135	14.17S	39.01W
Conway, N.H., U.S.	140	43.58N	71.07W
Conway, S.C., U.S.	138	33.50N	79.02W
Cook, Mount ʌ	126	43.36S	170.10 E
Cook Inlet ᴄ	144	60.30N	152.00W
Cook Islands ◻⁷	82	20.00S	158.00W
Cook Strait ᴜ	126	41.15S	174.30 E
Cooktown	122	15.28S	145.15 E
Cooperstown	140	42.42N	74.55W
Coos Bay	142	43.22N	124.12W
Copenhagen → København	89	55.40N	12.35 E
Copiapó	134	27.22S	70.20W
Copper ≃	144	60.30N	144.50W
Coral Sea ᴛ²	82	20.00S	158.00 E
Córdoba, Arg.	134	31.24S	64.11W
Córdoba, Mex.	128	18.53N	96.56W
Córdoba, Spain	94	37.53N	4.46W
Cordova	144	60.33N	145.46W
Corfu → Kérkira ɪ	98	39.40N	19.42 E
Corinth, Gulf of → Korinthiakós Kólpos ᴄ	98	38.19N	22.04 E
Cork	88	51.54N	8.28W
Çorlu	98	41.09N	27.48 E
Corner Brook	136	48.57N	57.57W
Corning	140	42.08N	77.03W
Cornwall	140	45.02N	74.44W
Coro	132	11.25N	69.41W
Coromandel Coast ≛²	111	14.00N	80.10 E
Coromandel Peninsula ➤¹	126	36.50S	175.35 E
Coronel Pringles	134	37.58S	61.22W
Corpus Christi	138	27.48N	97.23W
Corrientes	134	27.28S	58.50W
Corrientes, Cabo ➤, Col.	132	5.30N	77.34W

Name	Page No.	Lat.	Long.
Corrientes, Cabo ⌐, Cuba	130	21.45N	84.31W
Corrientes, Cabo ⌐, Mex.	128	20.25N	105.42W
Corry	140	41.55N	79.38W
Corse (Corsica) I	96	42.00N	9.00 E
Corse, Cap ⌐	96	43.00N	9.25 E
Corsica → Corse I	96	42.00N	9.00 E
Corsicana	128	32.05N	96.28W
Cortland	140	42.36N	76.10W
Corumbá	132	19.01S	57.39W
Cosenza	96	39.17N	16.15 E
Coshocton	140	40.16N	81.51W
Costa Rica □¹	130	10.00N	84.00W
Cote d'Ivoire □¹	104	8.00N	5.00W
Cotonou	104	6.21N	2.26 E
Cottbus	90	51.45N	14.19 E
Coubre, Pointe de la ⌐	92	45.41N	1.13W
Council Bluffs	138	41.15N	95.51W
Coventry	88	52.25N	1.30W
Covilhã	94	40.17N	7.30W
Covington	140	39.05N	84.30W
Cowansville	140	45.12N	72.45W
Cozumel, Isla de I	128	20.25N	86.55W
Craiova	98	44.19N	23.48 E
Crane Mountain ∧	142	42.04N	120.13W
Crasna (Kraszna) ≃	90	48.09N	22.20 E
Crater Lake ⌷	142	42.56N	122.06W
Crater Lake National Park ♦	142	42.49N	122.08W
Craters of the Moon National Monument ♦	142	43.20N	113.35W
Crawley	92	51.07N	0.12W
Cremona	96	45.07N	10.02 E
Cres, Otok I	96	44.50N	14.25 E
Crescent	142	43.27N	121.41W
Crete → Kríti I	98	35.29N	24.42 E
Crete, Sea of → Kritikón Pélagos ₹²	98	35.46N	23.54 E
Cristóbal Colón, Pico ∧	132	10.50N	73.41W
Croatia □¹	96	45.10N	15.30 E
Crooked Island I	130	22.45N	74.13W
Crooked Island Passage ⌣	130	22.55N	74.35W
Crystal City	128	28.40N	99.49W
Cuango	106	6.17S	16.41 E
Cuango (Kwango) ≃	106	3.14S	17.23 E
Cuba □¹	130	21.30N	80.00W
Cubango (Okavango) ≃	106	18.50S	22.25 E
Cúcuta	132	7.54N	72.31W
Čudskoje Ozero (Peipsi Järv) ⌷	100	58.45N	27.30 E
Cuenca, Ec.	132	2.53S	78.59W
Cuenca, Spain	94	40.04N	2.08W
Cuernavaca	128	18.55N	99.15W
Cuiabá	132	15.35S	56.05W
Culiacán	128	24.48N	107.24W
Cumaná	132	10.28N	64.10W
Cumberland	140	39.39N	78.45W
Cunene ≃	106	17.20S	11.50 E
Cuneo	96	44.23N	7.32 E
Curaçao I	130	12.11N	69.00W
Curitiba	134	25.25S	49.15W
Curvelo	135	18.45S	44.25W
Čusovoj	86	58.17N	57.49 E
Cuttack	112	20.30N	85.50 E
Cuxhaven	90	53.52N	8.42 E
Cuzco	132	13.31S	71.59W
Cyclades → Kikládhes II	98	37.30N	25.00 E
Cynthiana	140	38.23N	84.17W
Cyprus □¹	109	35.00N	33.00 E
Cyprus, North □¹	109	35.15N	33.40 E
Czech Republic □¹	86	49.30N	17.00 E
Częstochowa	90	50.49N	19.06 E
D			
Da → Black ≃	120	21.15N	105.20 E
Dacca → Dhaka	112	23.43N	90.25 E
Dachau	90	48.15N	11.27 E
Dādra and Nagar Haveli □⁸	111	20.05N	73.00 E
Dahlak Archipelago II	108	15.45N	40.30 E
Daimiel	94	39.04N	3.37W
Dakar	104	14.40N	17.26W
Dakhla	104	23.43N	15.57W
Dalälven ≃	89	60.38N	17.27 E
Da Lat	120	11.56N	108.25 E
Dalhart	138	36.03N	102.30W
Dalian	114	38.53N	121.35 E
Dallas	138	32.46N	96.47W
Dalmacija □⁹	96	43.00N	17.00 E
Dalwallinu	122	30.17S	116.40 E
Damān □⁸	111	20.10N	73.00 E
Damascus → Dimashq	109	33.30N	36.18 E
Damāvand, Qolleh-ye ∧	86	35.56N	52.08 E
Dampier Archipelago II	122	20.35S	116.35 E
Da Nang	120	16.04N	108.13 E
Danbury	140	41.23N	73.27W
Dandong	114	40.08N	124.20 E
Danforth	140	45.39N	67.52W
Dansville	140	42.33N	77.41W
Danube (Donau) (Dunaj) (Duna) ≃	90	45.20N	29.40 E
Danville, Ky., U.S.	140	37.42N	84.46W
Danville, Pa., U.S.	140	40.57N	76.36W
Danzig, Gulf of ⊂	90	54.40N	19.15 E
Darchan	114	49.29N	105.55 E
Dardanelles → Çanakkale Boğazı ⌣	98	40.15N	26.25 E
Dar es Salaam	106	6.48S	39.17 E
Dargaville	126	35.56S	173.53 E
Darling ≃	124	34.07S	141.55 E
Darling Range ⌀	122	32.00S	116.30 E
Darmstadt	90	49.53N	8.40 E
Dartmouth	136	44.40N	63.34W
Daru	118	9.04S	143.21 E
Darwin	122	12.28S	130.50 E
Datong	114	40.08N	113.13 E
Daugava (Zapadnaja Dvina) ≃	100	57.04N	24.03 E
Daugavpils	100	55.53N	26.32 E
Dauphin	136	51.09N	100.03W
Davao	118	7.04N	125.36 E
Davenport	138	41.31N	90.34W
David	130	8.26N	82.26W
Davis Strait ⌣	136	67.00N	57.00W
Dawa (Daua) ≃	108	4.11N	42.06 E
Dawei	120	14.05N	98.12 E
Dawson	136	64.04N	139.25W
Dayr az-Zawr	109	35.20N	40.09 E
Dayton	140	39.45N	84.11W
Daytona Beach	138	29.12N	81.01W
De Aar	106	30.39S	24.00 E
Dead Sea ⌷	109	31.30N	35.30 E
Deán Funes	134	30.26S	64.21W
Dearborn	140	42.18N	83.10W
Death Valley ⋁	142	36.30N	117.00W
Death Valley National Monument ♦	142	36.30N	117.00W

Name	Page No.	Lat.	Long.
Debrecen	90	47.32 N	21.38 E
Decatur	140	40.50 N	84.56 W
Deccan ⫽¹	110	17.00 N	78.00 E
Děčín	90	50.48 N	14.13 E
Deckerville	140	43.31 N	82.44 W
Deep River	140	46.06 N	77.30 W
Defiance	140	41.17 N	84.21 W
Dehiwala-Mount Lavinia	111	6.51 N	79.52 E
Dehra Dūn	112	30.19 N	78.02 E
Dej	98	47.09 N	23.52 E
Delano	142	35.46 N	119.14 W
Delaware □³	138	39.10 N	75.30 W
Delaware ⫽	140	39.20 N	75.25 W
Delaware Bay ⊂	140	39.05 N	75.15 W
Delhi	112	28.40 N	77.13 E
Delicias	128	28.13 N	105.28 W
Del Rio	138	29.21 N	100.53 W
Demirci	98	39.03 N	28.40 E
Denain	92	50.20 N	3.23 E
Denali National Park ◆	144	63.30 N	150.00 W
Den Helder	90	52.54 N	4.45 E
Denison	138	33.45 N	96.32 W
Denizli	98	37.46 N	29.06 E
Denmark □¹	86	56.00 N	10.00 E
Denpasar	118	8.39 S	115.13 E
Denton	140	38.53 N	75.49 W
D'Entrecasteaux Islands II	122	9.30 S	150.40 E
Denver	138	39.44 N	104.59 W
Dera Ghāzi Khān	110	30.03 N	70.38 E
Dera Ismāïl Khān	112	31.50 N	70.54 E
Derby	88	52.55 N	1.29 W
Derby Line	140	45.00 N	72.05 W
Dese	108	11.05 N	39.41 E
Des Moines	138	41.36 N	93.36 W
Des Moines ⫽	138	40.22 N	91.26 W
Dessau	90	51.50 N	12.14 E
Detmold	90	51.56 N	8.52 E
Detroit	140	42.20 N	83.03 W
Deutsche Bucht ⊂	90	54.30 N	7.30 E
Deva	98	45.53 N	22.55 E
Deventer	90	52.15 N	6.10 E
Devon Island I	136	75.00 N	87.00 W
Devonport	126	36.49 S	174.48 E
Dexter	140	45.01 N	69.17 W
Dezfūl	108	32.23 N	48.24 E
Dhaka	112	23.43 N	90.25 E
Dhodhekánisos (Dodecanese) II	98	36.30 N	27.00 E
Dhorāji	112	21.44 N	70.27 E
Diable, Île du I	132	5.17 N	52.35 W
Diablo Range ⫽	142	37.00 N	121.20 W
Diamantina	132	18.15 S	43.36 W
Diamond Peak ʌ	142	43.33 N	122.09 W
Dieppe	92	49.56 N	1.05 E
Digby	136	44.37 N	65.46 W
Dijon	92	47.19 N	5.01 E
Dili	118	8.33 S	125.35 E
Dillingham	144	59.02 N	158.29 W
Dillon	138	45.12 N	112.38 W
Dimashq (Damascus)	109	33.30 N	36.18 E
Dimitrovgrad	98	42.03 N	25.36 E
Dimlang ʌ	104	8.24 N	11.47 E
Dinant	90	50.16 N	4.55 E
Dinara (Dinaric Alps) ⫽	96	43.50 N	16.35 E
Dingle	88	52.08 N	10.15 W
Dingwall	88	57.35 N	4.29 W
Dire Dawa	108	9.37 N	41.52 E
Diriamba	130	11.51 N	86.14 W
Disappointment, Cape ⟩	138	46.18 N	124.03 W
Disappointment, Lake ⌐	122	23.30 S	122.50 E
Diu	112	20.42 N	70.59 E
Diu □³	112	20.42 N	70.59 E
Divinópolis	132	20.09 S	44.54 W
Diyarbakir	86	37.55 N	40.14 E
Dja ⫽	104	2.02 N	15.12 E
Djerba, Île de I	104	33.48 N	10.54 E
Djibouti	108	11.36 N	43.09 E
Djibouti □¹	108	11.30 N	43.00 E
Dnepr → Dnieper ⫽	86	46.30 N	32.18 E
Dnepropetrovsk → Dnipropetrovs'k	86	48.27 N	34.59 E
Dnieper ⫽	86	46.30 N	32.18 E
Dniester ⫽	86	46.18 N	30.17 E
Dnipropetrovs'k	86	48.27 N	34.59 E
Doberai, Jazirah ⟩¹	118	1.30 S	132.30 E
Dobrič	98	43.34 N	27.50 E
Dodecanese → Dhodhekánisos II	98	36.30 N	27.00 E
Dodge City	138	37.45 N	100.01 W
Dodoma	106	6.11 S	35.45 E
Doha → Ad-Dawḥah	108	25.17 N	51.32 E
Dolbeau	136	48.53 N	72.14 W
Dolisie	106	4.12 S	12.41 E
Dolomiti ⫽	96	46.25 N	11.50 E
Dominica □¹	130	15.30 N	61.20 W
Dominican Republic □¹	130	19.00 N	70.40 W
Don ⫽	86	47.04 N	39.18 E
Donau → Danube ⫽	90	45.20 N	29.40 E
Don Benito	94	38.57 N	5.52 W
Dondra Head ⟩	111	5.55 N	80.35 E
Doneck → Donets'k	86	48.00 N	37.48 E
Donegal	88	54.39 N	8.07 W
Donets'k	86	48.00 N	37.48 E
Donga ⫽	104	8.19 N	9.58 E
Dongara	122	29.15 S	114.56 E
Dongting Hu ☺	114	29.20 N	112.54 E
Dordogne ⫽	92	45.02 N	0.35 W
Dordrecht	90	51.49 N	4.40 E
Dores do Indaiá	135	19.27 S	45.36 W
Dortmund	90	51.31 N	7.28 E
Dothan	138	31.13 N	85.23 W
Douala	104	4.03 N	9.42 E
Doubtless Bay ⊂	126	34.55 S	173.25 E
Douglas	88	54.09 N	4.28 W
Dourados	135	22.13 S	54.48 W
Douro (Duero) ⫽	94	41.08 N	8.40 W
Dover, Eng., U.K.	88	51.08 N	1.19 E
Dover, De., U.S.	140	39.09 N	75.31 W
Dover, N.H., U.S.	140	43.11 N	70.52 W
Dover, Strait of (Pas de Calais) ʯ	92	51.00 N	1.30 E
Dra'a, Hamada du ◆²	104	29.00 N	6.45 W
Drâa, Oued ∨	104	28.43 N	11.09 W
Drachten	90	53.06 N	6.05 E
Drakensberg ⫽	106	27.00 S	30.00 E
Drake Passage ʯ	85	58.00 S	70.00 W
Dráma	98	41.09 N	24.08 E
Drammen	89	59.44 N	10.15 E
Dranov, Ostrovul I	98	44.52 N	29.15 E
Drava (Dráva) (Drau) ⫽	90	45.33 N	18.55 E
Dresden	90	51.03 N	13.44 E
Drina ⫽	98	44.53 N	19.21 E
Drobeta-Turnu-Severin	98	44.38 N	22.39 E
Drogheda	88	53.43 N	6.21 W
Drummondville	140	45.53 N	72.29 W
Duarte, Pico ʌ	130	19.02 N	70.59 W
Dubayy	108	25.18 N	55.18 E
Dubbo	122	32.15 S	148.36 E
Dublin (Baile Átha Cliath)	88	53.20 N	6.15 W
Du Bois	140	41.07 N	78.45 W

Name	Page No.	Lat.	Long.
Dubrovnik	98	42.38N	18.07 E
Duero (Douro) ≃	94	41.08N	8.40W
Dufourspitze ∧	92	45.55N	7.52 E
Dugi Otok I	96	44.00N	15.04 E
Duisburg	90	51.25N	6.46 E
Duluth	138	46.45N	92.07W
Dumfries	88	55.04N	3.37W
Dumyât	109	31.25N	31.48 E
Duna			
→ Danube ≃	90	45.20N	29.40 E
Dunaj			
→ Danube ≃	90	45.20N	29.40 E
Dunaújváros	90	46.58N	18.57 E
Dundalk	88	54.01N	6.25W
Dundee	88	56.28N	3.00W
Dunedin	126	45.52S	170.30 E
Dungarvan	88	52.05N	7.37W
Dunkirk, In., U.S.	140	40.22N	85.12W
Dunkirk, N.Y., U.S.	140	42.28N	79.20W
Dunkirk, Oh., U.S.	140	40.47N	83.38W
Dun Laoghaire	88	53.17N	6.08W
Dunnville	140	42.54N	79.36W
Durance ≃	94	43.55N	4.44 E
Durango	128	24.02N	104.40W
Durban	106	29.55S	30.56 E
Durham	140	44.10N	80.49W
Durmitor ∧	98	43.08N	19.01 E
Durness	88	58.33N	4.45W
Durrësi	98	41.19N	19.26 E
D'Urville Island I	126	40.50S	173.52 E
Dušanbe	110	38.35N	68.48 E
Düsseldorf	90	51.12N	6.47 E
Dzaoudzi	106	12.47S	45.17 E
Dzierżoniów			
(Reichenbach)	90	50.44N	16.39 E
E			
Eagle Pass	138	28.42N	100.29W
East Aurora	140	42.46N	78.36W
East Cape ⊁	126	37.41S	178.33 E
East China Sea ⊤²	114	30.00N	126.00 E
Eastern Ghāts ⊀	111	14.00N	78.50 E
East Falkland I	134	51.55S	59.00W
East Lansing	140	42.44N	84.29W
East Liverpool	140	40.37N	80.34W
East London			
(Oos-Londen)	106	33.00S	27.55 E
Eastmain	136	52.15N	78.30W
Easton	140	40.41N	75.13W
East Stroudsburg	140	40.59N	75.10W
East Tawas	140	44.16N	83.29W
Eau Claire	138	44.48N	91.29W
Eberswalde	90	52.50N	13.49 E
Ebro ≃	94	40.43N	0.54 E
Ebro, Delta del ≃²	94	40.43N	0.54 E
Écija	94	37.32N	5.05W
Ecuador □¹	132	2.00S	77.30W
Edinburg, Tx., U.S.	128	26.18N	98.09W
Edinburg, Va., U.S.	140	38.49N	78.33W
Edinburgh	88	55.57N	3.13W
Edirne	98	41.40N	26.34 E
Edmonton	136	53.33N	113.28W
Edremit	98	39.35N	27.01 E
Edson	136	53.35N	116.26W
Eel ≃	142	40.40N	124.20W
Efate I	127b	17.40S	168.25 E
Eganville	140	45.32N	77.06W
Eger	90	47.54N	20.23 E
Egypt □¹	104	27.00N	30.00 E
Eindhoven	90	51.26N	5.28 E
Eisenach	90	50.59N	10.19 E
Eisenhüttenstadt	90	52.10N	14.39 E
Eisenstadt	90	47.51N	16.32 E
Eisleben	90	51.31N	11.32 E

Name	Page No.	Lat.	Long.
Ekwan ≃	136	53.14N	82.13W
El Aaiún	104	27.09N	13.12W
Elat	109	29.33N	34.57 E
Elba, Isola d' I	96	42.46N	10.17 E
El Banco	130	9.00N	73.58W
Elbasani	98	41.06N	20.05 E
Elbe (Labe) ≃	90	53.50N	9.00 E
Elbląg (Elbing)	90	54.10N	19.25 E
El'brus, Gora ∧	86	43.21N	42.26 E
El Cajon	142	32.47N	116.57W
El Campo	128	29.11N	96.16W
El Capitan ∧	138	46.01N	114.23W
Elche	94	38.15N	0.42W
Elda	94	38.29N	0.47W
El Djazaïr (Algiers)	104	36.47N	3.03 E
El Djouf ◆²	104	20.30N	8.00W
El Dorado	138	33.12N	92.39W
Eldoret	106	0.31N	35.17 E
El Encanto	132	1.37S	73.14W
Elephant Mountain ∧	140	44.46N	70.46W
El Estor	130	15.32N	89.21W
Eleuthera I	130	25.10N	76.14W
Elgin	88	57.39N	3.20W
Elizabeth City	138	36.18N	76.13W
Ełk	90	53.50N	22.22 E
El Kef	96	36.11N	8.43 E
Elkins	140	38.55N	79.50W
Elko	142	40.49N	115.45W
Elk Rapids	140	44.53N	85.24W
Elkton	140	39.36N	75.50W
Ellesmere Island I	84	81.00N	80.00W
Ellsworth	140	44.32N	68.25W
Elmer	140	39.35N	75.10W
Elmira	140	42.05N	76.48W
Elmore	124	36.30S	144.37 E
Elmshorn	90	53.45N	9.39 E
El Nevado, Cerro ∧	134	35.35S	68.30W
El Palmar	130	7.58N	61.53W
El Paso	138	31.45N	106.29W
El Progreso	130	15.21N	87.49W
El Salvador □¹	130	13.50N	88.55W
El Sauce	130	12.53N	86.32W
El Tigre	132	8.55N	64.15W
El Turbio	134	51.41S	72.05W
Elvas	94	38.53N	7.10W
Ely	142	39.14N	114.53W
Embarcación	134	23.13S	64.06W
Emden	90	53.22N	7.12 E
Emerald	122	23.32S	148.10 E
Empoli	96	43.43N	10.57 E
Emporia	138	38.24N	96.10W
Emporium	140	41.30N	78.14W
Encarnación	134	27.20S	55.54W
Encontrados	130	9.03N	72.14W
Enderby Land ◆¹	85	67.30S	53.00 E
Endicott	140	42.05N	76.02W
Engel's	86	51.30N	46.07 E
England □⁸	88	52.30N	1.30W
English Channel (La			
Manche) ᵁ	92	50.20N	1.00W
Enns ≃	96	48.14N	14.32 E
Enschede	90	52.12N	6.53 E
Ensenada	128	31.52N	116.37W
Entebbe	106	0.04N	32.28 E
Enugu	104	6.27N	7.27 E
Eolie, Isole II	96	38.30N	15.00 E
Épinal	92	48.11N	6.27 E
Equatorial Guinea □¹	104	2.00N	9.00 E
Erechim	134	27.38S	52.17W
Erfurt	90	50.58N	11.01 E
Erie	140	42.07N	80.05W
Erie, Lake ⊜	138	42.15N	81.00W
Eritrea □¹, Afr.	108	15.20N	39.00 E
Erlangen	90	49.36N	11.01 E
Eromanga I	127b	18.45S	169.05 E
Erzurum	86	39.55N	41.17 E

Name	Page No.	Lat.	Long.
Esbjerg	89	55.28N	8.27 E
Esch-sur-Alzette	90	49.30N	5.59 E
Escondido	142	33.07N	117.05W
Escuintla	130	14.18N	90.47W
Eṣfahān	108	32.40N	51.38 E
Eskilstuna	89	59.22N	16.30 E
Eskimo Point	136	61.07N	94.03W
Eskişehir	86	39.46N	30.32 E
Esmeraldas	132	0.59N	79.42W
Esperance	122	33.51S	121.53 E
Espinhaço, Serra do ⚲	132	17.30S	43.30W
Espíritu Santo ∎	127b	15.50S	166.50 E
Espoo (Esbo)	89	60.13N	24.40 E
Esquel	134	42.54S	71.19W
Essen	90	51.28N	7.01 E
Estados, Isla de los ∎	134	54.47S	64.15W
Estelí	130	13.05N	86.23W
Estonia □[1]	86	59.00N	26.00 E
Estrela ⚲	94	40.19N	7.37W
Ethiopia □[1]	108	9.00N	39.00 E
Etna, Monte ⋀[1]	96	37.46N	15.00 E
Ettelbruck	90	49.52N	6.05 E
Eucla	122	31.43S	128.52 E
Eugene	138	44.03N	123.05W
Eugenia, Punta ➤	138	27.50N	115.05W
Euphrates (Al-Furāt) ≃	108	31.00N	47.25 E
Eureka, Ca., U.S.	142	40.48N	124.09W
Eureka, Nv., U.S.	142	39.30N	115.57W
Europa, Île ∎	106	22.20S	40.22 E
Europe ⚊[1]	82	50.00N	20.00 E
Evansville	138	37.58N	87.33W
Everest, Mount ⋀	112	27.59N	86.56 E
Everglades National Park ♦	130	25.27N	80.53W
Évora	94	38.34N	7.54W
Évreux	92	49.01N	1.09 E
Evrótas ≃	98	36.48N	22.40 E
Évvoia ∎	98	38.34N	23.50 E
Exeter	88	50.43N	3.31W
Exuma Sound ⋃	130	24.15N	76.00W
Eyre North, Lake ⊜	124	28.40S	137.10 E
Eyre Peninsula ➤[1]	124	34.00S	135.45 E
Eyre South, Lake ⊜	124	29.30S	137.20 E
F			
Fada	104	17.14N	21.33 E
Faenza	96	44.17N	11.53 E
Faeroe Islands □[2]	86	62.00N	7.00W
Fairbanks	144	64.51N	147.43W
Fairfield, Ca., U.S.	142	38.14N	122.02W
Fairfield, Oh., U.S.	140	39.20N	84.33W
Fairlie	126	44.06S	170.50 E
Fairmont	140	39.29N	80.08W
Fairview	140	44.43N	84.03W
Fairweather, Mount ⋀	136	58.54N	137.32W
Fais ∎	118	9.46N	140.31 E
Faisalabad	110	31.25N	73.05 E
Falevai	127e	13.55S	171.59W
Falfurrias	128	27.13N	98.08W
Falkland Islands □[2]	134	51.45S	59.00W
Falköping	89	58.10N	13.31 E
Fallon	142	39.28N	118.46W
Fall River	140	41.42N	71.09W
Falun	89	60.36N	15.38 E
Faradofay	106	25.02S	47.00 E
Farāh	110	32.22N	62.07 E
Farewell, Cape ➤	126	40.30S	172.41 E
Fargo	138	46.52N	96.47W
Farmington	138	36.43N	108.13W
Faro	94	37.01N	7.56W
Farquhar Group ∎∎	106	10.10S	51.10 E
Farvel, Kap ➤	136	59.45N	44.00W
Farwell	140	43.50N	84.52W
Fayetteville	138	35.03N	78.52W
Fazzān (Fezzan) ➡[1]	104	26.00N	14.00 E
Feira de Santana	132	12.15S	38.57W
Fenton	140	42.47N	83.42W
Fernando de Noronha, Ilha ∎	132	3.51S	32.25W
Fernandópolis	135	20.16S	50.14W
Fernando Póo → Bioko ∎	104	3.30N	8.40 E
Ferrara	96	44.50N	11.35 E
Fès	104	34.05N	4.57W
Feuilles, Rivière aux ≃	136	58.47N	70.04W
Feyzābād	110	35.01N	58.46 E
Fianarantsoa	106	21.26S	47.05 E
Fichtelberg ⋀	90	50.26N	12.57 E
Figueira da Foz	94	40.09N	8.52W
Figueras	94	42.16N	2.58 E
Fiji □[1]	82	18.00S	175.00W
Filchner Ice Shelf ⋈	85	79.00S	40.00W
Findlay	140	41.02N	83.39W
Finland □[1]	86	64.00N	26.00 E
Finland, Gulf of c	89	60.00N	27.00 E
Firenze (Florence)	96	43.46N	11.15 E
Fitchburg	140	42.35N	71.48W
Fitzroy, Monte (Cerro Chaltel) ⋀	134	49.17S	73.05W
Flagstaff	138	35.11N	111.39W
Flemingsburg	140	38.25N	83.44W
Flensburg	90	54.47N	9.26 E
Flinders Island ∎	124	40.00S	148.00 E
Flinders Range ⚲	122	31.00S	139.00 E
Flin Flon	136	54.46N	101.53W
Flint	140	42.59N	83.45W
Florence → Firenze	96	43.46N	11.15 E
Florencia	132	1.36N	75.36W
Flores ∎	118	8.30S	121.00 E
Flores, Laut (Flores Sea) ▿[2]	118	8.00S	120.00 E
Florianópolis	134	27.35S	48.34W
Florida	130	21.32N	78.14W
Florida □[3]	138	28.00N	82.00W
Florida, Straits of ⋃	130	25.00N	79.45W
Florida Keys ∎∎	138	24.45N	81.00W
Fly ≃	118	8.30S	143.41 E
Focşani	98	45.41N	27.11 E
Foggia	96	41.27N	15.34 E
Folkestone	88	51.05N	1.11 E
Fond du Lac	136	59.19N	107.10W
Fontainebleau	92	48.24N	2.42 E
Fontur ➤	86	66.23N	14.30W
Formiga	135	20.27S	45.25W
Formosa	134	26.11S	58.11W
Forrest	122	30.51S	128.06 E
Forst	90	51.44N	14.39 E
Fortaleza	132	3.43S	38.30W
Fort Chipewyan	136	58.42N	111.08W
Fort-de-France	130	14.36N	61.05W
Fort Fitzgerald	136	59.53N	111.37W
Fort Franklin	136	65.11N	123.46W
Fort Good Hope	136	66.15N	128.38W
Forth, Firth of c[1]	88	56.05N	2.55W
Fort-Lamy → N'Djamena	104	12.07N	15.03 E
Fort Lauderdale	138	26.07N	80.08W
Fort Macleod	136	49.43N	113.25W
Fort McMurray	136	56.44N	111.23W
Fort Myers	130	26.38N	81.52W
Fort Nelson	136	58.49N	122.39W
Fort Norman	136	64.54N	125.34W
Fort Peck Lake ⊜[1]	136	47.45N	106.50W
Fort Reliance	136	62.42N	109.08W
Fort Resolution	136	61.10N	113.40W
Fort Saint John	136	56.15N	120.51W
Fort Simpson	136	61.52N	121.23W
Fort Smith	138	35.23N	94.23W
Fort Stockton	138	30.53N	102.52W

Name	Page No.	Lat.	Long.
Fort Wayne	138	41.07N	85.07W
Fort Worth	138	32.43N	97.19W
Fort Yukon	144	66.34N	145.17W
Foshan	114	23.03N	113.09 E
Fostoria	140	41.09N	83.25W
Foveaux Strait ṵ	126	46.35S	168.00 E
Foxe Basin ᴄ	136	68.25N	77.00W
Fox Islands ɪɪ	144	54.00N	168.00W
Framingham	140	42.16N	71.25W
France □ [1]	86	46.00N	2.00 E
Franceville	106	1.38S	13.35 E
Francistown	106	21.11S	27.32 E
Frankfort	138	38.12N	84.52W
Frankfurt am Main	90	50.07N	8.40 E
Frankfurt an der Oder	90	52.20N	14.33 E
Fraser ≃	136	49.09N	123.12W
Fraserburgh	88	57.42N	2.00W
Fraser Island ɪ	124	25.15S	153.10 E
Fredericia	89	55.35N	9.46 E
Frederick	140	39.24N	77.24W
Fredericksburg, Tx., U.S.	128	30.16N	98.52W
Fredericksburg, Va., U.S.	140	38.18N	77.27W
Fredericton	136	45.58N	66.39W
Frederikshåb	136	62.00N	49.43W
Frederikshavn	89	57.26N	10.32 E
Fredrikstad	89	59.13N	10.57 E
Freels, Cape ⱱ	136	49.15N	53.28W
Freeport, N.Y., U.S.	140	40.39N	73.35W
Freeport, Tx., U.S.	128	28.57N	95.21W
Freer	128	27.52N	98.37W
Freetown	104	8.30N	13.15W
Freiberg	90	50.54N	13.20 E
Freiburg → Fribourg	92	46.48N	7.09 E
Freiburg [im Breisgau]	90	47.59N	7.51 E
Freising	90	48.23N	11.44 E
Fréjus	92	43.26N	6.44 E
French Guiana □ [2]	132	4.00N	53.00W
French Polynesia □ [2]	82	15.00S	140.00W
Fresnillo	128	23.10N	102.53W
Fresno	142	36.44N	119.46W
Fria, Cape ⱱ	106	18.30S	12.01 E
Fribourg (Freiburg)	92	46.48N	7.09 E
Friedrichshafen	90	47.39N	9.28 E
Friesland □ [9]	90	53.00N	5.40 E
Frome, Lake ⊜	124	30.48S	139.48 E
Frostburg	140	39.39N	78.55W
Fuji-san ⌃ [1]	116	35.22N	138.44 E
Fukui	116	36.04N	136.13 E
Fukuoka	116	33.35N	130.24 E
Fukushima	116	37.45N	140.28 E
Fukuyama	116	34.29N	133.22 E
Fulda	90	50.33N	9.41 E
Fulton	140	43.19N	76.25W
Funchal	104	32.38N	16.54W
Furneaux Group ɪɪ	124	40.10S	148.05 E
Fürstenwalde	90	52.21N	14.04 E
Fürth	90	49.28N	10.59 E
Fushun	114	41.52N	123.53 E
Fuzhou	114	26.06N	119.17 E
Fyn ɪ	89	55.20N	10.30 E
G			
Gaalkacyo	108	6.49N	47.23 E
Gabbs	142	38.52N	117.55W
Gabon □ [1]	106	1.00S	11.45 E
Gaborone	106	24.45S	25.55 E
Gabrovo	98	42.52N	25.19 E
Gadsden	138	34.00N	86.00W
Gaferut ɪ	118	9.14N	145.23 E
Gagnon	136	51.53N	68.10W
Gainesville	138	29.39N	82.19W

Name	Page No.	Lat.	Long.
Gairdner, Lake ⊜	122	31.35S	136.00 E
Galán, Cerro ⌃	134	25.55S	66.52W
Galapagos Islands → Colón, Archipiélago de ɪɪ	82	0.30S	90.30W
Galashiels	88	55.37N	2.49W
Galați	98	45.26N	28.03 E
Galicia □ [9]	90	49.50N	21.00 E
Gallarate	96	45.40N	8.47 E
Galle	111	6.02N	80.13 E
Gallipolis	140	38.48N	82.12W
Gällivare	89	67.07N	20.45 E
Galloo Island ɪ	140	43.54N	76.25W
Gallup	138	35.31N	108.44W
Galveston	138	29.17N	94.47W
Galveston Island ɪ	128	29.13N	94.55W
Galway	88	53.16N	9.03W
Gamarra	130	8.20N	73.45W
Gambia □ [1]	104	13.30N	15.30W
Gand → Gent	90	51.03N	3.43 E
Gandía	94	38.58N	0.11W
Ganges (Ganga) (Padma) ≃	112	23.22N	90.32 E
Gangtok	112	27.20N	88.37 E
Ganzhou	114	25.54N	114.55 E
Gao	104	16.16N	0.03W
Garda, Lago di ⊜	96	45.40N	10.41 E
Garden City	138	37.58N	100.52W
Gardēz	112	33.37N	69.07 E
Gardner	140	42.34N	71.59W
Gardnerville	142	38.56N	119.44W
Garies	106	30.30S	18.00 E
Garonne ≃	92	45.02N	0.36W
Garrett	140	41.20N	85.08W
Gary	138	41.35N	87.20W
Gata, Cabo de ⱱ	94	36.43N	2.12W
Gátas, Akrotírion ⱱ	109	34.34N	33.02 E
Gatere, Mount ⌃	127a	7.49S	158.54 E
Gatineau, Parc ♦	140	45.30N	76.05W
Gävle	89	60.40N	17.10 E
Gaziantep	109	37.05N	37.22 E
Gdańsk (Danzig)	90	54.23N	18.40 E
Gdynia	90	54.32N	18.33 E
Gearhart Mountain ⌃	142	42.30N	120.53W
Geelong	122	38.08S	144.21 E
Gejiu	114	23.22N	103.06 E
Gelibolu	98	40.24N	26.40 E
Gelibolu Yarımadası (Gallipoli Peninsula) ⱱ [1]	98	40.20N	26.30 E
General Eugenio A. Garay	132	20.31S	62.08W
General Pinedo	134	27.19S	61.17W
General Roca	134	39.02S	67.35W
Geneva, In., U.S.	140	40.35N	84.57W
Geneva, N.Y., U.S.	140	42.52N	77.00W
Geneva, Lake ⊜	92	46.25N	6.30 E
Genève (Geneva)	92	46.12N	6.09 E
Genk	90	50.58N	5.30 E
Genova (Genoa)	96	44.25N	8.57 E
Genova, Golfo di ᴄ	92	44.10N	8.55 E
Gent (Gand)	90	51.03N	3.43 E
George ≃	136	58.49N	66.10W
Georgetown, On., Can.	140	43.39N	79.55W
George-Town, Cay. Is.	130	19.18N	81.23W
Georgetown, Guy.	132	6.48N	58.10W
George Town (Pinang), Malay.	120	5.25N	100.20 E
Georgetown, Oh., U.S.	140	38.51N	83.54W
Georgetown, Tx., U.S.	128	30.37N	97.40W
Georgia □ [1]	86	42.00N	43.30 E
Georgia □ [3]	138	32.50N	83.15W
Georgian Bay ᴄ	140	45.15N	80.50W
Gera	90	50.52N	12.04 E
Geraldton, Austl.	122	28.46S	114.36 E

Name	Page No.	Lat.	Long.
Geraldton, On., Can.	136	49.44N	86.57W
Gerlachovský Štít ▲	90	49.12N	20.08 E
Germany □¹	86	53.00N	12.00 E
Gerona	94	41.59N	2.49 E
Ghana □¹	104	8.00N	2.00W
Ghanzi	106	21.38S	21.45 E
Gharbīyah, Aṣ-Ṣaḥrā' al- (Western Desert)			
◆²	104	27.00N	27.00 E
Ghardaïa	104	32.31N	3.37 E
Ghazāl, Baḥr al- ≃	104	9.31N	30.25 E
Ghaznī	112	33.33N	68.26 E
Ghazzah (Gaza)	109	31.30N	34.28 E
Gibeon	106	25.09S	17.43 E
Gibraltar	94	36.09N	5.21W
Gibraltar □²	86	36.11N	5.22W
Gibraltar, Strait of (Estrecho de Gibraltar) ᴜ	94	35.57N	5.36W
Gibson Desert ◆²	122	24.30S	126.00 E
Giessen	90	50.35N	8.40 E
Gifu	116	35.25N	136.45 E
Gijón	94	43.32N	5.40W
Gimli	136	50.38N	96.59W
Gironde c¹	92	45.20N	0.45W
Gisborne	126	38.40S	178.01 E
Gizo	127a	8.06S	156.51 E
Gjandza	86	40.40N	46.22 E
Gjirokastra	98	40.05N	20.10 E
Gjoa Haven	136	68.38N	95.57W
Glace Bay	136	46.12N	59.57W
Glacier Bay National Park ◆	144	58.45N	136.30W
Gladwin	140	43.58N	84.29W
Gláma ≃	89	59.12N	10.57 E
Glasgow	88	55.53N	4.15W
Glenns Ferry	142	42.57N	115.18W
Glens Falls	140	43.18N	73.38W
Glittertinden ▲	89	61.39N	8.33 E
Glorieuses, Îles ‖	106	11.30S	47.20 E
Gloucester, Eng., U.K.	88	51.53N	2.14W
Gloucester, Ma., U.S.	140	42.36N	70.39W
Gloversville	140	43.03N	74.20W
Gniezno	90	52.31N	17.37 E
Goa □⁸	111	14.20N	74.00 E
Gobi ◆²	114	43.00N	105.00 E
Godāvari ≃	111	17.00N	81.45 E
Godhavn	136	69.15N	53.33W
Godthåb	82	64.11N	51.44W
Godwin Austen → K2 ▲	112	35.53N	76.30 E
Goiânia	132	16.40S	49.16W
Gökçeada ‖	98	40.10N	25.50 E
Gómez Palacio	128	25.34N	103.30W
Gonaïves	130	19.27N	72.41W
Gonâve, Golfe de la c	130	19.00N	73.30W
Gonâve, Île de la ‖	130	18.51N	73.03W
Gonder	108	12.40N	37.30 E
Good Hope, Cape of ≻	106	34.24S	18.30 E
Good Hope Mountain ▲	136	51.09N	124.10W
Gooding	142	42.56N	114.42W
Goodland	138	39.21N	101.42W
Gorakhpur	112	26.45N	83.22 E
Gore, Eth.	108	8.08N	35.33 E
Gore, N.Z.	126	46.06S	168.58 E
Gorgān	86	36.50N	54.29 E
Gorki → Nižnij Novgorod	100	56.20N	44.00 E
Gorontalo	118	0.33N	123.03 E
Göteborg (Gothenburg)	89	57.43N	11.58 E
Gotland ‖	89	57.30N	18.33 E
Göttingen	90	51.32N	9.55 E
Gouin, Réservoir ⊜¹	136	48.38N	74.54W
Governador Valadares	132	18.51S	41.56W
Gowanda	140	42.27N	78.56W
Goya	134	29.08S	59.16W
Graaff-Reinet	106	32.14S	24.32 E
Gracias a Dios, Cabo ≻	130	15.00N	83.10W
Grafton	122	29.41S	152.56 E
Grampian Mountains ≮	88	56.45N	4.00W
Granada, Nic.	130	11.56N	85.57W
Granada, Spain	94	37.13N	3.41W
Granby	140	45.24N	72.44W
Gran Canaria ‖	104	28.00N	15.36W
Gran Chaco ≃	134	23.00S	60.00W
Grand Bahama ‖	130	26.38N	78.25W
Grand Bank	136	47.06N	55.46W
Grand Bend	140	43.15N	81.45W
Grande ≃	135	19.52S	50.20W
Grande, Bahía c³	134	50.45S	68.45W
Grande, Ilha ‖	135	23.09S	44.14W
Grande, Rio (Bravo del Norte) ≃	138	25.55N	97.09W
Grand Erg de Bilma ◆²	104	18.30N	14.00 E
Grand Erg Occidental ◆²	104	30.30N	0.30 E
Grand Erg Oriental ◆²	104	30.30N	7.00 E
Grande-Terre ‖	130	16.20N	61.25W
Grand Forks, B.C., Can.	136	49.02N	118.27W
Grand Forks, N.D., U.S.	138	47.55N	97.01W
Grand Island	138	40.55N	98.20W
Grand Junction	138	39.03N	108.33W
Grand Rapids, Mb., Can.	136	53.08N	99.20W
Grand Rapids, Mi., U.S.	140	42.58N	85.40W
Grand-Saint-Bernard, Tunnel du ◆⁵	92	45.51N	7.11 E
Grand Teton ▲	138	43.44N	110.48W
Grand Turk	130	21.28N	71.08W
Granollers	94	41.37N	2.18 E
Grants Pass	142	42.26N	123.19W
Grantsville	140	38.55N	81.05W
Gravenhurst	140	44.55N	79.22W
Grayling	140	44.39N	84.42W
Graz	90	47.05N	15.27 E
Great Abaco ‖	130	26.28N	77.05W
Great Artesian Basin ≃¹	124	25.00S	143.00 E
Great Astrolabe Reef ◆²	127c	18.52S	178.31 E
Great Australian Bight c³	122	35.00S	130.00 E
Great Barrier Island ‖	126	36.10S	175.25 E
Great Barrier Reef ◆²	122	18.00S	145.50 E
Great Basin ≃¹	138	40.00N	117.00W
Great Bear Lake ⊜	136	66.00N	120.00W
Great Channel ᴜ	120	6.25N	94.20 E
Great Dividing Range ≮	122	25.00S	147.00 E
Greater Antilles ‖	130	20.00N	74.00W
Greater Sunda Islands ‖	118	2.00S	110.00 E
Great Exuma ‖	138	23.32N	75.50W
Great Falls	138	47.30N	111.17W
Great Himalaya Range ≮	112	29.00N	83.00 E
Great Inagua ‖	130	21.05N	73.18W
Great Indian Desert (Thar Desert) ◆²	112	28.00N	72.00 E
Great Karroo ≮¹	106	32.25S	22.40 E
Great Salt Lake ⊜	138	41.10N	112.30W
Great Salt Lake Desert ◆²	142	40.40N	113.30W
Great Sandy Desert ◆², Austl.	122	21.30S	125.00 E

Name	Page No.	Lat.	Long.
Great Sandy Desert			
◆², Or., U.S.	142	43.35N	120.15W
Great Slave Lake ⊜	136	61.30N	114.00W
Great Victoria Desert			
◆²	122	28.30S	127.45 E
Great Yarmouth	88	52.37N	1.44 E
Gréboun, Mont ▲	104	20.00N	8.35 E
Greece □¹	86	39.00N	22.00 E
Green Bay	138	44.31N	88.01W
Greenfield	140	42.35N	72.36W
Greenland □²	82	70.00N	40.00W
Greenland Sea ▼²	84	77.00N	1.00W
Green Mountains ✗	140	43.45N	72.45W
Greenock	88	55.57N	4.45W
Greensboro	138	36.04N	79.47W
Greensburg	140	40.18N	79.32W
Greenville, Mi., U.S.	140	43.10N	85.15W
Greenville, S.C., U.S.	138	34.51N	82.23W
Greenville, Tx., U.S.	138	33.08N	96.06W
Greenwood	138	33.30N	90.10W
Greifswald	90	54.05N	13.23 E
Grenada □¹	130	12.07N	61.40W
Grenoble	92	45.10N	5.43 E
Greymouth	126	42.28S	171.12 E
Grey Range ✗	124	27.00S	143.35 E
Grimsby	88	53.35N	0.05W
Grodno	100	53.41N	23.50 E
Groningen	90	53.13N	6.33 E
Groote Eylandt I	122	14.00S	136.40 E
Grosseto	96	42.46N	11.08 E
Grossglockner ▲	90	47.04N	12.42 E
Grove City	140	41.09N	80.05W
Groznyj	86	43.20N	45.42 E
Grudziądz	90	53.29N	18.45 E
Guadalajara, Mex.	128	20.40N	103.20W
Guadalajara, Spain	94	40.38N	3.10W
Guadalcanal I	127a	9.32S	160.12 E
Guadalquivir ≃	94	36.47N	6.22W
Guadalupe	128	25.41N	100.15W
Guadalupe Peak ▲	128	31.50N	104.52W
Guadeloupe □²	130	16.15N	61.35W
Guadiana ≃	94	37.14N	7.22W
Guam □²	118	13.28N	144.47 E
Guanajuato	128	21.01N	101.15W
Guangzhou (Canton)	114	23.06N	113.16 E
Guantánamo	130	20.08N	75.12W
Guaratinguetá	135	22.49S	45.13W
Guardafui, Cape ⌐	108	11.48N	51.22 E
Guatemala	130	14.38N	90.31W
Guatemala □¹	130	15.30N	90.15W
Guayaquil	132	2.10S	79.50W
Guayaquil, Golfo de c	132	3.00S	80.30W
Guaymas	128	27.56N	110.54W
Gubkin	86	51.18N	37.32 E
Guelma	96	36.28N	7.26 E
Guernsey □²	92	49.28N	2.35W
Guildford	88	51.14N	0.35W
Guilin	114	25.11N	110.09 E
Guinea □¹	104	11.00N	10.00W
Guinea, Gulf of c	104	2.00N	2.30 E
Guinea-Bissau □¹	104	12.00N	15.00W
Güines	130	22.50N	82.02W
Güiria	130	10.34N	62.18W
Guiyang	114	26.35N	106.43 E
Gujarat □³	112	22.00N	72.00 E
Gujrānwāla	110	32.26N	74.33 E
Gujrāt	110	32.34N	74.05 E
Gulfport	128	30.22N	89.05W
Guntūr	111	16.18N	80.27 E
Guyana □¹	132	5.00N	59.00W
Gwalior	112	26.13N	78.10 E
Gwanda	106	20.57S	29.01 E
Gweru	106	19.27S	29.49 E
Gydanskaja Guba c	102	71.20N	76.30 E
Gyöngyös	90	47.47N	19.56 E
Győr	90	47.42N	17.38 E

Name	Page No.	Lat.	Long.
H			
Haarlem	90	52.23N	4.38 E
Haast	126	43.53S	169.03 E
Hachinohe	116	40.30N	141.29 E
Hachiōji	116	35.39N	139.20 E
Hadera	109	32.26N	34.55 E
Ha Dong	120	20.58N	105.46 E
Haḍūr Shu'ayb ▲	108	15.18N	43.59 E
Hagerstown	140	39.37N	77.45W
Ha Giang	120	22.50N	104.59 E
Haikou	114	20.06N	110.21 E
Hainan □⁴	114	19.00N	109.30 E
Hainan Dao I	120	19.00N	109.30 E
Hai Phong	120	20.52N	106.41 E
Haiti □¹	130	19.00N	72.25W
Hakodate	116a	41.45N	140.43 E
Halab (Aleppo)	109	36.12N	37.10 E
Haleakala Crater ▲⁶	143	20.43N	156.13W
Halifax	136	44.39N	63.36W
Halle	90	51.29N	11.58 E
Hallowell	140	44.17N	69.47W
Halls Creek	122	18.16S	127.46 E
Halmahera I	118	1.00N	128.00 E
Halmstad	89	56.39N	12.50 E
Haltiatunturi ▲	89	69.18N	21.16 E
Hamadān	108	34.48N	48.30 E
Ḥamāh	109	35.08N	36.45 E
Hamamatsu	116	34.42N	137.44 E
Hamar	89	60.48N	11.06 E
Hamburg	90	53.33N	9.59 E
Hämeenlinna	89	61.00N	24.27 E
Hameln	90	52.06N	9.21 E
Hamhŭng	114	39.54N	127.32 E
Hamilton, Ber.	138	32.17N	64.46W
Hamilton, On., Can.	136	43.15N	79.51W
Hamilton, N.Z.	126	37.47S	175.17 E
Hamilton, Oh., U.S.	140	39.23N	84.33W
Hammamet, Golfe de			
c	96	36.05N	10.40 E
Hammam Lif	96	36.44N	10.20 E
Hammerfest	89	70.40N	23.42 E
Hammond	128	30.30N	90.27W
Handan	114	36.37N	114.29 E
Hangzhou	114	30.15N	120.10 E
Hannover	90	52.24N	9.44 E
Ha Noi	120	21.02N	105.51 E
Hanover	140	39.48N	76.59W
Hanzhong	114	32.59N	107.11 E
Happy Valley-Goose			
Bay	136	53.20N	60.25W
Harare	106	17.50S	31.03 E
Harbin	114	45.45N	126.41 E
Hardangerfjorden c²	89	60.10N	6.00 E
Harer	108	9.18N	42.08 E
Hargeysa	108	9.30N	44.03 E
Harlingen	128	26.11N	97.41W
Harney Basin ≝¹	142	43.15N	120.40W
Härnösand	89	62.38N	17.56 E
Harrisburg	140	40.16N	76.53W
Harrison, Cape ⌐	136	54.55N	57.55W
Harrisonburg	140	38.26N	78.52W
Harrisville, Mi., U.S.	140	44.39N	83.17W
Harrisville, N.Y., U.S.	140	43.35N	75.31W
Harstad	89	68.46N	16.30 E
Hartford	140	41.46N	72.41W
Harts ≃	106	28.24S	24.17 E
Haryana □³	112	29.20N	76.20 E
Haskovo	98	41.56N	25.33 E
Hastings, N.Z.	126	39.38S	176.51 E
Hastings, Eng., U.K.	88	50.51N	0.36 E
Hattiesburg	138	31.19N	89.17W
Hat Yai	120	7.01N	100.28 E
Haugesund	89	59.25N	5.18 E
Havana			
→ La Habana	130	23.08N	82.22W

Name	Page No.	Lat.	Long.	Name	Page No.	Lat.	Long.
Havelock	140	44.26N	77.53W	Homer	144	59.39N	151.33W
Haverhill	140	42.46N	71.04W	Honduras □[1]	130	15.00N	86.30W
Havre-Saint-Pierre	136	50.14N	63.36W	Honduras, Gulf of c	130	16.10N	87.50W
Hawaii □[3]	143	20.00N	157.45W	Hønefoss	89	60.10N	10.18 E
Hawaii I	143	19.30N	155.30W	Honesdale	140	41.34N	75.15W
Hawaiian Islands II	82	24.00N	167.00W	Hon Gai	120	20.57N	107.05 E
Hawera	126	39.35S	174.17 E	Hong Kong	114	22.15N	114.10 E
Hawick	88	55.25N	2.47W	Honguedo, Détroit d'			
Hawke Bay c	126	39.20S	177.30 E	⋃	136	49.15N	64.00W
Hawthorne	142	38.31N	118.37W	Honiara	127a	9.26S	159.57 E
Hay	122	34.30S	144.51 E	Honolulu	143	21.18N	157.51W
Hayden Peak ∧	142	42.59N	116.39W	Honshū I	116	36.00N	138.00 E
Hayrabolu	98	41.12N	27.06 E	Hood, Mount ∧	138	45.23N	121.41W
Hay River	136	60.51N	115.40W	Hooghly ⋍	112	21.56N	88.04 E
Hays	138	38.52N	99.19W	Hoonah	144	58.07N	135.26W
Hazleton	140	40.57N	75.58W	Hooper Bay	144	61.31N	166.06W
Hearst	136	49.41N	83.40W	Hoover Dam ◆ [6]	142	36.00N	114.27W
Hebrides II	86	57.00N	6.30W	Hopedale	136	55.28N	60.13W
Hebron	136	58.12N	62.38W	Hormuz, Strait of ⋃	108	26.34N	56.15 E
Hecate Strait ⋃	136	53.00N	131.00W	Horn, Cape			
Hefa (Haifa)	109	32.50N	35.00 E	→ Hornos, Cabo de			
Hefei	114	31.51N	117.17 E	⅄	134	55.59S	67.16W
Hegang	114	47.24N	130.17 E	Hornell	140	42.19N	77.39W
Heidelberg	90	49.25N	8.43 E	Hornos, Cabo de (Cape			
Heidenheim	90	49.01N	10.44 E	Horn) ⅄	134	55.59S	67.16W
Heilbronn	90	49.08N	9.13 E	Horqin Youyi Qianqi	114	46.05N	122.05 E
Heilongjiang (Amur) ⋍	102	52.56N	141.10 E	Hospitalet	94	41.22N	2.08 E
Helena	138	46.35N	112.02W	Hot Springs National			
Helen Island I	118	2.58N	131.49 E	Park	138	34.30N	93.04W
Hellín	94	38.31N	1.41W	Houghton Lake	140	44.18N	84.45W
Helmand ⋍	110	31.12N	61.34 E	Houston	138	29.45N	95.21W
Helmsdale	88	58.07N	3.40W	Howard City	140	43.23N	85.28W
Helsingborg	89	56.03N	12.42 E	Howe, Cape ⅄	122	37.31S	149.59 E
Helsinki (Helsingfors)	89	60.10N	24.58 E	Howell	140	42.36N	83.55W
Hengyang	114	26.51N	112.30 E	Howland	140	45.14N	68.39W
Henzada	120	17.38N	95.28 E	Howrah	112	22.35N	88.20 E
Herāt	110	34.20N	62.07 E	Hradec Králové	90	50.12N	15.50 E
Hereford	88	52.04N	2.43W	Hranice	90	49.33N	17.44 E
Herford	90	52.06N	8.40 E	Hsinchu	114	24.48N	120.58 E
Hermosillo	128	29.04N	110.58W	Hsinkao Shan ∧	114	23.28N	120.57 E
Herning	89	56.08N	8.59 E	Hua Hin	120	12.34N	99.58 E
Hibbing	138	47.25N	92.56W	Huainan	114	32.40N	117.00 E
Hidalgo del Parral	128	26.56N	105.40W	Huallanca	132	8.49S	77.52W
Hilo	143	19.43N	155.05W	Huambo	106	12.44S	15.47 E
Himachal Pradesh □[8]	112	32.00N	77.00 E	Huancayo	132	12.04S	75.14W
Himalayas ⋌	112	28.00N	84.00 E	Huang (Hwang Ho) ⋍	114	37.32N	118.19 E
Himeji	116	34.49N	134.42 E	Huangshi	114	30.13N	115.05 E
Hims (Homs)	109	34.44N	36.43 E	Huánuco	132	9.55S	76.14W
Hindu Kush ⋌	112	36.00N	71.30 E	Huaras	132	9.32S	77.32W
Hinganghāt	111	20.34N	78.50 E	Huascarán, Nevado ∧	132	9.07S	77.37W
Hinnøya I	89	68.30N	16.00 E	Huasco	134	28.28S	71.14W
Hinton	136	53.25N	117.34W	Hudiksvall	89	61.44N	17.07 E
Hirosaki	116	40.35N	140.28 E	Hudson	140	42.15N	73.47W
Hiroshima	116	34.24N	132.27 E	Hudson ⋍	140	40.42N	74.02W
Hispaniola I	130	19.00N	71.00W	Hudson Bay	136	52.52N	102.25W
Hitachi	116	36.36N	140.39 E	Hudson Bay c	136	60.00N	86.00W
Hjørring	89	57.28N	9.59 E	Hudson Strait ⋃	136	62.30N	72.00W
Hobart	122	42.53S	147.19 E	Hue	120	16.28N	107.36 E
Hobbs	128	32.42N	103.08W	Huehuetenango	130	15.20N	91.28W
Hochalmspitze ∧	90	47.01N	13.19 E	Huelva	94	37.16N	6.57W
Hochschwab ∧	90	47.37N	15.09 E	Huesca	94	42.08N	0.25W
Hódmezővásárhely	90	46.25N	20.20 E	Hughenden	122	20.51S	144.12 E
Höfu	116	34.03N	131.34 E	Huixtla	128	15.09N	92.28W
Hohe Tauern ⋌	90	47.10N	12.30 E	Hull	140	45.26N	75.43W
Hohhot	114	40.51N	111.40 E	Humboldt ⋍	142	40.02N	118.31W
Hokitika	126	42.43S	170.58 E	Humboldt, Mont ∧	127b	21.53S	166.25 E
Hokkaidō I	116a	44.00N	143.00 E	Humphreys Peak ∧	138	35.20N	111.40W
Holbrook	138	34.54N	110.09W	Hunedoara	98	45.45N	22.54 E
Holden	140	37.49N	82.03W	Hungary □[1]	86	47.00N	20.00 E
Holguín	130	20.53N	76.15W	Hunkurāb, Ra's ⅄	109	24.34N	35.10 E
Hollister	142	36.51N	121.24W	Huntington	140	38.25N	82.26W
Holstebro	89	56.21N	8.38 E	Huntly	88	57.27N	2.47W
Holy Cross	144	62.12N	159.47W	Huntsville, On., Can.	140	45.20N	79.13W
Holyhead	88	53.19N	4.38W	Huntsville, Al., U.S.	138	34.43N	86.35W
Holyoke	140	42.12N	72.37W	Huntsville, Tx., U.S.	128	30.43N	95.33W
Hombori Tondo ∧	104	15.16N	1.40W	Huron, Lake ⊜	138	44.30N	82.15W

Name	Page No.	Lat.	Long.
Hutchinson	138	38.03N	97.55W
Hvannadalshnúkur ▲	86	64.01N	16.41W
Hwange	106	18.22S	26.29 E
Hwang Ho			
→ Huang ≃	114	37.32N	118.19 E
Hyannis	140	41.39N	70.17W
Hyde Park	140	41.47N	73.56W
Hyderābād, India	111	17.23N	78.29 E
Hyderābād, Pak.	110	25.22N	68.22 E
Hyères	92	43.07N	6.07 E
Hyvinkää	89	60.38N	24.52 E

I

Name	Page No.	Lat.	Long.
Ialomița ≃	98	44.42N	27.51 E
Iași	98	47.10N	27.35 E
Ibadan	104	7.17N	3.30 E
Ibagué	132	4.27N	75.14W
Ibapah Peak ▲	142	39.50N	113.55W
Ibérico, Sistema ↗	94	41.00N	2.30W
Ibiza I	94	39.00N	1.25 E
Ica	132	14.04S	75.42W
Içá (Putumayo) ≃	132	3.07S	67.58W
Iceland □¹	86	65.00N	18.00W
Ich Bogd Uul ↗	114	44.55N	100.20 E
Idaho □³	138	45.00N	115.00W
Idaho Falls	138	43.28N	112.02W
Ídhi Óros ▲	98	35.18N	24.43 E
Iforas, Adrar des ↗	104	20.00N	2.00 E
Iglesias	96	39.19N	8.32 E
Igloolik	136	69.24N	81.49W
Iguala	128	18.21N	99.32W
Iguéla	106	1.55S	9.19 E
Iguîdi, 'Erg ⇌⁸	104	26.35N	5.40W
Ijill, Kediet ▲	104	22.38N	12.33W
IJsselmeer (Zuiderzee)			
⇌²	90	52.45N	5.25 E
Ikaría I	98	37.41N	26.20 E
Ilhéus	132	14.49S	39.02W
Iliamna Lake ◎	144	59.30N	155.00W
Ilion	140	43.00N	75.02W
Illimani, Nevado ▲	132	16.39S	67.48W
Illinois □³	138	40.00N	89.00W
Ilo	132	17.38S	71.20W
Iloilo	118	10.42N	122.34 E
Imabari	116	34.03N	133.00 E
Imperia	96	43.53N	8.03 E
Imperial Valley ⋎	142	32.50N	115.30W
Inari	89	68.54N	27.01 E
Inari ◎	89	69.00N	28.00 E
Inch'ŏn	114	37.28N	126.38 E
India □¹	110	20.00N	77.00 E
Indiana	140	40.37N	79.09W
Indiana □³	138	40.00N	86.15W
Indianapolis	138	39.46N	86.09W
Indian Ocean ⇌¹	82	10.00S	70.00 E
Indian Peak ▲	142	38.16N	113.53W
Indian Springs	142	36.34N	115.40W
Indigirka ≃	102	70.48N	148.54 E
Indio	142	33.43N	116.12W
Indispensable Strait ⋃	127a	9.00S	160.30 E
Indonesia □¹	118	5.00S	120.00 E
Indore	112	22.43N	75.50 E
Indus ≃	112	24.20N	67.47 E
İnegöl	98	40.05N	29.31 E
Inez	140	37.51N	82.32W
Infiernillo, Presa del			
◎¹	128	18.35N	101.45W
In Guezzam	104	19.32N	5.42 E
Inhambane	106	23.51S	35.29 E
Inharrime	106	24.29S	35.01 E
Injasuti ▲	106	29.09S	29.23 E
Inn (En) ≃	92	48.35N	13.28 E

Name	Page No.	Lat.	Long.
Inner Mongolia			
→ Nei Monggol			
Zizhiqu □⁴	114	43.00N	115.00 E
Innsbruck	90	47.16N	11.24 E
Inowrocław	90	52.48N	18.15 E
In Salah	104	27.12N	2.28 E
Interlaken	92	46.41N	7.51 E
International Falls	138	48.36N	93.24W
Inthanon, Doi ▲	120	18.35N	98.29 E
Inukjuak	136	58.27N	78.06W
Inuvik	136	68.25N	133.30W
Invercargill	126	46.24S	168.21 E
Inverness	88	57.27N	4.15W
Inyangani ▲	106	18.20S	32.50 E
Ioánnina	98	39.40N	20.50 E
Ionia	140	42.59N	85.04W
Ionian Islands			
→ Iónioi Nísoi II	98	38.30N	20.30 E
Ionian Sea ⇌²	86	39.00N	19.00 E
Iónioi Nísoi II	98	38.30N	20.30 E
Iowa □³	138	42.15N	93.15W
Ipeiros ◆¹	98	39.40N	20.50 E
Ipiaú	135	14.08S	39.44W
Ipoh	120	4.35N	101.05 E
Ipswich, Austl.	122	27.36S	152.46 E
Ipswich, Eng., U.K.	88	52.04N	1.10 E
Iqaluit	136	63.44N	68.28W
Iquique	132	20.13S	70.10W
Iquitos	132	3.46S	73.15W
Iráklion	98	35.20N	25.09 E
Iran □¹	82	32.00N	53.00 E
Irapuato	128	20.41N	101.21W
Iraq □¹	108	33.00N	44.00 E
Irbil	86	36.11N	44.01 E
Ireland □¹	86	53.00N	8.00W
Iringa	106	7.46S	35.42 E
Irish Sea ⇌²	88	53.30N	5.20W
Irkutsk	102	52.16N	104.20 E
Iron Gate Reservoir ◎¹	98	44.30N	22.00 E
Iroquois	140	44.51N	75.19W
Irtyš ≃	102	61.04N	68.52 E
Irún	94	43.21N	1.47W
Isabelia, Cordillera ↗	130	13.45N	85.15W
Isar ≃	92	48.49N	12.58 E
Ise	116	34.29N	136.42 E
Isim	102	56.09N	69.27 E
İskenderun	109	36.37N	36.07 E
Islāmābād	110	33.42N	73.10 E
Island Pond	140	44.48N	71.52W
Islas Malvinas			
→ Falkland Islands			
□²	134	51.45S	59.00W
Isle of Man □²	86	54.15N	4.30W
Israel □¹	109	31.30N	35.00 E
İstanbul	98	41.01N	28.58 E
İstanbul Boğazı			
(Bosporus) ⋃	98	41.06N	29.04 E
Itabira	135	19.37S	43.13W
Itabuna	132	14.48S	39.16W
Itajaí	134	26.53S	48.39W
Itajubá	135	22.26S	45.27W
Italy □¹	86	42.50N	12.50 E
Itapetinga	135	15.15S	40.15W
Itapetininga	135	23.36S	48.03W
Itararé	135	24.07S	49.20W
Ithaca	140	42.26N	76.29W
Ituiutaba	132	18.58S	49.28W
Itumbiara	135	18.25S	49.13W
Itzehoe	90	53.55N	9.31 E
Ivano-Frankivs'k	86	48.55N	24.43 E
Ivanovo	100	57.00N	40.59 E
Ivory Coast			
→ Cote d'Ivoire □¹	104	8.00N	5.00W
Iwaki (Taira)	116	37.03N	140.55 E
Iwakuni	116	34.09N	132.11 E
Iwo	104	7.38N	4.11 E

Name	Page No.	Lat.	Long.
Iževsk	86	56.51N	53.14 E
Izmayil	86	45.21N	28.50 E
İzmir	98	38.25N	27.09 E
Izu-shotō II	116	34.30N	139.30 E
J			
Jabalpur	112	23.10N	79.57 E
Jablonec nad Nisou	90	50.44N	15.10 E
Jacarèzinho	135	23.09S	49.59W
Jackson, Mi., U.S.	140	42.14N	84.24W
Jackson, Ms., U.S.	138	32.17N	90.11W
Jacksonville, Fl., U.S.	138	30.19N	81.39W
Jacksonville, Tx., U.S.	128	31.57N	95.16W
Jacobābād	112	28.17N	68.26 E
Jacques-Cartier, Mont			
ᴧ	136	48.59N	65.57W
Jaén, Peru	132	5.42S	78.47W
Jaén, Spain	94	37.46N	3.47W
Jaffna	111	9.40N	80.00 E
Jaipur	112	26.55N	75.49 E
Jakarta	118	6.10S	106.48 E
Jakobstad (Pietarsaari)	89	63.40N	22.42 E
Jakutsk	102	62.13N	129.49 E
Jalālābād	112	34.26N	70.28 E
Jalapa Enríquez	128	19.32N	96.55W
Jamaica □¹	130	18.15N	77.30W
Jamal, Poluostrov ⊁¹	102	70.00N	70.00 E
Jambi	118	1.36S	103.37 E
Jambol	98	42.29N	26.30 E
James Bay c	136	53.30N	80.30W
Jamestown	140	42.05N	79.14W
Jammu	112	32.42N	74.52 E
Jammu and Kashmir			
□²	112	34.00N	76.00 E
Jāmnagar	112	22.28N	70.04 E
Jamshedpur	112	22.48N	86.11 E
Jamsk	102	59.35N	154.10 E
Jamuna ≃	112	23.51N	89.45 E
Japan □¹	114	36.00N	138.00 E
Japan, Sea of ₮²	114	40.00N	135.00 E
Japurá (Caquetá) ≃	132	3.08S	64.46W
Jaqué	130	7.31N	78.10W
Jaroslavl'	100	57.37N	39.52 E
Jarosław	90	50.02N	22.42 E
Jataí	135	17.53S	51.43W
Játiva	94	38.59N	0.31W
Jawa (Java) I	118	7.30S	110.00 E
Jawa, Laut (Java Sea)			
₮²	118	5.00S	110.00 E
Jaya, Puncak ᴧ	118	4.05S	137.11 E
Jayapura			
(Sukarnapura)	118	2.32S	140.42 E
Jefferson City	138	38.34N	92.10W
Jekaterinburg	102	56.51N	60.36 E
Jelec	100	52.37N	38.30 E
Jelenia Góra			
(Hirschberg)	90	50.55N	15.46 E
Jena	90	50.56N	11.35 E
Jenisej ≃	102	71.50N	82.40 E
Jenisejsk	102	58.27N	92.10 E
Jennings	128	30.13N	92.39W
Jequié	132	13.51S	40.05W
Jérémie	130	18.39N	74.07W
Jerevan	86	40.11N	44.30 E
Jerez de la Frontera	94	36.41N	6.08W
Jerome	142	42.43N	114.31W
Jersey □²	92	49.15N	2.10W
Jersey City	140	40.43N	74.04W
Jerusalem			
→ Yerushalayim	109	31.46N	35.14 E
Jessore	112	23.10N	89.13 E
Jezerce ᴧ	98	42.26N	19.49 E
Jhang Maghiāna	110	31.16N	72.19 E
Jhānsi	112	25.26N	78.35 E
Jhelum	112	32.56N	73.44 E
Jiddah	108	21.30N	39.12 E
Jilin	114	43.51N	126.33 E
Jima	108	7.36N	36.50 E
Jinan (Tsinan)	114	36.40N	116.57 E
Jingdezhen	114	29.16N	117.11 E
Jinsha (Yangtze) ≃	120	26.40N	102.55 E
Jinzhou	114	41.07N	121.08 E
Jirjā	104	26.20N	31.53 E
Jixi	114	45.17N	130.59 E
João Pessoa	132	7.07S	34.52W
Jodhpur	112	26.17N	73.02 E
Joensuu	89	62.36N	29.46 E
Johannesburg	106	26.15S	28.00 E
Johnstown	140	40.19N	78.55W
Johor Baharu	120	1.28N	103.45 E
Joinvile	134	26.18S	48.50W
Joliet	138	41.31N	88.04W
Joliette	140	46.01N	73.27W
Jonesboro	138	35.50N	90.42W
Jönköping	89	57.47N	14.11 E
Joplin	138	37.05N	94.30W
Jordan □¹	109	31.00N	36.00 E
Jordan ≃	109	31.46N	35.33 E
Jos	104	9.55N	8.53 E
Joseph, Lac ⊜	136	52.45N	65.15W
Joseph Bonaparte Gulf			
c	122	14.15S	128.30 E
Joškar-Ola	86	56.38N	47.52 E
Juàzeiro do Norte	132	7.12S	39.20W
Jūbā	104	4.51N	31.37 E
Jubba ≃	108	0.12N	42.40 E
Juiz de Fora	132	21.45S	43.20W
Juliaca	132	15.30S	70.08W
Juliana Top ᴧ	132	3.41N	56.32W
Julianehåb	136	60.43N	46.01W
Junction	128	30.29N	99.46W
Juneau	144	58.20N	134.27W
Jungfrau ᴧ	92	46.32N	7.58 E
Junín de los Andes	134	39.56S	71.05W
Jura �	92	46.45N	6.30 E
Juticalpa	130	14.42N	86.15W
Juventud, Isla de la			
(Isla de Pinos) I	130	21.40N	82.50W
Južno-Sachalinsk	102	46.58N	142.42 E
Jylland ⊁¹	89	56.00N	9.15 E
Jyväskylä	89	62.14N	25.44 E
K			
K2 (Qogir Feng) ᴧ	112	35.53N	76.30 E
Kābol	110	34.31N	69.12 E
Kabwe (Broken Hill)	106	14.27S	28.27 E
Kaduna	104	10.33N	7.27 E
Kaédi	104	16.09N	13.30W
Kaesŏng	114	37.59N	126.33 E
Kagoshima	116	31.36N	130.33 E
Kahoolawe I	143	20.33N	156.37W
Kaikoura	126	42.25S	173.41 E
Kailua Kona	143	19.22N	155.59W
Kaipara Harbour c	126	36.25S	174.13 E
Kairouan	96	35.41N	10.07 E
Kaitangata	126	46.18S	169.51 E
Kaiwi Channel ⪙	143	21.15N	157.30W
Kajaani	89	64.14N	27.41 E
Kalahari Desert ➝²	106	24.00S	21.30 E
Kalámai	98	37.04N	22.07 E
Kalasin	120	16.29N	103.30 E
Kalašnikovo	100	57.17N	35.13 E
Kalemie (Albertville)	106	5.56S	29.12 E
Kalgoorlie	122	30.45S	121.28 E
Kalimantan			
→ Borneo I	118	0.30N	114.00 E
Kaliningrad			
(Königsberg)	100	54.43N	20.30 E

Name	Page No.	Lat.	Long.
Kalispell	138	48.11 N	114.18 W
Kalixälven ⇌	89	65.50 N	23.11 E
Kalmar	89	56.40 N	16.22 E
Kaluga	100	54.31 N	36.16 E
Kamália	112	30.44 N	72.39 E
Kamčatka, Poluostrov ⊁[1]	102	56.00 N	160.00 E
Kamen'-na-Obi	102	53.47 N	81.20 E
Kamensk-Ural'skij	102	56.28 N	61.54 E
Kamina	106	8.44 S	25.00 E
Kamloops	136	50.40 N	120.20 W
Kampala	106	0.19 N	32.25 E
Kampen	90	52.33 N	5.54 E
Kâmpóng Cham	120	12.00 N	105.27 E
Kâmpóng Chhnäng	120	12.15 N	104.40 E
Kâmpóng Thum	120	12.42 N	104.54 E
Kâmpôt	120	10.37 N	104.11 E
Kananga (Luluabourg)	106	5.54 S	22.25 E
Kanazawa	116	36.34 N	136.39 E
Kanchanaburi	120	14.01 N	99.32 E
Kandavu I	127c	19.03 S	178.13 E
Kandavu Passage ⋃	127c	18.45 S	178.00 E
Kandy	111	7.18 N	80.38 E
Kane	140	41.39 N	78.48 W
Kangaroo Island I	124	35.50 S	137.06 E
Kangiqsualujjuaq	136	58.32 N	65.54 W
Kangiqsujuaq	136	61.36 N	71.58 W
Kangirsuk	136	60.01 N	70.01 W
Kankakee	138	41.07 N	87.51 W
Kankan	104	10.23 N	9.18 W
Kano	104	12.00 N	8.30 E
Känpur	112	26.28 N	80.21 E
Kansas □[3]	138	38.45 N	98.15 W
Kansas City, Ks., U.S.	138	39.06 N	94.37 W
Kansas City, Mo., U.S.	138	39.05 N	94.34 W
Kansk	102	56.13 N	95.41 E
Kanye	106	24.59 S	25.19 E
Kaohsiung	114	22.38 N	120.17 E
Kaolack	104	14.09 N	16.04 W
Kapfenberg	90	47.26 N	15.18 E
Kaposvár	90	46.22 N	17.47 E
Kapuas ⇌	118	0.25 S	109.40 E
Kapuskasing	136	49.25 N	82.26 W
Karaçaköy	98	41.24 N	28.22 E
Karáchi	110	24.52 N	67.03 E
Karakoram Range ⋌	112	35.30 N	77.00 E
Karamea Bight ⊂[3]	126	41.30 S	171.40 E
Karasburg	106	28.00 S	18.43 E
Karawanken ⋌	96	46.30 N	14.25 E
Karcag	90	47.19 N	20.56 E
Kardhítsa	98	39.21 N	21.55 E
Kărdžali	98	41.39 N	25.22 E
Kariba, Lake ⊜[1]	106	17.00 S	28.00 E
Karigasniemi	89	69.24 N	25.50 E
Karlovac	96	45.29 N	15.34 E
Karlovy Vary	90	50.11 N	12.52 E
Karlskoga	89	59.20 N	14.31 E
Karlskrona	89	56.10 N	15.35 E
Karlsruhe	90	49.03 N	8.24 E
Karlstad	89	59.22 N	13.30 E
Kárpathos I	98	35.40 N	27.10 E
Karskoje More (Kara Sea) ⇥[2]	102	76.00 N	80.00 E
Karviná	90	49.50 N	18.30 E
Kasai (Cassai) ⇌	106	3.06 S	16.57 E
Kasanga	106	8.28 S	31.09 E
Kashi (Kashgar)	114	39.29 N	75.59 E
Kasr, Ra's ⊁	104	18.02 N	38.35 E
Kassalá	104	15.28 N	36.24 E
Kassel	90	51.19 N	9.29 E
Kasugai	116	35.14 N	136.58 E
Kasür	112	31.07 N	74.27 E
Katahdin, Mount ⋀	140	45.55 N	68.55 W
Katerini	98	40.16 N	22.30 E
Katherine	122	14.28 S	132.16 E
Kāthiāwār ⊁[1]	112	22.00 N	71.00 E
Kăthmăndău	112	27.43 N	85.19 E
Katmandu → Kăthmăndău	112	27.43 N	85.19 E
Katowice	90	50.16 N	19.00 E
Kātrīnā, Jabal ⋀	109	28.31 N	33.57 E
Katrineholm	89	59.00 N	16.12 E
Katsina	104	13.00 N	7.32 E
Kattegat ⋃	89	57.00 N	11.00 E
Kauai I	143	22.00 N	159.30 W
Kauai Channel ⋃	143	21.45 N	158.50 W
Kaulakah Channel ⋃	143	22.00 N	159.53 W
Kaunas	100	54.54 N	23.54 E
Kavála	98	40.56 N	24.25 E
Kawasaki	116	35.32 N	139.43 E
Kayes	104	14.27 N	11.26 W
Kayseri	86	38.43 N	35.30 E
Kazakhstan □[1]	86	48.00 N	68.00 E
Kazan'	86	55.49 N	49.08 E
Kazanlăk	98	42.38 N	25.21 E
Kebnekaise ⋀	89	67.53 N	18.33 E
Kecskemét	90	46.54 N	19.42 E
Keele Peak ⋀	136	63.26 N	130.19 W
Keene	140	42.56 N	72.16 W
Keetmanshoop	106	26.36 S	18.08 E
Kefallinía I	98	38.15 N	20.35 E
Keg River	136	57.48 N	117.52 W
Kékes ⋀	90	47.55 N	20.02 E
Kelibia	96	36.51 N	11.06 E
Kelowna	136	49.53 N	119.29 W
Keluang	120	2.02 N	103.19 E
Kemerovo	102	55.20 N	86.05 E
Kemi	89	65.49 N	24.32 E
Kemijoki ⇌	89	65.47 N	24.30 E
Kempten [Allgäu]	90	47.43 N	10.19 E
Kemptville	140	45.01 N	75.38 W
Kenai	144	60.33 N	151.15 W
Kenai Peninsula ⊁[1]	144	60.10 N	150.00 W
Kenhardt	106	29.19 S	21.12 E
Kenora	136	49.47 N	94.29 W
Kent	140	41.09 N	81.21 W
Kentucky □[3]	138	37.30 N	85.15 W
Kentucky ⇌	140	38.40 N	85.09 W
Kenya □[1]	106	1.00 N	38.00 E
Kenya, Mount → Kirinyaga ⋀	106	2.43 N	36.51 E
Kerala □[3]	111	10.00 N	76.30 E
Kerinci, Gunung ⋀	118	1.42 S	101.16 E
Kérkira (Corfu)	98	39.36 N	19.56 E
Kérkira (Corfu) I	98	39.40 N	19.42 E
Kermän	108	30.17 N	57.05 E
Kermit	128	31.51 N	103.05 W
Ket' ⇌	102	58.55 N	81.32 E
Ketchikan	144	55.21 N	131.35 W
Kettering	140	39.41 N	84.10 W
Key West	138	24.33 N	81.46 W
Khadaungnge ⋀	120	18.57 N	94.37 E
Khalkidhikí □[9]	98	40.25 N	23.27 E
Khalkís	98	38.28 N	23.36 E
Khambhāt, Gulf of ⊂	112	21.00 N	72.30 E
Khānābād	112	36.41 N	69.07 E
Khānewāl	112	30.18 N	71.56 E
Khaniá	98	35.31 N	24.02 E
Kharkiv	86	50.00 N	36.15 E
Kharkov → Kharkiv	86	50.00 N	36.15 E
Khartoum → Al-Kharţūm	104	15.36 N	32.32 E
Kherson	86	46.38 N	32.35 E
Khíos	98	38.22 N	26.08 E
Khíos I	98	38.22 N	26.00 E
Kholm	112	36.42 N	67.41 E
Khon Kaen	120	16.26 N	102.50 E
Khulna	112	22.48 N	89.33 E
Khunjerab Pass)(	112	36.52 N	75.27 E
Khyber Pass)(	112	34.05 N	71.10 E
Kiel	90	54.20 N	10.08 E

Name	Page No.	Lat.	Long.
Kielce	90	50.52N	20.37 E
Kieler Bucht c	90	54.35N	10.35 E
Kiev			
→ Kyyiv	86	50.26N	30.31 E
Kigali	106	1.57S	30.04 E
Kikinda	98	45.50N	20.28 E
Kikládhes II	98	37.30N	25.00 E
Kikwit	106	5.02S	18.49 E
Kilauea Crater ± 6	143	19.25N	155.17 W
Kilimanjaro ʌ	106	3.04S	37.22 E
Kilkenny	88	52.39N	7.15 W
Killarney	140	45.58N	81.31 W
Killeen	138	31.07N	97.43 W
Kilmarnock	88	55.36N	4.30 W
Kimberley	106	28.43S	24.46 E
Kimberley Plateau ⤢ 1	122	17.00S	127.00 E
Kimch'aek	114	40.41N	129.12 E
Kinabalu, Gunong ʌ	118	6.05N	116.33 E
Kindersley	136	51.27N	109.10 W
Kindu	106	2.57S	25.56 E
King Island I	124	39.50S	144.00 E
Kingman	142	35.11N	114.03 W
Kings Canyon National			
Park ♦	142	36.48N	118.30 W
King's Lynn	88	52.45N	0.24 E
Kingston, On., Can.	136	44.14N	76.30 W
Kingston, Jam.	130	18.00N	76.48 W
Kingston, N.Z.	126	45.20S	168.42 E
Kingston, N.Y., U.S.	140	41.55N	73.59 W
Kingston upon Hull	88	53.45N	0.20 W
Kingstown	130	13.09N	61.14 W
Kingsville	128	27.30N	97.51 W
Kinshasa			
(Léopoldville)	106	4.18S	15.18 E
Kinyeti ʌ	108	3.57N	32.54 E
Kiparissiakós Kólpos c	98	37.37N	21.24 E
Kira Kira	127a	10.27S	161.55 E
Kirensk	102	57.46N	108.08 E
Kiribati □ 1	82	4.00S	175.00 E
Kirínia	109	35.20N	33.19 E
Kirinyaga ʌ	106	2.43N	36.51 E
Kirkcaldy	88	56.07N	3.10 W
Kırklareli	98	41.44N	27.12 E
Kirksville	138	40.11N	92.34 W
Kirkūk	108	35.28N	44.28 E
Kirkwall	88	58.59N	2.58 W
Kirov	100	54.05N	34.20 E
Kirovohrad	86	48.30N	32.18 E
Kīrthar Range ⤢	112	27.00N	67.10 E
Kiruna	89	67.51N	20.16 E
Kiryū	116	36.24N	139.20 E
Kisangani			
(Stanleyville)	106	0.30N	25.12 E
Kishinev			
→ Chişinău	98	47.00N	28.50 E
Kishiwada	116	34.28N	135.22 E
Kišin'ov			
→ Chişinău	98	47.00N	28.50 E
Kiskörei-víztároló ⊜ 1	90	47.35N	20.40 E
Kiskunfélegyháza	90	46.43N	19.52 E
Kiskunhalas	90	46.26N	19.30 E
Kismaayo	106	0.23S	42.30 E
Kissidougou	104	9.11N	10.06 W
Kita	104	13.03N	9.29 W
Kitakyūshū	116	33.53N	130.50 E
Kitami	116a	43.48N	143.54 E
Kitchener	136	43.27N	80.29 W
Kíthira I	98	36.20N	22.58 E
Kitwe	106	12.49S	28.13 E
Kjustendil	98	42.17N	22.41 E
Kladno	90	50.08N	14.05 E
Klagenfurt	90	46.38N	14.18 E
Klamath ≃	142	41.33N	124.04 W
Klamath Falls	138	42.13N	121.46 W
Klamath Mountains ⤢	142	41.40N	123.20 W
Klarälven ≃	89	59.23N	13.32 E
Klerksdorp	106	26.58S	26.39 E
Klincy	100	52.47N	32.14 E
Kłodzko	90	50.27N	16.39 E
Klondike □ 9	144	63.30N	139.00 W
Kl'učevskaja Sopka,			
Vulkan ʌ 1	102	56.04N	160.38 E
Kneža	98	43.30N	24.05 E
Knoxville	138	35.57N	83.55 W
Kōbe	116	34.41N	135.10 E
København			
(Copenhagen)	89	55.40N	12.35 E
Koblenz	90	50.21N	7.35 E
Kochi, India	110	9.58N	76.15 E
Kōchi, Japan	116	33.33N	133.33 E
Kodiak	144	57.48N	152.23 W
Kodiak Island I	144	57.30N	153.30 W
Koes	106	25.59S	19.08 E
Kōfu	116	35.39N	138.35 E
Kokkola			
(Gamlakarleby)	89	63.50N	23.07 E
Koksoak ≃	136	58.32N	68.10 W
Kola Peninsula			
→ Kol'skij			
Poluostrov ⤢ 1	102	67.30N	37.00 E
Kolhāpur	111	16.42N	74.13 E
Koliganek	144	59.48N	157.25 W
Köln (Cologne)	90	50.56N	6.59 E
Kolovrat, Mount ʌ	127a	9.10S	161.05 E
Kolpaševo	102	58.20N	82.50 E
Kol'skij Poluostrov			
(Kola Peninsula) ⤢ 1	102	67.30N	37.00 E
Kolwezi	106	10.43S	25.28 E
Kolyma ≃	102	69.30N	161.00 E
Komárno	90	47.45N	18.09 E
Komatsu	116	36.24N	136.27 E
Komló	90	46.12N	18.16 E
Kommunizma, Pik			
(Communism Peak)			
ʌ	110	38.57N	72.01 E
Komotiní	98	41.08N	25.25 E
Komsomolec, Ostrov I	102	80.30N	95.00 E
Komsomol'sk-na-Amure	102	50.35N	137.02 E
Kona Coast ± 2	143	19.25N	155.55 W
Koné	127b	21.04S	164.52 E
Kŏng, Kaôh I	120	11.20N	103.00 E
Königsberg			
→ Kaliningrad	100	54.43N	20.30 E
Konin	90	52.13N	18.16 E
Könkämäälven ≃	89	68.29N	22.17 E
Konstanz	90	47.40N	9.10 E
Kontagora	104	10.24N	5.28 E
Konya	86	37.52N	32.31 E
Kor'akskoje Nagorje ⤢	102	62.30N	172.00 E
Korça	98	40.37N	20.46 E
Korea, North □ 1	114	40.00N	127.00 E
Korea, South □ 1	114	36.30N	128.00 E
Korinthiakós Kólpos c	98	38.19N	22.04 E
Kórinthos (Corinth)	98	37.56N	22.56 E
Korolevu	127c	18.13S	177.44 E
Koro Sea ⫪ 2	127c	18.00S	179.50 E
Korsør	89	55.20N	11.09 E
Kortrijk (Courtrai)	90	50.50N	3.16 E
Kos I	98	36.50N	27.10 E
Kosciusko, Mount ʌ	124	36.27S	148.16 E
Košice	90	48.43N	21.15 E
Kosovska Mitrovica	98	42.53N	20.52 E
Kostroma	100	57.46N	40.55 E
Koszalin (Köslin)	90	54.12N	16.09 E
Kota Baharu	120	6.08N	102.15 E
Kota Kinabalu	118	5.59N	116.04 E
Kotel'nyj, Ostrov I	102	75.45N	138.44 E
Kotka	89	60.28N	26.55 E
Kotuj ≃	102	71.55N	102.05 E
Kotzebue Sound ⵡ	144	66.20N	163.00 W
Koussi, Emi ʌ	104	19.50N	18.30 E
Kouvola	89	60.52N	26.42 E

Name	Page No.	Lat.	Long.
Kowloon	114	22.18N	114.10 E
Koyukuk ≃	144	64.56N	157.30W
Koza	117b	26.20N	127.50 E
Kozhikode	111	11.15N	75.46 E
Kra, Isthmus of ≛ [3]	120	10.20N	99.00 E
Krâchéh	120	12.29N	106.01 E
Kragerø	89	58.52N	9.25 E
Kragujevac	98	44.01N	20.55 E
Kraków	90	50.03N	19.58 E
Kraljevo	98	43.43N	20.41 E
Kranj	96	46.15N	14.21 E
Krasnodar	86	45.02N	39.00 E
Krasnojarsk	102	56.01N	92.50 E
Krasnokamsk	86	58.04N	55.48 E
Krasnoural'sk	102	58.21N	60.03 E
Krems an der Donau	90	48.25N	15.36 E
Kričov	100	53.42N	31.43 E
Kristiansand	89	58.10N	8.00 E
Kristianstad	89	56.02N	14.08 E
Kristiansund	89	63.07N	7.45 E
Krìti I	98	35.29N	24.42 E
Kritikón Pélagos ₮ [2]	98	35.46N	23.54 E
Krnov	90	50.05N	17.41 E
Kroonstad	106	27.46S	27.12 E
Kropotkin	102	58.30N	115.17 E
Krung Thep (Bangkok)	120	13.45N	100.31 E
Kruševac	98	43.35N	21.20 E
Kryvyy Rih	86	47.55N	33.21 E
Ksar-el-Kebir	94	35.01N	5.54W
Kuala Lumpur	120	3.10N	101.42 E
Kuala Terengganu	120	5.20N	103.08 E
Kuching	120	1.33N	110.20 E
Kuhmo	89	64.08N	29.31 E
Kujbyšev			
→ Samara, Russia	86	53.12N	50.09 E
Kujbyšev, Russia	102	55.27N	78.19 E
Kula Kangri ᴧ	112	28.03N	90.27 E
Kumagaya	116	36.08N	139.23 E
Kumajri	86	40.48N	43.50 E
Kumamoto	116	32.48N	130.43 E
Kumanovo	98	42.08N	21.43 E
Kumasi	104	6.41N	1.35W
Kumo	104	10.03N	11.13 E
Kumon Range ⋋	120	26.30N	97.15 E
Kunlun Shan ⋋	112	36.30N	88.00 E
Kunming	114	25.05N	102.40 E
Kuopio	89	62.54N	27.41 E
Kupang	118	10.10S	123.35 E
Kupino	102	54.22N	77.18 E
Kurashiki	116	34.35N	133.46 E
Kure	116	34.14N	132.34 E
Kurgan	102	55.26N	65.18 E
Kuril'skije Ostrova			
(Kuril Islands) II	102	46.10N	152.00 E
Kurmuk	104	10.33N	34.17 E
Kursk	86	51.42N	36.12 E
Kuruman	106	27.28S	23.28 E
Kurume	116	33.19N	130.31 E
Kuskokwim ≃	144	60.17N	162.27W
Kûstî	104	13.10N	32.40 E
Kutch, Gulf of C	112	22.36N	69.30 E
Kutno	90	52.15N	19.23 E
Kuwait ◻ [1]	108	29.30N	47.45 E
Kwangju	114	35.09N	126.54 E
Kwekwe	106	18.55S	29.49 E
Kyle of Lochalsh	88	57.17N	5.43W
Kyoga, Lake ⊜	106	1.30N	33.00 E
Kyōto	116	35.00N	135.45 E
Kyrgyzstan ◻ [1]	82	41.00N	75.00 E
Kyūshū I	116	33.00N	131.00 E
Kyyiv (Kiev)	86	50.26N	30.31 E
Kyzyl	102	51.42N	94.27 E

Name	Page No.	Lat.	Long.
L			
Labe (Elbe) ≃	90	53.50N	9.00 E
La Blanquilla I	130	11.51N	64.37W
Labrador ◆ [1]	136	54.00N	62.00W
Labrador City	136	52.57N	66.55W
Labrador Sea ₮ [2]	136	57.00N	53.00W
Labutta	120	16.09N	94.46 E
Laccadive Sea ₮ [2]	111	8.00N	75.00 E
La Ceiba	130	15.47N	86.50W
Lachlan ≃	124	34.21S	143.57 E
La Chorrera	130	8.53N	79.47W
Lac la Biche	136	54.46N	111.58W
Lac-Mégantic	140	45.36N	70.53W
Laconia	140	43.31N	71.28W
La Coruña	94	43.22N	8.23W
La Crosse	138	43.48N	91.14W
Ladožskoje Ozero			
(Lake Ladoga) ⊜	89	61.00N	31.30 E
Ladysmith	106	28.34S	29.45 E
Lafayette	138	30.13N	92.01W
Laghouat	104	33.50N	2.59 E
Lagos	104	6.27N	3.24 E
Lagrange	140	41.39N	85.25W
La Gran Sabana ≏	132	5.30N	61.30W
La Guajira, Península			
de ⋗ [1]	132	12.00N	71.40W
Laguna Beach	142	33.32N	117.46W
Lagunillas	132	19.38S	63.43W
La Habana (Havana)	130	23.08N	82.22W
Lahaina	143	20.52N	156.40W
Lahore	110	31.35N	74.18 E
Lahti	89	60.58N	25.40 E
Laingsburg	106	33.11S	20.51 E
Lake Charles	138	30.13N	93.13W
Lake Harbour	136	62.51N	69.53W
Lake Havasu City	142	34.29N	114.19W
Lake Placid	140	44.16N	73.58W
Lake Pleasant	140	43.28N	74.25W
Lakeview	142	42.11N	120.20W
Lakonikós Kólpos C	98	36.25N	22.37 E
Lakshadweep ◻ [3]	111	10.00N	73.00 E
Lakshadweep II	111	10.00N	73.00 E
La Loche	136	56.29N	109.27W
La Mancha ◆ [1]	94	39.05N	3.00W
La Manche (English			
Channel) Ⴑ	92	50.20N	1.00W
Lamap	127b	16.26S	167.43 E
Lambaréné	106	0.42S	10.13 E
Lambasa	127c	16.26S	179.24 E
Lambert's Bay	106	32.05S	18.17 E
Lamesa	128	32.44N	101.57W
Lamía	98	38.54N	22.26 E
Lamont	142	35.15N	118.54W
Lampang	120	18.18N	99.31 E
Lamphun	120	18.35N	99.01 E
Lamu	106	2.16S	40.54 E
Lanai I	143	20.50N	156.55W
Lanai City	143	20.49N	156.55W
Lancaster, On., Can.	140	45.15N	74.30W
Lancaster, Eng., U.K.	88	54.03N	2.48W
Lancaster, Ca., U.S.	142	34.41N	118.08W
Lancaster, Oh., U.S.	140	39.43N	82.36W
Lancaster, Pa., U.S.	140	40.02N	76.18W
Lancaster Sound Ⴑ	136	74.13N	84.00W
Lanchow			
→ Lanzhou	114	36.03N	103.41 E
Land's End ⋗	88	50.03N	5.44W
Landshut	90	48.33N	12.09 E
Langenhagen	90	52.27N	9.44 E
Langsa	120	4.28N	97.58 E
L'Annonciation	140	46.25N	74.52W
Lansing	140	42.43N	84.33W
Lanzhou	114	36.03N	103.41 E
Laos ◻ [1]	118	18.00N	105.00 E
La Palma	130	8.25N	78.09W

Name	Page No.	Lat.	Long.
La Paragua	132	6.50N	63.20W
La Paz, Bol.	132	16.30S	68.09W
La Paz, Mex.	128	24.10N	110.18W
La Perouse Strait			
(Sōya-kaikyō) ⊔	116a	45.45N	142.00 E
La Piedad [Cavadas]	128	20.21N	102.00W
Lapland ◆¹	89	68.00N	25.00 E
La Plata, Arg.	134	34.55S	57.57W
La Plata, Md., U.S.	140	38.31N	76.58W
Lappeenranta	89	61.04N	28.11 E
Laptevych, More			
(Laptev Sea) ⊤²	102	76.00N	126.00 E
La Quiaca	134	22.06S	65.37W
L'Aquila	96	42.22N	13.22 E
Larache	94	35.12N	6.10W
Laramie	138	41.18N	105.35W
Laredo	138	27.30N	99.30W
La Rioja	134	29.26S	66.51W
Lárisa	98	39.38N	22.25 E
Lārkāna	112	27.33N	68.13 E
La Rochelle	92	46.10N	1.10W
La Roche-sur-Yon	92	46.40N	1.26W
La Ronge	136	55.06N	105.17W
La Sarre	136	48.48N	79.12W
Las Cruces	128	32.18N	106.46W
La Serena	134	29.54S	71.16W
Las Flores	134	36.03S	59.07W
Las Lomitas	134	24.42S	60.36W
Las Minas, Cerro ⋏	130	14.33N	88.39W
Las Palmas de Gran			
Canaria	104	28.06N	15.24W
La Spezia	96	44.07N	9.50 E
Lassen Peak ⋏¹	142	40.29N	121.31W
Las Vegas	142	36.10N	115.08W
La Tortuga, Isla I	130	10.56N	65.20W
La Tuque	136	47.26N	72.47W
Lātūr	111	18.24N	76.35 E
Latvia □¹	86	57.00N	25.00 E
Lauchhammer	90	51.30N	13.47 E
Lau Group II	127c	18.20S	178.30W
Launceston	122	41.26S	147.08 E
La Union	130	13.20N	87.57W
Laurel	128	31.41N	89.07W
Lausanne	92	46.31N	6.38 E
Lautoka	127c	17.37S	177.27 E
Laval, P.Q., Can.	140	45.33N	73.44W
Laval, Fr.	92	48.04N	0.46W
Lavapié, Punta ≻	134	37.09S	73.35W
La Vela, Cabo de ≻	130	12.13N	72.11W
Lavras	135	21.14S	45.00W
Lawrenceburg	140	39.05N	84.51W
Lawton	138	34.36N	98.23W
Lead	138	44.21N	103.45W
Leamington	140	42.03N	82.36W
Lebanon, N.H., U.S.	140	43.38N	72.15W
Lebanon, Pa., U.S.	140	40.20N	76.24W
Lebanon □¹	109	33.50N	35.50 E
Lecce	96	40.23N	18.11 E
Lecco	96	45.51N	9.23 E
Leeds	88	53.50N	1.35W
Leeuwarden	90	53.12N	5.46 E
Leeward Islands II	130	17.00N	63.00W
Legnica (Liegnitz)	90	51.13N	16.09 E
Le Havre	92	49.30N	0.08 E
Lehighton	140	40.50N	75.42W
Leicester	88	52.38N	1.05W
Leinster □⁹	88	53.05N	7.00W
Leipzig	90	51.19N	12.20 E
Leland	140	45.01N	85.45W
Lemanmanu Mission	127a	5.02S	154.35 E
Le Mans	92	48.00N	0.12 E
Leme	135	22.12S	47.24W
Lemesós (Limassol)	109	34.40N	33.02 E
Lemmon	138	45.56N	102.09W
Lena ≏	102	72.25N	126.40 E
Lenakel	127b	19.32S	169.16 E
Leningrad			
→ Sankt-Peterburg	100	59.55N	30.15 E
Leninsk-Kuzneckij	102	54.38N	86.10 E
Lens	92	50.26N	2.50 E
Leoben	90	47.23N	15.06 E
León, Nic.	130	12.26N	86.53W
León, Spain	94	42.36N	5.34W
León [de los Aldamas]	128	21.07N	101.40W
Leonora	122	28.53S	121.20 E
Leopoldina	135	21.32S	42.38W
Lérida	94	41.37N	0.37 E
Lerwick	88	60.09N	1.09W
Lesbos			
→ Lésvos I	98	39.10N	26.20 E
Les Cayes	130	18.12N	73.45W
Leskovac	98	42.59N	21.57 E
Lesotho □¹	106	29.30S	28.30 E
Lesozavodsk	102	45.28N	133.27 E
Lesser Antilles II	130	15.00N	61.00W
Lesser Sunda Islands II	118	9.00S	120.00 E
Lésvos I	98	39.10N	26.20 E
Leszno	90	51.51N	16.35 E
Letea, Ostrovul I	98	45.20N	29.20 E
Lethbridge	136	49.42N	112.50W
Lethem	132	3.23N	59.48W
Leticia	132	4.09S	69.57W
Levanger	89	63.45N	11.18 E
Leverkusen	90	51.03N	6.59 E
Levin	126	40.37S	175.17 E
Levkás I	98	38.39N	20.27 E
Lewis, Isle of I	88	58.10N	6.40W
Lewiston, Id., U.S.	138	46.25N	117.01W
Lewiston, Me., U.S.	140	44.06N	70.12W
Lewistown	140	40.35N	77.34W
Lexington, Ky., U.S.	140	38.02N	84.30W
Lexington, Ma., U.S.	140	42.26N	71.13W
Lexington Park	140	38.16N	76.27W
Leyte I	118	10.50N	124.50 E
Leyte Gulf c	118	10.50N	125.25 E
Lhasa	114	29.40N	91.09 E
Lianyungang	114	34.39N	119.16 E
Liaoyuan	114	42.54N	125.07 E
Liberal	138	37.02N	100.55W
Liberec	90	50.46N	15.03 E
Liberia	130	10.38N	85.27W
Liberia □¹	104	6.00N	10.00W
Libertad	130	8.20N	69.37W
Lībīyah, Aṣ-Ṣaḥrā' al-			
(Libyan Desert) ◆²	104	24.00N	25.00 E
Libreville	106	0.23N	9.27 E
Libya □¹	104	27.00N	17.00 E
Licata	96	37.05N	13.56 E
Lichinga	106	13.18S	35.14 E
Liechtenstein □¹	86	47.09N	9.35 E
Liège	90	50.38N	5.34 E
Lier	90	51.08N	4.34 E
Liezen	90	47.35N	14.15 E
Lifou, Île I	127b	20.53S	167.13 E
Ligurian Sea ⊤²	92	43.00N	8.00 E
Lihue	143	21.58N	159.22W
Likasi (Jadotville)	106	10.59S	26.44 E
Lille	92	50.38N	3.04 E
Lilongwe	106	13.59S	33.44 E
Lima, Peru	132	12.03S	77.03W
Lima, Oh., U.S.	140	40.44N	84.06W
Limeira	135	22.34S	47.24W
Limerick	88	52.40N	8.38W
Límnos I	98	39.54N	25.21 E
Limoges	92	45.50N	1.16 E
Limón, C.R.	130	10.00N	83.02W
Limón, Hond.	130	15.52N	85.33W
Limpopo ≏	106	25.15S	33.30 E
Linares	94	38.05N	3.38W
Lincoln, Eng., U.K.	88	53.14N	0.33W
Lincoln, Ne., U.S.	138	40.48N	96.40W
Lindi	106	10.00S	39.43 E

Name	Page No.	Lat.	Long.	Name	Page No.	Lat.	Long.
Lingga, Kepulauan II	118	0.05S	104.35 E	Louisiade Archipelago			
Linköping	89	58.25N	15.37 E	II	122	11.00S	153.00 E
Lins	135	21.40S	49.45W	Louisiana □³	138	31.15N	92.15W
Linton	138	46.16N	100.13W	Louis Trichardt	106	23.01S	29.43 E
Linz	90	48.18N	14.18 E	Louisville	138	38.15N	85.45W
Lion, Golfe du c	92	43.00N	4.00 E	Lourdes	92	43.06N	0.03W
Lipeck	100	52.37N	39.35 E	Lourenço Marques			
Lippstadt	90	51.40N	8.19 E	→ Maputo	106	25.58S	32.35 E
Lisboa (Lisbon)	94	38.43N	9.08W	Loveč	98	43.08N	24.43 E
Lismore	122	28.48S	153.17 E	Lovelock	142	40.10N	118.28W
Lithuania □¹	86	56.00N	24.00 E	Lowell	140	42.38N	71.19W
Little Current	140	45.58N	81.56W	Lower Hutt	126	41.13S	174.55 E
Little Inagua I	130	21.30N	73.00W	Loyauté, Îles (Loyalty			
Little Minch ⅄	88	57.35N	6.45W	Islands) II	127b	21.00S	167.00 E
Little Rock	138	34.44N	92.17W	Lualaba ≃	106	0.26N	25.20 E
Liuzhou	114	24.22N	109.32 E	Luanda	106	8.48S	13.14 E
Livermore Falls	140	44.28N	70.11W	Luanguinga ≃	106	15.11S	22.56 E
Liverpool	88	53.25N	2.55W	Luanshya	106	13.08S	28.24 E
Livingston	138	45.39N	110.33W	Luao	106	12.12S	15.52 E
Livingstone	106	17.50S	25.53 E	Lubango	106	14.55S	13.30 E
Livny	100	52.25N	37.37 E	Lubbock	138	33.34N	101.51W
Livonia	140	42.22N	83.21W	Lübeck	90	53.52N	10.40 E
Livorno (Leghorn)	96	43.33N	10.19 E	Lublin	90	51.15N	22.35 E
Ljubljana	96	46.03N	14.31 E	Lubudi	106	6.51S	21.18 E
Ljusnan ≃	89	61.12N	17.08 E	Lubumbashi			
Llanos ≃	132	5.00N	70.00W	(Élisabethville)	106	11.40S	27.28 E
Lloydminster	136	53.17N	110.00W	Lucasville	140	38.52N	82.59W
Lobito	106	12.20S	13.34 E	Lucena	94	37.24N	4.29W
Lochgilphead	88	56.03N	5.26W	Luckenwalde	90	52.05N	13.10 E
Lochinver	88	58.09N	5.15W	Lucknow	112	26.51N	80.55 E
Lock Haven	140	41.08N	77.26W	Ludlow	140	43.23N	72.42W
Lockport	140	43.10N	78.41W	Ludwigsburg	90	48.53N	9.11 E
Lodi	142	38.07N	121.16W	Ludwigshafen	90	49.29N	8.26 E
Łódź	90	51.46N	19.30 E	Lufkin	128	31.20N	94.43W
Lofoten II	89	68.30N	15.00 E	Lugano	92	46.01N	8.58 E
Logan, Mount ⋀	136	60.34N	140.24W	Luganville	127b	15.32S	167.08 E
Logroño	94	42.28N	2.27W	Lugo	94	43.00N	7.34W
Loire ≃	92	47.16N	2.11W	Lugoj	98	45.41N	21.54 E
Loja	132	4.00S	79.13W	Luhans'k	86	48.34N	39.20 E
Lom	98	43.49N	23.14 E	Lukeville	128	31.52N	112.48W
Loma Mansa ⋀	104	9.13N	11.07W	Luleå	89	65.34N	22.10 E
Lombok I	118	8.45S	116.30 E	Luleälven ≃	89	65.35N	22.03 E
Lomé	104	6.08N	1.13 E	Lüleburgaz	98	41.24N	27.21 E
Lompoc	142	34.38N	120.27W	Lund	89	55.42N	13.11 E
Łomża	90	53.11N	22.05 E	Lüneburg	90	53.15N	10.23 E
London, On., Can.	140	42.59N	81.14W	Luoyang	114	34.41N	112.28 E
London, Eng., U.K.	88	51.30N	0.10W	Lupeni	98	45.22N	23.13 E
Londonderry	88	55.00N	7.19W	Luray	140	38.39N	78.27W
Londrina	135	23.18S	51.09W	Lusaka	106	15.25S	28.17 E
Long Beach	142	33.46N	118.11W	Lushnja	98	40.56N	19.42 E
Long Branch	140	40.18N	73.59W	Lūt, Dasht-e ◆²	108	33.00N	57.00 E
Long Island I, Bah.	130	23.15N	75.07W	Luton	88	51.53N	0.25W
Long Island I, N.Y.,				Luts'k	86	50.44N	25.20 E
U.S.	140	40.50N	73.00W	Luwegu ≃	106	8.31S	37.23 E
Long Point ≻¹	140	42.34N	80.15W	Luxembourg	90	49.36N	6.09 E
Longview	128	32.30N	94.44W	Luxembourg □¹	86	49.45N	6.05 E
Longwy	92	49.31N	5.46 E	Luzern	92	47.03N	8.18 E
Long Xuyen	120	10.23N	105.25 E	Luzhou	114	28.54N	105.27 E
Lop Buri	120	14.48N	100.37 E	Luzon I	118	16.00N	121.00 E
Lorain	140	41.27N	82.10W	Luzon Strait ⅄	118	20.30N	121.00 E
Lorca	94	37.40N	1.42W	L'viv	86	49.50N	24.00 E
Lord Howe Island I	122	31.33S	159.05 E	L'vov			
Lordsburg	128	32.21N	108.42W	→ L'viv	86	49.50N	24.00 E
Lorica	130	9.14N	75.49W	Lynch, Lac ⊜	140	46.25N	77.05W
Lorient	92	47.45N	3.22W	Lynn	140	42.28N	70.57W
Lorraine □⁹	92	49.00N	6.00 E	Lynn Lake	136	56.51N	101.03W
Los Alamos	138	35.53N	106.19W	Lyon	92	45.45N	4.51 E
Los Ángeles, Chile	134	37.28S	72.21W				
Los Angeles, Ca., U.S.	142	34.03N	118.14W				
Los Banos	142	37.03N	120.50W	**M**			
Los Blancos	134	23.36S	62.36W				
Los Mochis	128	25.45N	108.57W	Ma'ān	109	30.12N	35.44 E
Los Roques, Islas II	130	11.50N	66.45W	Maastricht	90	50.52N	5.43 E
Los Vilos	134	31.55S	71.31W	Macaé	135	22.23S	41.47W
Louang Namtha	120	20.57N	101.25 E	Macapá	132	0.02N	51.03W
Louangphrabang	120	19.52N	102.08 E	Macau	114	22.14N	113.35 E

Name	Page No.	Lat.	Long.
Macau □²	114	22.10N	113.33 E
Macdonnell Ranges ⋌	122	23.45S	133.20 E
Macedonia □⁹	98	41.00N	23.00 E
Macedonia □¹	98	41.50N	22.00 E
Maceió	132	9.40S	35.43W
Macerata	96	43.18N	13.27 E
Machačkala	86	42.58N	47.30 E
Machias	140	44.42N	67.27W
Machupicchu	132	13.07S	72.34W
Macina ◆¹	104	14.30N	5.00W
Mackay	122	21.09S	149.11 E
Mackay, Lake ⊜	122	22.30S	129.00 E
Mackenzie ≈	136	69.15N	134.08W
Mackenzie Bay c	136	69.00N	136.30W
Mackenzie Mountains ⋌	136	64.00N	130.00W
Mackinac, Straits of ṳ	138	45.49N	84.42W
Mackinaw City	140	45.47N	84.43W
Mâcon, Fr.	92	46.18N	4.50 E
Macon, Ga., U.S.	138	32.50N	83.37W
Madagascar □¹	106	19.00S	46.00 E
Madeira ≈	132	3.22S	58.45W
Madeira, Arquipélago da (Madeira Islands) II	104	32.40N	16.45W
Mädelegabel ⋀	96	47.18N	10.18 E
Madera	142	36.57N	120.03W
Madhya Pradesh □³	112	23.00N	79.00 E
Madison, W.V., U.S.	140	38.04N	81.49W
Madison, Wi., U.S.	138	43.04N	89.24W
Madiun	118	7.37S	111.31 E
Madras → Chennai	111	13.05N	80.17 E
Madre, Laguna c, Mex.	128	25.00N	97.40W
Madre, Laguna c, Tx., U.S.	128	27.00N	97.35W
Madre, Sierra ⋌	128	15.30N	92.35W
Madre del Sur, Sierra ⋌	128	17.00N	100.00W
Madre Occidental, Sierra ⋌	128	25.00N	105.00W
Madre Oriental, Sierra ⋌	128	22.00N	99.30W
Madrid	94	40.24N	3.41W
Madura I	118	7.00S	113.20 E
Madurai	111	9.56N	78.07 E
Madyan ◆¹	109	27.40N	35.35 E
Maebashi	116	36.23N	139.04 E
Maewo I	127b	15.10S	168.10 E
Magadan	102	59.34N	150.48 E
Magallanes, Estrecho de (Strait of Magellan) ṳ	134	54.00S	71.00W
Magangué	132	9.14N	74.45W
Magdalena	132	13.20S	64.08W
Magdalena ≈	132	11.06N	74.51W
Magdeburg	90	52.07N	11.38 E
Maghāghah	109	28.39N	30.50 E
Magnitogorsk	86	53.27N	59.04 E
Magog	140	45.16N	72.09W
Magway	120	20.09N	94.55 E
Mahābhārat Range ⋌	112	27.40N	84.30 E
Mahajanga	106	15.43S	46.19 E
Mahārāshtra □³	111	19.00N	76.00 E
Mahia Peninsula ⊁¹	126	39.10S	177.53 E
Mahón	94	39.53N	4.15 E
Maiduguri	104	11.51N	13.10 E
Mai-Ndombe, Lac ⊜	106	2.00S	18.20 E
Maine □³	138	45.15N	69.15W
Mainland I	88	59.00N	3.10W
Mainz	90	50.01N	8.16 E
Maipo, Volcán ⋀¹	134	34.10S	69.50W
Maipú	134	36.52S	57.52W
Maiquetía	130	10.36N	66.57W
Majorca → Mallorca I	94	39.30N	3.00 E
Makasar, Selat (Makassar Strait) ṳ	118	2.00S	117.30 E
Makgadikgadi Pans ≈	106	20.45S	25.30 E
Makinsk	102	52.37N	70.26 E
Makkah (Mecca)	108	21.27N	39.49 E
Makó	90	46.13N	20.29 E
Makunudu Atoll I¹	111	6.20N	72.36 E
Makurdi	104	7.45N	8.32 E
Malabar Coast ⋅²	111	10.00N	76.15 E
Malabo	104	3.45N	8.47 E
Malacca, Strait of ṳ	120	2.30N	101.20 E
Málaga	94	36.43N	4.25W
Malaita I	127a	9.00S	161.00 E
Malakāl	104	9.31N	31.39 E
Malang	118	7.59S	112.37 E
Malange	106	9.32S	16.20 E
Malatya	86	38.21N	38.19 E
Malawi □¹	106	13.30S	34.00 E
Malaya □⁹	120	4.00N	102.00 E
Malay Peninsula ⊁¹	120	6.00N	101.00 E
Malaysia □¹	118	2.30N	112.30 E
Malbork	90	54.02N	19.01 E
Maldive Islands II	111	5.00N	73.00 E
Maldives □¹	111	3.15N	73.00 E
Malekula I	127b	16.15S	167.30 E
Malheur, South Fork ≈	142	43.33N	118.10W
Mali □¹	104	17.00N	4.00W
Malik, Wādī al- V	104	18.02N	30.58 E
Malino, Bukit ⋀	118	0.45N	120.47 E
Malkara	98	40.53N	26.54 E
Mallaig	88	57.00N	5.50W
Mallawī	104	27.44N	30.50 E
Mallorca I	94	39.30N	3.00 E
Malmö	89	55.36N	13.00 E
Małopolska ◆¹	90	50.10N	21.30 E
Malpelo, Isla de I	132	3.59N	81.35W
Malta □¹	86	35.50N	14.35 E
Malta I	96	35.53N	14.27 E
Maluku (Moluccas) II	118	2.00S	128.00 E
Maluku, Laut (Molucca Sea) ⊤²	118	0.00	125.00 E
Mamagota	127a	6.46S	155.24 E
Manado	118	1.29N	124.51 E
Managua	130	12.09N	86.17W
Manakara	106	22.08S	48.01 E
Manaus	132	3.08S	60.01W
Manawai	127a	9.05S	161.11 E
Manchester, Eng., U.K.	88	53.30N	2.15W
Manchester, N.H., U.S.	140	42.59N	71.27W
Manchester, Vt., U.S.	140	43.09N	73.04W
Manchuria □⁹	114	47.00N	125.00 E
Mandal	89	58.02N	7.27 E
Mandalay	120	22.00N	96.05 E
Mandeb, Bāb el- ṳ	108	12.40N	43.20 E
Manfredonia	96	41.38N	15.55 E
Manfredonia, Golfo di c	96	41.35N	16.05 E
Mangalore	111	12.52N	74.53 E
Manhattan	138	39.11N	96.34W
Manhuaçu	135	20.15S	42.02W
Manila	118	14.35N	121.00 E
Manipur □⁸	112	25.00N	94.00 E
Manitoba □⁴	136	54.00N	97.00W
Manitoba, Lake ⊜	136	51.00N	98.45W
Manitoulin Island I	140	45.45N	82.30W
Manizales	132	5.05N	75.32W
Mankato	138	44.09N	93.59W
Mannar, Gulf of c	111	8.30N	79.00 E
Mannheim	90	49.29N	8.29 E
Mannington	140	39.31N	80.20W
Manono	106	7.18S	27.25 E
Manresa	94	41.44N	1.50 E
Mansfield	140	40.45N	82.30W
Mansfield, Mount ⋀	140	44.33N	72.49W
Manta	132	0.57S	80.44W
Mantes-la-Jolie	92	48.59N	1.43 E

Name	Page No.	Lat.	Long.	Name	Page No.	Lat.	Long.
Manton	140	44.24N	85.23W	Massena	140	44.55N	74.53W
Mantova	96	45.09N	10.48 E	Massillon	140	40.48N	81.32W
Manzanares	94	39.00N	3.22W	Masterton	126	40.57S	175.40 E
Manzanillo, Cuba	130	20.21N	77.07W	Matadi	106	5.49S	13.27 E
Manzanillo, Mex.	128	19.03N	104.20W	Matagalpa	130	12.55N	85.55W
Maoke, Pegunungan ⋌	118	4.00S	138.00 E	Matagorda Island I	128	28.15N	96.30W
Mapire	130	7.45N	64.42W	Matamoros	128	25.53N	97.30W
Maputo (Lourenço				Matanzas	130	23.03N	81.35W
Marques)	106	25.58S	32.35 E	Matías Romero	128	16.53N	95.02W
Maqat	86	47.39N	53.19 E	Mato Grosso, Planalto			
Maracaibo	132	10.40N	71.37W	do ⋌ [1]	132	15.30S	56.00W
Maracaibo, Lago de ⊜	130	9.50N	71.30W	Matsue	116	35.28N	133.04 E
Maracay	132	10.15N	67.36W	Matsumoto	116	36.14N	137.58 E
Maragogipe	135	12.46S	38.55W	Matsuyama	116	33.50N	132.45 E
Marañón ≃	132	4.30S	73.27W	Mattagami ≃	136	50.43N	81.29W
Marathon	136	48.40N	86.25W	Mattawamkeag	140	45.30N	68.21W
Maravovo	127a	9.17S	159.38 E	Matterhorn ⋀	92	45.59N	7.43 E
Marcy, Mount ⋀	140	44.07N	73.56W	Matthew Town	130	20.57N	73.40W
Mardān	112	34.12N	72.02 E	Maturín	132	9.45N	63.11W
Mar del Plata	134	38.00S	57.33W	Maubeuge	92	50.17N	3.58 E
Maré, Île I	127b	21.30S	168.00 E	Maug Islands II	118	20.01N	145.13 E
Margarita, Isla de I	130	11.00N	64.00W	Maui I	143	20.45N	156.15W
Margherita Peak ⋀	106	0.22N	29.51 E	Maumee	140	41.33N	83.39W
Mariana Islands II	118	16.00N	145.30 E	Mauna Loa ⋀ [1]	143	19.29N	155.36W
Marianao	130	23.05N	82.26W	Maunath Bhanjan	112	25.57N	83.33 E
Marías, Islas II	128	21.25N	106.28W	Mauritania □ [1]	104	20.00N	12.00W
Maribor	96	46.33N	15.39 E	Mauritius □ [1]	106	20.17S	57.33 E
Mariental	106	24.36S	17.59 E	Mawlamyine	120	16.30N	97.38 E
Marietta	140	39.24N	81.27W	Mayaguana I	130	22.23N	72.57W
Marília	135	22.13S	49.56W	Mayagüez	130	18.12N	67.09W
Marinette	138	45.06N	87.37W	Maymyo	120	22.02N	96.28 E
Maringá	134	23.25S	51.55W	Mayotte □ [2]	106	12.50S	45.10 E
Marion, Mi., U.S.	140	44.06N	85.08W	Mayotte I	106	12.50S	45.10 E
Marion, Oh., U.S.	140	40.35N	83.07W	Maysville	140	38.38N	83.44W
Maripa	130	7.26N	65.09W	Mazara del Vallo	96	37.39N	12.36 E
Mariscal Estigarribia	134	22.02S	60.38W	Mazār-e-Sharīf	112	36.42N	67.06 E
Maritime Alps ⋌	92	44.15N	7.10 E	Mazatlán	128	23.13N	106.25W
Mariupol'	86	47.06N	37.33 E	Mazury ◆ [1]	90	53.45N	21.00 E
Markham, Mount ⋀	85	82.51S	161.21 E	Mbabane	106	26.18S	31.06 E
Marlborough	140	42.20N	71.33W	Mbala	106	8.50S	31.22 E
Marmara Denizi (Sea				Mbale	106	1.05N	34.10 E
of Marmara) ⊤ [2]	98	40.40N	28.15 E	Mbandaka			
Marmara Gölü ⊜	98	38.37N	28.02 E	(Coquilhatville)	106	0.04N	18.16 E
Marmet	140	38.14N	81.34W	Mbomou (Bomu) ≃	104	4.08N	22.26 E
Marne ≃	92	48.49N	2.24 E	Mbuji-Mayi			
Maroa	132	2.43N	67.33W	(Bakwanga)	106	6.09S	23.38 E
Maromokotro ⋀	106	14.01S	48.59 E	McAdam	140	45.36N	67.20W
Maroua	104	10.36N	14.20 E	McAlester	138	34.56N	95.46W
Marovoay	106	16.06S	46.39 E	McAllen	128	26.12N	98.13W
Marquette	138	46.32N	87.23W	McComb	128	31.14N	90.27W
Marrah, Jabal ⋀	104	14.04N	24.21 E	McConnellsburg	140	39.55N	77.59W
Marrakech	104	31.38N	8.00W	McCook	138	40.12N	100.37W
Marsabit	108	2.20N	37.59 E	McGill	142	39.24N	114.46W
Marsala	96	37.48N	12.26 E	Mcgrath	144	62.58N	155.38W
Marseille	92	43.18N	5.24 E	McKinley, Mount ⋀	144	63.30N	151.00W
Marshall	138	32.32N	94.22W	M'Clintock Channel ⨆	136	71.00N	101.00W
Marsh Island I	128	29.35N	91.53W	McLoughlin, Mount ⋀	142	42.27N	122.19W
Marsing	142	43.32N	116.48W	Mead, Lake ⊜ [1]	142	36.05N	114.25W
Martaban, Gulf of ⊂	120	16.30N	97.00 E	Meadville	140	41.38N	80.09W
Martha's Vineyard I	140	41.25N	70.40W	Meander River	136	59.02N	117.42W
Martigny	92	46.06N	7.04 E	Meath □ [9]	88	53.36N	6.54W
Martigues	92	43.24N	5.03 E	Mecca			
Martin	90	49.05N	18.55 E	→ Makkah	108	21.27N	39.49 E
Martinique □ [2]	130	14.40N	61.00W	Mechelen	90	51.02N	4.28 E
Martinsburg	140	39.27N	77.57W	Mecklenburg □ [9]	90	53.30N	13.00 E
Maryborough	122	25.32S	152.42 E	Medan	118	3.35N	98.40 E
Maryland □ [3]	138	39.00N	76.45W	Medellín	132	6.15N	75.35W
Marysville	142	39.08N	121.35W	Médenine	104	32.21N	10.30 E
Masai Steppe ⋌ [1]	106	4.45S	37.00 E	Medford	142	42.19N	122.52W
Mascarene Islands II	106	21.00S	57.00 E	Medgidia	98	44.15N	28.16 E
Masherbrum ⋀	112	35.38N	76.18 E	Medicine Hat	136	50.03N	110.40W
Mason City	138	43.09N	93.12W	Mediterranean Sea ⊤ [2]	82	35.00N	20.00 E
Masqaṭ (Muscat)	108	23.37N	58.35 E	Medjerda, Monts de la			
Massa	96	44.01N	10.09 E	⋌	96	36.35N	8.15 E
Massachusetts □ [3]	138	42.15N	71.50W	Meekatharra	122	26.36S	118.29 E
Massachusetts Bay ⊂	140	42.20N	70.50W	Meerut	112	28.59N	77.42 E

Name	Page No.	Lat.	Long.
Meiktila	120	20.52N	95.52E
Meiningen	90	50.34N	10.25E
Meissen	90	51.10N	13.28E
Mekambo	106	1.01N	13.56E
Mekong ≈	120	10.33N	105.24E
Melaka	120	2.12N	102.15E
Melanesia II	82	13.00S	164.00E
Melbourne, Austl.	122	37.49S	144.58E
Melbourne, Fl., U.S.	138	28.04N	80.36W
Melby House	88	60.18N	1.39W
Melilla	104	35.19N	2.58W
Melita	136	49.16N	101.00W
Melitopol'	86	46.50N	35.22E
Melville Island I, Austl.	122	11.40S	131.00E
Melville Island I, N.T., Can.	136	75.15N	110.00W
Melville Peninsula ≻1	136	68.00N	84.00W
Memmingen	90	47.59N	10.11E
Memphis	138	35.08N	90.02W
Mendocino, Cape ≻	142	40.25N	124.25W
Mendoza	134	32.53S	68.49W
Menorca I	94	40.00N	4.00E
Mentawai, Kepulauan II	118	2.00S	99.30E
Menzel Bourguiba	96	37.10N	9.48E
Merano (Meran)	96	46.40N	11.09E
Merced	142	37.18N	120.28W
Mercedes	134	33.40S	65.28W
Mergui (Myeik)	120	12.26N	98.36E
Mergui Archipelago II	120	12.00N	98.00E
Mérida, Mex.	128	20.58N	89.37W
Mérida, Spain	94	38.55N	6.20W
Mérida, Ven.	130	8.30N	71.10W
Meriden	140	41.32N	72.48W
Meridian	138	32.21N	88.42W
Merseburg	90	51.21N	11.59E
Mersin	109	36.48N	34.38E
Merthyr Tydfil	88	51.46N	3.23W
Mesa	138	33.25N	111.49W
Mesopotamia ◆1	108	34.00N	44.00E
Mesquite	142	36.48N	114.03W
Messina, Italy	96	38.11N	15.33E
Messina, S. Afr.	106	22.23S	30.00E
Metán	134	25.29S	64.57W
Metz	92	49.08N	6.10E
Meuse (Maas) ≈	90	51.49N	5.01E
Mexicali	128	32.40N	115.29W
Mexico	138	39.10N	91.52W
Mexico □1	128	23.00N	102.00W
Mexico, Gulf of ⊂	128	24.00N	93.00W
Mexico City → Ciudad de México	128	19.24N	99.09W
Meymaneh	112	35.55N	64.47E
Miami	138	25.46N	80.11W
Miānwāli	112	32.35N	71.33E
Miass	86	54.59N	60.06E
Michigan □3	138	44.00N	85.00W
Michigan, Lake ⊜	138	44.00N	87.00W
Micronesia II	82	11.00N	159.00E
Micronesia, Federated States of □1	118	5.00N	152.00E
Mičurinsk	100	52.54N	40.30E
Middelburg	106	31.30S	25.00E
Middlebury	140	44.00N	73.10W
Middlesbrough	88	54.35N	1.14W
Middletown, N.Y., U.S.	140	41.26N	74.25W
Middletown, Oh., U.S.	140	39.30N	84.23W
Midland, On., Can.	140	44.45N	79.53W
Midland, Mi., U.S.	140	43.36N	84.14W
Midland, Tx., U.S.	138	31.59N	102.04W
Mielec	90	50.18N	21.25E
Miguel Alemán, Presa ⊜1	128	18.13N	96.32W
Mihajlovgrad	98	43.25N	23.13E
Mikkeli	89	61.41N	27.15E
Milan → Milano, Italy	96	45.28N	9.12E
Milan, Mi., U.S.	140	42.05N	83.40W
Milano (Milan)	96	45.28N	9.12E
Mildura	122	34.12S	142.09E
Miles City	138	46.24N	105.50W
Milford	140	38.54N	75.25W
Milford Haven	88	51.40N	5.02W
Millau	92	44.06N	3.05E
Millinocket	140	45.39N	68.42W
Milltown Malbay	88	52.52N	9.23W
Mílos I	98	36.41N	24.15E
Milparinka	122	29.44S	141.53E
Milwaukee	138	43.02N	87.54W
Minas	134	34.23S	55.14W
Minas, Sierra de las ⋏	130	15.10N	89.40W
Minatitlán	128	17.59N	94.31W
Mindanao I	118	8.00N	125.00E
Minden	128	32.36N	93.17W
Mindoro I	118	12.50N	121.05E
Mineral Wells	138	32.48N	98.06W
Minho (Miño) ≈	94	41.52N	8.51W
Minneapolis	138	44.58N	93.15W
Minnesota □3	138	46.00N	94.15W
Miño (Minho) ≈	94	41.52N	8.51W
Minorca → Menorca I	94	40.00N	4.00E
Minot	138	48.13N	101.17W
Minsk	100	53.54N	27.34E
Minto, Lac ⊜	136	51.00N	73.37W
Minüf	109	30.28N	30.56E
Mirtóön Pélagos ⊤2	98	36.51N	23.18E
Miskolc	90	48.06N	20.47E
Mississippi □3	138	32.50N	89.30W
Mississippi ≈	138	29.00N	89.15W
Mississippi Delta ≊2	138	29.10N	89.15W
Missoula	138	46.52N	113.59W
Missouri □3	138	38.30N	93.30W
Missouri ≈	138	38.50N	90.08W
Mistassini, Lac ⊜	136	51.00N	73.37W
Mitilíni	98	39.06N	26.32E
Mito	116	36.22N	140.28E
Mitsiwa	108	15.38N	39.28E
Mitú	132	1.08N	70.03W
Mitumba, Monts ⋏	106	6.00S	29.00E
Miyakonojō	116	31.44N	131.04E
Miyazaki	116	31.54N	131.26E
Mizoram □8	112	23.30N	93.00E
Mladá Boleslav	90	50.23N	14.59E
Mobile	138	30.41N	88.02W
Moçambique	106	15.03S	40.42E
Mochudi	106	24.28S	26.05E
Mococa	135	21.28S	47.01W
Modena	96	44.40N	10.55E
Modesto	142	37.38N	120.59W
Moffat	88	55.20N	3.27W
Moga	112	30.48N	75.10E
Mogaung	120	25.18N	96.56E
Mogil'ov	100	53.54N	30.21E
Mohave, Lake ⊜1	142	35.25N	114.38W
Mohawk ≈	140	42.47N	73.42W
Moisie ≈	136	50.12N	66.04W
Mojave Desert ◆2	142	35.00N	117.00W
Mokp'o	114	34.48N	126.22E
Moldavia □9	98	46.30N	27.00E
Molde	89	62.44N	7.11E
Moldova □1	86	47.00N	29.00E
Moldoveanu ⋀	98	45.36N	24.44E
Molfetta	96	41.12N	16.36E
Mollendo	132	17.02S	72.01W
Mölndal	89	57.39N	12.01E
Molokai I	143	21.07N	157.00W
Molopo ≈	106	28.30S	20.13E
Moluccas → Maluku II	118	2.00S	128.00E
Mombasa	106	4.03S	39.40E

Name	Page No.	Lat.	Long.	Name	Page No.	Lat.	Long.
Momi	127c	17.55 S	177.17 E	Most	90	50.32 N	13.39 E
Monaco □ 1	86	43.45 N	7.25 E	Mostar	96	43.20 N	17.49 E
Mončegorsk	86	67.54 N	32.58 E	Motala	89	58.33 N	15.03 E
Mönchengladbach	90	51.12 N	6.28 E	Motherwell	88	55.48 N	4.00 W
Monclova	128	26.54 N	101.25 W	Moulins	92	46.34 N	3.20 E
Moncton	136	46.06 N	64.47 W	Moundou	104	8.34 N	16.05 E
Monessen	140	40.08 N	79.53 W	Moundsville	140	39.55 N	80.44 W
Monfalcone	96	45.49 N	13.32 E	Mountain Home	142	43.07 N	115.41 W
Mongolia □ 1	114	46.00 N	105.00 E	Mountain Nile (Baḥr			
Mono Lake ◎	142	38.00 N	119.00 W	al-Jabal) ≃	108	9.30 N	30.30 E
Monroe, La., U.S.	138	32.30 N	92.07 W	Mount Forest	140	43.59 N	80.44 W
Monroe, Mi., U.S.	140	41.54 N	83.23 W	Mount Gambier	122	37.50 S	140.46 E
Monrovia	104	6.18 N	10.47 W	Mount Isa	122	20.44 S	139.30 E
Montana □ 3	138	47.00 N	110.00 W	Mount Magnet	122	28.04 S	117.49 E
Montargis	92	48.00 N	2.45 E	Mount Morris	140	42.43 N	77.52 W
Montauban	92	44.01 N	1.21 E	Mount Olivet	140	38.31 N	84.02 W
Montauk	140	41.02 N	71.57 W	Mount Pleasant	140	43.35 N	84.46 W
Montceau [-les-Mines]	92	46.40 N	4.22 E	Mount Union	140	40.23 N	77.52 W
Mont-de-Marsan	92	43.53 N	0.30 W	Mozambique □ 1	106	18.15 S	35.00 E
Monte Caseros	134	30.15 S	57.39 W	Mozambique Channel			
Monte Comán	134	34.36 S	67.54 W	⋃	106	19.00 S	41.00 E
Montego Bay	130	18.28 N	77.55 W	Mozyr'	86	52.03 N	29.14 E
Montenegro □ 3	98	42.30 N	19.20 E	Mrhila, Djebel ∧	96	35.25 N	9.14 E
Monterey	142	36.36 N	121.53 W	Mtwara	106	10.16 S	40.11 E
Monterey Bay c	142	36.45 N	121.55 W	Muang Không	120	14.07 N	105.51 E
Montería	132	8.46 N	75.53 W	Muang Khôngxédôn	120	15.34 N	105.49 E
Monterrey	128	25.40 N	100.19 W	Muang Xaignabouri	120	19.15 N	101.45 E
Montes Claros	132	16.43 S	43.52 W	Muar (Bandar			
Montevideo	134	34.53 S	56.11 W	Maharani)	120	2.02 N	102.34 E
Montgomery	138	32.23 N	86.18 W	Muchinga Mountains ⋌	106	12.00 S	31.45 E
Montluçon	92	46.21 N	2.36 E	Mudanjiang	114	44.35 N	129.36 E
Montpelier	140	44.15 N	72.34 W	Mufulira	106	12.33 S	28.14 E
Montpellier	92	43.36 N	3.53 E	Muhammad, Ra's ⋗	109	27.44 N	34.15 E
Montréal	140	45.31 N	73.34 W	Mühlviertel ➧ 1	90	48.25 N	14.10 E
Montrose	140	41.50 N	75.52 W	Mukden			
Montserrat □ 2	130	16.45 N	62.12 W	→ Shenyang	114	41.48 N	123.27 E
Monywa	120	22.05 N	95.08 E	Mulatupo	130	8.57 N	77.45 W
Monza	96	45.35 N	9.16 E	Mulhacén ∧	94	37.03 N	3.19 W
Moorea ⅼ	127d	17.32 S	149.50 W	Mulhouse	92	47.45 N	7.20 E
Moosehead Lake ◎	140	45.40 N	69.40 W	Mull, Island of ⅼ	88	56.27 N	6.00 W
Moose Jaw	136	50.23 N	105.32 W	Multān	110	30.11 N	71.29 E
Mooselookmeguntic				Mumbai (Bombay)	111	18.58 N	72.50 E
Lake ◎	140	44.53 N	70.48 W	München (Munich)	90	48.08 N	11.34 E
Moosonee	136	51.17 N	80.39 W	Munhango	106	12.12 S	18.42 E
Mopti	104	14.30 N	4.12 W	Munich			
Morādābād	112	28.50 N	78.47 E	→ München	90	48.08 N	11.34 E
Morava □ 9	90	49.20 N	17.00 E	Münster	90	51.57 N	7.37 E
Morawhanna	132	8.16 N	59.45 W	Munster □ 9	88	52.25 N	8.20 W
Morden	136	49.11 N	98.05 W	Muqdisho (Mogadishu)	108	2.01 N	45.20 E
More, Ben ∧	88	56.23 N	4.31 W	Mura (Mur) ≃	90	46.18 N	16.53 E
More Assynt, Ben ∧	88	58.07 N	4.51 W	Murcia	94	37.59 N	1.07 W
Morehead	140	38.11 N	83.25 W	Murcia □ 9	94	38.30 N	1.45 W
Morelia	128	19.42 N	101.07 W	Mureş (Maros) ≃	90	46.15 N	20.13 E
Morena, Sierra ⋌	94	38.00 N	5.00 W	Murfreesboro	138	35.50 N	86.23 W
Morgantown	140	39.37 N	79.57 W	Murmansk	86	68.58 N	33.05 E
Moriah, Mount ∧	142	39.17 N	114.12 W	Murom	100	55.34 N	42.02 E
Morioka	116	39.42 N	141.09 E	Muroran	116a	42.18 N	140.59 E
Morocco □ 1	104	32.00 N	5.00 W	Murray ≃	124	35.22 S	139.22 E
Morogoro	106	6.49 S	37.40 E	Murraysburg	106	31.58 S	23.47 E
Moro Gulf c	118	6.51 N	123.00 E	Murrumbidgee ≃	124	34.43 S	143.12 E
Morondava	106	20.17 S	44.17 E	Murupara	126	38.28 S	176.42 E
Morón de la Frontera	94	37.08 N	5.27 W	Mürzzuschlag	90	47.36 N	15.41 E
Moroni	106	11.41 S	43.16 E	Mūsā, Jabal (Mount			
Morrisville	126	37.39 S	175.32 E	Sinai) ∧	109	28.32 N	33.59 E
Moscos Islands ⅠⅠ	120	14.00 N	97.45 E	Musala ∧	98	42.11 N	23.34 E
Moscow				Muscat			
→ Moskva	100	55.45 N	37.35 E	→ Masqaṭ	108	23.37 N	58.35 E
Mosel (Moselle) ≃	92	50.22 N	7.36 E	Mustafakemalpaşa	98	40.02 N	28.24 E
Moselle (Mosel) ≃	92	50.22 N	7.36 E	Mutá, Ponta do ⋗	135	13.52 S	38.56 W
Moskva (Moscow)	100	55.45 N	37.35 E	Mutare	106	18.58 S	32.40 E
Moskva ≃	100	55.05 N	38.50 E	Mwanza	106	2.31 S	32.54 E
Mosquitos, Golfo de				Myanaung	120	18.17 N	95.19 E
los c	130	9.00 N	81.15 W	Myanmar (Burma) □ 1	118	22.00 N	98.00 E
Mossburn	126	45.40 S	168.15 E	Myingyan	120	21.28 N	95.23 E
Mosselbaai	106	34.11 S	22.08 E	Myitkyinā	120	25.23 N	97.24 E
Mossoró	132	5.11 S	37.20 W	Mykolayiv	86	46.58 N	32.00 E

Name	Page No.	Lat.	Long.
Mymensingh	112	24.45 N	90.24 E
Myrtle Point	142	43.03 N	124.08 W
Mysore	111	12.18 N	76.39 E
N			
Naalehu	143	19.03 N	155.35 W
Naas	88	53.13 N	6.39 W
Nabeul	96	36.27 N	10.44 E
Nābulus	109	32.13 N	35.16 E
Nacogdoches	138	31.36 N	94.39 W
Næstved	89	55.14 N	11.46 E
Naga	118	13.37 N	123.11 E
Nāgāland □ 3	112	26.00 N	95.00 E
Nagano	116	36.39 N	138.11 E
Nagaoka	116	37.27 N	138.51 E
Nagasaki	116	32.48 N	129.55 E
Nagoya	116	35.10 N	136.55 E
Nāgpur	112	21.09 N	79.06 E
Nagykanizsa	90	46.27 N	17.00 E
Naha	117b	26.13 N	127.40 E
Nain	136	56.32 N	61.41 W
Nairobi	106	1.17 S	36.49 E
Najin	114	42.15 N	130.18 E
Nakhon Pathom	120	13.49 N	100.03 E
Nakhon Ratchasima	120	14.58 N	102.07 E
Nakhon Sawan	120	15.41 N	100.07 E
Nakhon Si Thammarat	120	8.26 N	99.58 E
Nakuru	106	0.17 S	36.04 E
Nal'čik	86	43.29 N	43.37 E
Namangan	110	41.00 N	71.40 E
Nam Dinh	120	20.25 N	106.10 E
Namib Desert ← 2	106	23.00 S	15.00 E
Namibe	106	15.10 S	12.09 E
Namibia □ 1	106	22.00 S	17.00 E
Nampa	138	43.32 N	116.33 W
Namp'o	114	38.45 N	125.23 E
Nampula	106	15.07 S	39.15 E
Namsos	89	64.29 N	11.30 E
Nanchang	114	28.41 N	115.53 E
Nanchong	114	30.48 N	106.04 E
Nancy	92	48.41 N	6.12 E
Nanda Devi ∧	112	30.23 N	79.59 E
Nānga Parbat ∧	112	35.15 N	74.36 E
Nanjing (Nanking)	114	32.03 N	118.47 E
Nanling ⤬	114	25.00 N	112.00 E
Nanning	114	22.48 N	108.20 E
Nansei-shotō (Ryukyu Islands) ❚❚	114	26.30 N	128.00 E
Nantes	92	47.13 N	1.33 W
Nantong	114	32.02 N	120.53 E
Nantucket Island ❙	140	41.16 N	70.03 W
Nanuque	132	17.50 S	40.21 W
Napanee	140	44.15 N	76.57 W
Napier	126	39.29 S	176.55 E
Naples → Napoli	96	40.51 N	14.17 E
Napo ≃	132	3.20 S	72.40 W
Napoleon	140	41.23 N	84.07 W
Napoli (Naples)	96	40.51 N	14.17 E
Nara	116	34.41 N	135.50 E
Narathiwat	120	6.26 N	101.50 E
Nārāyanganj	112	23.37 N	90.30 E
Narbonne	92	43.11 N	3.00 E
Narew ≃	90	52.26 N	20.42 E
Narmada ≃	112	21.38 N	72.36 E
Narodnaja, Gora ∧	102	65.04 N	60.09 E
Narva	100	59.23 N	28.12 E
Narvik	89	68.26 N	17.25 E
Nashua	140	42.45 N	71.28 W
Nashville	138	36.09 N	86.47 W
Nāsik	111	19.59 N	73.48 E
Nassau	130	25.05 N	77.21 W
Nasser, Lake ⊜ 1	108	22.40 N	32.00 E
Natal	132	5.47 S	35.13 W
Natchez	138	31.33 N	91.24 W
Natchitoches	128	31.45 N	93.05 W
Natuna Besar ❙	120	4.00 N	108.15 E
Naumburg	90	51.09 N	11.48 E
Nausori	127c	18.02 S	175.32 E
Navojoa	128	27.06 N	109.26 W
Nawābganj	112	24.36 N	88.17 E
Nawābshāh	112	26.15 N	68.25 E
Náxos ❙	98	37.02 N	25.35 E
Nazaré	135	13.02 S	39.00 W
Nazca	132	14.50 S	74.57 W
Naze	117b	28.23 N	129.30 E
Nazilli	98	37.55 N	28.21 E
N'Djamena (Fort-Lamy)	104	12.07 N	15.03 E
Ndola	106	12.58 S	28.38 E
Néa Páfos (Paphos)	109	34.45 N	32.25 E
Near Islands ❚❚	144	52.40 N	173.30 E
Nebraska □ 3	138	41.30 N	100.00 W
Nechí ≃	130	8.07 N	74.46 W
Neepawa	136	50.13 N	99.29 W
Negele	108	5.20 N	39.36 E
Negombo	111	7.13 N	79.50 E
Negra, Punta ➤	132	6.06 S	81.09 W
Negro ≃, Arg.	134	41.02 S	62.47 W
Negro ≃, S.A.	132	3.08 S	59.55 W
Negros ❙	118	10.00 N	123.00 E
Nei Monggol Zizhiqu (Inner Mongolia) □ 4	114	43.00 N	115.00 E
Neisse ≃	90	52.04 N	14.46 E
Neiva	132	2.56 N	75.18 W
Nelson, B.C., Can.	136	49.29 N	117.17 W
Nelson, N.Z.	126	41.17 S	173.17 E
Neman (Nemunas) ≃	100	55.18 N	21.23 E
Nemunas (Neman) ≃	100	55.18 N	21.23 E
Nemuro	116a	43.20 N	145.35 E
Nemuro Strait ⨆	116a	44.00 N	145.20 E
Nenana	144	64.34 N	149.07 W
Nepal □ 1	110	28.00 N	84.00 E
Nerastro, Sarīr ← 2	104	24.20 N	20.37 E
Ness, Loch ⊜	88	57.15 N	4.30 W
Netherlands □ 1	86	52.15 N	5.30 E
Netherlands Antilles □ 2	130	12.15 N	69.00 W
Neubrandenburg	90	53.33 N	13.15 E
Neuchâtel, Lac de ⊜	92	46.52 N	6.50 E
Neumünster	90	54.04 N	9.59 E
Neunkirchen	90	49.20 N	7.10 E
Neusiedler See ⊜	96	47.50 N	16.46 E
Neustrelitz	90	53.21 N	13.04 E
Nevada □ 3	138	39.00 N	117.00 W
Nevada, Sierra ⤬	142	38.00 N	119.15 W
Nevers	92	47.00 N	3.09 E
Nevinnomyssk	86	44.38 N	41.56 E
Nevis, Ben ∧	88	56.48 N	5.01 W
New Amsterdam	132	6.15 N	57.31 W
Newark, N.J., U.S.	140	40.44 N	74.10 W
Newark, Oh., U.S.	140	40.04 N	82.24 W
New Bedford	140	41.38 N	70.56 W
New Braunfels	128	29.42 N	98.07 W
New Brunswick	140	40.29 N	74.27 W
New Brunswick □ 4	136	46.30 N	66.15 W
Newburgh	140	41.30 N	74.00 W
New Caledonia □ 2	127b	21.30 S	165.30 E
Newcastle, Austl.	122	32.56 S	151.46 E
Newcastle, N.B., Can.	136	47.00 N	65.34 W
New Castle, Pa., U.S.	140	41.00 N	80.20 W
Newcastle upon Tyne	88	54.59 N	1.35 W
Newcastle Waters	122	17.24 S	133.24 E
New Delhi	112	28.36 N	77.12 E
Newfoundland □ 4	136	52.00 N	56.00 W
Newfoundland ❙	136	48.30 N	56.00 W
New Georgia ❙	127a	8.15 S	157.30 E
New Georgia Group ❚❚	127a	8.30 S	157.20 E
New Glasgow	136	45.35 N	62.39 W
New Guinea ❙	118	5.00 S	140.00 E
New Hampshire □ 3	138	43.35 N	71.40 W

Name	Page No.	Lat.	Long.
New Haven	140	41.18N	72.56W
New Hebrides			
→ Vanuatu □ ¹	127b	16.00S	167.00 E
New Jersey □ ³	138	40.15N	74.30W
New Liskeard	136	47.30N	79.40W
New London	140	41.21N	72.07W
Newmarket	140	43.04N	70.56W
New Martinsville	140	39.38N	80.51W
New Mexico □ ³	138	34.30N	106.00W
New Orleans	138	29.57N	90.04W
New Philadelphia	140	40.30N	81.27W
New Plymouth	126	39.04S	174.05 E
Newport, Wales, U.K.	88	51.35N	3.00W
Newport, R.I., U.S.	140	41.29N	71.18W
Newport, Vt., U.S.	140	44.56N	72.12W
Newport News	138	36.58N	76.25W
New Providence I	130	25.02N	77.24W
Newry	88	54.11N	6.20W
New South Wales □ ³	122	33.00S	146.00 E
Newton Stewart	88	54.57N	4.29W
Newtownards	88	54.36N	5.41W
New York	140	40.43N	74.01W
New York □ ³	138	43.00N	75.00W
New Zealand □ ¹	126	41.00S	174.00 E
Nezahualcóyotl, Presa ◙ ¹	128	17.10N	93.40W
Nguigmi	104	14.15N	13.07 E
Nha Trang	120	12.15N	109.11 E
Niagara Falls, On., Can.	136	43.06N	79.04W
Niagara Falls, N.Y., U.S.	140	43.05N	79.03W
Niamey	104	13.31N	2.07 E
Nias, Pulau I	120	1.05N	97.35 E
Nicaragua □ ¹	130	13.00N	85.00W
Nicaragua, Lago de ◙	130	11.30N	85.30W
Nice	92	43.42N	7.15 E
Nicholasville	140	37.52N	84.34W
Nicobar Islands II	120	8.00N	93.30 E
Nicosia	109	35.10N	33.22 E
Nicoya, Península de ﹥¹	130	10.00N	85.25W
Nienburg	90	52.38N	9.13 E
Niger □ ¹	104	16.00N	8.00 E
Niger ≙	104	5.33N	6.33 E
Nigeria □ ¹	104	10.00N	8.00 E
Niigata	116	37.55N	139.03 E
Niihama	116	33.58N	133.16 E
Niihau I	143	21.55N	160.10W
Niitsu	116	37.48N	139.07 E
Nijmegen	90	51.50N	5.50 E
Nikkō	116	36.45N	139.37 E
Nile (Nahr an-Nīl) ≙	104	30.10N	31.06 E
Nimba, Mont ʌ	104	7.37N	8.25W
Nîmes	92	43.50N	4.21 E
Nine Degree Channel ꙉ	111	9.00N	73.00 E
Ningbo	114	29.52N	121.31 E
Niort	92	46.19N	0.27W
Nipigon, Lake ◙	136	49.50N	88.30W
Nipissing, Lake ◙	140	46.17N	80.00W
Niš	98	43.19N	21.54 E
Niterói	132	22.53S	43.07W
Nitra	90	48.20N	18.05 E
Nivelles	90	50.36N	4.20 E
Nižn'aja Tunguska ≙	102	65.48N	88.04 E
Nižneudinsk	102	54.54N	99.03 E
Nižnij Novgorod	100	56.20N	44.00 E
Nižnij Tagil	102	57.55N	59.57 E
Njazidja I	106	11.35S	43.20 E
Noatak	144	67.34N	162.59W
Nogales	128	31.20N	110.56W
Nokia	89	61.28N	23.30 E
Nome	144	64.30N	165.24W
Nordhausen	90	51.30N	10.47 E
Nordhorn	90	52.27N	7.05 E
Nordkapp ﹥	89	71.11N	25.48 E
Norfolk	138	36.50N	76.17W
Noril'sk	102	69.20N	88.06 E
Normandie □ ⁹	92	49.00N	0.05W
Normanton	122	17.40S	141.05 E
Norristown	140	40.07N	75.20W
Norrköping	89	58.36N	16.11 E
Norseman	122	32.12S	121.46 E
North Adams	140	42.42N	73.06W
Northam	122	31.39S	116.40 E
North America ≛ ¹	82	45.00N	100.00W
Northampton, Eng., U.K.	88	52.14N	0.54W
Northampton, Ma., U.S.	140	42.19N	72.38W
North Bay	136	46.19N	79.28W
North Cape ﹥, N.Z.	126	34.25S	173.02 E
→ Nordkapp ﹥, Nor.	89	71.11N	25.48 E
North Caribou Lake ◙	136	52.50N	90.40W
North Carolina □ ³	138	35.30N	80.00W
North Channel ꙉ, On., Can.	140	46.02N	82.50W
North Channel ꙉ, U.K.	88	55.10N	5.40W
North Dakota □ ³	138	47.30N	100.15W
North East	140	42.12N	79.50W
Northern Ireland □ ⁸	88	54.40N	6.45W
Northern Territory □ ⁸	122	20.00S	134.00 E
North Island I	126	39.00S	176.00 E
North Magnetic Pole ✦	84	76.16N	99.55W
North Platte ≙	138	41.15N	100.45W
North Pole ✦	84	90.00N	0.00
North Sea ᴛ ²	86	55.20N	3.00 E
Northwest Territories □ ⁴	136	70.00N	100.00W
Norton Sound ꙉ	144	63.50N	164.00W
Norwalk	140	41.14N	82.36W
Norway □ ¹	86	62.00N	10.00 E
Norwegian Sea ᴛ ²	84	70.00N	2.00 E
Norwich, Eng., U.K.	88	52.38N	1.18 E
Norwich, N.Y., U.S.	140	42.31N	75.31W
Noshiro	116	40.12N	140.02 E
Notodden	89	59.34N	9.17 E
Notre Dame, Monts ⸗	136	48.10N	68.00W
Nottaway ≙	136	51.22N	79.55W
Nottingham	88	52.58N	1.10W
Nouadhibou	104	20.54N	17.04W
Nouakchott	104	18.06N	15.57W
Nouméa	127b	22.16S	166.27 E
Nouvelle-Calédonie I	127b	21.30S	165.30 E
Nova Friburgo	135	22.16S	42.32W
Nova Iguaçu	135	22.45S	43.27W
Novaja Sibir', Ostrov I	102	75.00N	149.00 E
Novaja Zeml'a II	102	74.00N	57.00 E
Nova Lima	135	19.59S	43.51W
Nova Lisboa → Huambo	106	12.44S	15.47 E
Novara	92	45.28N	8.38 E
Nova Scotia □ ⁴	136	45.00N	63.00W
Nové Zámky	90	47.59N	18.11 E
Novgorod	100	58.31N	31.17 E
Novi Pazar, Bul.	98	43.21N	27.12 E
Novi Pazar, Yugo.	98	43.08N	20.31 E
Novi Sad	98	45.15N	19.50 E
Novokuzneck	102	53.45N	87.06 E
Novomoskovsk	100	54.05N	38.13 E
Novorossijsk	86	44.45N	37.45 E
Novosibirsk	102	55.02N	82.55 E
Novosibirskije Ostrova II	102	75.00N	142.00 E
Novyj Port	102	67.40N	72.52 E
Nowa Sól (Neusalz)	90	51.48N	15.44 E
Nowy Sącz	90	49.38N	20.42 E
Nubian Desert ✦⸗ ²	108	20.30N	33.00 E
Nueces ≙	128	27.50N	97.30W

Name	Page No.	Lat.	Long.
Nueva Rosita	128	27.57N	101.13W
Nueva San Salvador	130	13.41N	89.17W
Nueve de Julio	134	35.27S	60.52W
Nuevitas	130	21.33N	77.16W
Nuevo Laredo	128	27.30N	99.31W
Numazu	116	35.06N	138.52 E
Nunivak Island I	144	60.00N	166.30W
Nürnberg	90	49.27N	11.04 E
Nyala	104	12.03N	24.53 E
Nyanda	106	20.05S	30.50 E
Nyasa, Lake ☉	106	12.00S	34.30 E
Nyaunglebin	120	17.57N	96.44 E
Nyíregyháza	90	47.59N	21.43 E
Nykøbing	89	55.55N	11.41 E
Nyköping	89	58.45N	17.00 E
Nyngan	124	31.34S	147.11 E
Nysa	90	50.29N	17.20 E
Nzérékoré	104	7.45N	8.49W

O

Name	Page No.	Lat.	Long.
Oahu I	143	21.30N	158.00W
Oak Hill	140	37.58N	81.08W
Oakland, Ca., U.S.	142	37.48N	122.16W
Oakland, Or., U.S.	142	43.25N	123.17W
Oakville	140	43.27N	79.41W
Oamaru	126	45.06S	170.58 E
Oaxaca [de Juárez]	128	17.03N	96.43W
Ob' ≃	102	66.45N	69.30 E
Oberwart	90	47.17N	16.13 E
Obihiro	116a	42.55N	143.12 E
Obskaja Guba c	102	69.00N	73.00 E
Ocaña	130	8.15N	73.20W
Occidental, Cordillera			
↗	132	10.00S	77.00W
Ocean City, Md., U.S.	140	38.20N	75.05W
Ocean City, N.J., U.S.	140	39.16N	74.34W
Oceanside	142	33.11N	117.22W
Ochotsk	102	59.23N	143.18 E
Ocotlán	128	20.21N	102.46W
Ōdate	116	40.16N	140.34 E
Odawara	116	35.15N	139.10 E
Ödemiş	98	38.13N	27.59 E
Odense	89	55.24N	10.23 E
Oder (Odra) ≃	90	53.32N	14.38 E
Odesa	86	46.28N	30.44 E
Odessa			
→ Odesa, Ukr.	86	46.28N	30.44 E
Odessa, Tx., U.S.	138	31.50N	102.22W
Odra (Oder) ≃	90	53.32N	14.38 E
Offenbach	90	50.08N	8.47 E
Ōgaki	116	35.21N	136.37 E
Ogallala	138	41.07N	101.43W
Ogbomosho	104	8.08N	4.15 E
Ogden	138	41.13N	111.58W
Ogdensburg	140	44.41N	75.29W
Ohio □³	138	40.15N	82.45W
Ohio ≃	138	36.59N	89.08W
Ohrid, Lake ☉	98	41.02N	20.43 E
Oil City	140	41.26N	79.42W
Oildale	142	35.25N	119.01W
Ōita	116	33.14N	131.36 E
Ojos del Salado, Nevado ⋀	134	27.06S	68.32W
Oka ≃	100	56.20N	43.59 E
Okahandja	106	21.59S	16.58 E
Okaihau	126	35.19S	173.47 E
Okavango (Cubango) ≃	106	18.50S	22.25 E
Okavango Swamp ☲	106	18.45S	22.45 E
Okayama	116	34.39N	133.55 E
Okazaki	116	34.57N	137.10 E
Okeechobee, Lake ☉	138	26.55N	80.45W
Okhotsk, Sea of (Ochotskoje More) ⛝²	102	53.00N	150.00 E

Name	Page No.	Lat.	Long.
Oki-guntō II	116	36.15N	133.15 E
Okinawa-jima I	117b	26.30N	128.00 E
Oklahoma □³	138	35.30N	98.00W
Oklahoma City	138	35.28N	97.30W
Oksskolten ⋀	89	65.59N	14.15 E
Okt'abr'skoj Revol'ucii, Ostrov I	102	79.30N	97.00 E
Öland I	89	56.45N	16.38 E
Olcott	140	43.20N	78.42W
Old Bahama Channel ⛝	130	22.30N	78.50W
Old Crow	136	67.35N	139.50W
Oldenburg	90	53.08N	8.13 E
Old Forge	140	43.42N	74.58W
Old Town	140	44.56N	68.38W
Olean	140	42.04N	78.25W
Oléron, Île d' I	92	45.56N	1.15W
Olimarao I¹	118	7.41N	145.52 E
Ólimbos ⋀, Cyp.	109	34.56N	32.52 E
Ólimbos ⋀, Grc.	98	40.05N	22.21 E
Olimpia	135	20.44S	48.54W
Olinda	132	8.01S	34.51W
Oliveira	135	20.41S	44.49W
Ollagüe	134	21.14S	68.16W
Olmos	132	5.59S	79.46W
Olomouc	90	49.36N	17.16 E
Olsztyn (Allenstein)	90	53.48N	20.29 E
Oltul ≃	98	43.43N	24.51 E
Olympia	138	47.02N	122.53W
Olympus, Mount → Ólimbos ⋀, Grc.	98	40.05N	22.21 E
Olympus, Mount ⋀, Wa., U.S.	138	47.48N	123.43W
Omagh	88	54.36N	7.18W
Omaha	138	41.15N	95.56W
Oman □¹	108	22.00N	58.00 E
Oman, Gulf of c	108	24.30N	58.30 E
Omarama	126	44.29S	169.58 E
Ometepe, Isla de I	130	11.30N	85.35W
Ōmiya	116	35.54N	139.38 E
Omsk	102	55.00N	73.24 E
Ōmuta	116	33.02N	130.27 E
Ondangua	106	17.55S	16.00 E
Oneida	140	43.05N	75.39W
Oneida Lake ☉	140	43.13N	76.00W
Oneonta	140	42.27N	75.03W
Onslow	122	21.39S	115.06 E
Ontario	138	44.01N	116.57W
Ontario □⁴	136	51.00N	85.00W
Ontario, Lake ☉	138	43.45N	78.00W
Ooldea	122	30.27S	131.50 E
Oostende (Ostende)	90	51.13N	2.55 E
Opava	90	49.56N	17.54 E
Opelousas	128	30.32N	92.04W
Opole (Oppeln)	90	50.41N	17.55 E
Opotiki	126	38.00S	177.17 E
Opunake	126	39.27S	173.51 E
Oradea	98	47.03N	21.57 E
Orange, Austl.	122	33.17S	149.06 E
Orange, Tx., U.S.	128	30.05N	93.44W
Orange, Va., U.S.	140	38.14N	78.06W
Orange (Oranje) ≃	106	28.41S	16.28 E
Orange Walk	130	18.06N	88.33W
Oranjestad	130	12.33N	70.06W
Orchon ≃	114	50.21N	106.05 E
Örebro	89	59.17N	15.13 E
Orechovo-Zujevo	100	55.49N	38.59 E
Oregon □³	138	44.00N	121.00W
Orenburg	86	51.54N	55.06 E
Orense	94	42.20N	7.51W
Oriental, Cordillera ↗	132	11.00S	74.00W
Orillia	140	44.37N	79.25W
Orinoco ≃	132	8.37N	62.15W
Orissa □³	111	20.00N	84.00 E
Orizaba, Pico de ⋀¹	128	19.01N	97.16W
Orkney Islands II	88	59.00N	3.00W

Name	Page No.	Lat.	Long.
Orlando	138	28.32 N	81.22 W
Orléanais □⁹	92	47.50 N	2.00 E
Orléans	92	47.55 N	1.54 E
Örnsköldsvik	89	63.18 N	18.43 E
Orohena, Mont ʌ	127d	17.37 S	149.28 W
Or'ol	100	52.59 N	36.05 E
Oroville	142	39.30 N	121.33 W
Orša	100	54.30 N	30.24 E
Orsk	86	51.12 N	58.34 E
Orŭmīyeh	86	37.33 N	45.04 E
Oruro	132	17.59 S	67.09 W
Osa, Península de ➤¹	130	8.34 N	83.31 W
Ōsaka	116	34.40 N	135.30 E
Osăm ≃	98	43.42 N	24.51 E
Oscoda	140	44.26 N	83.20 W
Oshawa	136	43.54 N	78.51 W
Oshkosh	138	44.01 N	88.32 W
Oshogbo	104	7.47 N	4.34 E
Osijek	98	45.33 N	18.41 E
Oskemen	102	49.58 N	82.38 E
Oslo	89	59.55 N	10.45 E
Osmaniye	109	37.05 N	36.14 E
Osnabrück	90	52.16 N	8.02 E
Osorno	134	40.34 S	73.09 W
Ossa, Mount ʌ	122	41.54 S	146.01 E
Östersund	89	63.11 N	14.39 E
Ostfriesische Inseln ɪɪ	90	53.44 N	7.25 E
Ostrava	90	49.50 N	18.17 E
Ostrov	90	50.17 N	12.57 E
Ostrowiec Świętokrzyski	90	50.57 N	21.23 E
Ostrów Wielkopolski	90	51.39 N	17.49 E
Ōsumi-kaikyō ᴜ	116	31.00 N	131.00 E
Oswego	140	43.27 N	76.30 W
Otaru	116a	43.13 N	141.00 E
Otra ≃	89	58.09 N	8.00 E
Otranto, Strait of ≃¹	98	40.00 N	19.00 E
Ötscher ʌ	90	47.52 N	15.12 E
Ōtsu	116	35.00 N	135.52 E
Ottawa	140	45.25 N	75.42 W
Ottawa ≃	136	45.20 N	73.58 W
Ouagadougou	104	12.22 N	1.31 W
Ouahigouya	104	13.35 N	2.25 W
Ouarane •¹	104	21.00 N	10.30 W
Oubangui (Ubangi) ≃	104	1.15 N	17.50 E
Ouessant, Île d' ɪ	92	48.28 N	5.05 W
Oujda	104	34.41 N	1.45 W
Oulu	89	65.01 N	25.28 E
Oulujärvi ⊜	89	64.20 N	27.15 E
Ourinhos	135	22.59 S	49.52 W
Ouro Prêto	135	20.23 S	43.30 W
Ovalle	134	30.36 S	71.12 W
Ovamboland □⁹	106	17.45 S	16.30 E
Overton	142	36.32 N	114.26 W
Oviedo	94	43.22 N	5.50 W
Owens Lake ⊜	142	36.25 N	117.56 W
Owen Sound	136	44.34 N	80.56 W
Owen Stanley Range ⋌	122	9.20 S	147.55 E
Owenton	140	38.32 N	84.50 W
Owosso	140	42.59 N	84.10 W
Owyhee ≃	142	43.46 N	117.02 W
Oxford	88	51.46 N	1.15 W
Oxnard	142	34.11 N	119.10 W
Ozark Plateau ⋌¹	138	36.30 N	92.30 W
Ozarks, Lake of the ⊜¹	138	38.10 N	92.50 W
Ózd	90	48.14 N	20.18 E
P			
Paarl	106	33.45 S	18.56 E
Paauilo	143	20.02 N	155.22 W
Pābna	112	24.00 N	89.15 E
Pacasmayo	132	7.24 S	79.34 W
Pachuca [de Soto]	128	20.07 N	98.44 W
Pacific Ocean ᴛ¹	82	10.00 S	150.00 W
Padang	118	0.57 S	100.21 E
Padangsidimpaun	120	1.22 N	99.16 E
Paderborn	90	51.43 N	8.45 E
Padova	96	45.25 N	11.53 E
Paducah	138	37.05 N	88.36 W
Paektu-san ʌ	114	42.00 N	128.03 E
Pagan ɪ	118	18.07 N	145.46 E
Pagon, Bukit ʌ	118	4.18 N	115.19 E
Pago Pago	127e	14.16 S	170.42 W
Päijänne ⊜	89	61.35 N	25.30 E
Painesville	140	41.43 N	81.14 W
Pakanbaru	118	0.32 N	101.27 E
Pakaraima Mountains ⋌	132	5.30 N	60.40 W
Pakistan □¹	110	30.00 N	70.00 E
Pakokku	120	21.20 N	95.05 E
Pakxé	120	15.07 N	105.47 E
Palau □¹	118	7.30 N	134.30 E
Palawan ɪ	118	9.30 N	118.30 E
Palembang	118	2.55 S	104.45 E
Palencia	94	42.01 N	4.32 W
Palermo	96	38.07 N	13.21 E
Palestine	128	31.45 N	95.37 W
Palestine □⁹	109	32.00 N	35.15 E
Palk Strait ᴜ	111	10.00 N	79.45 E
Pallastunturi ʌ	89	68.06 N	24.00 E
Palliser, Cape ➤	126	41.37 S	175.17 E
Palma [de Mallorca]	94	39.34 N	2.39 E
Palmdale	142	34.34 N	118.06 W
Palmer	144	61.36 N	149.07 W
Palmerston	126	45.29 S	170.43 E
Palmerston North	126	40.21 S	175.37 E
Pamir ⋌	112	38.00 N	73.00 E
Pampa ←¹	134	35.00 S	63.00 W
Pamplona	92	42.49 N	1.38 W
Panamá	130	8.58 N	79.32 W
Panama □¹	130	9.00 N	80.00 W
Panamá, Golfo de ᴄ	130	8.00 N	79.30 W
Panamá, Istmo de ⋤³	130	9.00 N	79.00 W
Panay ɪ	118	11.15 N	122.30 E
Pančevo	98	44.52 N	20.39 E
Pandharpur	111	17.40 N	75.20 E
Pangkalpinang	118	2.08 S	106.08 E
Panié, Mont ʌ	127b	20.36 S	164.46 E
Pápa	90	47.19 N	17.28 E
Papeete	127d	17.32 S	149.34 W
Papineau, Parc de ♦	140	45.55 N	75.20 W
Papua, Gulf of ᴄ	118	8.30 S	145.00 E
Papua New Guinea □¹	82	6.00 S	143.00 E
Paracatu	135	17.13 S	46.52 W
Paradise	142	39.44 N	121.38 W
Paraguaçu Paulista	135	22.25 S	50.34 W
Paraguaná, Península de ⋌¹	130	11.55 N	70.00 W
Paraguarí	134	25.38 S	57.09 W
Paraguay □¹	134	23.00 S	58.00 W
Paraíba do Sul ≃	135	21.37 S	41.03 W
Paramaribo	132	5.50 N	55.10 W
Paraná	134	31.44 S	60.32 W
Paraná ≃, Braz.	135	12.30 S	48.14 W
Paraná ≃, S.A.	134	33.43 S	59.15 W
Paranaguá	134	25.31 S	48.30 W
Paranavaí	135	23.04 S	52.28 W
Pardubice	90	50.02 N	15.47 E
Parecis, Chapada dos ⋌	132	13.00 S	60.00 W
Parent	136	47.55 N	74.37 W
Parepare	118	4.01 S	119.38 E
Paris, Fr.	92	48.52 N	2.20 E
Paris, Ky., U.S.	140	38.12 N	84.15 W
Parker	142	34.09 N	114.17 W
Parkersburg	140	39.16 N	81.33 W
Parma, Italy	96	44.48 N	10.20 E
Parma, Oh., U.S.	140	41.24 N	81.43 W
Parnaíba	132	2.54 S	41.47 W
Pärnu	100	58.24 N	24.32 E
Paro	110	27.26 N	89.25 E

Name	Page No.	Lat.	Long.	Name	Page No.	Lat.	Long.
Páros I	98	37.08 N	25.12 E	Peterborough, Austl.	122	32.58 S	138.50 E
Parry Sound	136	45.21 N	80.02 W	Peterborough, On.,			
Parsons	138	37.20 N	95.15 W	Can.	136	44.18 N	78.19 W
Pasadena	142	34.08 N	118.08 W	Peterborough, Eng.,			
Paso de Indios	134	43.52 S	69.06 W	U.K.	88	52.35 N	0.15 W
Passau	90	48.35 N	13.28 E	Petersburg	144	56.49 N	132.57 W
Passo Fundo	134	28.15 S	52.24 W	Petoskey	140	45.22 N	84.57 W
Passos	135	20.43 S	46.37 W	Petrič	98	41.24 N	23.13 E
Pasto	132	1.13 N	77.17 W	Petrolina	132	9.24 S	40.30 W
Patagonia ✦ ¹	134	44.00 S	68.00 W	Petropavl	102	54.54 N	69.06 E
Paternò	96	37.34 N	14.54 E	Petropavlovsk-Kamčatskij	102	53.01 N	158.39 E
Paterson	140	40.55 N	74.10 W	Petrópolis	132	22.31 S	43.10 W
Pathein	120	16.47 N	94.44 E	Petroşani	98	45.25 N	23.22 E
Pátmos I	98	37.20 N	26.33 E	Petrozavodsk	86	61.47 N	34.20 E
Patna	112	25.36 N	85.07 E	Pforzheim	90	48.54 N	8.42 E
Patos de Minas	135	18.35 S	46.32 W	Phan Rang	120	11.34 N	108.59 E
Patquía	134	30.03 S	66.53 W	Phan Si Pang ∧	120	22.15 N	103.46 E
Pátrai	98	38.15 N	21.44 E	Phan Thiet	120	10.56 N	108.06 E
Patrocínio	135	18.57 S	46.59 W	Phet Buri	120	13.06 N	99.57 E
Patuca ≃	130	15.50 N	84.17 W	Philadelphia	140	39.57 N	75.09 W
Pau	92	43.18 N	0.22 W	Philippi	140	39.09 N	80.02 W
Paulo Afonso	132	9.21 S	38.14 W	Philippines □ ¹	118	13.00 N	122.00 E
Paungde	120	18.29 N	95.30 E	Philippine Sea ▼ ²	82	20.00 N	135.00 E
Pavlodar	102	52.18 N	76.57 E	Philipsburg	140	40.53 N	78.13 W
Paysandú	134	32.19 S	58.05 W	Phitsanulok	120	16.50 N	100.15 E
Pazardžik	98	42.12 N	24.20 E	Phnum Pénh	120	11.33 N	104.55 E
Peace River	136	56.14 N	117.17 W	Phoenix	138	33.26 N	112.04 W
Pearl ≃	128	30.11 N	89.32 W	Phôngsali	120	21.41 N	102.06 E
Pearl Harbor c	143	21.22 N	157.58 W	Phra Nakhon Si			
Peć	98	42.40 N	20.19 E	Ayutthaya	120	14.21 N	100.33 E
Pečora	102	65.10 N	57.11 E	Phuket	120	7.53 N	98.24 E
Pečora ≃	102	68.13 N	54.15 E	Phu Quoc, Dao I	120	10.12 N	104.00 E
Pecos	128	31.25 N	103.29 W	Piacenza	96	45.01 N	9.40 E
Pecos ≃	128	29.42 N	101.22 W	Piatra-Neamţ	98	46.56 N	26.22 E
Pécs	90	46.05 N	18.13 E	Picardie □ ⁹	92	50.00 N	3.30 E
Pedregal	130	11.01 N	70.08 W	Pickford	140	46.09 N	84.21 W
Pedro Juan Caballero	135	22.34 S	55.37 W	Pidurutalagala ∧	111	7.00 N	80.46 E
Peekskill	140	41.17 N	73.55 W	Piedras Negras, Guat.	130	17.11 N	91.15 W
Pegasus Bay c	126	43.20 S	173.00 E	Piedras Negras, Mex.	128	28.42 N	100.31 W
Peking				Pieksämäki	89	62.18 N	27.08 E
→ Beijing	114	39.55 N	116.25 E	Pielinen ⊜	89	63.15 N	29.40 E
Pelagie, Isole II	96	35.40 N	12.40 E	Pierre	138	44.22 N	100.21 W
Pelée, Montagne ∧	130	14.48 N	61.10 W	Pietermaritzburg	106	29.37 S	30.16 E
Pelly Mountains ⋌	136	62.00 N	133.00 W	Pietersburg	106	23.54 S	29.25 E
Pelopónnisos				Pietrosul ∧	98	47.08 N	25.11 E
(Peloponnesus) ✦ ¹	98	37.30 N	22.00 E	Pietrosu, Vîrful ∧	98	47.36 N	24.38 E
Pelotas	134	31.46 S	52.20 W	Pikes Peak ∧	138	38.51 N	105.03 W
Pematangsiantar	118	2.57 N	99.03 E	Piła (Schneidemühl)	90	53.10 N	16.44 E
Pemba	106	12.58 S	40.30 E	Pilica ≃	90	51.52 N	21.17 E
Pemba Island I	106	7.31 S	39.25 E	Pinang			
Pembroke	136	45.49 N	77.07 W	→ George Town	120	5.25 N	100.20 E
Penápolis	135	21.24 S	50.04 W	Pinar del Río	130	22.25 N	83.42 W
Pennines ⋌	88	54.10 N	2.05 W	Píndhos óros ⋌	98	39.49 N	21.14 E
Pennsylvania □ ³	138	40.45 N	77.30 W	Pine Bluff	138	34.13 N	92.00 W
Penobscot ≃	140	44.30 N	68.50 W	Pins, Île des I	127b	22.37 S	167.30 E
Pensacola	138	30.25 N	87.13 W	Pinsk	100	52.07 N	26.04 E
Pentecost Island I	127b	15.42 S	168.10 E	Piombino	96	42.55 N	10.32 E
Penza	86	53.13 N	45.00 E	Piotrków Trybunalski	90	51.25 N	19.42 E
Peoria	138	40.41 N	89.35 W	Pipmouacane,			
Pereira	132	4.49 N	75.43 W	Réservoir ⊜ ¹	136	49.35 N	70.30 W
Périgueux	92	45.11 N	0.43 E	Piqua	140	40.08 N	84.14 W
Perijá, Sierra de ⋌	130	10.00 N	73.00 W	Piracicaba	135	22.43 S	47.38 W
Perm'	86	58.00 N	56.15 E	Piraiévs (Piraeus)	98	37.57 N	23.38 E
Pernik	98	42.36 N	23.02 E	Piraju	135	23.12 S	49.23 W
Perpignan	92	42.41 N	2.53 E	Pirapora	135	17.21 S	44.56 W
Perryville	144	55.54 N	159.10 W	Pirmasens	90	49.12 N	7.36 E
Persian Gulf c	108	27.00 N	51.00 E	Pisa	96	43.43 N	10.23 E
Perth, Austl.	122	31.56 S	115.50 E	Pisco	132	13.42 S	76.13 W
Perth, Scot., U.K.	88	56.24 N	3.28 W	Pisticci	96	40.23 N	16.34 E
Perth Amboy	140	40.30 N	74.15 W	Piteå	89	65.20 N	21.30 E
Peru □ ¹	132	10.00 S	76.00 W	Piteşti	98	44.52 N	24.52 E
Perugia	96	43.08 N	12.22 E	Pittsburgh	140	40.26 N	79.59 W
Pesaro	96	43.54 N	12.55 E	Pittsfield	140	42.27 N	73.14 W
Pescara	96	42.28 N	14.13 E	Piura	132	5.12 S	80.38 W
Peshāwar	112	34.01 N	71.33 E	Placetas	130	22.19 N	79.40 W
Petaluma	142	38.13 N	122.38 W	Planeta Rica	130	8.25 N	75.36 W

Name	Page No.	Lat.	Long.
Plata, Río de la c [1]	134	35.00S	57.00W
Platte ≃	138	39.16N	94.50W
Plattsburgh	140	44.41N	73.27W
Plauen	90	50.30N	12.08 E
Plenty, Bay of c	126	37.40S	177.00 E
Plétipi, Lac ⊜	136	51.44N	70.06W
Pleven	98	43.25N	24.37 E
Płock	90	52.33N	19.43 E
Ploieşti	98	44.56N	26.02 E
Plovdiv	98	42.09N	24.45 E
Plymouth, Eng., U.K.	88	50.23N	4.10W
Plymouth, Ma., U.S.	140	41.57N	70.40W
Plzeň	90	49.45N	13.23 E
Po ≃	96	44.57N	12.04 E
Pobeda, Gora ⋀	102	65.12N	146.12 E
Pocatello	138	42.52N	112.26W
Poços de Caldas	135	21.48S	46.34W
Podgorica	98	42.26N	19.14 E
Podlasie ◆ [1]	90	52.30N	23.00 E
Podol'sk	100	55.26N	37.33 E
Podor	104	16.40N	14.57W
Pofadder	106	29.10S	19.22 E
Poiana Ruşcăi, Munţii ⋪	98	45.41N	22.30 E
Pointe-Noire	106	4.48S	11.51 E
Point Pleasant	140	40.04N	74.04W
Point Reyes National Seashore ◆	142	38.00N	122.58W
Poitiers	92	46.35N	0.20 E
Poland ▢ [1]	86	52.00N	19.00 E
Polevskoj	86	56.26N	60.11 E
Poltava	86	49.35N	34.34 E
Poltimore	140	45.47N	75.43W
Polynesia II	82	4.00S	156.00W
Pomerania ▢ [9]	90	54.00N	16.00 E
Pomeranian Bay c	90	54.00N	14.15 E
Ponca City	138	36.42N	97.05W
Ponce	130	18.01N	66.37W
Pondicherry ▢ [8]	111	11.56N	79.50 E
Ponta Grossa	134	25.05S	50.09W
Pontchartrain, Lake ⊜	128	30.10N	90.10W
Ponte Nova	135	20.24S	42.54W
Pontevedra	94	42.26N	8.38W
Pontiac	140	42.38N	83.17W
Pontianak	118	0.02S	109.20 E
Poopó, Lago ⊜	132	18.45S	67.07W
Popayán	132	2.27N	76.36W
Poplar Bluff	138	36.45N	90.23W
Popocatépetl, Volcán ⋀ [1]	128	19.02N	98.38W
Popomanaseu, Mount ⋀	122	9.42S	160.04 E
Poprad	90	49.03N	20.18 E
Pordenone	96	45.57N	12.39 E
Pori	89	61.29N	21.47 E
Porlamar	130	10.57N	63.51W
Poronajsk	102	49.14N	143.04 E
Portadown	88	54.26N	6.27W
Portage	140	42.12N	85.34W
Port Allegany	140	41.48N	78.16W
Port Arthur	138	29.53N	93.55W
Port Augusta	122	32.30S	137.46 E
Port-au-Prince	130	18.32N	72.20W
Port Austin	140	44.02N	82.59W
Port Blair	120	11.40N	92.45 E
Port Clyde	140	43.55N	69.15W
Port Elgin	140	44.26N	81.24W
Port Elizabeth	106	33.58S	25.40 E
Port Ellen	88	55.39N	6.12W
Porterville	142	36.03N	119.00W
Port-Gentil	106	0.43S	8.47 E
Port Harcourt	104	4.43N	7.05 E
Port Hedland	122	20.19S	118.34 E
Port Henry	140	44.02N	73.27W
Port Huron	140	42.58N	82.25W
Portland, Austl.	122	38.21S	141.36 E
Portland, Me., U.S.	140	43.39N	70.15W
Portland, Or., U.S.	138	45.31N	122.40W
Port Lavaca	128	28.36N	96.37W
Port Lincoln	122	34.44S	135.52 E
Port Louis	106	20.10S	57.30 E
Port Macquarie	122	31.26S	152.55 E
Port Moresby	122	9.30S	147.10 E
Port Nolloth	106	29.17S	16.51 E
Porto	94	41.11N	8.36W
Pôrto Alegre	134	30.04S	51.11W
Porto Amboim	106	10.44S	13.44 E
Portobelo	130	9.33N	79.39W
Port of Spain	130	10.39N	61.31W
Porto-Novo	104	6.29N	2.37 E
Port Orford	142	42.44N	124.29W
Porto-Vecchio	96	41.35N	9.16 E
Pôrto Velho	132	8.46S	63.54W
Port Pirie	122	33.11S	138.01 E
Port Said → Būr Sa'īd	104	31.16N	32.18 E
Port Shepstone	106	30.46S	30.22 E
Portsmouth, Eng., U.K.	88	50.48N	1.05W
Portsmouth, N.H., U.S.	140	43.04N	70.45W
Portsmouth, Oh., U.S.	140	38.43N	82.59W
Porttipahdan tekojärvi ⊜ [1]	89	68.08N	26.40 E
Portugal ▢ [1]	86	39.30N	8.00W
Portugalete	94	43.19N	3.01W
Posadas	134	27.23S	55.53W
Potenza	96	40.38N	15.49 E
Potgietersrus	106	24.15S	28.55 E
Potomac ≃	140	38.00N	76.18W
Potosí	132	19.35S	65.45W
Potsdam	90	52.24N	13.04 E
Poughkeepsie	140	41.42N	73.55W
Poume	127b	20.14S	164.02 E
Pouso Alegre	135	22.13S	45.56W
Poŭthĭsăt	120	12.32N	103.55 E
Povungnituk	136	60.02N	77.10W
Powassan	140	46.05N	79.22W
Powell, Lake ⊜ [1]	138	37.25N	110.45W
Poza Rica de Hidalgo	128	20.33N	97.27W
Poznań	90	52.25N	16.55 E
Prague → Praha	90	50.05N	14.26 E
Praha (Prague)	90	50.05N	14.26 E
Preparis North Channel ᴜ	120	15.27N	94.05 E
Preparis South Channel ᴜ	120	14.40N	94.00 E
Presidente Epitácio	135	21.46S	52.06W
Presidente Prudente	132	22.07S	51.22W
Presidio	128	29.33N	104.22W
Prešov	90	49.00N	21.15 E
Prespa, Lake ⊜	98	40.55N	21.00 E
Presque Isle	138	46.40N	68.00W
Preston, Eng., U.K.	88	53.46N	2.42W
Preston, Id., U.S.	138	42.05N	111.52W
Pretoria	106	25.45S	28.10 E
Prey Vêng	120	11.29N	105.19 E
Příbram	90	49.42N	14.01 E
Prievidza	90	48.47N	18.37 E
Prilep	98	41.20N	21.33 E
Prince Albert	136	53.12N	105.46W
Prince Edward Island ▢ [4]	136	46.20N	63.20W
Prince George	136	53.55N	122.45W
Prince of Wales Island I, N.T., Can.	136	72.40N	99.00W
Prince of Wales Island I, Ak., U.S.	144	55.47N	132.50W
Prince Rupert	136	54.19N	130.19W
Princeton	140	40.20N	74.39W

Name	Page No.	Lat.	Long.
Priština	98	42.39N	21.10 E
Prizren	98	42.12N	20.44 E
Proctor	140	43.39N	73.02W
Prokopjevsk	102	53.53N	86.45 E
Prome (Pyè)	120	18.49N	95.13 E
Prostějov	90	49.29N	17.07 E
Provence □[9]	92	44.00N	6.00 E
Providence	140	41.49N	71.24W
Providence, Cape ➤	126	46.01S	166.28 E
Provincetown	140	42.03N	70.10W
Provo	138	40.14N	111.39W
Prudhoe Bay ⊂	144	70.20N	148.20W
Pruszków	90	52.11N	20.48 E
Prut ≙	98	45.30N	28.12 E
Przemyśl	90	49.47N	22.47 E
Pskov	100	57.50N	28.20 E
Puapua	127e	13.34S	172.09W
Pucallpa	132	8.23S	74.32W
Pudukkottai	111	10.23N	78.49 E
Puebla [de Zaragoza]	128	19.03N	98.12W
Pueblo	138	38.15N	104.36W
Puerto Aisén	134	45.24S	72.42W
Puerto Armuelles	130	8.17N	82.52W
Puerto Asís	132	0.30N	76.31W
Puerto Barrios	130	15.43N	88.36W
Puerto Berrío	132	6.29N	74.24W
Puerto Cabello	130	10.28N	68.01W
Puerto Cabezas	130	14.02N	83.23W
Puerto Carreño	132	6.12N	67.22W
Puerto Casado	134	22.20S	57.55W
Puerto Cortés, C.R.	130	8.58N	83.32W
Puerto Cortés, Hond.	130	15.48N	87.56W
Puerto Cumarebo	130	11.29N	69.21W
Puerto de Nutrias	132	8.05N	69.18W
Puerto Deseado	134	47.45S	65.54W
Puerto la Cruz	132	10.13N	64.38W
Puerto Leguízamo	132	0.12S	74.46W
Puertollano	94	38.41N	4.07W
Puerto Lobos	134	42.00S	65.06W
Puerto Madryn	134	42.46S	65.03W
Puerto Maldonado	132	12.36S	69.11W
Puerto Montt	134	41.28S	72.57W
Puerto Natales	134	51.44S	72.31W
Puerto Rico □[2]	130	18.15N	66.30W
Puerto Vallarta	128	20.37N	105.15W
Pula	96	44.52N	13.50 E
Pulaski	140	43.34N	76.07W
Puławy	90	51.25N	21.57 E
Pune (Poona)	111	18.32N	73.52 E
Punjab □[3]	112	31.00N	75.30 E
Puno	132	15.50S	70.02W
Punta Arenas	134	53.09S	70.55W
Puntarenas	130	9.58N	84.50W
Punto Fijo	132	11.42N	70.13W
Puri	112	19.48N	85.51 E
Purnea	112	25.47N	87.31 E
Purus (Purús) ≙	132	3.42S	61.28W
Pusan	114	35.06N	129.03 E
Puto	127a	5.41S	154.43 E
Putumayo (Içá) ≙	132	3.07S	67.58W
Puy de Sancy ⋀	92	45.32N	2.49 E
Pyinmana	120	19.44N	96.13 E
P'yŏngyang	114	39.01N	125.45 E
Pyramid Lake ◎	142	40.00N	119.35W
Pyrenees ⋌	94	42.40N	1.00 E
Pyu	120	18.29N	96.26 E

Q

Name	Page No.	Lat.	Long.
Qacentina	104	36.22N	6.37 E
Qaidam Pendi ⩳[1]	114	37.00N	95.00 E
Qalāt	112	32.07N	66.54 E
Qamar, Ghubbat al- ⊂	108	16.00N	52.30 E
Qandahār	112	31.32N	65.30 E
Qaraghandy	102	49.50N	73.10 E

Name	Page No.	Lat.	Long.
Qatar □[1]	108	25.00N	51.10 E
Qinā	109	26.10N	32.43 E
Qingdao (Tsingtao)	114	36.06N	120.19 E
Qinhuangdao	114	39.56N	119.36 E
Qiqihar	114	47.19N	123.55 E
Qom	108	34.39N	50.54 E
Qostanay	86	53.10N	63.35 E
Quanzhou	114	24.54N	118.35 E
Quartzsite	142	33.39N	114.13W
Québec	136	46.49N	71.14W
Quebec (Québec) □[4]	136	52.00N	72.00W
Quedlinburg	90	51.48N	11.09 E
Queen Charlotte Islands ❙❙	136	53.00N	132.00W
Queen Charlotte Sound ⊍	136	51.30N	129.30W
Queen Maud Land ➤[1]	85	72.30S	12.00 E
Queen Maud Mountains ⋌	85	86.00S	160.00W
Queensland □[3]	122	22.00S	145.00 E
Queenstown, N.Z.	126	45.02S	168.40 E
Queenstown, S. Afr.	106	31.52S	26.52 E
Quelimane	106	17.53S	36.51 E
Querétaro	128	20.36N	100.23W
Quetta	112	30.12N	67.00 E
Quezon City	118	14.38N	121.00 E
Quibdó	132	5.42N	76.40W
Quilpie	122	26.37S	144.15 E
Quimper	92	48.00N	4.06W
Quincemil	132	13.16S	70.38W
Qui Nhon	120	13.46N	109.14 E
Quiros, Cape ➤	127b	14.55S	167.01 E
Quito	132	0.13S	78.30W
Qūṣ	109	25.55N	32.45 E

R

Name	Page No.	Lat.	Long.
Rabat (Victoria), Malta	96	36.02N	14.14 E
Rabat, Mor.	104	34.02N	6.51W
Rach Gia	120	10.01N	105.05 E
Racibórz (Ratibor)	90	50.06N	18.13 E
Radom	90	51.25N	21.10 E
Radomsko	90	51.05N	19.25 E
Raetihi	126	39.26S	175.17 E
Rafaela	134	31.16S	61.29W
Rafaḥ	109	31.18N	34.15 E
Ragusa	96	36.55N	14.44 E
Rahīmyār Khān	112	28.25N	70.18 E
Raiatea ⊚	127d	16.50S	151.25W
Rāichūr	111	16.12N	77.22 E
Raipur	112	21.14N	81.38 E
Rājahmundry	111	16.59N	81.47 E
Rajang ≙	118	2.04N	111.12 E
Rājapālaiyam	111	9.27N	77.34 E
Rājasthān □[4]	112	27.00N	74.00 E
Rajčichinsk	102	49.46N	129.25 E
Rājkot	112	22.18N	70.47 E
Raleigh	138	35.46N	78.38W
Rama	130	12.09N	84.15W
Ramm, Jabal ⋀	109	29.35N	35.24 E
Rāmpur	112	28.49N	79.02 E
Ramree Island ❙	120	19.06N	93.48 E
Ramu ≙	118	5.00S	144.40 E
Rancagua	134	34.10S	70.45W
Rānchī	112	23.21N	85.20 E
Randers	89	56.28N	10.03 E
Randolph	140	43.55N	72.39W
Rangeley	140	44.57N	70.38W
Rangitikei ≙	126	40.18S	175.14 E
Rangoon (Yangon)	120	16.47N	96.10 E
Rangpur	112	25.45N	89.15 E
Rankin Inlet	136	62.45N	92.10W
Rann of Kutch ⩳	112	24.00N	70.00 E
Rantauprapat	120	2.06N	99.50 E
Rapid City	138	44.04N	103.13W

Name	Page No.	Lat.	Long.
Ras Dashen Terara ∧	108	13.10N	38.26 E
Rasht	86	37.16N	49.36 E
Rat Islands II	144	52.00N	178.00 E
Ratlām	112	23.19N	75.04 E
Rauma	89	61.08N	21.30 E
Ravena	140	42.28N	73.49W
Ravenna	96	44.25N	12.12 E
Ravensburg	90	47.47N	9.37 E
Ravenshoe	122	17.37S	145.29 E
Ravensthorpe	122	33.35S	120.02 E
Rāwalpindi	112	33.36N	73.04 E
Rawson	134	43.18S	65.06W
Raz, Pointe du ≻	92	48.02N	4.44W
R'azan'	100	54.38N	39.44 E
Razgrad	98	43.32N	26.31 E
Ré, Île de I	92	46.12N	1.25W
Reading, Eng., U.K.	88	51.28N	0.59W
Reading, Pa., U.S.	140	40.20N	75.55W
Real, Cordillera ⋀	132	19.00S	66.30W
Realicó	134	35.02S	64.15W
Recherche, Cape ≻	127a	10.11S	161.19 E
Recife	132	8.03S	34.54W
Recklinghausen	90	51.36N	7.13 E
Red (Hong) (Yuan) ≃, Asia	120	20.17N	106.34 E
Red ≃, U.S.	138	31.00N	91.40W
Red Deer	136	52.16N	113.48W
Redding	142	40.35N	122.23W
Red Lake	136	51.03N	93.49W
Red Sea ▾ [2]	108	20.00N	38.00 E
Reed City	140	43.52N	85.30W
Reefton	126	42.07S	171.52 E
Regensburg	90	49.01N	12.06 E
Reggio di Calabria	96	38.07N	15.39 E
Reggio nell'Emilia	96	44.43N	10.36 E
Regina	136	50.25N	104.39W
Rehoboth Beach	140	38.43N	75.04W
Reḥovot	109	31.54N	34.49 E
Reims	92	49.15N	4.02 E
Remada	104	32.19N	10.24 E
Rendsburg	90	54.18N	9.40 E
Renfrew	140	45.28N	76.41W
Rennes	92	48.05N	1.41W
Reno	142	39.31N	119.48W
Reschenpass)(	92	46.50N	10.30 E
Resistencia	134	27.27S	58.59W
Reşiţa	98	45.17N	21.53 E
Réthimnon	98	35.22N	24.29 E
Reunion □ [2]	106	21.06S	55.36 E
Reus	94	41.09N	1.07 E
Reutlingen	90	48.29N	9.11 E
Revelstoke	136	50.59N	118.12W
Revillagigedo, Islas II	128	19.00N	111.30W
Rewa	112	24.32N	81.18 E
Rewāri	112	28.11N	76.37 E
Rey, Isla del I	130	8.22N	78.55W
Reyes	132	14.19S	67.23W
Reykjavík	86	64.09N	21.51W
Reynosa	128	26.07N	98.18W
Rhaetian Alps ⋀	92	46.30N	10.00 E
Rhein → Rhine ≃	90	51.52N	6.02 E
Rheine	90	52.17N	7.26 E
Rhine (Rhein) (Rhin) ≃	90	51.52N	6.02 E
Rhinelander	138	45.38N	89.24W
Rhode Island □ [3]	138	41.40N	71.30W
Rhodes → Ródhos I	98	36.10N	28.00 E
Rhodope Mountains ⋀	98	41.30N	24.30 E
Rhône ≃	92	43.20N	4.50 E
Riau, Kepulauan II	120	1.00N	104.30 E
Ribeirão Prêto	132	21.10S	47.48W
Riberalta	132	10.59S	66.06W
Richfield, Id., U.S.	142	43.02N	114.09W
Richfield, Ut., U.S.	138	38.46N	112.05W
Richmond, In., U.S.	140	39.49N	84.53W
Richmond, Ky., U.S.	140	37.44N	84.17W
Richmond, Va., U.S.	138	37.33N	77.27W
Richwood	140	38.13N	80.32W
Riesa	90	51.18N	13.17 E
Rieti	96	42.24N	12.51 E
Rif ⋀	94	35.00N	4.00W
Rift Valley V	106	3.00S	29.00 E
Rīga	100	56.57N	24.06 E
Riga, Gulf of ⊂	100	57.30N	23.35 E
Rīgestān ◆ [1]	110	31.00N	65.00 E
Rijeka	96	45.20N	14.27 E
Rimini	96	44.04N	12.34 E
Ringgold Isles II	127c	16.15S	179.25W
Ringvassøya I	89	69.55N	19.15 E
Riobamba	132	1.40S	78.38W
Rio Branco	132	9.58S	67.48W
Río Cuarto	134	33.08S	64.21W
Rio de Janeiro	132	22.54S	43.14W
Río Gallegos	134	51.38S	69.13W
Río Grande, Arg.	134	53.47S	67.42W
Rio Grande, Braz.	134	32.02S	52.05W
Ríohacha	132	11.33N	72.55W
Río Hato	130	8.23N	80.10W
Río Mayo	134	45.41S	70.16W
Rio Verde	135	17.43S	50.56W
Ripley	140	38.49N	81.42W
Ritter, Mount ∧	142	37.42N	119.12W
Rivas	130	11.26N	85.50W
Rivera	134	30.54S	55.31W
Riverhead	140	40.55N	72.39W
Riverina ◆ [1]	124	35.30S	145.30 E
Riverside	142	33.57N	117.23W
Rivne	86	50.37N	26.15 E
Riyadh → Ar-Riyāḍ	108	24.38N	46.43 E
Rizzuto, Capo ≻	96	38.54N	17.06 E
Roanne	92	46.02N	4.04 E
Roanoke	138	37.16N	79.56W
Roberts Peak ∧	136	52.57N	120.32W
Roberval	136	48.31N	72.13W
Roboré	132	18.20S	59.45W
Rocha	134	34.29S	54.20W
Rochefort	92	45.57N	0.58W
Rochester, Mn., U.S.	138	44.01N	92.28W
Rochester, N.H., U.S.	140	43.18N	70.58W
Rochester, N.Y., U.S.	140	43.09N	77.36W
Rockefeller Plateau ⋀ [1]	85	80.00S	135.00W
Rockford, Il., U.S.	138	42.16N	89.05W
Rockford, Mi., U.S.	140	43.07N	85.33W
Rockhampton	122	23.23S	150.31 E
Rock Island	138	41.30N	90.34W
Rockland	140	44.06N	69.06W
Rock Springs	138	41.35N	109.12W
Rockville	140	39.05N	77.09W
Rocky Mountains ⋀	82	48.00N	116.00W
Rodez	92	44.21N	2.35 E
Ródhos (Rhodes)	98	36.26N	28.13 E
Ródhos I	98	36.10N	28.00 E
Roebourne	122	20.47S	117.09 E
Roeselare	90	50.57N	3.08 E
Rogue ≃	142	42.26N	124.25W
Rohtak	112	28.54N	76.34 E
Roma (Rome)	96	41.54N	12.29 E
Roman	98	46.55N	26.56 E
Romania □ [1]	86	46.00N	25.30 E
Romans [-sur-Isère]	92	45.03N	5.03 E
Rome → Roma, Italy	96	41.54N	12.29 E
Rome, Ga., U.S.	138	34.15N	85.09W
Rome, N.Y., U.S.	140	43.12N	75.27W
Romeo	140	42.48N	83.00W
Ron, Mui ≻	120	18.07N	106.22 E
Roncador, Serra do ⋀ [1]	132	12.00S	52.00W
Ronne Ice Shelf ⊠	85	78.30S	61.00W
Roosevelt Island I	85	79.30S	162.00W

Name	Page No.	Lat.	Long.
Roraima, Mount ʌ	132	5.12N	60.44W
Rosario	134	32.57S	60.40W
Roscommon	88	53.38N	8.11W
Roseau	130	15.18N	61.24W
Roseburg	142	43.13N	123.20W
Rosenheim	90	47.51N	12.07 E
Ross Ice Shelf ⋈	85	81.30S	175.00W
Rosslare	88	52.17N	6.23W
Ross Sea ⋝²	85	76.00S	175.00W
Rostock	90	54.05N	12.07 E
Rostov-na-Donu	86	47.14N	39.42 E
Roswell	138	33.23N	104.31W
Rotorua	126	38.09S	176.15 E
Rotterdam	90	51.55N	4.28 E
Roubaix	92	50.42N	3.10 E
Rouen	92	49.26N	1.05 E
Rouyn-Noranda	136	48.15N	79.01W
Rovaniemi	89	66.34N	25.48 E
Royan	92	45.37N	1.01W
Ruapehu ʌ	126	39.17S	175.34 E
Rubcovsk	102	51.33N	81.10 E
Ruby	144	64.44N	155.30W
Ruby Lake ☲	142	40.10N	115.30W
Rudolf, Lake ⊜	108	3.30N	36.00 E
Rügen ı	90	54.25N	13.24 E
Rukwa, Lake ⊜	106	8.00S	32.25 E
Rump Mountain ʌ	140	45.12N	71.04W
Rupert	142	42.37N	113.40W
Ruse	98	43.50N	25.57 E
Rüsselsheim	90	50.00N	8.25 E
Russia □¹	86	60.00N	100.00 E
Rutland	140	43.36N	72.58W
Ruvuma (Rovuma) ≃	106	10.29S	40.28 E
Rwanda □¹	106	2.30S	30.00 E
Rybinsk	100	58.03N	38.52 E
Rybinskoje Vodochranilišče ⊜¹	100	58.30N	38.25 E
Rysy ʌ	90	49.12N	20.04 E
Ryukyu Islands → Nansei-shotō ıı	114	26.30N	128.00 E
Rzeszów	90	50.03N	22.00 E

S

Saarbrücken	90	49.14N	6.59 E
Saaremaa ı	100	58.25N	22.30 E
Sab, Tônlé ⊜	120	13.00N	104.00 E
Sabinas Hidalgo	128	26.30N	100.10W
Sabine ≃	128	30.00N	93.45W
Sable, Île de ı	122	19.15S	159.56 E
Sachalin, Ostrov (Sakhalin) ı	102	51.00N	143.00 E
Šachty	86	47.42N	40.13 E
Sacramento	142	38.34N	121.29W
Sacramento ≃	142	38.03N	121.56W
Sacramento Valley v	142	39.15N	122.00W
Sado ı	116	38.00N	138.25 E
Saga	116	33.15N	130.18 E
Sagami-nada c	116	35.00N	139.30 E
Sāgar	112	23.50N	78.45 E
Saginaw	140	43.25N	83.56W
Saginaw Bay c	140	43.50N	83.40W
Sagua de Tánamo	130	20.35N	75.14W
Sagua la Grande	130	22.49N	80.05W
Saguaro National Monument ✦	128	32.12N	110.38W
Sagunto	94	39.41N	0.16W
Sahara ⬥²	104	26.00N	13.00 E
Sahāranpur	112	29.58N	77.33 E
Saidpur	112	25.47N	88.54 E
Saigon → Thanh Pho Ho Chi Minh	120	10.45N	106.40 E
Saint Anthony	136	51.22N	55.35W
Saint Augustine	138	29.53N	81.18W

Name	Page No.	Lat.	Long.
Saint-Augustin-Saguenay	136	51.14N	58.39W
Saint-Brieuc	92	48.31N	2.47W
Saint Catharines	140	43.10N	79.15W
Saint-Chamond	92	45.28N	4.30 E
Saint Christopher (Saint Kitts) ı	130	17.20N	62.45W
Saint Clair	140	42.48N	82.29W
Saint Croix ı	130	17.45N	64.45W
Saint-Denis, Fr.	92	48.56N	2.22 E
Saint-Denis, Reu.	106	20.52S	55.28 E
Saint-Dizier	92	48.38N	4.57 E
Saint Elias, Mount ʌ	144	60.18N	140.55W
Saint-Étienne	92	45.26N	4.24 E
Saint George	122	28.02S	148.35 E
Saint George's	130	12.03N	61.45W
Saint George's Bay c	136	48.20N	59.00W
Saint George's Channel ᚢ	88	52.00N	6.00W
Saint Helier	92	49.12N	2.37W
Saint-Hyacinthe	140	45.38N	72.57W
Saint James	140	45.45N	85.30W
Saint James, Cape ≻	136	51.56N	131.01W
Saint-Jean	140	45.19N	73.16W
Saint-Jérôme	140	45.46N	74.00W
Saint John	136	45.16N	66.03W
Saint John, Cape ≻	136	50.00N	55.32W
Saint John's	136	47.34N	52.43W
Saint Johnsbury	140	44.25N	72.00W
Saint Joseph	138	39.46N	94.50W
Saint Joseph, Lake ⊜	136	51.05N	90.35W
Saint-Jovite	140	46.07N	74.36W
Saint Kilda ı	88	57.49N	8.36W
Saint Kitts → Saint Christopher ı	130	17.20N	62.45W
Saint Kitts and Nevis □¹	130	17.20N	62.45W
Saint Lawrence ≃	136	49.30N	67.00W
Saint Lawrence, Gulf of c	136	48.00N	62.00W
Saint Lawrence Island ı	144	63.30N	170.30W
Saint-Lô	92	49.07N	1.05W
Saint-Louis, Sen.	104	16.02N	16.30W
Saint Louis, Mo., U.S.	138	38.37N	90.11W
Saint Lucia □¹	130	13.53N	60.58W
Saint-Malo	92	48.39N	2.01W
Saint-Malo, Golfe de c	92	48.45N	2.00W
Sainte-Marie, Cap ≻	106	25.36S	45.08 E
Saint Marys	140	41.25N	78.33W
Saint-Nazaire	92	47.17N	2.12W
Saint Paul	138	44.57N	93.05W
Saint Peter Port	92	49.27N	2.32W
Saint Petersburg → Sankt-Peterburg, Russia	100	59.55N	30.15 E
Saint Petersburg, Fl., U.S.	138	27.46N	82.40W
Saint Pierre and Miquelon □²	136	46.55N	56.10W
Saint-Quentin	92	49.51N	3.17 E
Saintes	92	45.45N	0.52W
Saint Thomas	140	42.47N	81.12W
Saint Vincent, Gulf c	124	35.00S	138.05 E
Saint Vincent and the Grenadines □¹	130	13.15N	61.12W
Saipan ı	118	15.12N	145.45 E
Sairecábur, Cerro ʌ	132	22.43S	67.54W
Saito	116	32.06N	131.24 E
Sajama, Nevado ʌ	132	18.06S	68.54W
Sakai	116	34.35N	135.28 E
Sakata	116	38.55N	139.50 E
Sakau	127b	16.49S	168.24 E
Sakhalin → Sachalin, Ostrov ı	102	51.00N	143.00 E
Saku	116	36.09N	138.26 E
Sakurai	116	34.30N	135.51 E

Name	Page No.	Lat.	Long.
Salamanca	94	40.58N	5.39W
Saldanha	106	33.00S	17.56 E
Salem, Ma., U.S.	140	42.31N	70.53W
Salem, Oh., U.S.	140	40.54N	80.51W
Salem, Or., U.S.	138	44.56N	123.02W
Salerno	96	40.41N	14.47 E
Salgótarján	90	48.07N	19.48 E
Salihli	98	38.29N	28.09 E
Salinas	142	36.40N	121.39W
Salinas ≃	142	36.45N	121.48W
Salisbury, Eng., U.K.	88	51.05N	1.48W
Salisbury, Md., U.S.	140	38.21N	75.35W
Salmon River Mountains ⋏	138	44.45N	115.00W
Salonika → Thessaloníki	98	40.38N	22.56 E
Sal'sk	86	46.28N	41.33 E
Salta	134	24.47S	65.25W
Saltillo	128	25.25N	101.00W
Salt Lake City	138	40.45N	111.53W
Salto	134	31.23S	57.58W
Salton Sea ∈	142	33.19N	115.50W
Salvador	132	12.59S	38.31W
Salween (Nu) ≃	120	16.31N	97.37 E
Salyersville	140	37.45N	83.04W
Salzburg	90	47.48N	13.02 E
Salzgitter	90	52.10N	10.25 E
Samar I	118	12.00N	125.00 E
Samara	86	53.12N	50.09 E
Samarinda	118	0.30S	117.09 E
Samarkand	110	39.40N	66.48 E
Sambalpur	112	21.27N	83.58 E
Samoa Islands II	127e	14.00S	171.00W
Sámos I	98	37.48N	26.44 E
Samothráki (Samothrace) I	98	40.30N	25.32 E
Sam Rayburn Reservoir ∈1	138	31.27N	94.37W
Samsun	86	41.17N	36.20 E
Samui, Ko I	120	9.30N	100.00 E
Samut Prakan	120	13.36N	100.36 E
San ≃	90	50.45N	21.51 E
San'ā'	108	15.23N	44.12 E
San Agustin, Cape ⋗	118	6.16N	126.11 E
San Andrés	130	12.35N	81.42W
San Andrés, Isla de I	130	12.32N	81.42W
San Angelo	138	31.27N	100.26W
San Antonio	138	29.25N	98.29W
San Antonio, Cabo ⋗	130	21.52N	84.57W
San Antonio Oeste	134	40.44S	64.56W
San Benedetto del Tronto	96	42.57N	13.53 E
San Benito	130	16.55N	89.54W
San Bernardino	142	34.07N	117.18W
San Bernardino Mountains ⋏	142	34.10N	117.00W
San Blas, Cape ⋗	138	29.40N	85.22W
San Carlos	130	11.07N	84.47W
San Carlos de Bariloche	134	41.09S	71.18W
San Carlos del Zulia	130	9.01N	71.55W
San Carlos de Río Negro	132	1.55N	67.04W
San Clemente	142	33.25N	117.36W
San Clemente Island I	142	32.54N	118.29W
San Cristóbal	132	7.46N	72.14W
San Cristóbal I	127a	10.36S	161.45 E
Sancti-Spíritus	130	21.56N	79.27W
Sandakan	118	5.50N	118.07 E
Sandia	132	14.17S	69.26W
San Diego	142	32.42N	117.09W
Sandnes	89	58.51N	5.44 E
Sandusky, Mi., U.S.	140	43.25N	82.49W
Sandusky, Oh., U.S.	140	41.26N	82.42W
Sandviken	89	60.37N	16.46 E
Sandy Hook	140	38.05N	83.07W
Sandy Lake ∈	136	53.00N	93.07W
San Felipe	130	10.20N	68.44W
San Fernando, Spain	94	36.28N	6.12W
San Fernando, Trin.	130	10.17N	61.28W
San Fernando de Apure	132	7.54N	67.28W
San Fernando de Atabapo	132	4.03N	67.42W
Sanford	140	43.26N	70.46W
San Francisco	142	37.46N	122.25W
San Francisco de Macorís	130	19.18N	70.15W
San Gabriel Mountains ⋏	142	34.20N	118.00W
Sängli	111	16.52N	74.34 E
San Gottardo, Passo del ⋌	92	46.33N	8.34 E
San Jacinto	130	9.50N	75.08W
San Joaquin ≃	142	38.03N	121.50W
San Joaquin Valley V	142	36.50N	120.10W
San Jorge, Golfo c	134	46.00S	67.00W
San José, C.R.	130	9.56N	84.05W
San Jose, Ca., U.S.	142	37.20N	121.53W
San José de Chiquitos	132	17.51S	60.47W
San José de Guanipa	130	8.54N	64.09W
San José del Guaviare	132	2.35N	72.38W
San Juan, Arg.	134	31.32S	68.31W
San Juan, P.R.	130	18.28N	66.07W
San Juan ≃	130	10.56N	83.42W
San Juan del Norte	130	10.55N	83.42W
San Juan de los Cayos	130	11.10N	68.25W
San Juan de los Morros	130	9.55N	67.21W
San Julián	134	49.18S	67.43W
San Justo	134	30.47S	60.35W
Sankt Gallen	92	47.25N	9.23 E
Sankt Moritz	92	46.30N	9.50 E
Sankt-Peterburg (Saint Petersburg)	100	59.55N	30.15 E
Sankt Pölten	90	48.12N	15.37 E
Şanlıurfa	109	37.08N	38.46 E
San Lucas, Cabo ⋗	128	22.52N	109.53W
San Luis, Guat.	130	16.14N	89.27W
San Luis, Ven.	130	11.07N	69.42W
San Luis Obispo	142	35.16N	120.39W
San Luis Potosí	128	22.09N	100.59W
San Luis Río Colorado	128	32.29N	114.48W
San Marcos	128	29.52N	97.56W
San Marino	96	43.55N	12.28 E
San Marino □1	86	43.56N	12.25 E
San Mateo, Ca., U.S.	142	37.33N	122.19W
San Mateo, Ven.	130	9.45N	64.33W
San Miguel	130	13.29N	88.11W
San Miguel de Tucumán	134	26.49S	65.13W
San Nicolas Island I	142	33.15N	119.31W
San Onofre	130	9.44N	75.32W
San Pedro, Punta ⋗	134	25.30S	70.38W
San Pedro de las Colonias	128	25.45N	102.59W
San Pedro de Macorís	130	18.27N	69.18W
San Pedro Sula	130	15.27N	88.02W
San Rafael, Arg.	134	34.36S	68.20W
San Rafael, Mex.	128	25.01N	100.33W
San Remo	96	43.49N	7.46 E
San Salvador	130	13.41N	89.17W
San Salvador de Jujuy	134	24.11S	65.18W
San Sebastián	94	43.19N	1.59W
San Severo	96	41.41N	15.23 E
Santa Ana, Bol.	132	15.31S	67.30W
Santa Ana, Hond.	130	13.59N	89.34W
Santa Ana, Ca., U.S.	142	33.44N	117.52W
Santa Barbara	142	34.25N	119.42W
Santa Barbara Channel ⍩	142	34.15N	119.55W

Name	Page No.	Lat.	Long.
Santa Catalina, Gulf of c	142	33.20N	117.45W
Santa Clara, Cuba	130	22.24N	79.58W
Santa Clara, Ca., U.S.	142	37.20N	121.56W
Santa Cruz, Bol.	132	17.48S	63.10W
Santa Cruz, Ca., U.S.	142	36.58N	122.01W
Santa Cruz de Tenerife	104	28.27N	16.14W
Santa Cruz Island I	142	34.01N	119.45W
Santa Fe, Arg.	134	31.38S	60.42W
Santa Fe, N.M., U.S.	138	35.41N	105.56W
Santa Fe de Bogotá	132	4.36N	74.05W
Santa Isabel I	127a	8.00S	159.00 E
Santa Lucia Range ⊀	142	36.00N	121.20W
Santa Maria, Braz.	134	29.41S	53.48W
Santa Maria, Ca., U.S.	142	34.57N	120.26W
Santa Maria, Cabo de ↘	106	13.25S	12.32 E
Santa María Island I	127b	14.15S	167.30 E
Santa Marta	132	11.15N	74.13W
Santana do Livramento	134	30.53S	55.31W
Santander	94	43.28N	3.48W
Santarém	132	2.26S	54.42W
Santa Rosa, Arg.	134	36.37S	64.17W
Santa Rosa, Arg.	134	32.20S	65.12W
Santa Rosa, Ca., U.S.	142	38.26N	122.42W
Santa Rosa Island I	142	33.58N	120.06W
Santiago	134	33.27S	70.40W
Santiago de Compostela	94	42.53N	8.33W
Santiago de Cuba	130	20.01N	75.49W
Santiago del Estero	134	27.47S	64.16W
Santiago [de los Caballeros]	130	19.27N	70.42W
Santo André	135	23.40S	46.31W
Santo Ángelo	134	28.18S	54.16W
Santo Antônio de Jesus	135	12.58S	39.16W
Santo Domingo	130	18.28N	69.54W
Santos	132	23.57S	46.20W
San Valentín, Cerro ⋀	134	46.36S	73.20W
San Vicente	130	13.38N	88.48W
San Vicente de Baracaldo	94	43.18N	2.59W
San Vito, Capo ⋗	96	38.11N	12.43 E
São Carlos	135	22.01S	47.54W
São Francisco ≃	132	10.30S	36.24W
São José do Rio Prêto	132	20.48S	49.23W
São José dos Campos	135	23.11S	45.53W
São Leopoldo	134	29.46S	51.09W
São Luís	132	2.31S	44.16W
São Mateus	132	18.44S	39.51W
Saône ≃	90	46.05N	4.45 E
São Paulo	132	23.32S	46.37W
São Roque, Cabo de ⋗	132	5.29S	35.16W
São Sebastião, Ilha de I	135	23.50S	45.18W
São Sebastião, Ponta ⋗	106	22.07S	35.30 E
São Tomé	106	0.20N	6.44 E
São Tomé, Cabo de ⋗	135	21.59S	40.59W
Sao Tome and Principe □ [1]	106	1.00N	7.00 E
São Vicente, Cabo de ⋗	94	37.01N	9.00W
Sapitwa ⋀	106	15.57S	35.36 E
Sapporo	116a	43.03N	141.21 E
Sarajevo	98	43.52N	18.25 E
Saransk	86	54.11N	45.11 E
Sarapul	86	56.28N	53.48 E
Sarasota	138	27.20N	82.31W
Saratoga Springs	140	43.04N	73.47W
Saratov	86	51.34N	46.02 E
Sardegna (Sardinia) I	96	40.00N	9.00 E
Sargodha	112	32.05N	72.40 E
Sarh	104	9.09N	18.23 E
Sarmiento	134	45.36S	69.05W
Sarnia	136	42.58N	82.23W
Saronikós Kólpos c	98	37.54N	23.12 E
Sarthe ≃	92	47.30N	0.32W
Sasamungga	127a	7.02S	156.47 E
Sasebo	116	33.10N	129.43 E
Saskatchewan □ [4]	136	54.00N	105.00W
Saskatoon	136	52.07N	106.38W
Sassandra ≃	104	4.58N	6.05W
Sassari	96	40.44N	8.33 E
Sātāra	111	17.41N	73.59 E
Sataua	127e	13.28S	172.40W
Satna	112	24.35N	80.50 E
Satsunan-shotō II	117b	29.00N	130.00 E
Satu Mare	98	47.48N	22.53 E
Saudi Arabia □ [1]	108	25.00N	45.00 E
Sauerland ⬦ [1]	90	51.10N	8.00 E
Saugerties	140	42.04N	73.57W
Sault Sainte Marie, On., Can.	136	46.31N	84.20W
Sault Sainte Marie, Mi., U.S.	138	46.30N	84.21W
Saumur	92	47.16N	0.05W
Saurimo	106	9.39S	20.24 E
Sava ≃	98	44.50N	20.26 E
Savai'i I	127e	13.35S	172.25W
Savannah	138	32.05N	81.06W
Savannakhét	120	16.33N	104.45 E
Savona	96	44.17N	8.30 E
Savusavu	127c	16.16S	179.21 E
Sawdā', Qurnat as- ⋀	109	34.18N	36.07 E
Sawhāj	104	26.33N	31.42 E
Sawu, Laut (Savu Sea) ⊽ [2]	122	9.40S	122.00 E
Sayan Mountains (Sajany) ⊀	102	52.45N	96.00 E
Sayaxché	130	16.31N	90.10W
Schaffhausen	92	47.42N	8.38 E
Schefferville	136	54.48N	66.50W
Schenectady	140	42.48N	73.56W
Schleswig	90	54.31N	9.33 E
Schwaben □ [9]	90	48.20N	10.30 E
Schwäbisch Gmünd	90	48.48N	9.47 E
Schwarzwald ⊀	90	48.00N	8.15 E
Schwedt	90	53.03N	14.17 E
Schweinfurt	90	50.03N	10.14 E
Schwerin	90	53.38N	11.25 E
Sciacca	96	37.30N	13.06 E
Scotland □ [8]	88	57.00N	4.00W
Scott Islands II	136	50.48N	128.40W
Scottsbluff	138	41.52N	103.40W
Scranton	140	41.24N	75.39W
Scutari, Lake ⊜	98	42.12N	19.18 E
Searsport	140	44.27N	68.55W
Seattle	138	47.36N	122.19W
Sebastian, Cape ⋗	142	42.19N	124.26W
Sebastián Vizcaíno, Bahía c	128	28.00N	114.30W
Ségou	104	13.27N	6.16W
Segovia	94	40.57N	4.07W
Seguin	128	29.34N	97.57W
Seine ≃	92	49.26N	0.26 E
Seine, Baie de la ≃	92	49.30N	0.30W
Sekondi-Takoradi	104	4.59N	1.43W
Selawik	144	66.37N	160.03W
Seldovia	144	59.27N	151.43W
Šelichova, Zaliv c	102	60.00N	158.00 E
Selma	138	32.24N	87.01W
Selva	134	29.46S	62.03W
Selvas ⬦ [3]	132	5.00S	68.00W
Selwyn Mountains ⊀	136	63.10N	130.20W
Semara	104	26.44N	14.41W
Semarang	118	6.58S	110.25 E
Semey	102	50.28N	80.13 E
Sendai	116	38.15N	140.53 E
Seneca Lake ⊜	140	42.40N	76.57W
Senegal □ [1]	104	14.00N	14.00W
Sénégal ≃	104	15.48N	16.32W
Senigallia	96	43.43N	13.13 E
Senja I	89	69.20N	17.30 E
Senmonorom	120	12.27N	107.12 E

Name	Page No.	Lat.	Long.
Senneterre	136	48.23N	77.15W
Seoul			
→ Sŏul	114	37.33N	126.58 E
Sepi	127a	8.33S	159.50 E
Sept-Îles (Seven Islands)	136	50.12N	66.23W
Sequoia National Park ◆	142	36.30N	118.30W
Seram (Ceram) I	118	3.00S	129.00 E
Seram, Laut (Ceram Sea) ☞²	118	2.30S	128.00 E
Serbia □³	98	44.00N	21.00 E
Seremban	120	2.43N	101.56 E
Serengeti Plain ≝	106	2.50S	35.00 E
Sergijev Posad	86	56.18N	38.08 E
Serov	102	59.29N	60.31 E
Serowe	106	22.25S	26.44 E
Sérrai	98	41.05N	23.32 E
Serrat, Cap ⋟	96	37.14N	9.13 E
Sesfontein	106	19.07S	13.39 E
Sète	92	43.24N	3.41 E
Sete Lagoas	132	19.27S	44.14W
Seto-naikai ☞²	116	34.20N	133.30 E
Setúbal	94	38.32N	8.54W
Sevastopol'	86	44.36N	33.32 E
Severn ≃	88	51.35N	2.40W
Severnaja Dvina ≃	86	64.32N	40.30 E
Severodvinsk	86	64.34N	39.50 E
Severo-Kuril'sk	102	50.40N	156.08 E
Sevilla	94	37.23N	5.59W
Seward	144	60.06N	149.26W
Seward Peninsula ⋟¹	144	65.00N	164.00W
Seychelles □¹	106	4.35S	55.40 E
Seyđisfjörđur	86	65.16N	14.00W
Sfax	104	34.44N	10.46 E
's-Gravenhage (The Hague)	90	52.06N	4.18 E
Shabeelle (Shebele) ≃	108	0.50N	42.10 E
Shache	114	38.25N	77.16 E
Shāhjahānpur	112	27.53N	79.55 E
Shakawe	106	18.23S	21.50 E
Shalqar	86	47.50N	59.36 E
Shām, Jabal ash- ᴧ	108	23.13N	57.16 E
Shamattawa	136	55.52N	92.05W
Shamokin	140	40.47N	76.33W
Shandī	104	16.42N	33.26 E
Shanghai	114	31.14N	121.28 E
Shangqiu	114	34.27N	115.42 E
Shannon ≃	88	52.36N	9.41W
Shantou	114	23.23N	116.41 E
Shaoguan	114	24.50N	113.37 E
Shaoyang	114	27.06N	111.25 E
Sharon	140	41.13N	80.29W
Sharqīyah, Aş-Şaḥrā' ash- (Arabian Desert) ◆²	109	28.00N	32.00 E
Shashi ≃	106	22.14S	29.20 E
Shasta, Mount ᴧ¹	142	41.20N	122.20W
Shasta Lake ⊜¹	142	40.50N	122.25W
Shaykh, Jabal ash- ᴧ	109	33.26N	35.51 E
Shebele (Shabeelle) ≃	108	0.50N	43.10 E
Sheberghān	112	36.41N	65.45 E
Sheffield, N.J.	126	43.23S	172.01 E
Sheffield, Eng., U.K.	88	53.23N	1.30W
Shelburne	136	43.46N	65.19W
Shenandoah National Park ◆	140	38.48N	78.12W
Shenyang	114	41.48N	123.27 E
Sherbro Island I	104	7.45N	12.55W
Sherbrooke	140	45.25N	71.54W
Sheridan	138	44.47N	106.57W
Sherman Station	140	45.53N	68.25W
Shetland Islands II	88	60.30N	1.30W
Shibīn al-Kawm	104	30.33N	31.01 E
Shijiazhuang	114	38.03N	114.28 E
Shikārpur	112	27.57N	68.38 E
Shikoku I	116	33.45N	133.30 E
Shillong	112	25.34N	91.53 E
Shimodate	116	36.18N	139.59 E
Shimonoseki	116	33.57N	130.57 E
Shingū	116	33.44N	135.59 E
Shīrāz	108	29.36N	52.32 E
Shiroishi	116	38.00N	140.37 E
Shizuoka	116	34.58N	138.23 E
Shkodra	98	42.05N	19.30 E
Sholāpur	111	17.41N	75.55 E
Shreveport	138	32.30N	93.44W
Shwebo	120	22.34N	95.42 E
Siālkot	112	32.30N	74.31 E
Sian			
→ Xi'an	114	34.15N	108.52 E
Šiauliai	100	55.56N	23.19 E
Šibenik	96	43.44N	15.54 E
Siberia			
→ Sibir' ◆¹	102	65.00N	110.00 E
Sibir' (Siberia) ◆¹	102	65.00N	110.00 E
Sibiu	98	45.48N	24.09 E
Sibsāgar	112	26.59N	94.38 E
Sichote-Alin' ↗	102	48.00N	138.00 E
Sicilia (Sicily) I	96	37.30N	14.00 E
Sicuani	132	14.16S	71.13W
Sidi bel Abbès	86	35.13N	0.10W
Sidi el Hani, Sebkher ⊜	96	35.33N	10.25 E
Sidney	138	47.43N	104.09W
Siegen	90	50.52N	8.02 E
Siĕmréab	120	13.22N	103.51 E
Siena	96	43.19N	11.21 E
Sierra Colorada	134	40.35S	67.48W
Sierra Leone □¹	104	8.30N	11.30W
Sierre	92	46.18N	7.32 E
Sighetul Marmaţiei	98	47.56N	23.54 E
Sighişoara	98	46.13N	24.48 E
Sīkar	112	27.37N	75.09 E
Sikasso	104	11.19N	5.40W
Sikkim □³	112	27.35N	88.35 E
Silīguri	112	26.42N	88.26 E
Silistra	98	44.07N	27.16 E
Silkeborg	89	56.10N	9.34 E
Silver City	138	32.46N	108.16W
Silver Lake	142	43.07N	121.02W
Simanovsk	102	52.00N	127.42 E
Simcoe	140	42.50N	80.18W
Simcoe, Lake ⊜	140	44.20N	79.20W
Simeulue, Pulau I	120	2.35N	96.00 E
Simferopol'	86	44.57N	34.06 E
Simla	112	31.06N	77.10 E
Simplon Pass ⋊	96	46.15N	8.02 E
Simpson Desert ◆²	122	25.00S	137.00 E
Sīnā', Shibh Jazīrat (Sinai Peninsula) ⋟¹	108	29.30N	34.00 E
Sincelejo	130	9.18N	75.24W
Singapore	120	1.17N	103.51 E
Singapore □¹	118	1.22N	103.48 E
Singapore Strait ⋓	120	1.15N	104.00 E
Sinkiang			
→ Xinjiang Uygur Zizhiqu □⁴	114	40.00N	85.00 E
Sinŭiju	114	40.05N	124.24 E
Sioux City	138	42.30N	96.24W
Sioux Falls	138	43.33N	96.42W
Sioux Lookout	136	50.06N	91.55W
Siple, Mount ᴧ	85	73.15S	126.06W
Siracusa	96	37.04N	15.17 E
Sirājganj	112	24.27N	89.43 E
Siret ≃	98	45.24N	28.01 E
Sirhān, Wādī as- ꙮ	109	30.30N	38.00 E
Sisak	96	45.29N	16.23 E
Siskiyou Pass ⋊	142	42.03N	122.36W
Sitka	144	57.03N	135.02W
Sittwe (Akyab)	120	20.09N	92.54 E
Sivas	86	39.45N	37.02 E
Skagerrak ⋓	89	57.45N	9.00 E

Name	Page No.	Lat.	Long.	Name	Page No.	Lat.	Long.
Skagway	144	59.28N	135.19W	South Carolina □³	138	34.00N	81.00W
Skarżysko-Kamienna	90	51.08N	20.53 E	South China Sea ᴛ²	114	19.00N	115.00 E
Skeldon	132	5.53N	57.08W	South Dakota □³	138	44.15N	100.00W
Skelleftea	89	64.46N	20.57 E	Southend-on-Sea	88	51.33N	0.43 E
Skellefteälven ≊	89	64.42N	21.06 E	Southern Alps ⚹	126	43.30S	170.30 E
Skien	89	59.12N	9.36 E	Southern Cross	122	31.13S	119.19 E
Skíros	98	38.53N	24.33 E	South Georgia I	134	54.15S	36.45W
Skíros I	98	38.53N	24.32 E	South Indian Lake	136	56.46N	98.57W
Skopje	98	41.59N	21.26 E	South Island I	126	43.00S	171.00 E
Skye, Island of I	88	57.15N	6.10W	South Orkney Islands II	85	60.35S	45.30W
Slanské Vrchy ⚹	90	48.50N	21.30 E	South Platte ≊	138	41.07N	100.42W
Slavgorod	102	53.00N	78.40 E	South Point ⟩	124	39.00S	146.20 E
Slavonija ◆¹	96	45.00N	18.00 E	South Pole ◆	85	90.00S	0.00
Slavonski Brod	98	45.10N	18.01 E	Southport, Austl.	124	27.58S	153.25 E
Sligo	88	54.17N	8.28W	Southport, Eng., U.K.	88	53.39N	3.01 W
Sliven	98	42.40N	26.19 E	South Sandwich			
Slovakia □¹	90	49.00N	19.30 E	Islands II	85	57.45S	26.30W
Slovenia □¹	96	46.15N	15.10 E	South Shetland Islands			
Słupsk (Stolp)	90	54.28N	17.01 E	II	85	62.00S	58.00W
Smederevo	98	44.40N	20.56 E	South West Cape ⟩	124	43.34S	146.02 E
Smiths Falls	140	44.54N	76.01W	Sovetskaja Gavan'	102	48.58N	140.18 E
Smithton	122	40.51S	145.07 E	Spain □¹	86	40.00N	4.00W
Smokey Dome ▲	142	43.29N	114.56W	Spanish North Africa			
Smolensk	100	54.47N	32.03 E	□²	94	35.53N	5.19W
Smoljan	98	41.35N	24.41 E	Spanish Town	130	17.59N	76.57W
Smythe, Mount ▲	136	57.54N	124.53W	Sparks	142	39.32N	119.45W
Snake ≊	138	46.12N	119.02W	Spárti (Sparta)	98	37.05N	22.27 E
Snake River Plain ≊	142	43.00N	113.00W	Spassk-Dal'nij	102	44.37N	132.48 E
Snina	90	48.59N	22.07 E	Spencer Gulf c	124	34.00S	137.00 E
Snøtinden ▲	89	66.38N	14.00 E	Speyer	90	49.19N	8.26 E
Snow Hill	140	38.10N	75.23W	Split	96	43.31N	16.27 E
Snyder	128	32.43N	100.55W	Spokane	138	47.39N	117.25W
Sobat ≊	108	9.22N	31.33 E	Spoleto	96	42.44N	12.44 E
Sobral	132	3.42S	40.21W	Springbok	106	29.43S	17.55 E
Soči	86	43.35N	39.45 E	Springdale	136	49.30N	56.04W
Société, Îles de la				Springfield, Il., U.S.	138	39.48N	89.38W
(Society Islands) II	127d	17.00S	150.00W	Springfield, Ma., U.S.	140	42.06N	72.35W
Soc Trang	120	9.36N	105.58 E	Springfield, Mo., U.S.	138	37.12N	93.17W
Söderhamn	89	61.18N	17.03 E	Springfield, Oh., U.S.	140	39.55N	83.48W
Sofija (Sofia)	98	42.41N	23.19 E	Springfontein	106	30.19S	25.36 E
Sognafjorden c²	89	61.06N	5.10 E	Springhill	136	45.39N	64.03W
Soissons	92	49.22N	3.20 E	Springs	106	26.13S	28.25 E
Söke	98	37.45N	27.24 E	Spruce Knob ▲	140	38.42N	79.32W
Sokoto	104	13.04N	5.16 E	Squillace, Golfo di c	96	38.50N	16.50 E
Solbad Hall in Tirol	90	47.17N	11.31 E	Srednesibirskoje			
Soligorsk	100	52.48N	27.32 E	Ploskogorje ⚹¹	102	65.00N	105.00 E
Solikamsk	86	59.39N	56.47 E	Sri Lanka □¹	110	7.00N	81.00 E
Solimões				Sri Lanka I	111	7.00N	81.00 E
→ Amazon ≊	132	0.05S	50.00W	Srinagar	112	34.05N	74.49 E
Solomon Islands □¹	82	8.00S	159.00 E	Stade	90	53.36N	9.28 E
Solomon Sea ᴛ²	122	8.00S	155.00 E	Stafford	88	52.48N	2.07W
Solothurn	92	47.13N	7.32 E	Stalingrad			
Somalia □¹	108	10.00N	49.00 E	→ Volgograd	86	48.44N	44.25 E
Sombor	98	45.46N	19.07 E	Stamford	140	41.03N	73.32W
Somerset	138	37.05N	84.36W	Standish	140	43.58N	83.57W
Somerset Island I	136	73.15N	93.30W	Stanke Dimitrov	98	42.16N	23.07 E
Someşu Mic ≊	98	47.09N	23.55 E	Stanley Falls			
Somosomo	127c	16.46S	179.58W	→ Boyoma Falls ʟ	106	0.15N	25.30 E
Songkhla	120	7.12N	100.36 E	Stanovoje Nagorje			
Sonneberg	90	50.22N	11.10 E	(Stanovoy			
Sopron	90	47.41N	16.36 E	Mountains) ⚹	102	56.00N	114.00 E
Sorel	140	46.02N	73.07W	Stanton	140	37.50N	83.51W
Sorocaba	135	23.29S	47.27W	Starachowice	90	51.03N	21.04 E
Sorol I¹	118	8.08N	140.23 E	Staraja Russa	100	58.00N	31.23 E
Sørøya I	89	70.36N	22.46 E	Stara Planina (Balkan			
Sorsatunturi ▲	89	67.24N	29.38 E	Mountains) ⚹	98	43.15N	25.00 E
Souk Ahras	96	36.23N	8.00 E	Stara Zagora	98	42.25N	25.38 E
Sŏul (Seoul)	114	37.33N	126.58 E	Starogard Gdański	90	53.59N	18.33 E
Sousse	96	35.49N	10.38 E	State College	140	40.47N	77.51W
South Africa □¹	106	30.00S	26.00 E	Staunton	140	38.08N	79.04W
South America ▲¹	82	15.00S	60.00W	Stavanger	89	58.58N	5.45 E
Southampton	88	50.55N	1.25W	Stavropol'	86	45.02N	41.59 E
Southampton Island I	136	64.20N	84.40W	Steinkjer	89	64.01N	11.30 E
South Australia □³	122	30.00S	135.00 E	Stelvio, Passo dello ⤬	92	46.32N	10.27 E
Southbridge	126	43.49S	172.15 E	Stendal	90	52.36N	11.51 E
South Cape ⟩	127c	17.01S	179.55 E	Sterling	138	40.37N	103.12W

Name	Page No.	Lat.	Long.
Sterlitamak	86	53.37N	55.58 E
Steubenville	140	40.22N	80.38W
Stewart	136	55.56N	129.59W
Stewart Island I	126	47.00S	167.50 E
Steyr	90	48.03N	14.25 E
Stockerau	90	48.23N	16.13 E
Stockholm	89	59.20N	18.03 E
Stockton	142	37.57N	121.17W
Stoke-on-Trent	88	53.00N	2.10W
Stowe	140	44.27N	72.41W
Stralsund	90	54.19N	13.05 E
Strasbourg	92	48.35N	7.45 E
Strasburg	140	38.59N	78.21W
Stratford	140	43.22N	80.57W
Stratford-upon-Avon	88	52.12N	1.41W
Stratton	140	45.08N	70.26W
Straubing	90	48.53N	12.34 E
Struma (Strimón) ≃	98	40.47N	23.51 E
Sturgis	140	41.47N	85.25W
Stuttgart	90	48.46N	9.11 E
Subotica	98	46.06N	19.39 E
Suceava	98	47.39N	26.19 E
Suchumi	86	43.01N	41.02 E
Sucre	132	19.02S	65.17W
Sudan □[1]	104	15.00N	30.00 E
Sudan ◆[1]	104	10.00N	20.00 E
Sudbury	136	46.30N	81.00W
Sukkur	112	27.42N	68.52 E
Sula, Kepulauan II	118	1.52S	125.22 E
Sulaimān Range ⋀	112	30.30N	70.10 E
Sulawesi (Celebes) I	118	2.00S	121.00 E
Sullana	132	4.53S	80.41W
Sulmona	96	42.03N	13.55 E
Sulu Archipelago II	118	6.00N	121.00 E
Sulu Sea ▾[2]	118	8.00N	120.00 E
Sumatera (Sumatra) I	118	0.05S	102.00 E
Sumba I	118	10.00S	120.00 E
Sumbawa I	118	8.40S	118.00 E
Šumen	98	43.16N	26.55 E
Summit Lake	136	54.17N	122.38W
Sumoto	116	34.21N	134.54 E
Sumy	86	50.55N	34.45 E
Sunbury	140	40.51N	76.47W
Sunderland	88	54.55N	1.23W
Sundsvall	89	62.23N	17.18 E
Sunnyvale	142	37.22N	122.02W
Superior, Lake ⊜	138	48.00N	88.00W
Suquṭrā (Socotra) I	108	12.30N	54.00 E
Ṣūr (Tyre)	109	33.16N	35.11 E
Surabaya	118	7.15S	112.45 E
Surakarta	118	7.35S	110.50 E
Surat	112	21.10N	72.50 E
Surat Thani (Ban Don)	120	9.08N	99.19 E
Surendranagar	112	22.42N	71.41 E
Suretamati, Mount ∧	127b	13.47S	167.29 E
Surgut	102	61.14N	73.20 E
Suriname □[1]	132	4.00N	56.00W
Surt	104	31.12N	16.35 E
Surt, Khalīj C	104	31.30N	18.00 E
Surud Ad ∧	108	10.41N	47.18 E
Susquehanna ≃	140	39.33N	76.05W
Sutlej (Satluj) (Langchuhe) ≃	112	29.23N	71.02 E
Suva	127c	18.08S	178.25 E
Suwa	116	36.02N	138.08 E
Suways, Khalīj as- (Gulf of Suez) C	109	29.00N	32.50 E
Suways, Qanāt as- (Suez Canal) ≅	109	29.55N	32.33 E
Suzhou	114	31.18N	120.37 E
Svartenhuk ≻[1]	136	71.55N	55.00W
Svinecea ∧	98	44.48N	22.09 E
Svobodnyj	102	51.24N	128.08 E
Swan River	136	52.06N	101.16W
Swansea	88	51.38N	3.57W
Swaziland □[1]	106	26.30S	31.30 E
Sweden □[1]	86	62.00N	15.00 E
Sweetwater	138	32.28N	100.24W
Swellendam	106	34.02S	20.26 E
Świdnica (Schweidnitz)	90	50.51N	16.29 E
Świnoujście (Swinemünde)	90	53.53N	14.14 E
Switzerland □[1]	86	47.00N	8.00 E
Sydney	122	33.52S	151.13 E
Syktyvkar	86	61.40N	50.46 E
Sylhet	112	24.54N	91.52 E
Syracuse	140	43.02N	76.08W
Syria □[1]	109	35.00N	38.00 E
Syzran'	86	53.09N	48.27 E
Szczecin (Stettin)	90	53.24N	14.32 E
Szczecinek (Neustettin)	90	53.43N	16.42 E
Szeged	90	46.15N	20.09 E
Székesfehérvár	90	47.12N	18.25 E
Szolnok	90	47.10N	20.12 E
Szombathely	90	47.14N	16.38 E
T			
Tábor, Czech. Rep.	90	49.25N	14.41 E
Tabor, Russia	102	71.16N	150.12 E
Tabora	106	5.01S	32.48 E
Tabou	104	4.25N	7.21W
Tabrīz	86	38.05N	46.18 E
Tacna	132	18.01S	70.15W
Tacoma	138	47.15N	122.26W
Tadinou	127b	21.33S	167.52 E
Tadoule Lake ⊜	136	58.36N	98.20W
Taegu	114	35.52N	128.35 E
Taga	127e	13.46S	172.28W
Tagus (Tejo) (Tajo) ≃	94	38.40N	9.24W
Tahaa I	127d	16.48S	151.30W
Tahat ∧	104	23.18N	5.47 E
Tahoe, Lake ⊜	142	38.58N	120.00W
Tahoua	104	14.54N	5.16 E
Taiarapu, Presqu'île de ≻[1]	127d	17.47S	149.14W
T'aichung	114	24.09N	120.41 E
Taihape	126	39.40S	175.48 E
T'ainan	114	23.00N	120.12 E
T'aipei	114	25.03N	121.30 E
Taiping	120	4.51N	100.44 E
Taiwan □[1]	114	23.30N	121.00 E
Taiwan Strait ⋓	114	24.00N	119.00 E
Taiyuan	114	37.55N	112.30 E
Taizhou	114	32.30N	119.58 E
Tajikistan □[1]	110	39.00N	71.00 E
Tajmyr, Poluostrov ≻[1]	102	76.00N	104.00 E
Tajšet	102	55.57N	98.00 E
Tajumulco, Volcán ∧[1]	130	15.02N	91.55W
Takada	116	37.06N	138.15 E
Takaka	126	40.51S	172.48 E
Takamatsu	116	34.20N	134.03 E
Takaoka	116	36.45N	137.01 E
Takapuna	126	36.47S	174.47 E
Takasaki	116	36.20N	139.01 E
Takatsuki	116	34.51N	135.37 E
Takefu	116	35.54N	136.10 E
Takêv	120	10.59N	104.47 E
Takla Makan → Taklimakan Shamo ◆[2]	114	39.00N	83.00 E
Taklimakan Shamo ◆[2]	114	39.00N	83.00 E
Takuam, Mount ∧	127a	6.27S	155.36 E
Talara	132	4.34S	81.17W
Talaud, Kepulauan II	118	4.20N	126.50 E
Talavera de la Reina	94	39.57N	4.50W
Talca	134	35.26S	71.40W
Talcahuano	134	36.43S	73.07W
Tallahassee	138	30.26N	84.16W
Tallinn	100	59.25N	24.45 E
Tamale	104	9.25N	0.50W

Name	Page No.	Lat.	Long.
Tambov	100	52.43N	41.25 E
Tamel Aike	134	48.19S	70.58W
Tamenghest	104	22.56N	5.30 E
Tamil Nadu □³	111	11.00N	78.15 E
Tampa	138	27.56N	82.27W
Tampere	89	61.30N	23.45 E
Tampico	128	22.13N	97.51W
Tamworth	122	31.05S	150.55 E
Tana, Lake ⬤	108	12.00N	37.20 E
Tananarive			
— Antananarivo	106	18.55S	47.31 E
Tandil	134	37.19S	59.09W
Tando Ādam	112	25.46N	68.40 E
Tanega-shima I	117b	30.40N	131.00 E
Tanga	106	5.04S	39.06 E
Tanganyika, Lake ⬤	106	6.00S	29.30 E
Tanger (Tangier)	104	35.48N	5.45W
Tangshan	114	39.38N	118.11 E
Tanimbar, Kepulauan			
II	118	7.30S	131.30 E
Tanjungbalai	120	2.58N	99.48 E
Tanjungpinang	120	0.55N	104.27 E
Tanoriki	127b	14.59S	168.09 E
Tanță	104	30.47N	31.00 E
Tanzania □¹	106	6.00S	35.00 E
Tapachula	128	14.54N	92.17W
Tapajós ≈	132	2.24S	54.41W
Tāpi ≈	111	21.06N	72.41 E
Tapuaenuku ʌ	126	42.00S	173.40 E
Tara	102	56.54N	74.22 E
Țarābulus (Tripoli), Leb.	109	34.26N	35.51 E
Țarābulus (Tripoli), Libya	104	32.54N	13.11 E
Țarābulus (Tripolitania) ◆¹	104	31.00N	15.00 E
Taranto	96	40.28N	17.15 E
Taranto, Golfo di c	96	40.10N	17.20 E
Tărgoviște, Bul.	98	43.15N	26.34 E
Tarija	132	21.31S	64.45W
Tarim Pendi ≌¹	114	39.00N	83.00 E
Tarnów	90	50.01N	21.00 E
Tarragona	94	41.07N	1.15 E
Tarrasa	94	41.34N	2.01 E
Tartu	100	58.23N	26.43 E
Tarutung	120	2.01N	98.58 E
Tashi Gang Dzong	112	27.19N	91.34 E
Tasikmalaya	118	7.20S	108.12 E
Taškent	110	41.20N	69.18 E
Tasman Bay c	126	41.00S	173.20 E
Tasmania □³	122	43.00S	147.00 E
Tasman Sea ᵥ²	122	37.00S	157.00 E
Taštagol	102	52.47N	87.53 E
Tatabánya	90	47.34N	18.26 E
Tatarsk	102	55.13N	75.58 E
Taumarunui	126	38.52S	175.17 E
Taunggyi	120	20.47N	97.02 E
Taupo	126	38.41S	176.05 E
Taupo, Lake ⬤	126	38.49S	175.55 E
Tauranga	126	37.42S	176.10 E
Tauroa Point ➤	126	35.10S	173.04 E
Tautira	127d	17.44S	149.09W
Tavda	102	58.03N	65.15 E
Tawkar	104	18.26N	37.44 E
Tbilisi	86	41.43N	44.49 E
Tchibanga	106	2.51S	11.02 E
Te Anau	126	45.25S	167.43 E
Te Anau, Lake ⬤	126	45.12S	167.48 E
Tebessa	96	35.28N	8.09 E
Tecuci	98	45.50N	27.26 E
Tegucigalpa	130	14.06N	87.13W
Tehrān	86	35.40N	51.26 E
Tehuacán	128	18.27N	97.23W
Tehuantepec	128	16.20N	95.14W
Tehuantepec, Golfo de c	128	16.00N	94.50W

Name	Page No.	Lat.	Long.
Tehuantepec, Istmo de ▴³	128	17.00N	95.00W
Tejo			
→ Tagus ≈	94	38.40N	9.24W
Tekirdağ	98	40.59N	27.31 E
Te Kuiti	126	38.20S	175.10 E
Tel Aviv-Yafo	109	32.04N	34.46 E
Telén	134	36.16S	65.30W
Teleño ʌ	94	42.21N	6.23W
Telescope Peak ʌ	142	36.10N	117.05W
Telok Anson	120	4.02N	101.01 E
Tembeling ≈	120	4.04N	102.20 E
Temirtau	102	50.05N	72.56 E
Temple	128	31.05N	97.20W
Temuco	134	38.44S	72.36W
Tenāli	111	16.15N	80.35 E
Tende, Col de)(	92	44.09N	7.34 E
Ténéré ◆²	104	19.00N	10.30 E
Tenerife I	104	28.19N	16.34W
Tennant Creek	122	19.40S	134.10 E
Tennessee □³	138	35.50N	85.30W
Tenterfield	122	29.03S	152.01 E
Teófilo Otoni	135	17.51S	41.30W
Tepelena	98	40.18N	20.01 E
Tepic	128	21.30N	104.54W
Teramo	96	42.39N	13.42 E
Teresina	132	5.05S	42.49W
Terre Haute	138	39.28N	87.24W
Tete	106	16.13S	33.35 E
Tetiaroa I¹	127d	17.05S	149.32W
Tétouan	94	35.34N	5.23W
Tetovo	98	42.01N	20.58 E
Tevere (Tiber) ≈	92	41.44N	12.14 E
Texarkana	138	33.25N	94.02W
Texas □³	138	31.30N	99.00W
Texas City	128	29.23N	94.54W
Thabazimbi	106	24.41S	27.21 E
Thailand □¹	118	15.00N	100.00 E
Thailand, Gulf of c	120	10.00N	101.00 E
Thai Nguyen	120	21.36N	105.50 E
Thames	126	37.08S	175.33 E
Thames ≈	88	51.28N	0.43 E
Thamesville	140	42.33N	81.59W
Thāna	111	19.12N	72.58 E
Thanh Hoa	120	19.48N	105.46 E
Thanh Pho Ho Chi Minh (Saigon)	120	10.45N	106.40 E
Thar Desert (Great Indian Desert) ◆²	110	27.00N	71.00 E
Thásos I	98	40.41N	24.47 E
Thaton	120	16.55N	97.22 E
Thayetmyo	120	19.19N	95.11 E
The Everglades ≋	130	26.00N	81.00W
The Hague			
→ 's-Gravenhage	90	52.06N	4.18 E
Theodore	122	24.57S	150.05 E
Thermaïkós Kólpos c	98	40.23N	22.47 E
The Slot ʉ	127a	8.00S	158.10 E
Thessalía ◆¹	98	39.30N	22.00 E
Thessalon	140	46.15N	83.34W
Thessaloníki (Salonika)	98	40.38N	22.56 E
Thetford Mines	140	46.05N	71.18W
Thiel Mountains ʌ	85	85.15S	91.00W
Thielsen, Mount ʌ	142	43.09N	122.04W
Thimphu	114	27.28N	89.39 E
Thionville	92	49.22N	6.10 E
Thíra I	98	36.24N	25.29 E
Thisted	89	56.57N	8.42 E
Thívai (Thebes)	98	38.21N	23.19 E
Thongwa	120	16.46N	96.32 E
Thonze	120	17.38N	95.47 E
Thrakikón Pélagos ᵥ²	98	40.15N	24.28 E
Thunder Bay	136	48.23N	89.15W
Thüringer Wald ⤸	92	50.30N	10.30 E
Tianjin	114	39.08N	117.12 E
Tibasti, Sarīr ◆²	104	24.15N	17.15 E

Name	Page No.	Lat.	Long.
Tiber			
→ Tevere ≃	92	41.44N	12.14 E
Tibesti ⊀	104	21.30N	17.30 E
Tibet			
→ Xizang Zizhiqu			
□ 9	114	31.00N	88.00 E
Tiburón, Isla I	128	29.00N	112.23W
Tichoreck	86	45.51N	40.09 E
Ticonderoga	140	43.50N	73.25W
Tien Shan ⊀	114	42.00N	80.00 E
Tientsin			
→ Tianjin	114	39.08N	117.12 E
Tierra de Campos ◆¹	94	42.10N	4.50W
Tierra del Fuego I	134	54.00S	69.00W
Tietê ≃	135	20.40S	51.35W
Tifton	138	31.27N	83.30W
Tigre ≃	132	4.26S	74.05W
Tigris (Dijlah) ≃	108	31.00N	47.25 E
Tīh, Jabal at- ⊀¹	109	29.30N	34.00 E
Tijuana	128	32.32N	117.01W
Tilburg	90	51.34N	5.05 E
Tilimsen	104	34.52N	1.15W
Tillabéry	104	14.13N	1.27 E
Timaru	126	44.24S	171.15 E
Timbuktu			
→ Tombouctou	104	16.46N	3.01W
Timişoara	98	45.45N	21.13 E
Timmins	136	48.28N	81.20W
Timor I	118	9.00S	125.00 E
Timor Sea ⊤²	122	11.00S	128.00 E
Tinaco	130	9.42N	68.26W
Tinian I	118	15.00N	145.38 E
Tínos I	98	37.38N	25.10 E
Tinsukia	112	27.30N	95.22 E
Tipperary	88	52.29N	8.10W
Tiquisate	130	14.17N	91.22W
Tiranë	98	41.20N	19.50 E
Tire	98	38.04N	27.45 E
Tîrgovişte, Rom.	98	44.56N	25.27 E
Tîrgu Mureş	98	46.33N	24.33 E
Tîrgu Ocna	98	46.15N	26.37 E
Tîrgu Vâlcea	98	45.02N	23.17 E
Tiruchchirāppalli	111	10.49N	78.41 E
Tirunelveli	111	8.44N	77.42 E
Tiruppur	111	11.06N	77.21 E
Tiruvannāmalai	111	12.13N	79.04 E
Tisza (Tisa) ≃	98	45.15N	20.17 E
Titicaca, Lago ☻	132	15.50S	69.20W
Tivoli	96	41.58N	12.48 E
Tlētē Ouâte Gharbī,			
Jabal ʌ	109	35.20N	39.13 E
Toamasina	106	18.10S	49.23 E
Toba, Danau ☻	120	2.35N	98.50 E
Tobago I	130	11.15N	60.40W
Tocantins ≃	132	1.45S	49.10W
Togo □¹	104	8.00N	1.10 E
Toiyabe Range ⊀	142	39.10N	117.10W
Tōkamachi	116	37.08N	138.46 E
Toki	116	35.21N	137.11 E
Tokushima	116	34.04N	134.34 E
Tokuyama	116	34.03N	131.49 E
Tōkyō	116	35.42N	139.46 E
Toledo, Spain	94	39.52N	4.01W
Toledo, Oh., U.S.	140	41.39N	83.33W
Toliara	106	23.21S	43.40 E
Toljatti	86	53.31N	49.26 E
Tomakomai	116a	42.38N	141.36 E
Tomaniivi, Mount ʌ	127c	17.37S	178.01 E
Tomaszów			
Mazowiecki	90	51.32N	20.01 E
Tombigbee ≃	138	31.04N	87.58W
Tombouctou			
(Timbuktu)	104	16.46N	3.01W
Tomini, Teluk c	118	0.20S	121.00 E
Tomsk	102	56.30N	84.58 E
Tone ≃	116	35.44N	140.51 E
Tonga □¹	82	20.00S	175.00W
Tonkin, Gulf of c	120	20.00N	108.00 E
Tonopah	142	38.04N	117.13W
Tønsberg	89	59.17N	10.25 E
Toowoomba	122	27.33S	151.57 E
Topeka	138	39.02N	95.40W
Torino (Turin)	96	45.03N	7.40 E
Torneträsk ☻	89	68.20N	19.10 E
Torokina	127a	6.14S	155.03 E
Toronto	136	43.39N	79.23W
Toros Dağları ⊀	109	37.00N	33.00 E
Torquay (Torbay)	88	50.28N	3.30W
Torrens, Lake ☻	122	31.00S	137.50 E
Torreón	128	25.33N	103.26W
Torres Islands II	127b	13.15S	166.37 E
Torres Strait ⊔	122	10.25S	142.10 E
Torrington	140	41.48N	73.07W
Tortona	96	44.54N	8.52 E
Toruń	90	53.02N	18.35 E
Tostado	134	29.14S	61.46W
Tottori	116	35.30N	134.14 E
Toubkal, Jbel ʌ	104	31.05N	7.55W
Touggourt	104	33.10N	6.00 E
Toulon	92	43.07N	5.56 E
Toulouse	92	43.36N	1.26 E
Toungoo	120	18.56N	96.26 E
Tours	92	47.23N	0.41 E
Townsville	122	19.16S	146.48 E
Toyama	116	36.41N	137.13 E
Toyohashi	116	34.46N	137.23 E
Toyota	116	35.05N	137.09 E
Tracy	142	37.44N	121.25W
Tralee	88	52.16N	9.42W
Trancas	134	26.13S	65.17W
Transkei □9	106	31.20S	29.00 E
Transylvania □9	98	46.30N	24.00 E
Transylvanian Alps			
→ Carpaţii			
Meridionali ⊀	98	45.30N	24.15 E
Trapani	96	38.01N	12.31 E
Traverse City	140	44.45N	85.37W
Tra Vinh	120	9.56N	106.20 E
Treinta y Tres	134	33.14S	54.23W
Trelew	134	43.15S	65.18W
Tremblant, Mont ʌ	140	46.16N	74.35W
Trenčín	90	48.54N	18.04 E
Trento	96	46.04N	11.08 E
Trenton, On., Can.	140	44.06N	77.35W
Trenton, N.J., U.S.	140	40.13N	74.44W
Tres Arroyos	134	38.23S	60.17W
Três Corações	135	21.42S	45.16W
Três Lagoas	135	20.48S	51.43W
Três Pontas	135	21.22S	45.31W
Tres Puntas, Cabo ﹥	134	47.06S	65.53W
Treviso	96	45.40N	12.15 E
Trichūr	111	10.31N	76.13 E
Trier	90	49.45N	6.38 E
Trieste	96	45.40N	13.46 E
Triglav ʌ	96	46.23N	13.50 E
Tríkala	98	39.34N	21.46 E
Trincomalee	111	8.34N	81.14 E
Trinidad, Bol.	132	14.47S	64.47W
Trinidad, Co., U.S.	138	37.10N	104.30W
Trinidad I	130	10.30N	61.15W
Trinidad and Tobago			
□¹	130	11.00N	61.00W
Tripoli			
→ Tarābulus, Leb.	109	34.26N	35.51 E
Tripoli			
→ Tarābulus, Libya	104	32.54N	13.11 E
Trípolis	98	37.31N	22.21 E
Tripura □4	112	24.00N	92.00 E
Trivandrum	111	8.29N	76.55 E
Trnava	90	48.23N	17.35 E
Trobriand Islands II	122	8.35S	151.05 E
Trois-Rivières	140	46.21N	72.33W

Name	Page No.	Lat.	Long.
Tromelin I	106	15.52 S	54.25 E
Tromsø	89	69.40 N	18.58 E
Trondheim	89	63.25 N	10.25 E
Trondheimsfjorden C²	89	63.39 N	10.49 E
Troy, N.Y., U.S.	140	42.43 N	73.41 W
Troy, Oh., U.S.	140	40.02 N	84.12 W
Troyes	92	48.18 N	4.05 E
Truckee ≈	142	39.51 N	119.24 W
Trujillo, Peru	132	8.07 S	79.02 W
Trujillo, Ven.	130	9.22 N	70.26 W
Trutnov	90	50.34 N	15.55 E
Tsingtao			
→ Qingdao	114	36.06 N	120.19 E
Tsu	116	34.43 N	136.31 E
Tsuchiura	116	36.05 N	140.12 E
Tsugaru-kaikyō ⊻	116	41.35 N	141.00 E
Tsumeb	106	19.13 S	17.42 E
Tsuruga	116	35.39 N	136.04 E
Tsuruoka	116	38.44 N	139.50 E
Tsuyama	116	35.03 N	134.00 E
Tual	118	5.40 S	132.45 E
Tubarão	134	28.30 S	49.01 W
Tübingen	90	48.31 N	9.02 E
Tucson	138	32.13 N	110.55 W
Tucumcari	138	35.10 N	103.43 W
Tucupita	130	9.04 N	62.03 W
Tudmur (Palmyra)	109	34.33 N	38.17 E
Tuktoyaktuk	136	69.27 N	133.02 W
Tula	100	54.12 N	37.37 E
Tulancingo	128	20.05 N	98.22 W
Tulare	142	36.12 N	119.20 W
Tulcán	132	0.48 N	77.43 W
Tulcea	98	45.11 N	28.48 E
Tulsa	138	36.09 N	95.59 W
Tulun	102	54.35 N	100.33 E
Tumaco	132	1.49 N	78.46 W
Tumbes	132	3.34 S	80.28 W
T'umen'	102	57.09 N	65.32 E
Tumeremo	132	7.18 N	61.30 W
Tumuc-Humac			
Mountains ⋌	132	2.20 N	55.00 W
Tundža (Tunca) ≈	98	41.40 N	26.34 E
Tunis	104	36.48 N	10.11 E
Tunisia □¹	104	34.00 N	9.00 E
Tunja	132	5.31 N	73.22 W
Tuolumne ≈	142	37.36 N	121.10 W
Tupã	135	21.56 S	50.30 W
Tupaciguara	135	18.35 S	48.42 W
Tupelo	138	34.15 N	88.42 W
Tupper Lake	140	44.13 N	74.29 W
Turbo	132	8.06 N	76.43 W
Turda	98	46.34 N	23.47 E
Turgutlu	98	38.30 N	27.43 E
Turin			
→ Torino	96	45.03 N	7.40 E
Turkey □¹	86	39.00 N	35.00 E
Turkmenistan □¹	86	40.00 N	60.00 E
Turks and Caicos			
Islands □²	130	21.45 N	71.35 W
Turks Islands II	130	21.24 N	71.07 W
Turku (Åbo)	89	60.27 N	22.17 E
Turquino, Pico ⋏	130	19.59 N	76.50 W
Turuchansk	102	65.49 N	87.59 E
Tuscaloosa	138	33.12 N	87.34 W
Tuticorin	111	8.47 N	78.08 E
Tutuila I	127e	14.18 S	170.42 W
Tuxpan de Rodríguez			
Cano	128	20.57 N	97.24 W
Tuxtla Gutiérrez	128	16.45 N	93.07 W
Tuzla	96	44.32 N	18.41 E
Tver'	100	56.52 N	35.55 E
Twin Falls	138	42.33 N	114.27 W
Tyler	138	32.21 N	95.18 W
Tyrrhenian Sea (Mare			
Tirreno) ⲧ²	96	40.00 N	12.00 E

Name	Page No.	Lat.	Long.
U			
Ubá	135	21.07 S	42.56 W
Ubangi (Oubangui) ≈	104	1.15 N	17.50 E
Ube	116	33.56 N	131.15 E
Úbeda	94	38.01 N	3.22 W
Uberaba	132	19.45 S	47.55 W
Uberlândia	132	18.56 S	48.18 W
Ubon Ratchathani	120	15.14 N	104.54 E
Ucayali ≈	132	4.30 S	73.27 W
Uchta	102	63.33 N	53.38 E
Udaipur	112	24.35 N	73.41 E
Uddevalla	89	58.21 N	11.55 E
Udine	96	46.03 N	13.14 E
Udon Thani	120	17.26 N	102.46 E
Ueda	116	36.24 N	138.16 E
Ufa	86	54.44 N	55.56 E
Uganda □¹	106	1.00 N	32.00 E
Uitenhage	106	33.40 S	25.28 E
Ujiji	106	4.55 S	29.41 E
Ujungpandang	118	5.07 S	119.24 E
Ukiah	142	39.09 N	123.12 W
Ukraine □¹	86	49.00 N	32.00 E
Ulaanbaatar	114	47.55 N	106.53 E
Ulan Bator			
→ Ulaanbaatar	114	47.55 N	106.53 E
Ulan-Ude	102	51.50 N	107.37 E
Uleza	98	41.41 N	19.54 E
Uljanovsk	86	54.20 N	48.24 E
Ullŭng-do I	116	37.29 N	130.52 E
Ulm	90	48.24 N	10.00 E
Umeå	89	63.50 N	20.15 E
Umm Durmān			
(Omdurman)	104	15.38 N	32.30 E
Umnak Island I	144	53.25 N	168.10 W
Umpqua ≈	142	43.42 N	124.03 W
Unalakleet	144	63.53 N	160.47 W
Unalaska Island I	144	53.45 N	166.45 W
'Unayzah	108	26.06 N	43.56 E
Uncompahgre Peak ⋏	138	38.04 N	107.28 W
Undu Cape ⟩	127c	16.08 S	179.57 W
Ungava, Péninsule d'			
⟩¹	136	60.00 N	74.00 W
Ungava Bay C	136	59.30 N	67.30 W
Unimak Island I	144	54.50 N	164.00 W
Uniontown	140	39.54 N	79.44 W
United Arab Emirates			
□¹	108	24.00 N	54.00 E
United Kingdom □¹	86	54.00 N	2.00 W
United States □¹	138	38.00 N	97.00 W
Uozu	116	36.48 N	137.24 E
Upata	130	8.01 N	62.24 W
Upington	106	28.25 S	21.15 E
Upolu I	127e	13.55 S	171.45 W
Upper Arlington	140	40.00 N	83.03 W
Upper Klamath Lake ⊜	142	42.23 N	122.55 W
Upper Volta			
→ Burkina Faso □¹	104	13.00 N	2.00 W
Uppsala	89	59.52 N	17.38 E
Ural ≈	86	47.00 N	51.48 E
Ural'skije Gory ⋌	102	66.00 N	63.00 E
Urbana	140	40.06 N	83.45 W
Uruapan [del Progreso]	128	19.25 N	102.04 W
Uruguaiana	134	29.45 S	57.05 W
Uruguay □¹	134	33.00 S	56.00 W
Uruguay (Uruguai) ≈	134	34.12 S	58.18 W
Ürümqi	114	43.48 N	87.35 E
Usa	116	33.31 N	131.22 E
Uşak	98	38.41 N	29.25 E
Ushibuka	116	32.11 N	130.01 E
Ushuaia	134	54.48 S	68.18 W
Ussuri (Wusulijiang) ≈	102	48.27 N	135.04 E
Ussurijsk	102	43.48 N	131.59 E
Ust'-Čaun	102	68.47 N	170.30 E
Ústí nad Labem	90	50.40 N	14.02 E
Ust'-Kut	102	56.46 N	105.40 E

Name	Page No.	Lat.	Long.
Usuki	116	33.08N	131.49 E
Usumacinta ≃	128	18.24N	92.38W
Utah □³	138	39.30N	111.30W
Utica	140	43.06N	75.13W
Utrecht	90	52.05N	5.08 E
Utsunomiya	116	36.33N	139.52 E
Uttar Pradesh □³	112	27.00N	80.00 E
Uvalde	128	29.12N	99.47W
Uvéa, Île I	127b	20.30S	166.35 E
Uwajima	116	33.13N	132.34 E
'Uwaynāt, Jabal al- ʌ	104	21.54N	24.58 E
Uyuni	132	20.28S	66.50W
Uzbekistan □¹	82	41.00N	64.00 E
Užice	98	43.51N	19.51 E
Uzunköprü	98	41.16N	26.41 E

V

Name	Page No.	Lat.	Long.
Vaasa (Vasa)	89	63.06N	21.36 E
Vác	90	47.47N	19.08 E
Vadsø	89	70.05N	29.46 E
Vaduz	92	47.09N	9.31 E
Vaganski Vrh ʌ	96	44.22N	15.31 E
Vaileka	127c	17.23S	178.09 E
Vākhān ≃	112	37.00N	72.40 E
Valdez	144	61.07N	146.16W
Valdivia	134	39.48S	73.14W
Valdosta	138	30.49N	83.16W
Valença	135	13.22S	39.05W
Valence	92	44.56N	4.54 E
Valencia, Spain	94	39.28N	0.22W
Valencia, Ven.	132	10.11N	68.00W
Valencia □⁹	94	39.30N	0.40W
Valencia, Golfo de c	94	39.50N	0.30 E
Valenciennes	92	50.21N	3.32 E
Valentine	138	42.52N	100.33W
Valera	132	9.19N	70.37W
Valkeakoski	89	61.16N	24.02 E
Valladolid	94	41.39N	4.43W
Valle de la Pascua	130	9.13N	66.00W
Valledupar	130	10.29N	73.15W
Vallejo	142	38.06N	122.15W
Vallenar	134	28.35S	70.46W
Valletta	96	35.54N	14.31 E
Valleyfield	140	45.15N	74.08W
Valparaíso	134	33.02S	71.38W
Vancouver	136	49.16N	123.07W
Vancouver Island I	136	49.45N	126.00W
Vanderbilt	140	45.08N	84.39W
Vandergrift	140	40.36N	79.33W
Vänern ⊜	89	58.55N	13.30 E
Vangunu, Mount ʌ	127a	8.42S	158.00 E
Vannes	92	47.39N	2.46W
Vanrhynsdorp	106	31.36S	18.44 E
Vanua Levu I	127c	16.33S	179.15 E
Vanuatu □¹	127b	16.00S	167.00 E
Vārānasi (Benares)	112	25.20N	83.00 E
Varangerfjorden c²	89	70.00N	30.00 E
Varangerhalvøya ≯¹	89	70.25N	29.30 E
Varaždin	96	46.19N	16.20 E
Vardar (Axiós) ≃	98	40.31N	22.43 E
Vardø	89	70.21N	31.02 E
Varese	96	45.48N	8.48 E
Varkaus	89	62.19N	27.55 E
Varna	98	43.13N	27.55 E
Varunga Point ≯	127a	7.11S	157.17 E
Vassar	140	43.22N	83.35W
Västerås	89	59.37N	16.33 E
Vatican City (Città del Vaticano) □¹	96	41.54N	12.27 E
Vatnajökull ⋈	86	64.25N	16.50W
Vättern ⊜	89	58.24N	14.36 E
Vatu-i-Ra Channel ⋃	127c	17.17S	178.31 E
Växjö	89	56.52N	14.49 E
Velika Morava ≃	98	44.43N	21.03 E

Name	Page No.	Lat.	Long.
Velikije Luki	100	56.20N	30.32 E
Veliki Vitorog ʌ	96	44.07N	17.03 E
Veliko Tărnovo	98	43.04N	25.39 E
Vellore	111	12.56N	79.08 E
Venado Tuerto	134	33.45S	61.58W
Venezia (Venice)	96	45.27N	12.21 E
Venezuela □¹	132	8.00N	66.00W
Venezuela, Golfo de c	132	11.30N	71.00W
Venice			
→ Venezia	96	45.27N	12.21 E
Venice, Gulf of c	96	45.15N	13.00 E
Ventura	142	34.16N	119.17W
Veracruz [Llave]	128	19.12N	96.08W
Verāval	112	20.54N	70.22 E
Vercelli	96	45.19N	8.25 E
Verchojanskij Chrebet ⋏	102	67.00N	129.00 E
Verdun, P.Q., Can.	140	45.27N	73.34W
Verdun, Fr.	92	49.10N	5.23 E
Vereeniging	106	26.38S	27.57 E
Vermont □³	138	43.50N	72.45W
Vernon	140	41.49N	72.28W
Véroia	98	40.31N	22.12 E
Verona	96	45.27N	11.00 E
Versailles, Fr.	92	48.48N	2.08 E
Versailles, Ky., U.S.	140	38.03N	84.43W
Verviers	90	50.35N	5.52 E
Vesterålen II	89	68.45N	15.00 E
Vestfjorden c²	89	68.08N	15.00 E
Vesuvio ʌ¹	96	40.49N	14.26 E
Veszprém	90	47.06N	17.55 E
Viangchan (Vientiane)	120	17.58N	102.36 E
Viareggio	96	43.52N	10.14 E
Viborg	89	56.26N	9.24 E
Vicenza	96	45.33N	11.33 E
Vichy	92	46.08N	3.26 E
Vicksburg	128	32.21N	90.52W
Victoria, B.C., Can.	136	48.25N	123.22W
Victoria, Sey.	106	4.38S	55.27 E
Victoria, Tx., U.S.	138	28.48N	97.00W
Victoria □³	122	38.00S	145.00 E
Victoria, Lake ⊜	106	1.00S	33.00 E
Victoria Island I	136	71.00N	114.00W
Victoria Peak ʌ	130	16.48N	88.37W
Victoriaville	140	46.03N	71.57W
Victorville	142	34.32N	117.17W
Vidin	98	43.59N	22.52 E
Viedma	134	40.48S	63.00W
Vienna			
→ Wien	90	48.13N	16.20 E
Vienne ≃	92	47.13N	0.05 E
Vientiane			
→ Viangchan	120	17.58N	102.36 E
Vietnam □¹	118	16.00N	108.00 E
Vigo	94	42.14N	8.43W
Vijayawāda	111	16.31N	80.37 E
Vila	127b	17.44S	168.19 E
Vila Nova de Gaia	94	41.08N	8.37W
Vila Velha	135	20.20S	40.17W
Vilhelmina	89	64.37N	16.39 E
Villa Bella	132	10.23S	65.24W
Villa Bruzual	130	9.20N	69.06W
Villach	90	46.36N	13.50 E
Villa Hayes	134	25.06S	57.34W
Villahermosa	128	17.59N	92.55W
Villalonga	134	39.53S	62.35W
Villa María	134	32.25S	63.15W
Villavicencio	132	4.09N	73.37W
Villeneuve-sur-Lot	92	44.25N	0.42 E
Ville-Saint-Georges	140	46.07N	70.40W
Villeurbanne	92	45.46N	4.53 E
Vilnius	100	54.41N	25.19 E
Vindhya Range ↗	112	23.00N	77.00 E
Vineland	140	39.29N	75.01W
Vinh	120	18.40N	105.40 E
Vinh Long	120	10.15N	105.58 E

Name	Page No.	Lat.	Long.
Vinnytsya	86	49.14N	28.29 E
Vinson Massif ∧	85	78.35S	85.25W
Virden	136	49.51N	100.55W
Virginia □³	106	28.12S	26.49 E
Virginia □³	138	37.30N	78.45W
Virgin Islands □²	130	18.20N	64.50W
Virudunagar	111	9.36N	77.58 E
Visalia	142	36.19N	119.17W
Visby	89	57.38N	18.18 E
Viscount Melville			
Sound ☷	136	74.10N	113.00W
Vishākhapatnam	110	17.43N	83.19 E
Visnagar	112	23.42N	72.33 E
Viso, Monte ∧	96	44.40N	7.07 E
Vista	142	33.12N	117.14W
Vistula			
→ Wisła ☷	90	54.22N	18.55 E
Vitebsk	100	55.12N	30.11 E
Viterbo	96	42.25N	12.06 E
Viti Levu I	127c	18.00S	178.00 E
Vitória, Braz.	132	20.19S	40.21W
Vitoria, Spain	94	42.51N	2.40W
Vitória da Conquista	132	14.51S	40.51W
Vittoria	96	36.57N	14.32 E
Vizianagaram	111	18.07N	83.25 E
Vjosa ☷	98	40.37N	19.20 E
Vladikavkaz	86	43.03N	44.40 E
Vladimir	100	56.10N	40.25 E
Vladivostok	102	43.10N	131.56 E
Vlissingen (Flushing)	90	51.26N	3.35 E
Vlora	98	40.27N	19.30 E
Vltava ☷	90	50.21N	14.30 E
Vöcklabruck	90	48.01N	13.39 E
Volga ☷	86	45.55N	47.52 E
Volgograd (Stalingrad)	86	48.44N	44.25 E
Volgogradskoje			
Vodochranilišče ☷¹	86	49.20N	45.00 E
Vologda	100	59.12N	39.55 E
Vólos	98	39.21N	22.56 E
Vol'sk	86	52.02N	47.23 E
Volta, Lake ☷¹	104	7.30N	0.15 E
Volta Redonda	132	22.32S	44.07W
Volžskij	86	48.50N	44.44 E
Voríai Sporádhes II	98	39.17N	23.23 E
Vorkuta	102	67.27N	63.58 E
Voronež	86	51.40N	39.10 E
Vosges ∢	92	48.30N	7.10 E
Voss	89	60.39N	6.26 E
Vostočno-Sibirskoje			
More (East Siberian			
Sea) ▼²	102	74.00N	166.00 E
Votuporanga	135	20.24S	49.59W
Vraca	98	43.12N	23.33 E
Vrangel'a, Ostrov I	102	71.00N	179.30W
Vryburg	106	26.55S	24.45 E
Vunisea	127c	19.03S	178.09 E
Vuoksenniska	89	61.13N	28.49 E
Vyborg	100	60.42N	28.45 E
Vyšnij Voločok	100	57.35N	34.34 E
W			
Wabash ☷	138	37.46N	88.02W
Wabowden	136	54.55N	98.38W
Waco	138	31.32N	97.08W
Waddeneilanden II	90	53.26N	5.30 E
Waddenzee ▼²	90	53.15N	5.15 E
Waddington, Mount ∧	138	51.23N	125.15W
Wādī Ḥalfā`	104	21.56N	31.20 E
Wad Madanī	104	13.25N	33.28 E
Wagga Wagga	122	35.07S	147.22 E
Wah	112	33.48N	72.42 E
Wahiawa	143	21.30N	158.01W
Wahpeton	138	46.15N	96.36W
Wahran (Oran)	104	35.43N	0.43W

Name	Page No.	Lat.	Long.
Waiau	126	42.39S	173.03 E
Waihi	126	37.24S	175.51 E
Waipara	126	43.04S	172.45 E
Waipukurau	126	40.00S	176.34 E
Wairoa	126	39.02S	177.25 E
Waitato ☷	126	37.43S	176.14 E
Wakayama	116	34.13N	135.11 E
Wakkanai	116a	45.25N	141.40 E
Wakunai	127a	5.52S	155.13 E
Wałbrzych			
(Waldenburg)	90	50.46N	16.17 E
Waldron	140	41.43N	84.25W
Wales □⁸	88	52.30N	3.30W
Walgett	122	30.01S	148.07 E
Walker ☷	142	38.54N	118.47W
Walker Lake ☷	142	38.44N	118.43W
Walkerton	140	44.07N	81.09W
Wallaceburg	140	42.36N	82.23W
Wallachia □⁹	98	44.00N	25.00 E
Walla Walla	138	46.03N	118.20W
Walvis Bay	106	22.59S	14.31 E
Wanaka	126	44.42S	169.09 E
Wanganui	126	39.56S	175.03 E
Wanxian	114	30.52N	108.22 E
Warangal	111	18.00N	79.35 E
Wargla	104	31.59N	5.25 E
Warner Mountains ∢	142	41.40N	120.20W
Warren, Mi., U.S.	140	42.28N	83.01W
Warren, Oh., U.S.	140	41.14N	80.49W
Warren, Pa., U.S.	140	41.50N	79.08W
Warrenton	140	38.42N	77.47W
Warrnambool	122	38.23S	142.29 E
Warsaw			
→ Warszawa, Pol.	90	52.15N	21.00 E
Warsaw, Ky., U.S.	140	38.47N	84.54W
Warsaw, Va., U.S.	140	37.57N	76.45W
Warszawa (Warsaw)	90	52.15N	21.00 E
Washington, D.C.,			
U.S.	140	38.53N	77.02W
Washington, Pa., U.S.	140	40.10N	80.14W
Washington □³	138	47.30N	120.30W
Washington, Mount ∧	140	44.15N	71.15W
Washington Court			
House	140	39.32N	83.26W
Waspán	130	14.44N	83.58W
Waterbury	140	41.33N	73.02W
Waterford	88	52.15N	7.06W
Waterloo, On., Can.	140	43.28N	80.31W
Waterloo, Ia., U.S.	138	42.29N	92.20W
Watertown, N.Y., U.S.	140	43.58N	75.54W
Watertown, S.D., U.S.	136	44.53N	97.06W
Waterville	140	44.33N	69.37W
Watrous	136	51.40N	105.28W
Watson Lake	136	60.07N	128.48W
Wāw	104	7.42N	28.00 E
Wawa	136	47.59N	84.47W
Waycross	138	31.12N	82.21W
Waynesboro, Pa., U.S.	140	39.45N	77.34W
Waynesboro, Va., U.S.	140	38.04N	78.53W
Weatherford	128	32.45N	97.47W
Webster Springs	140	38.28N	80.24W
Weddell Sea ▼²	85	72.00S	45.00W
Weiden in der			
Oberpfalz	90	49.41N	12.10 E
Weifang	114	36.42N	19.04 E
Weirton	140	40.25N	80.35W
Welkom	106	27.59S	26.45 E
Wellington	126	41.18S	174.47 E
Wellington, Isla I	134	49.20S	74.40W
Wells	142	41.06N	114.57W
Wellsford	126	36.17S	174.31 E
Wellston	140	39.07N	82.31W
Wels	90	48.10N	14.02 E
Wendover	142	40.44N	114.02W
Wenzhou	114	28.01N	120.39 E
West Bengal □³	112	24.00N	88.00 E

Name	Page No.	Lat.	Long.	Name	Page No.	Lat.	Long.
Westerly	140	41.22N	71.49W	Winton, Austl.	122	22.23S	143.02 E
Western Australia □³	122	25.00S	122.00 E	Winton, N.Z.	126	46.09S	168.20 E
Western Ghâts ⋆	111	14.00N	75.00 E	Wisconsin □³	138	44.45N	89.30W
Western Sahara □²	104	24.30N	13.00W	Wisła ⋍	90	5.42N	18.55 E
Western Samoa □¹	127e	13.55S	172.00W	Wismar, Ger.	90	53.53N	11.28 E
Westerville	140	40.07N	82.55W	Wismar, Guy.	132	6.00N	58.18W
West Falkland I	134	51.50S	60.00W	Wittenberg	90	51.52N	12.39 E
Westfield	140	42.19N	79.34W	Wittenberge	90	53.00N	11.44 E
West Indies II	130	19.00N	70.00W	Woleai I¹	118	7.21N	143.52 E
West Liberty	140	37.55N	83.15W	Wolfsberg	90	46.51N	14.51 E
Westminster	140	39.34N	76.59W	Wolfsburg	90	52.25N	10.47 E
West Palm Beach	138	26.42N	80.03W	Wollongong	124	34.25S	150.54 E
Westport	126	41.45S	171.36 E	Wŏnsan	114	39.09N	127.25 E
West Virginia □³	138	38.45N	80.30W	Woodbridge	140	38.39N	77.15W
Wetaskiwin	136	52.58N	113.22W	Woodland	142	38.40N	121.46W
Wexford	88	52.20N	6.27W	Woodlark Island I	122	9.05S	152.50 E
Weymouth	88	50.36N	2.28W	Woods, Lake of the ◎	138	49.15N	94.45W
Whangarei	126	35.43S	174.19 E	Woodstock	140	43.08N	80.45W
Whataroa	126	43.17S	170.25 E	Woodsville	140	44.09N	72.02W
Wheeler Peak ⋏, Nv.,				Woodville	126	40.20S	175.52 E
U.S.	142	38.59N	114.19W	Woomera	122	31.31S	137.10 E
Wheeler Peak ⋏, N.M.,				Woonsocket	140	42.00N	71.30W
U.S.	138	36.34N	105.25W	Worcester, Eng., U.K.	88	52.11N	2.13W
Wheeling	140	40.03N	80.43W	Worcester, Ma., U.S.	140	42.15N	71.48W
Whitehaven	88	54.33N	3.35W	Wrangell	144	56.28N	132.23W
Whitehorse	136	60.43N	135.03W	Wrangell Mountains ⋆	144	62.00N	143.00W
White Mountains ⋆	140	44.10N	71.35W	Wrexham	88	53.03N	3.00W
White Nile (Al-Baḥr				Wrocław (Breslau)	90	51.06N	17.00 E
al-Abyaḍ) ⋍	108	15.38N	32.31 E	Wuhan	114	30.36N	114.17 E
White Plains	140	41.02N	73.45W	Wuhu	114	31.21N	118.22 E
White Sands National				Wuppertal	90	51.16N	7.11 E
Monument ◆	128	32.48N	106.20W	Würzburg	90	49.48N	9.56 E
White Volta (Volta				Wusulijiang (Ussuri) ⋍	102	48.27N	135.04 E
Blanche) ⋍	104	9.10N	1.15W	Wutongqiao	114	29.26N	103.51 E
Whitney, Mount ⋏	142	36.35N	118.18W	Wyndham	122	15.28S	128.06 E
Whyalla	124	33.02S	137.35 E	Wyoming □³	138	43.00N	107.30W
Wichita	138	37.41N	97.20W				
Wichita Falls	138	33.54N	98.29W	**X**			
Wielkopolska ◄¹	90	51.50N	17.20 E				
Wien (Vienna)	90	48.13N	16.20 E	Xai-Xai	106	25.02S	33.34 E
Wiener Neustadt	90	47.49N	16.15 E	Xam Nua	120	20.25N	104.02 E
Wieprz ⋍	90	51.34N	21.49 E	Xánthi	98	41.08N	24.53 E
Wieprz-Krzna, Kanał ≊	90	51.56N	22.56 E	Xenia	140	39.41N	83.55W
Wiesbaden	90	50.05N	8.14 E	Xi ⋍	114	22.25N	113.23 E
Wilhelm, Mount ⋏	118	5.45S	145.05 E	Xiamen	114	24.28N	118.07 E
Wilhelmshaven	90	53.31N	8.08 E	Xi'an (Sian)	114	34.15N	108.52 E
Wilkes-Barre	140	41.14N	75.52W	Xiangtan	114	27.51N	112.54 E
Wilkes Land ◄¹	85	69.00S	120.00 E	Xingu ⋍	132	1.30S	51.53W
Willard	140	41.03N	82.44W	Xining	114	36.38N	101.55 E
Willemstad	130	12.06N	68.56W	Xinjiang Uygur			
Williams Lake	136	52.08N	122.09W	Zizhiqu (Sinkiang)			
Williamsport	140	41.14N	76.59W	□⁴	114	40.00N	85.00 E
Williston	138	48.08N	103.38W	Xinxiang	114	35.20N	113.51 E
Wilmington, De., U.S.	140	39.44N	75.32W	Xinyang	114	32.19N	114.01 E
Wilmington, N.C.,				Xizang Zizhiqu □⁴	114	32.00N	88.00 E
U.S.	138	34.13N	77.56W	Xuzhou	114	34.16N	117.11 E
Wiluna	122	26.36S	120.13 E				
Winchester, In., U.S.	140	40.10N	84.58W	**Y**			
Winchester, Va., U.S.	140	39.11N	78.10W				
Windhoek	106	22.34S	17.06 E	Yaizu	116	34.52N	138.20 E
Windsor, N.S., Can.	136	44.59N	64.08W	Yakima	138	46.36N	120.30W
Windsor, On., Can.	136	42.18N	83.01W	Yakumo	116a	42.15N	140.16 E
Windsor, P.Q., Can.	140	45.34N	72.00W	Yakutat	144	59.33N	139.44W
Windsor, Eng., U.K.	88	51.29N	0.38W	Yakutsk			
Windward Islands II	130	13.00N	61.00W	→ Jakutsk	102	62.13N	129.49 E
Windward Passage ⋃	138	20.00N	73.50W	Yala	120	6.33N	101.18 E
Winisk	136	55.15N	85.12W	Yamagata	116	38.15N	140.20 E
Winisk Lake ◎	136	52.55N	87.22W	Yamaguchi	116	34.10N	131.29 E
Winnemucca	142	40.58N	117.44W	Yamoussoukro	104	6.49N	5.17W
Winnfield	128	31.55N	92.38W	Yamsay Mountain ⋏	142	42.56N	121.22W
Winnipeg	136	49.53N	97.09W	Yanbu'	108	24.05N	38.03 E
Winnipeg, Lake ◎	136	52.00N	97.00W	Yandoon	120	17.02N	95.39 E
Winnipesaukee, Lake ◎	140	43.35N	71.20W	Yangquan	114	37.52N	113.36 E
Winslow	140	44.32N	69.37W	Yangtze			
Winston-Salem	138	36.05N	80.14W	→ Chang ⋍	114	31.48N	121.10 E
Winterport	140	44.38N	68.51W				

Name	Page No.	Lat.	Long.
Yantai (Chefoo)	114	37.33 N	121.20 E
Yaoundé	104	3.52 N	11.31 E
Yap I	118	9.31 N	138.06 E
Yasawa Group II	127c	17.00 S	177.23 E
Yaté	127b	22.09 S	166.57 E
Yatsushiro	116	32.30 N	130.36 E
Yatta Plateau ✗ ¹	106	2.00 S	38.00 E
Yaviza	130	8.11 N	77.41 W
Yawatahama	116	33.27 N	132.24 E
Yazd	108	31.53 N	54.25 E
Yazoo City	128	32.51 N	90.24 W
Ye	120	15.15 N	97.51 E
Yekïbastüz	102	51.42 N	75.22 E
Yellow			
→ Huang ≏	114	37.32 N	118.19 E
Yellowknife	136	62.27 N	114.21 W
Yellow Sea ⊤ ²	114	36.00 N	123.00 E
Yellowstone ≏	138	47.58 N	103.59 W
Yellowstone Lake ☺	138	44.25 N	110.22 W
Yemen □ ¹	108	15.00 N	47.00 E
Yenangyaung	120	20.28 N	94.52 E
Yendéré	104	10.12 N	4.58 W
Yenisey			
→ Jenisej ≏	102	71.50 N	82.40 E
Yerevan			
→ Jerevan	86	40.11 N	44.30 E
Yerushalayim			
(Jerusalem)	109	31.46 N	35.14 E
Yiannitsá	98	40.48 N	22.25 E
Yibin	114	28.47 N	104.38 E
Yinchuan	114	38.30 N	106.18 E
Yingkou	114	40.40 N	122.14 E
Yining (Kuldja)	114	43.55 N	81.14 E
Yogyakarta	118	7.48 S	110.22 E
Yokkaichi	116	34.58 N	136.37 E
Yokohama	116	35.27 N	139.39 E
Yokosuka	116	35.18 N	139.40 E
Yonago	116	35.26 N	133.20 E
Yonezawa	116	37.55 N	140.07 E
Yonkers	140	40.55 N	73.53 W
York, Eng., U.K.	88	53.58 N	1.05 W
York, Pa., U.S.	140	39.57 N	76.43 W
York, Cape ➤	122	10.42 S	142.31 E
York Factory	136	57.00 N	92.18 W
Yorkton	136	51.13 N	102.28 W
Yoro	130	15.09 N	87.07 W
Yosemite National			
Park ✦	142	37.51 N	119.33 W
Yos Sudarsa, Pulau I	118	7.50 S	138.30 E
Youngstown	140	41.05 N	80.38 W
Yuba City	142	39.08 N	121.36 W
Yucatan Channel ⋃	130	21.45 N	85.45 W
Yucatan Peninsula ➤¹	128	19.30 N	89.00 W
Yucca	142	34.52 N	114.08 W
Yugoslavia □ ¹	86	44.00 N	20.00 E
Yukon □ ⁴	144	64.00 N	135.00 W
Yukon ≏	144	62.33 N	163.59 W
Yukuhashi	116	33.44 N	130.59 E
Yuma	138	32.43 N	114.37 W
Yumen	114	39.56 N	97.51 E
Yurimaguas	132	5.54 S	76.05 W

Z

Name	Page No.	Lat.	Long.
Zaandam	90	52.26 N	4.49 E
Zacapa	128	14.58 N	89.32 W
Zacatecas	128	22.47 N	102.35 W
Zagreb	96	45.48 N	15.58 E
Zāgros, Kūhhā-ye ✗	108	33.40 N	47.00 E
Zaḥlah	109	33.51 N	35.53 E
Zaire			
→ Congo,			
Democratic Republic			
of the □ ¹	106	4.00 S	25.00 E
Zákinthos I	98	37.52 N	20.44 E
Zalaegerszeg	90	46.51 N	16.51 E
Zambezi (Zambeze) ≏	106	18.55 S	36.04 E
Zambia □ ¹	106	15.00 S	30.00 E
Zamboanga	118	6.54 N	122.04 E
Zamora	94	41.30 N	5.45 W
Zamora de Hidalgo	128	19.59 N	102.16 W
Zamość	90	50.44 N	23.15 E
Zanesville	140	39.56 N	82.00 W
Zanzibar	106	6.10 S	39.11 E
Zanzibar Island I	106	6.10 S	39.20 E
Zapadnaja Dvina			
(Daugava) ≏	100	57.04 N	24.03 E
Zapadno-Sibirskaja			
Nizmennost' ⨆	102	60.00 N	75.00 E
Zapala	134	38.54 S	70.04 W
Zaporizhzhya	86	47.50 N	35.10 E
Zaragoza	94	41.38 N	0.53 W
Zárate	134	34.06 S	59.02 W
Zaraza	130	9.21 N	65.19 W
Zaria	104	11.07 N	7.44 E
Żary (Sorau)	90	51.38 N	15.09 E
Zawiercie	90	50.30 N	19.25 E
Zāwiyat al-Bayḍā'	104	32.46 N	21.43 E
Zaysan köli ☺	102	48.00 N	84.00 E
Zduńska Wola	90	51.36 N	18.57 E
Zeerust	106	25.33 S	26.06 E
Zeja	102	53.45 N	127.15 E
Zelee, Cape ➤	127a	9.45 S	161.34 E
Zgierz	90	51.52 N	19.25 E
Zhambyl	114	42.54 N	71.22 E
Zhangjiakou	114	40.50 N	114.53 E
Zhangzhou	114	24.33 N	117.39 E
Zhanjiang	114	21.16 N	110.28 E
Zhengzhou	114	34.48 N	113.39 E
Zhuzhou	114	27.50 N	113.09 E
Zhytomyr	86	50.16 N	28.40 E
Zigong	114	29.24 N	104.47 E
Ziguinchor	104	12.35 N	16.16 W
Žilina	90	49.14 N	18.46 E
Zimbabwe □ ¹	106	20.00 S	30.00 E
Zlín	90	49.13 N	17.41 E
Żłobin	100	52.54 N	30.03 E
Znojmo	90	48.52 N	16.02 E
Zomba	106	15.23 S	35.18 E
Zudañez	132	19.06 S	64.44 W
Zugspitze ⋀	90	47.25 N	10.59 E
Zuiderzee			
→ IJsselmeer ⊤ ²	90	52.45 N	5.25 E
Zululand □ ⁹	106	28.10 S	32.00 E
Zunyi	114	27.39 N	106.57 E
Zürich	92	47.23 N	8.32 E
Zvolen	90	48.35 N	19.08 E
Zwettl	90	48.37 N	15.10 E
Zwickau	90	50.44 N	12.29 E
Zwolle	90	52.30 N	6.05 E

World Flags

Afghanistan

Albania

Algeria

Andorra

Angola

Antigua and Barbuda

Argentina

Armenia

Australia

Austria

Azerbaijan

Bahamas

Bahrain

Bangladesh

Barbados

Belarus

Belgium

Belize

Benin

Bhutan

Bolivia

Bosnia and Herzegovina

Botswana

Brazil

Brunei

Bulgaria

Burkina Faso

Burundi

Cambodia

Cameroon

Canada

Cape Verde

Central African Republic

Chad

Chile

China

Colombia

Comoros

Congo

Congo, Democratic
Republic of the

Costa Rica

Cote d´Ivoire
(Ivory Coast)

Croatia

Cuba

Cyprus

Czech Republic

Denmark

Djibouti

Dominica

Dominican Republic

Ecuador

Egypt

El Salvador

Equatorial Guinea

Eritrea

Estonia

Ethiopia

Fiji

Finland

France

Gabon

Gambia

Georgia

Germany

Ghana

Greece

Greenland

Grenada

Guatemala

Guinea

Guinea-Bissau

Guyana

Haiti

Honduras

Hungary

Iceland

India

Indonesia

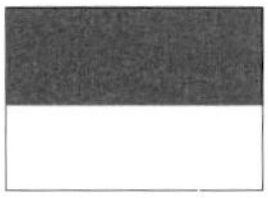

Iran

Iraq

Ireland

Israel

Italy

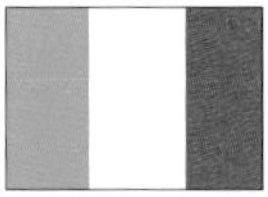

Jamaica

Japan

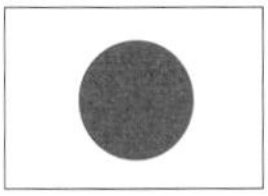

Jordan

Kazakhstan

Kenya

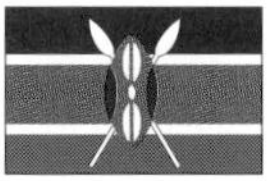

Kiribati

Korea, North

Korea, South

Kuwait

Kyrgyzstan

Laos

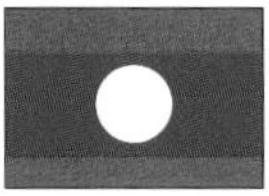

Latvia

Lebanon

Lesotho

Liberia

Libya

Liechtenstein

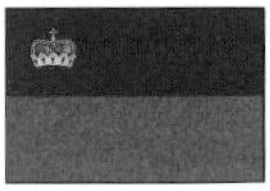

Lithuania

Luxembourg

Macedonia

Madagascar

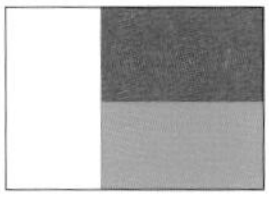

Malawi

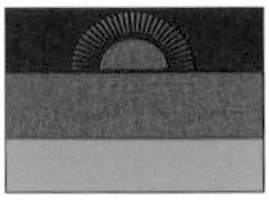

Malaysia

Maldives

Mali

Malta

Marshall Islands

Mauritania

Mauritius

Mexico

Micronesia,
Federated States of

Moldova

Monaco

Mongolia

Morocco

Mozambique

Myanmar (Burma)

Namibia

Nauru

Nepal

Netherlands

New Zealand

Nicaragua

Niger

Nigeria

Northern
Mariana Islands

Norway

Oman

Pakistan

Palau

Panama

Papua New Guinea

Paraguay

Peru

Philippines

Poland

Portugal

Qatar

Romania

Russia

Rwanda

St. Kitts and Nevis

St. Lucia

St. Vincent and
the Grenadines

Samoa

San Marino

Sao Tome
and Principe

Saudi Arabia

Senegal

Seychelles

Sierra Leone

Singapore

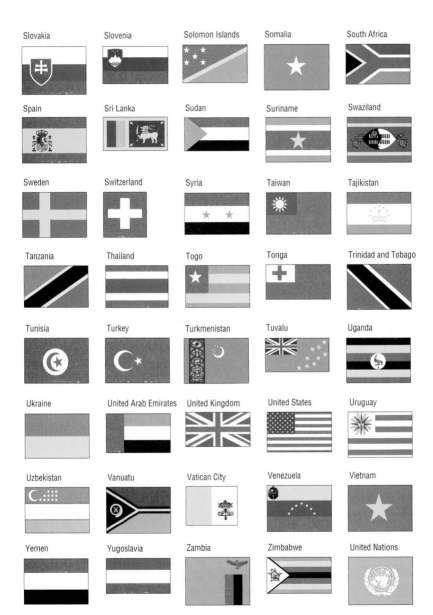

Slovakia

Slovenia

Solomon Islands

Somalia

South Africa

Spain

Sri Lanka

Sudan

Suriname

Swaziland

Sweden

Switzerland

Syria

Taiwan

Tajikistan

Tanzania

Thailand

Togo

Tonga

Trinidad and Tobago

Tunisia

Turkey

Turkmenistan

Tuvalu

Uganda

Ukraine

United Arab Emirates

United Kingdom

United States

Uruguay

Uzbekistan

Vanuatu

Vatican City

Venezuela

Vietnam

Yemen

Yugoslavia

Zambia

Zimbabwe

United Nations

Country Profiles

Afghanistan (Afghānestān)
Location: Southern Asia, landlocked
Area: 251,826 mi^2 (652,225 km^2)
Population: 22,780,000 (Urban: 20%)
Literacy: 29%
Capital: Kabōl, 1,424,400
Government: Transitional
Languages: Dari, Pashto, Uzbek, Turkmen
Ethnic Groups: Pathan 38%, Tajik 25%,
Hazara 19%, Uzbek 6%
Religions: Sunni Muslim 84%, Shiite
Muslim 15%
Currency: Afghani
Tel. Area Code: 93

Albania (Shqipëria)
Location: Southeastern Europe
Area: 11,100 mi^2 (28,748 km^2)
Population: 3,434,000 (Urban: 37%)
Literacy: 72%
Capital: Tiranë, 238,100
Government: Republic
Languages: Albanian, Greek
Ethnic Groups: Albanian (Illyrian) 90%,
Greek 8%
Religions: Muslim 70%, Greek
Orthodox 20%, Roman Catholic 10%
Currency: Lek
Tel. Area Code: 355

Algeria (Djazaïr)
Location: Northern Africa
Area: 919,595 mi^2 (2,381,741 km^2)
Population: 28,855,000 (Urban: 56%)
Literacy: 57%
Capital: El Djazaïr (Algiers), 1,507,241
Government: Republic
Languages: Arabic, Berber dialects, French
Ethnic Groups: Arab-Berber 99%
Religions: Sunni Muslim 99%, Christian and
Jewish 1%
Currency: Dinar
Tel. Area Code: 213

Angola
Location: Southern Africa
Area: 481,354 mi^2 (1,246,700 km^2)
Population: 11,105,000 (Urban: 32%)
Literacy: 42%
Capital: Luanda, 1,459,900
Government: Republic
Languages: Portuguese, indigenous
Ethnic Groups: Ovimbundu 37%,
Mbundu 25%, Kongo 13%, mulatto 2%,
European 1%
Religions: Animist 47%, Roman
Catholic 38%, Protestant 15%
Currency: Kwanza
Tel. Area Code: 244

Antigua and Barbuda
Location: Caribbean islands
Area: 171 mi^2 (442 km^2)
Population: 67,000 (Urban: 36%)
Literacy: 89%
Capital: St. John's, 24,359
Government: Parliamentary state
Languages: English, local dialects
Ethnic Groups: Black, British, Portuguese,
Lebanese, Syrian
Religions: Anglican, Protestant, Roman
Catholic
Currency: East Caribbean dollar
Tel. Area Code: 809

Argentina
Location: Southern South America
Area: 1,073,519 mi^2 (2,780,400 km^2)
Population: 34,465,000 (Urban: 88%)
Literacy: 95%
Capital: Buenos Aires (de facto), 2,960,976;
Viedma (future) 24,346
Government: Republic
Languages: Spanish, English, Italian,
German, French
Ethnic Groups: White 85%; mestizo,
Amerindian, and others 15%
Religions: Roman Catholic 90%, Jewish 2%,
Protestant 2%
Currency: Peso
Tel. Area Code: 54

Armenia (Hayastan)

Location: Southwestern Asia, landlocked
Area: 11,506 mi^2 (29,800 km^2)
Population: 3,571,000 (Urban: 69%)
Literacy: 99%
Capital: Jerevan, 1,199,000
Government: Republic
Languages: Armenian, Russian
Ethnic Groups: Armenian 93%, Azeri 3%, Russian 2%
Religions: Armenian Orthodox 94%
Currency: Dram
Tel. Area Code: 374

Australia

Location: Continent between South Pacific and Indian oceans
Area: 2,966,155 mi^2 (7,682,300 km^2)
Population: 18,430,000 (Urban: 85%)
Literacy: 100%
Capital: Canberra, 276,162
Government: Federal parliamentary state
Languages: English, indigenous
Ethnic Groups: Caucasian 95%, Asian 4%, Aboriginal and other 1%
Religions: Anglican 26%, Roman Catholic 26%, other Christian 24%
Currency: Dollar
Tel. Area Code: 61

Austria (Österreich)

Location: Central Europe, landlocked
Area: 32,377 mi^2 (83,856 km^2)
Population: 8,003,000 (Urban: 55%)
Literacy: 99%
Capital: Wien (Vienna), 1,539,848
Government: Federal republic
Languages: German
Ethnic Groups: German 99%
Religions: Roman Catholic 85%, Protestant 6%
Currency: Schilling
Tel. Area Code: 43

Azerbaijan (Azärbaycan)

Location: Southwestern Asia, landlocked
Area: 33,436 mi^2 (86,600 km^2)
Population: 7,837,000 (Urban: 56%)
Literacy: 97%
Capital: Baku, 1,080,500
Government: Republic
Languages: Azeri, Russian, Armenian
Ethnic Groups: Azeri 83%, Armenian 6%, Russian 6%

Religions: Muslim 87%, Russian Orthodox 6%, Armenian Orthodox 6%
Currency: Manat
Tel. Area Code: 994

Bahamas

Location: Caribbean islands
Area: 5,382 mi^2 (13,939 km^2)
Population: 258,000 (Urban: 87%)
Literacy: 90%
Capital: Nassau, 141,000
Government: Parliamentary state
Languages: English, Creole
Ethnic Groups: Black 85%, white 15%
Religions: Baptist 32%, Anglican 20%, Roman Catholic 19%, Methodist 6%
Currency: Dollar
Tel. Area Code: 809

Bahrain (Al-Baḥrayn)

Location: Southwestern Asian islands (in Persian Gulf)
Area: 267 mi^2 (691 km^2)
Population: 583,000 (Urban: 90%)
Literacy: 84%
Capital: Al-Manāmah (Manama), 82,700
Government: Monarchy
Languages: Arabic, English, Farsi, Urdu
Ethnic Groups: Bahraini 63%, Asian 13%, other Arab 10%
Religions: Shiite Muslim 70%, Sunni Muslim 30%
Currency: Dinar
Tel. Area Code: 973

Bangladesh

Location: Southern Asia
Area: 55,598 mi^2 (143,998 km^2)
Population: 129,500,000 (Urban: 18%)
Literacy: 35%
Capital: Dhaka, 3,637,892
Government: Republic
Languages: Bangla, English
Ethnic Groups: Bengali 98%
Religions: Muslim 83%, Hindu 16%
Currency: Taka
Tel. Area Code: 880

Barbados

Location: Caribbean island
Area: 166 mi^2 (430 km^2)
Population: 256,000 (Urban: 47%)
Literacy: 99%
Capital: Bridgetown, 5,928
Government: Parliamentary state

Languages: English
Ethnic Groups: Black 80%, mixed 16%, white 4%
Religions: Anglican 40%, Pentecostal 8%, Methodist 7%, Roman Catholic 4%
Currency: Dollar
Tel. Area Code: 809

Belarus (Byelarus')
Location: Eastern Europe, landlocked
Area: 80,155 mi^2 (207,600 km^2)
Population: 10,370,000 (Urban: 71%)
Literacy: 97%
Capital: Minsk, 1,633,600
Government: Republic
Languages: Byelorussian, Russian
Ethnic Groups: Byelorussian 78%, Russian 13%, Polish 4%, Ukrainian 3%
Religions: Russian Orthodox
Currency: Rubel
Tel. Area Code: 375

Belgium (Belgique, België)
Location: Western Europe
Area: 11,783 mi^2 (30,518 km^2)
Population: 10,175,000 (Urban: 97%)
Literacy: 99%
Capital: Bruxelles (Brussels), 136,424
Government: Constitutional monarchy
Languages: Dutch (Flemish), French, German
Ethnic Groups: Fleming 55%, Walloon 33%, mixed and others 12%
Religions: Roman Catholic 75%
Currency: Franc
Tel. Area Code: 32

Belize
Location: Central America
Area: 8,867 mi^2 (22,963 km^2)
Population: 217,000 (Urban: 47%)
Literacy: 91%
Capital: Belmopan, 5,256
Government: Parliamentary state
Languages: English, Spanish, Mayan, Garifuna
Ethnic Groups: Mestizo 44%, Creole 30%, Mayan 11%, Garifuna 7%
Religions: Roman Catholic 62%, Anglican 12%, Methodist 6%, Mennonite 4%
Currency: Dollar
Tel. Area Code: 501

Benin (Bénin)
Location: Western Africa
Area: 43,475 mi^2 (112,600 km^2)
Population: 5,617,000 (Urban: 31%)
Literacy: 23%
Capital: Porto-Novo (designated), 164,000; Cotonou (de facto), 533,212
Government: Republic
Languages: French, Fon, Yoruba, indigenous
Ethnic Groups: Fon 39%, Yoruba 12%, Adja 10%, others
Religions: Voodoo and other African religions 70%, Muslim 15%, Christian
Currency: CFA franc
Tel. Area Code: 229

Bhutan (Druk-Yul)
Location: Southern Asia, landlocked
Area: 17,954 mi^2 (46,500 km^2)
Population: 1,801,000 (Urban: 6%)
Capital: Thimphu, 12,000
Government: Monarchy (Indian protection)
Languages: Dzongkha, Tibetan and Nepalese dialects
Ethnic Groups: Bhotia 60%, Nepalese 25%, indigenous 15%
Religions: Buddhist 75%, Hindu 25%
Currency: Ngultrum, Indian rupee
Tel. Area Code: 975

Bolivia
Location: Central South America, landlocked
Area: 424,165 mi^2 (1,098,581 km^2)
Population: 7,487,000 (Urban: 61%)
Literacy: 80%
Capital: La Paz (seat of government), 713,378; Sucre (legal capital), 131,769
Government: Republic
Languages: Aymara, Quechua, Spanish
Ethnic Groups: Quechua 30%, Aymara 25%, mixed 25-30%, European 5-15%
Religions: Roman Catholic 95%, Methodist and other Protestant
Currency: Boliviano
Tel. Area Code: 591

Bosnia and Herzegovina (Bosna i Hercegovina)
Location: Eastern Europe
Area: 19,741 mi^2 (51,129 km^2)
Population: 3,215,000 (Urban: 49%)
Literacy: 86%
Capital: Sarajevo, 341,200

Government: Republic
Languages: Serbo-Croatian
Ethnic Groups: Muslim 44%, Serb 31%, Croat 17%
Religions: Muslim 40%, Orthodox 31%, Roman Catholic 15%
Currency: Yugoslavian dinar, Croatian dinar
Tel. Area Code: 387

Botswana

Location: Southern Africa, landlocked
Area: 224,711 mi² (582,000 km²)
Population: 1,495,000 (Urban: 28%)
Literacy: 76%
Capital: Gaborone, 133,468
Government: Republic
Languages: English, Tswana
Ethnic Groups: Tswana 95%; Kalanga, Baswara, and Kgalagadi 4%; white 1%
Religions: Khoisan 50%, Roman Catholic and other Christian 50%
Currency: Pula
Tel. Area Code: 267

Brazil (Brasil)

Location: Eastern South America
Area: 3,300,171 mi² (8,547,404 km²)
Population: 161,700,000 (Urban: 78%)
Literacy: 80%
Capital: Brasília, 1,513,470
Government: Federal republic
Languages: Portuguese, Spanish, English, French
Ethnic Groups: White 55%, mixed 38%, black 6%
Religions: Roman Catholic 90%
Currency: Real
Tel. Area Code: 55

Brunei

Location: Southeastern Asia (island of Borneo)
Area: 2,226 mi² (5,765 km²)
Population: 296,000 (Urban: 58%)
Literacy: 88%
Capital: Bandar Seri Begawan, 22,777
Government: Monarchy
Languages: Malay, English, Chinese
Ethnic Groups: Malay 64%, Chinese 20%, indigenous 8%, Tamil 3%
Religions: Muslim 63%, Buddhist 14%, Roman Catholic and other Christian 8%
Currency: Dollar
Tel. Area Code: 673

Bulgaria (Bălgarija)

Location: Southeastern Europe
Area: 42,855 mi² (110,994 km²)
Population: 8,405,000 (Urban: 71%)
Literacy: 98%
Capital: Sofija (Sofia), 1,136,875
Government: Republic
Languages: Bulgarian, Turkish
Ethnic Groups: Bulgarian (Slavic) 85%, Turkish 9%, Gypsy 3%, Macedonian 3%
Religions: Bulgarian Orthodox 85%, Muslim 13%
Currency: Lev
Tel. Area Code: 359

Burkina Faso

Location: Western Africa, landlocked
Area: 105,869 mi² (274,200 km²)
Population: 10,570,000 (Urban: 27%)
Literacy: 18%
Capital: Ouagadougou, 441,514
Government: Republic
Languages: French, indigenous
Ethnic Groups: Mossi 30%, Fulani, Lobi, Malinke, Bobo, Senufo, Gurunsi, others
Religions: Animist 65%, Muslim 25%, Roman Catholic and other Christian 10%
Currency: CFA franc
Tel. Area Code: 226

Burundi

Location: Eastern Africa, landlocked
Area: 10,745 mi² (27,830 km²)
Population: 6,331,000 (Urban: 8%)
Literacy: 50%
Capital: Bujumbura, 226,628
Government: Republic
Languages: French, Kirundi, Swahili
Ethnic Groups: Hutu 85%, Tutsi 14%, Twa (Pygmy) 1%
Religions: Roman Catholic 62%, Animist 32%, Protestant 5%, Muslim 1%
Currency: Franc
Tel. Area Code: 257

Cambodia (Kâmpŭchéa)

Location: Southeastern Asia
Area: 69,898 mi² (181,035 km²)
Population: 10,710,000 (Urban: 21%)
Literacy: 35%
Capital: Phnum Pénh (Phnom Penh), 620,000
Government: Constitutional monarchy
Languages: Khmer, French
Ethnic Groups: Khmer 90%, Vietnamese 5%

Religions: Buddhist 95%
Currency: Riel
Tel. Area Code: 855

Cameroon (Cameroun)

Location: Central Africa
Area: 183,568 mi^2 (475,440 km^2)
Population: 13,725,000 (Urban: 45%)
Literacy: 55%
Capital: Yaoundé, 560,785
Government: Republic
Languages: English, French, indigenous
Ethnic Groups: Cameroon Highlander 31%, Equatorial Bantu 19%, Kirdi 11%, Fulani 10%
Religions: Bangwa and other African religions 51%, Christian 33%, Muslim 16%
Currency: CFA franc
Tel. Area Code: 237

Canada

Location: Northern North America
Area: 3,849,674 mi^2 (9,970,610 km^2)
Population: 29,725,000 (Urban: 77%)
Literacy: 97%
Capital: Ottawa, 313,987
Government: Federal parliamentary state
Languages: English, French
Ethnic Groups: British origin 40%, French origin 27%, other European 23%, native Canadian 2%
Religions: Roman Catholic 47%, United Church 16%, Anglican 10%, other Christian
Currency: Dollar
Tel. Area Code: 1

Cape Verde (Cabo Verde)

Location: Western African islands
Area: 1,557 mi^2 (4,033 km^2)
Population: 443,000 (Urban: 54%)
Literacy: 63%
Capital: Praia, 61,644
Government: Republic
Languages: Portuguese, Crioulo
Ethnic Groups: Creole (mulatto) 71%, African 28%, European 1%
Religions: Roman Catholic, Nazarene and other Protestant
Currency: Escudo
Tel. Area Code: 238

Central African Republic (République centrafricaine)

Location: Central Africa, landlocked

Area: 240,535 mi^2 (622,984 km^2)
Population: 3,245,000 (Urban: 39%)
Literacy: 38%
Capital: Bangui, 596,800
Government: Republic
Languages: French, Sango, Arabic, indigenous
Ethnic Groups: Baya 34%, Banda 27%, Mandjia 21%, Sara 10%
Religions: Protestant 25%, Roman Catholic 24%, African religions 24%, Muslim 15%
Currency: CFA franc
Tel. Area Code: 236

Chad (Tchad)

Location: Central Africa, landlocked
Area: 495,755 mi^2 (1,284,000 km^2)
Population: 6,387,000 (Urban: 21%)
Literacy: 30%
Capital: N'Djamena, 500,000
Government: Republic
Languages: Arabic, French, indigenous
Ethnic Groups: Sara and other African, Arab
Religions: Muslim 44%, Christian 33%, Animist 23%
Currency: CFA franc
Tel. Area Code: 235

Chile

Location: Southern South America
Area: 292,135 mi^2 (756,626 km^2)
Population: 14,260,000 (Urban: 84%)
Literacy: 94%
Capital: Santiago, 232,667
Government: Republic
Languages: Spanish
Ethnic Groups: White and mestizo 95%, Amerindian 3%
Religions: Roman Catholic 89%, Pentecostal and other Protestant 11%
Currency: Peso
Tel. Area Code: 56

China (Zhongguo)

Location: Eastern Asia
Area: 3,689,631 mi^2 (9,556,100 km^2)
Population: 1,209,110,000 (Urban: 30%)
Literacy: 78%
Capital: Beijing (Peking), 6,710,000
Government: Socialist republic
Languages: Chinese dialects
Ethnic Groups: Han Chinese 93%, Zhuang, Uygur, Hui, Yi, Tibetan, Miao, Manchu, others

Religions: Taoist, Buddhist, and Muslim 3%
Currency: Yuan
Tel. Area Code: 86

Colombia
Location: Northern South America
Area: 440,831 mi^2 (1,141,748 km^2)
Population: 35,400,000 (Urban: 73%)
Literacy: 88%
Capital: Santa Fe de Bogotá, 3,982,941
Government: Republic
Languages: Spanish
Ethnic Groups: Mestizo 58%, white 20%, mulatto 14%, black 4%
Religions: Roman Catholic 95%
Currency: Peso
Tel. Area Code: 57

Comoros (Al Qumur, Comores)
Location: Southeastern African islands
Area: 863 mi^2 (2,235 km^2)
Population: 559,000 (Urban: 31%)
Literacy: 48%
Capital: Moroni, 23,432
Government: Federal Islamic republic
Languages: Arabic, French, Comoran
Ethnic Groups: African-Arab descent (Antalote, Cafre, Makoa, Oimatsaha, Sakalava)
Religions: Sunni Muslim 86%, Roman Catholic 14%
Currency: Franc
Tel. Area Code: 269

Congo
Location: Central Africa
Area: 132,047 mi^2 (342,000 km^2)
Population: 2,533,000 (Urban: 59%)
Literacy: 57%
Capital: Brazzaville, 693,712
Government: Republic
Languages: French, Lingala, Kikongo, indigenous
Ethnic Groups: Kongo 48%, Sangho 20%, Bateke 17%, Mbochi 12%
Religions: Christian 50%, Animist 48%, Muslim 2%
Currency: CFA franc
Tel. Area Code: 242

Congo, Democratic Republic of the (République démocratique du Congo)
Location: Central Africa
Area: 905,446 mi^2 (2,345,095 km^2)
Population: 44,765,000 (Urban: 29%)
Literacy: 72%
Capital: Kinshasa, 3,000,000
Government: Republic
Languages: French, Kikongo, Lingala, Swahili, Tshiluba, Kingwana
Ethnic Groups: Kongo, Luba, Mongo, Mangbetu-Azande, others
Religions: Roman Catholic 50%, Protestant 20%, Kimbanguist 10%, Muslim 10%
Currency: Zaire
Tel. Area Code: 243

Costa Rica
Location: Central America
Area: 19,730 mi^2 (51,100 km^2)
Population: 3,110,000 (Urban: 50%)
Literacy: 93%
Capital: San José, 278,600
Government: Republic
Languages: Spanish
Ethnic Groups: White and mestizo 96%, black 2%, Amerindian 1%
Religions: Roman Catholic 95%
Currency: Colon
Tel. Area Code: 506

Cote d'Ivoire (Côte d'Ivoire)
Location: Western Africa
Area: 124,518 mi^2 (322,500 km^2)
Population: 14,395,000 (Urban: 44%)
Literacy: 54%
Capital: Abidjan (de facto), 1,929,079; Yamoussoukro (future), 106,786
Government: Republic
Languages: French, Dioula and other indigenous
Ethnic Groups: Baule 23%, Bete 18%, Senoufou 15%, Malinke 11%, other African
Religions: Animist 63%, Muslim 25%, Christian 12%
Currency: CFA franc
Tel. Area Code: 225

Croatia (Hrvatska)
Location: Eastern Europe
Area: 21,829 mi^2 (56,538 km^2)
Population: 4,671,000 (Urban: 64%)
Literacy: 97%
Capital: Zagreb, 697,925
Government: Republic
Languages: Serbo-Croatian
Ethnic Groups: Croat 78%, Serb 12%, Muslim 1%

Religions: Roman Catholic 77%,
Orthodox 11%, Muslim 1%
Currency: Kuna
Tel. Area Code: 385

Cuba

Location: Caribbean island
Area: 42,804 mi^2 (110,861 km^2)
Population: 10,980,000 (Urban: 76%)
Literacy: 96%
Capital: La Habana (Havana), 2,119,059
Government: Socialist republic
Languages: Spanish
Ethnic Groups: Mulatto 51%, white 37%,
black 11%, Chinese 1%
Religions: Roman Catholic, Pentecostal,
Baptist
Currency: Peso
Tel. Area Code: 53

Cyprus (Kípros, Kıbrıs)

Location: Southern part of the island of
Cyprus
Area: 2,276 mi^2 (5,896 km^2)
Population: 605,000 (Urban: 54%)
Literacy: 94%
Capital: Nicosia (Levkosía), 48,221
Government: Republic
Languages: Greek, English
Ethnic Groups: Greek
Religions: Greek Orthodox
Currency: Pound
Tel. Area Code: 357

Czech Republic (Česká Republika)

Location: Eastern Europe, landlocked
Area: 30,450 mi^2 (78,864 km^2)
Population: 10,455,000 (Urban: 65%)
Literacy: 99%
Capital: Praha (Prague), 1,212,010
Government: Republic
Languages: Czech, Slovak
Ethnic Groups: Czech 94%, Slovak 3%
Religions: Roman Catholic 39%,
Protestant 5%, Orthodox 3%
Currency: Koruna
Tel. Area Code: 42

Denmark

Location: Northern Europe
Area: 16,639 mi^2 (43,094 km^2)
Population: 5,227,000 (Urban: 85%)
Literacy: 99%
Capital: København (Copenhagen), 464,566
Government: Constitutional monarchy

Languages: Danish
Ethnic Groups: Danish (Scandinavian),
German
Religions: Lutheran 91%
Currency: Krone
Tel. Area Code: 45

Djibouti

Location: Eastern Africa
Area: 8,958 mi^2 (23,200 km^2)
Population: 579,000 (Urban: 83%)
Literacy: 48%
Capital: Djibouti, 329,337
Government: Republic
Languages: French, Arabic, Somali, Afar
Ethnic Groups: Somali 60%, Afar 35%
Religions: Muslim 94%, Christian 6%
Currency: Franc
Tel. Area Code: 253

Dominica

Location: Caribbean island
Area: 305 mi^2 (790 km^2)
Population: 83,000 (Urban: 27%)
Literacy: 94%
Capital: Roseau, 9,348
Government: Republic
Languages: English, French
Ethnic Groups: Black 91%, mixed 6%, West
Indian 2%
Religions: Roman Catholic 77%,
Methodist 5%, Pentecostal 3%
Currency: East Caribbean dollar
Tel. Area Code: 809

Dominican Republic (República Dominicana)

Location: Caribbean island (eastern
Hispaniola)
Area: 18,704 mi^2 (48,442 km^2)
Population: 7,909,000 (Urban: 65%)
Literacy: 83%
Capital: Santo Domingo, 2,411,900
Government: Republic
Languages: Spanish
Ethnic Groups: Mulatto 73%, white 16%,
black 11%
Religions: Roman Catholic 95%
Currency: Peso
Tel. Area Code: 809

Ecuador

Location: Western South America
Area: 105,037 mi^2 (272,045 km^2)
Population: 10,560,000 (Urban: 58%)

Literacy: 87%
Capital: Quito, 1,100,847
Government: Republic
Languages: Spanish, Quechua, indigenous
Ethnic Groups: Mestizo 55%,
  Amerindian 25%, white 10%, black 10%
Religions: Roman Catholic 95%
Currency: Sucre
Tel. Area Code: 593

Egypt (Miṣr)

Location: Northeastern Africa
Area: 386,662 mi^2 (1,001,449 km^2)
Population: 60,080,000 (Urban: 45%)
Literacy: 48%
Capital: Al-Qāhirah (Cairo), 6,068,695
Government: Socialist republic
Languages: Arabic
Ethnic Groups: Egyptian (Eastern Hamitic)
  90%
Religions: Muslim 94%, Coptic Christian
  and others 6%
Currency: Pound
Tel. Area Code: 20

El Salvador

Location: Central America
Area: 8,124 mi^2 (21,041 km^2)
Population: 5,929,000 (Urban: 45%)
Literacy: 73%
Capital: San Salvador, 462,652
Government: Republic
Languages: Spanish, Nahua
Ethnic Groups: Mestizo 94%,
  Amerindian 5%, white 1%
Religions: Roman Catholic 75%
Currency: Colon
Tel. Area Code: 503

Equatorial Guinea (Guinea Ecuatorial)

Location: Central Africa
Area: 10,831 mi^2 (28,051 km^2)
Population: 425,000 (Urban: 42%)
Literacy: 62%
Capital: Malabo, 31,630
Government: Republic
Languages: Spanish, indigenous, English
Ethnic Groups: Fang 80%, Bubi 15%
Religions: Roman Catholic 83%, other
  Christian, tribal religionist
Currency: CFA franc
Tel. Area Code: 240

Eritrea (Ērtra)

Location: Eastern Africa
Area: 36,170 mi^2 (93,679 km^2)
Population: 3,740,000 (Urban: 17%)
Capital: Asmera, 358,100
Government: Republic
Languages: Tigre, Kunama, Cushitic
  dialects, Nora Bana, Arabic
Ethnic Groups: Tigray 50%, Tigre and
  Kunama 30%, Afar 4%, Saho 3%
Religions: Muslim, Coptic Christian,
  Roman Catholic, Protestant
Currency: Ethiopian birr
Tel. Area Code: 291

Estonia (Eesti)

Location: Eastern Europe
Area: 17,413 mi^2 (45,100 km^2)
Population: 1,499,000 (Urban: 73%)
Literacy: 100%
Capital: Tallinn, 481,500
Government: Republic
Languages: Estonian, Latvian, Lithuanian,
  Russian
Ethnic Groups: Estonian 62%, Russian 30%,
  Ukrainian 3%
Religions: Lutheran
Currency: Kroon
Tel. Area Code: 372

Ethiopia (Ītyop'iya)

Location: Eastern Africa, landlocked
Area: 446,953 mi^2 (1,157,603 km^2)
Population: 56,820,000 (Urban: 13%)
Literacy: 24%
Capital: Adis Abeba, 1,912,500
Government: Provisional military
  government
Languages: Amharic, Tigrinya, Orominga,
  Guaraginga, Somali, Arabic
Ethnic Groups: Oromo (Galla) 40%,
  Amhara and Tigrean 32%, Sidamo 9%,
  Shankella 6%, Somali 6%
Religions: Muslim 40-50%, Ethiopian
  Orthodox 35-40%, Animist 12%
Currency: Birr
Tel. Area Code: 251

Fiji (Viti)

Location: South Pacific islands
Area: 7,056 mi^2 (18,274 km^2)
Population: 778,000 (Urban: 40%)
Literacy: 87%
Capital: Suva, 69,665
Government: Republic

Languages: English, Fijian, Hindustani
Ethnic Groups: Fijian 49%, Indian 46%
Religions: Methodist and other
Christian 52%, Hindu 38%, Muslim 8%
Currency: Dollar
Tel. Area Code: 679

Finland (Suomi)

Location: Northern Europe
Area: 130,559 mi^2 (338,145 km^2)
Population: 5,117,000 (Urban: 63%)
Literacy: 100%
Capital: Helsinki, 501,514
Government: Republic
Languages: Finnish, Swedish, Lapp, Russian
Ethnic Groups: Finnish (mixed
Scandinavian and Baltic), Swedish,
Lappic, Gypsy, Tatar
Religions: Jehovah's Witness, Free Church,
Adventist, Confessional Lutheran
Currency: Markkaa
Tel. Area Code: 358

France

Location: Western Europe
Area: 211,208 mi^2 (547,026 km^2)
Population: 58,280,000 (Urban: 73%)
Literacy: 99%
Capital: Paris, 2,152,423
Government: Republic
Languages: French
Ethnic Groups: French (mixed Celtic, Latin,
and Teutonic)
Religions: Roman Catholic 90%,
Protestant 2%, Jewish 1%, Muslim 1%
Currency: Franc
Tel. Area Code: 33

French Guiana (Guyane)

Location: Northeastern South America
Area: 32,253 mi^2 (83,534 km^2)
Population: 148,000 (Urban: 77%)
Literacy: 83%
Capital: Cayenne, 38,091
Government: Overseas department (France)
Languages: French
Ethnic Groups: Black or mulatto 66%;
white 12%; East Indian, Chinese, and
Amerindian 12%
Religions: Roman Catholic
Currency: French franc
Tel. Area Code: 594

French Polynesia (Polynésie française)

Location: South Pacific islands
Area: 1,359 mi^2 (3,521 km^2)
Population: 222,000 (Urban: 65%)
Literacy: 98%
Capital: Papeete, 23,555
Government: Overseas territory (France)
Languages: French, Tahitian
Ethnic Groups: Polynesian 78%,
Chinese 12%, French descent 6%
Religions: Evangelical and other
Protestant 54%, Roman Catholic 30%
Currency: CFP franc
Tel. Area Code: 689

Gabon

Location: Central Africa
Area: 103,347 mi^2 (267,667 km^2)
Population: 1,164,000 (Urban: 50%)
Literacy: 61%
Capital: Libreville, 235,700
Government: Republic
Languages: French, Fang, indigenous
Ethnic Groups: Fang, Eshira, Bapounou,
Bateke
Religions: Roman Catholic and other
Christian 55-75%, Muslim
Currency: CFA franc
Tel. Area Code: 241

Gambia

Location: Western Africa
Area: 4,127 mi^2 (10,689 km^2)
Population: 1,131,000 (Urban: 26%)
Literacy: 27%
Capital: Banjul, 44,188
Government: Provisional military
government
Languages: English, Malinke, Wolof, Fula,
indigenous
Ethnic Groups: Malinke 42%, Fulani 18%,
Wolof 16%, Jola 10%, Serahuli 9%
Religions: Muslim 90%, Christian 9%, tribal
religionist 1%
Currency: Dalasi
Tel. Area Code: 220

Georgia (Sakartvelo)

Location: Southwestern Asia
Area: 26,911 mi^2 (69,700 km^2)
Population: 5,749,000 (Urban: 59%)
Literacy: 99%
Capital: Tbilisi, 1,279,000
Government: Republic

Languages: Georgian, Russian, Armenian, Azeri
Ethnic Groups: Georgian 70%, Armenian 8%, Russian 6%, Azeri 6%, Ossetian 3%, Abkhaz 2%
Religions: Georgian Orthodox 65%, Muslim 11%, Russian Orthodox 10%
Currency: Lari
Tel. Area Code: 7

Germany (Deutschland)

Location: Northern Europe
Area: 137,822 mi^2 (356,955 km^2)
Population: 81,800,000 (Urban: 87%)
Literacy: 99%
Capital: Berlin (designated), 3,433,695; Bonn (de facto), 292,234
Government: Federal republic
Languages: German
Ethnic Groups: German (Teutonic) 95%, Turkish 2%
Religions: Evangelical and other Protestant 45%, Roman Catholic 37%
Currency: Mark
Tel. Area Code: 49

Ghana

Location: Western Africa
Area: 92,098 mi^2 (238,533 km^2)
Population: 18,030,000 (Urban: 36%)
Literacy: 60%
Capital: Accra, 949,113
Government: Republic
Languages: English, Akan and other indigenous
Ethnic Groups: Akan 44%, Moshi-Dagomba 16%, Ewe 13%, Ga 8%
Religions: Tribal religionist 38%, Muslim 30%, Christian 24%
Currency: Cedi
Tel. Area Code: 233

Greece (Ellás)

Location: Southeastern Europe
Area: 50,949 mi^2 (131,957 km^2)
Population: 10,535,000 (Urban: 65%)
Literacy: 95%
Capital: Athínai (Athens), 748,110
Government: Republic
Languages: Greek, English, French
Ethnic Groups: Greek 98%
Religions: Greek Orthodox 98%, Muslim 1%
Currency: Drachma
Tel. Area Code: 30

Greenland (Kalaallit Nunaat, Grønland)

Location: North Atlantic island
Area: 840,004 mi^2 (2,175,600 km^2)
Population: 58,000 (Urban: 80%)
Capital: Godtháb, 12,217
Government: Self-governing territory (Danish protection)
Languages: Danish, Greenlandic, Inuit dialects
Ethnic Groups: Greenlander (Inuit and native-born whites) 86%, Danish 14%
Religions: Lutheran
Currency: Danish krone
Tel. Area Code: 299

Grenada

Location: Caribbean island
Area: 133 mi^2 (344 km^2)
Population: 94,000 (Urban: 15%)
Literacy: 98%
Capital: St. George's, 4,439
Government: Parliamentary state
Languages: English, French
Ethnic Groups: Black 82%, mixed 13%, East Indian 3%
Religions: Roman Catholic 59%, Anglican 17%, Seventh Day Adventist 6%
Currency: East Caribbean dollar
Tel. Area Code: 809

Guatemala

Location: Central America
Area: 42,042 mi^2 (108,889 km^2)
Population: 11,140,000 (Urban: 42%)
Literacy: 55%
Capital: Guatemala, 1,057,210
Government: Republic
Languages: Spanish, Amerindian
Ethnic Groups: Ladino (mestizo) 56%, Amerindian 44%
Religions: Roman Catholic, Protestant, tribal religionist
Currency: Quetzal
Tel. Area Code: 502

Guinea (Guinée)

Location: Western Africa
Area: 94,926 mi^2 (245,857 km^2)
Population: 6,628,000 (Urban: 30%)
Literacy: 24%
Capital: Conakry, 800,000
Government: Provisional military government
Languages: French, indigenous

Ethnic Groups: Fulani 35%, Malinke 30%,
Susu 20%, others
Religions: Muslim 85%, Christian 8%,
Animist 7%
Currency: Franc
Tel. Area Code: 224

Guinea-Bissau (Guiné-Bissau)

Location: Western Africa
Area: 13,948 mi^2 (36,125 km^2)
Population: 1,139,000 (Urban: 22%)
Literacy: 36%
Capital: Bissau, 125,000
Government: Republic
Languages: Portuguese, Crioulo, indigenous
Ethnic Groups: Balanta 30%, Fulani 20%,
Manjaca 14%, Malinke 13%, Papel 7%
Religions: Tribal religionist 65%,
Muslim 30%, Christian 5%
Currency: Peso
Tel. Area Code: 245

Guyana

Location: Northeastern South America
Area: 83,000 mi^2 (214,969 km^2)
Population: 721,000 (Urban: 36%)
Literacy: 96%
Capital: Georgetown, 78,500
Government: Republic
Languages: English, indigenous
Ethnic Groups: East Indian 51%, black 30%,
mixed 11%, Amerindian 5%
Religions: Anglican and other
Christian 57%, Hindu 33%, Muslim 9%
Currency: Dollar
Tel. Area Code: 592

Haiti (Haïti)

Location: Caribbean island (western
Hispaniola)
Area: 10,714 mi^2 (27,750 km^2)
Population: 7,199,000 (Urban: 32%)
Literacy: 35%
Capital: Port-au-Prince, 797,000
Government: Provisional military
government
Languages: Creole, French
Ethnic Groups: Black 95%, mulatto and
white 5%
Religions: Roman Catholic 80%,
Baptist 10%, Pentecostal 4%
Currency: Gourde
Tel. Area Code: 509

Honduras

Location: Central America
Area: 43,277 mi^2 (112,088 km^2)
Population: 6,004,000 (Urban: 44%)
Literacy: 73%
Capital: Tegucigalpa, 576,661
Government: Republic
Languages: Spanish, indigenous
Ethnic Groups: Mestizo 90%,
Amerindian 7%, black 2%, white 1%
Religions: Roman Catholic 97%
Currency: Lempira
Tel. Area Code: 504

Hong Kong (Xianggang)

Location: Eastern Asia (islands and
mainland area on China's southeastern
coast)
Area: 414 mi^2 (1,072 km^2)
Population: 5,540,000 (Urban: 95%)
Literacy: 77%
Capital: Hong Kong (Xianggang), 1,250,993
Government: Special administrative region
of China
Languages: Chinese (Cantonese), English,
Putonghua
Ethnic Groups: Chinese 98%
Religions: Buddhist and Taoist 90%,
Christian 10%
Currency: Dollar
Tel. Area Code: 852

Hungary (Magyarország)

Location: Eastern Europe, landlocked
Area: 35,919 mi^2 (93,030 km^2)
Population: 10,240,000 (Urban: 65%)
Literacy: 99%
Capital: Budapest, 2,016,774
Government: Republic
Languages: Hungarian
Ethnic Groups: Hungarian (Magyar) 90%,
Gypsy 4%, German 3%, Serb 2%
Religions: Roman Catholic 68%,
Calvinist 20%, Lutheran 5%
Currency: Forint
Tel. Area Code: 36

Iceland (Ísland)

Location: North Atlantic island
Area: 39,769 mi^2 (103,000 km^2)
Population: 267,000 (Urban: 92%)
Literacy: 100%
Capital: Reykjavík, 100,850
Government: Republic
Languages: Icelandic

Ethnic Groups: Icelander (mixed Norwegian and Celtic)
Religions: Lutheran 96%, other Christian 3%
Currency: Krona
Tel. Area Code: 354

India (Bharat)

Location: Southern Asia
Area: 1,237,062 mi^2 (3,203,975 km^2)
Population: 944,980,000 (Urban: 27%)
Literacy: 52%
Capital: New Delhi, 301,297
Government: Federal republic
Languages: English, Hindi, Telugu, Bengali, indigenous
Ethnic Groups: Indo-Aryan 72%, Dravidian 25%, Mongoloid and other 3%
Religions: Hindu 80%, Muslim 11%, Christian 2%, Sikh 2%
Currency: Rupee
Tel. Area Code: 91

Indonesia

Location: Southeastern Asian islands
Area: 752,410 mi^2 (1,948,732 km^2)
Population: 196,830,000 (Urban: 35%)
Literacy: 82%
Capital: Jakarta, 8,227,746
Government: Republic
Languages: Bahasa Indonesia (Malay), English, Dutch, indigenous
Ethnic Groups: Javanese 45%, Sundanese 14%, Madurese 8%, coastal Malay 8%
Religions: Muslim 87%, Protestant 6%, Catholic 3%, Hindu 2%
Currency: Rupiah
Tel. Area Code: 62

Iran (Īrān)

Location: Southwestern Asia
Area: 630,578 mi^2 (1,633,189 km^2)
Population: 65,340,000 (Urban: 59%)
Literacy: 66%
Capital: Tehrān, 6,042,584
Government: Islamic republic
Languages: Farsi, Turkish dialects, Kurdish
Ethnic Groups: Persian 51%, Azeri 24%, Kurdish 7%
Religions: Shiite Muslim 95%, Sunni Muslim 4%
Currency: Rial
Tel. Area Code: 98

Iraq (Al-'Irāq)

Location: Southwestern Asia
Area: 169,235 mi^2 (438,317 km^2)
Population: 21,015,000 (Urban: 75%)
Literacy: 89%
Capital: Baghdād, 3,841,268
Government: Republic
Languages: Arabic, Kurdish, Assyrian, Armenian
Ethnic Groups: Arab 75%-80%; Kurdish 15-20%; Turkoman, Assyrian, or other 5%
Religions: Shiite Muslim 60-65%, Sunni Muslim 32-37%, Christian and others 3%
Currency: Dinar
Tel. Area Code: 964

Ireland (Éire)

Location: Northwestern European island (five-sixths of Ireland)
Area: 27,137 mi^2 (70,285 km^2)
Population: 3,557,000 (Urban: 58%)
Literacy: 98%
Capital: Dublin, 502,749
Government: Republic
Languages: English, Irish Gaelic
Ethnic Groups: Irish (Celtic), English
Religions: Roman Catholic 93%, Church of Ireland 3%
Currency: Pound (punt)
Tel. Area Code: 353

Israel (Yisra'el, Isrā'īl)

Location: Southwestern Asia
Area: 8,019 mi^2 (20,770 km^2)
Population: 5,122,000 (Urban: 91%)
Literacy: 95%
Capital: Yerushalayim (Jerusalem), 524,500
Government: Republic
Languages: Hebrew, Arabic
Ethnic Groups: Jewish 83%, Arab and others 17%
Religions: Jewish 82%, Muslim 14%, Christian 2%, Druze 2%
Currency: Shekel
Tel. Area Code: 972

Italy (Italia)

Location: Southern Europe
Area: 116,336 mi^2 (301,309 km^2)
Population: 58,320,000 (Urban: 67%)
Literacy: 97%
Capital: Roma (Rome), 2,693,383
Government: Republic
Languages: Italian, German, French, Slovene

Ethnic Groups: Italian (Latin)
Religions: Roman Catholic
Currency: Lira
Tel. Area Code: 39

Jamaica

Location: Caribbean island
Area: 4,244 mi^2 (10,991 km^2)
Population: 2,584,000 (Urban: 54%)
Literacy: 98%
Capital: Kingston, 587,798
Government: Parliamentary state
Languages: English, Creole
Ethnic Groups: Black 75%, mixed 13%, East Indian 1%
Religions: Church of God 18%, Baptist 10%, Anglican 7%, Seventh-Day Adventist 7%
Currency: Dollar
Tel. Area Code: 809

Japan (Nihon)

Location: Eastern Asian islands
Area: 145,850 mi^2 (377,750 km^2)
Population: 125,760,000 (Urban: 78%)
Literacy: 99%
Capital: Tōkyō, 8,163,573
Government: Constitutional monarchy
Languages: Japanese
Ethnic Groups: Japanese 99%, Korean
Religions: Buddhist and Shinto
Currency: Yen
Tel. Area Code: 81

Jordan (Al-Urdun)

Location: Southwestern Asia
Area: 35,135 mi^2 (91,000 km^2)
Population: 4,154,000 (Urban: 72%)
Literacy: 83%
Capital: ʿAmmān, 936,300
Government: Constitutional monarchy
Languages: Arabic
Ethnic Groups: Arab 98%, Circassian 1%, Armenian 1%
Religions: Sunni Muslim 92%, Christian 8%
Currency: Dinar
Tel. Area Code: 962

Kazakhstan (Kazachstan)

Location: Central Asia, landlocked
Area: 1,049,156 mi^2 (2,717,300 km^2)
Population: 17,180,000 (Urban: 60%)
Literacy: 98%
Capital: Almaty (Alma-Ata), 1,156,200
Government: Republic
Languages: Kazakh, Russian

Ethnic Groups: Kazakh 42%, Russian 37%, Ukrainian 5%, German 5%
Religions: Muslim 47%, Russian Orthodox 15%, Lutheran
Currency: Tenge
Tel. Area Code: 7

Kenya

Location: Eastern Africa
Area: 224,961 mi^2 (582,646 km^2)
Population: 28,960,000 (Urban: 28%)
Literacy: 71%
Capital: Nairobi, 1,505,000
Government: Republic
Languages: English, Swahili, indigenous
Ethnic Groups: Kikuyu 21%, Luhya 14%, Luo 13%, Kamba 11%, Kalenjin 11%, Kisii 6 %, Meru 5%
Religions: Roman Catholic 28%, Protestant 26%, Animist 18%, Muslim 6%
Currency: Shilling
Tel. Area Code: 254

Kiribati

Location: Central Pacific islands
Area: 313 mi^2 (811 km^2)
Population: 80,000 (Urban: 36%)
Capital: Bairiki, 2,226
Government: Republic
Languages: English, Gilbertese
Ethnic Groups: Kiribatian (Micronesian) 98%
Religions: Roman Catholic 53%, Congregationalist 39%, Bahai 2%
Currency: Australian dollar
Tel. Area Code: 686

Korea, North (Chosŏn-minjujuǔi-inmĭn-konghwaguk)

Location: Eastern Asia
Area: 46,540 mi^2 (120,538 km^2)
Population: 23,700,000 (Urban: 61%)
Literacy: 99%
Capital: P'yŏngyang, 2,355,000
Government: Socialist republic
Languages: Korean
Ethnic Groups: Korean 100%
Religions: Buddhist, Chondoist, Confucian
Currency: Won
Tel. Area Code: 850

Korea, South (Taehan-min'guk)

Location: Eastern Asia
Area: 38,230 mi^2 (99,016 km^2)
Population: 45,040,000 (Urban: 81%)

Literacy: 96%
Capital: Sŏul (Seoul), 10,627,790
Government: Republic
Languages: Korean
Ethnic Groups: Korean
Religions: Christian 49%, Buddhist 47%,
  Confucian 3%
Currency: Won
Tel. Area Code: 82

Kuwait (Al-Kuwayt)

Location: Southwestern Asia
Area: 6,880 mi^2 (17,818 km^2)
Population: 1,802,000 (Urban: 97%)
Literacy: 74%
Capital: Al-Kuwayt (Kuwait), 44,335
Government: Constitutional monarchy
Languages: Arabic, English
Ethnic Groups: Kuwaiti 45%, other
  Arab 35%, South Asian 9%, Iranian 4%
Religions: Sunni Muslim 45%, Shiite
  Muslim 30%, Christian 6%
Currency: Dinar
Tel. Area Code: 965

Kyrgyzstan

Location: Central Asia, landlocked
Area: 76,641 mi^2 (198,500 km^2)
Population: 4,543,000 (Urban: 39%)
Literacy: 97%
Capital: Biškek (Frunze), 631,300
Government: Republic
Languages: Kirghiz, Russian
Ethnic Groups: Kirghiz 52%, Russian 22%,
  Uzbek 13%
Religions: Muslim 70%, Russian Orthodox
Currency: Som
Tel. Area Code: 7

Laos (Lao)

Location: Southeastern Asia, landlocked
Area: 91,429 mi^2 (236,800 km^2)
Population: 4,905,000 (Urban: 22%)
Literacy: 50%
Capital: Viangchan (Vientiane), 377,409
Government: Socialist republic
Languages: Lao, French, English
Ethnic Groups: Lao 50%; Thai 20%;
  Phoutheung 15%; Miao, Hmong, Yao, and
  others 15%
Religions: Buddhist 85%, Animist and
  others 15%
Currency: Kip
Tel. Area Code: 856

Latvia (Latvija)

Location: Eastern Europe
Area: 24,595 mi^2 (63,700 km^2)
Population: 2,522,000 (Urban: 73%)
Literacy: 100%
Capital: Rīga, 910,200
Government: Republic
Languages: Lettish, Lithuanian, Russian,
  other
Ethnic Groups: Latvian 52%, Russian 34%,
  Byelorussian 5%, Ukrainian 3%, Polish 2%
Religions: Lutheran, Roman Catholic,
  Russian Orthodox
Currency: Lat
Tel. Area Code: 371

Lebanon (Lubnān)

Location: Southwestern Asia
Area: 4,015 mi^2 (10,400 km^2)
Population: 3,737,000 (Urban: 87%)
Literacy: 80%
Capital: Bayrūt (Beirut), 509,000
Government: Republic
Languages: Arabic, French, Armenian,
  English
Ethnic Groups: Arab 95%, Armenian 4%
Religions: Muslim 70%, Christian 30%
Currency: Pound
Tel. Area Code: 961

Lesotho

Location: Southern Africa, landlocked
Area: 11,720 mi^2 (30,355 km^2)
Population: 2,017,000 (Urban: 23%)
Literacy: 59%
Capital: Maseru, 109,382
Government: Constitutional monarchy under
  military rule
Languages: English, Sesotho, Zulu, Xhosa
Ethnic Groups: Sotho 99%
Religions: Roman Catholic and other
  Christian 80%, tribal religionist 20%
Currency: Loti
Tel. Area Code: 266

Liberia

Location: Western Africa
Area: 38,250 mi^2 (99,067 km^2)
Population: 3,125,000 (Urban: 45%)
Literacy: 40%
Capital: Monrovia, 465,000
Government: Transitional
Languages: English, indigenous
Ethnic Groups: Indigenous African 95%,
  descendants of freed American slaves 5%

Religions: Animist 70%, Muslim 20%,
Christian 10%
Currency: Dollar
Tel. Area Code: 231

Libya (Lībiyā)

Location: Northern Africa
Area: 679,362 mi^2 (1,759,540 km^2)
Population: 5,342,000 (Urban: 86%)
Literacy: 64%
Capital: Ṭarābulus (Tripoli), 591,062
Government: Socialist republic
Languages: Arabic
Ethnic Groups: Arab-Berber 97%
Religions: Sunni Muslim 97%
Currency: Dinar
Tel. Area Code: 218

Liechtenstein

Location: Central Europe, landlocked
Area: 62 mi^2 (160 km^2)
Population: 31,000 (Urban: 21%)
Literacy: 100%
Capital: Vaduz, 4,887
Government: Constitutional monarchy
Languages: German
Ethnic Groups: Liechtensteiner (Alemannic)
95%
Religions: Roman Catholic 87%,
Protestant 8%
Currency: Swiss franc
Tel. Area Code: 4175

Lithuania (Lietuva)

Location: Eastern Europe
Area: 25,212 mi^2 (65,300 km^2)
Population: 4,012,000 (Urban: 72%)
Literacy: 98%
Capital: Vilnius, 596,900
Government: Republic
Languages: Lithuanian, Polish, Russian
Ethnic Groups: Lithuanian 80%,
Russian 9%, Polish 8%, Byelorussian 2%
Religions: Roman Catholic, Lutheran
Currency: Litas
Tel. Area Code: 370

Luxembourg (Lezebuurg)

Location: Western Europe, landlocked
Area: 998 mi^2 (2,586 km^2)
Population: 406,000 (Urban: 89%)
Literacy: 100%
Capital: Luxembourg, 75,377
Government: Constitutional monarchy

Languages: French, Luxembourgish,
German
Ethnic Groups: Luxembourger (mixed
Celtic, French, and German)
Religions: Roman Catholic 97%, Jewish and
Protestant 3%
Currency: Franc
Tel. Area Code: 352

Macau

Location: Eastern Asia (islands and
peninsula on China's southeastern coast)
Area: 6.6 mi^2 (17 km^2)
Population: 406,000 (Urban: 99%)
Literacy: 90%
Capital: Macau, 452,300
Government: Chinese territory under
Portuguese administration
Languages: Portuguese, Chinese (Cantonese)
Ethnic Groups: Chinese 95%, Portuguese 3%
Religions: Buddhist 45%, Roman
Catholic 7%
Currency: Pataca
Tel. Area Code: 853

Macedonia (Makedonija)

Location: Southeastern Europe, landlocked
Area: 9,928 mi^2 (25,713 km^2)
Population: 2,169,000 (Urban: 60%)
Literacy: 89%
Capital: Skopje, 444,900
Government: Republic
Languages: Macedonian, Albanian
Ethnic Groups: Macedonian 67%,
Albanian 21%, Turkish 4%, Serb 2%
Religions: Eastern Orthodox 59%,
Muslim 26%, Roman Catholic 4%
Currency: Denar
Tel. Area Code: 389

Madagascar (Madagasikara)

Location: Southeastern African island
Area: 226,658 mi^2 (587,041 km^2)
Population: 14,185,000 (Urban: 27%)
Literacy: 80%
Capital: Antananarivo, 1,250,000
Government: Republic
Languages: Malagasy, French
Ethnic Groups: Merina 15%,
Betsimisaraka 9%, Betsileo 7%,
Tsimihety 4%, Antaisaka 4 %, other tribes
Religions: Animist 52%, Christian 41%,
Muslim 7%
Currency: Franc
Tel. Area Code: 261

Malawi (Malaŵi)

Location: Southern Africa, landlocked
Area: 45,747 mi^2 (118,484 km^2)
Population: 9,937,000 (Urban: 14%)
Literacy: 48%
Capital: Lilongwe, 223,318
Government: Republic
Languages: Chichewa, English
Ethnic Groups: Chewa, Nyanja, Tumbuko, Yao, Lomwe, others
Religions: Protestant 55%, Roman Catholic 20%, Muslim 20%
Currency: Kwacha
Tel. Area Code: 265

Malaysia

Location: Southeastern Asia (includes part of the island of Borneo)
Area: 127,320 mi^2 (329,758 km^2)
Population: 19,940,000 (Urban: 54%)
Literacy: 78%
Capital: Kuala Lumpur, 919,610
Government: Federal constitutional monarchy
Languages: Malay, Chinese dialects, English, Tamil
Ethnic Groups: Malay and other indigenous 59%, Chinese 32%, Indian 9%
Religions: Muslim 53%, Buddhist 17%, Chinese religions 12%, Hindu 7%
Currency: Ringgit
Tel. Area Code: 60

Maldives

Location: Indian Ocean islands
Area: 115 mi^2 (298 km^2)
Population: 259,000 (Urban: 27%)
Literacy: 91%
Capital: Male', 55,130
Government: Republic
Languages: Divehi
Ethnic Groups: Maldivian (mixed Sinhalese, Dravidian, Arab, and black)
Religions: Sunni Muslim
Currency: Rufiyaa
Tel. Area Code: 960

Mali

Location: Western Africa, landlocked
Area: 482,077 mi^2 (1,248,574 km^2)
Population: 9,516,000 (Urban: 27%)
Literacy: 32%
Capital: Bamako, 658,275
Government: Republic
Languages: French, Bambara, indigenous
Ethnic Groups: Mande 50%, Fulani 17%, Voltaic 12%, Songhai 6%
Religions: Sunni Muslim 90%, Animist 9%, Christian 1%
Currency: CFA franc
Tel. Area Code: 223

Malta

Location: Mediterranean island
Area: 122 mi^2 (316 km^2)
Population: 371,000 (Urban: 90%)
Literacy: 84%
Capital: Valletta, 9,199
Government: Republic
Languages: English, Maltese
Ethnic Groups: Maltese (mixed Arab, Sicilian, Norman, Spanish, Italian, and English)
Religions: Roman Catholic 98%
Currency: Lira
Tel. Area Code: 356

Mauritania (Mūrītāniyā, Mauritanie)

Location: Western Africa
Area: 397,956 mi^2 (1,030,700 km^2)
Population: 2,299,000 (Urban: 54%)
Literacy: 35%
Capital: Nouakchott, 285,000
Government: Republic
Languages: Arabic, Pular, Soninke, Wolof
Ethnic Groups: Mixed Moor and black 40%, Moor 30%, black 30%
Religions: Sunni Muslim 100%
Currency: Ouguiya
Tel. Area Code: 222

Mauritius

Location: Indian Ocean island
Area: 788 mi^2 (2,040 km^2)
Population: 1,132,000 (Urban: 41%)
Literacy: 80%
Capital: Port Louis, 141,870
Government: Republic
Languages: English, Creole, Bhojpuri, French, Hindi, Tamil, others
Ethnic Groups: Indo-Mauritian 68%, Creole 27%, Sino-Mauritian 3%, Franco-Mauritian 2%
Religions: Hindu 52%, Roman Catholic 28%, Muslim 17%
Currency: Rupee
Tel. Area Code: 230

Mexico (México)

Location: Southern North America
Area: 759,534 mi^2 (1,967,183 km^2)
Population: 94,830,000 (Urban: 75%)
Literacy: 88%
Capital: Ciudad de México (Mexico City), 8,235,744
Government: Federal republic
Languages: Spanish, indigenous
Ethnic Groups: Mestizo 60%, Amerindian 30%, white 9%
Religions: Roman Catholic 89%, Protestant 6%
Currency: Peso
Tel. Area Code: 52

Moldova

Location: Eastern Europe, landlocked
Area: 13,012 mi^2 (33,700 km^2)
Population: 4,611,000 (Urban: 52%)
Literacy: 96%
Capital: Chişinău (Kishinev), 676,700
Government: Republic
Languages: Romanian (Moldovan), Russian
Ethnic Groups: Moldovan 65%, Ukrainian 14%, Russian 13%, Gagauz 4%, Jewish 2%
Religions: Eastern Orthodox 99%
Currency: Leu
Tel. Area Code: 373

Monaco

Location: Southern Europe (on the southeastern coast of France)
Area: 0.7 mi^2 (1.9 km^2)
Population: 32,000 (Urban: 100%)
Capital: Monaco, 32,000
Government: Constitutional monarchy
Languages: French, English, Italian, Monegasque
Ethnic Groups: French 47%, Monegasque 16%, Italian 16%, English 4%, Belgian 2 %, Swiss 1%
Religions: Roman Catholic 95%
Currency: French franc
Tel. Area Code: 33

Mongolia (Mongol Uls)

Location: Central Asia, landlocked
Area: 604,829 mi^2 (1,566,500 km^2)
Population: 2,526,000 (Urban: 61%)
Literacy: 90%
Capital: Ulaanbaatar (Ulan Bator), 575,000
Government: Republic
Languages: Khalkha Mongol, Turkish dialects, Russian, Chinese
Ethnic Groups: Mongol 90%, Kazakh 4%, Chinese 2%, Russian 2%
Religions: Shamanic, Tibetan Buddhist, Muslim
Currency: Tughrik
Tel. Area Code: 976

Morocco (Al-Magrib)

Location: Northwestern Africa
Area: 172,414 mi^2 (446,550 km^2)
Population: 27,430,000 (Urban: 48%)
Literacy: 50%
Capital: Rabat, 518,616
Government: Constitutional monarchy
Languages: Arabic, Berber dialects, French
Ethnic Groups: Arab-Berber 99%
Religions: Muslim 99%
Currency: Dirham
Tel. Area Code: 212

Mozambique (Moçambique)

Location: Southern Africa
Area: 308,642 mi^2 (799,380 km^2)
Population: 16,200,000 (Urban: 34%)
Literacy: 33%
Capital: Maputo, 1,069,727
Government: Republic
Languages: Portuguese, indigenous
Ethnic Groups: Makua, Lomwe, Thonga, others
Religions: Tribal religionist 60%, Roman Catholic and other Christian 30%, Muslim
Currency: Metical
Tel. Area Code: 258

Myanmar

Location: Southeastern Asia
Area: 261,228 mi^2 (676,577 km^2)
Population: 45,510,000 (Urban: 26%)
Literacy: 81%
Capital: Rangoon (Yangon), 2,513,023
Government: Provisional military government
Languages: Burmese, indigenous
Ethnic Groups: Bamar (Burmese) 69%, Shan 9%, Kayin 6%, Rakhine 5%
Religions: Buddhist 89%, Muslim 4%, Christian 4%
Currency: Kyat
Tel. Area Code: 95

Namibia

Location: Southern Africa
Area: 317,818 mi^2 (823,144 km^2)
Population: 1,680,000 (Urban: 37%)
Literacy: 38%
Capital: Windhoek, 114,500
Government: Republic
Languages: English, Afrikaans, German, indigenous
Ethnic Groups: Ovambo 49%, Kavango 9%, Damara 8%, Herero 7%, white 7%, mixed 7%
Religions: Lutheran and other Protestant, Roman Catholic, Animist
Currency: Dollar
Tel. Area Code: 264

Nepal (Nepāl)

Location: Southern Asia, landlocked
Area: 56,827 mi^2 (147,181 km^2)
Population: 21,820,000 (Urban: 14%)
Literacy: 26%
Capital: Kāṭmāṇḍaū (Kathmandu), 421,258
Government: Constitutional monarchy
Languages: Nepali, Maithali, Bhojpuri, other indigenous
Ethnic Groups: Newar, Indian, Tibetan, Gurung, Magar, Tamang, Bhotia, Sherpa, others
Religions: Hindu 90%, Buddhist 5%, Muslim 3%
Currency: Rupee
Tel. Area Code: 977

Netherlands (Nederland)

Location: Western Europe
Area: 16,164 mi^2 (41,864 km^2)
Population: 15,500,000 (Urban: 89%)
Literacy: 99%
Capital: Amsterdam (designated), 713,407; The Hague (seat of government), 445,287
Government: Constitutional monarchy
Languages: Dutch
Ethnic Groups: Dutch (mixed Scandinavian, French, and Celtic) 96%
Religions: Roman Catholic 36%, Dutch Reformed 19%, Calvinist 8%
Currency: Guilder
Tel. Area Code: 31

New Caledonia (Nouvelle-Calédonie)

Location: South Pacific islands
Area: 7,172 mi^2 (18,575 km^2)
Population: 187,000 (Urban: 62%)
Literacy: 91%
Capital: Nouméa, 65,110
Government: Overseas territory (France)
Languages: French, indigenous
Ethnic Groups: Melanesian (Kanak) 45%, French 34%, Wallisian 9%, Indonesian 3%, Tahitian 3%
Religions: Roman Catholic 60%, Protestant 30%
Currency: CFP franc
Tel. Area Code: 687

New Zealand

Location: South Pacific islands
Area: 104,454 mi^2 (270,534 km^2)
Population: 3,608,000 (Urban: 86%)
Literacy: 99%
Capital: Wellington, 150,301
Government: Parliamentary state
Languages: English, Maori
Ethnic Groups: European origin 86%, Maori 10%, Samoan and other Pacific islander 4%
Religions: Anglican 24%, Presbyterian 18%, Roman Catholic 15%, Methodist 5%
Currency: Dollar
Tel. Area Code: 64

Nicaragua

Location: Central America
Area: 50,054 mi^2 (129,640 km^2)
Population: 4,573,000 (Urban: 63%)
Literacy: 57%
Capital: Managua, 682,000
Government: Republic
Languages: Spanish, English, indigenous
Ethnic Groups: Mestizo 69%, white 17%, black 9%, Amerindian 5%
Religions: Roman Catholic 95%
Currency: Cordoba
Tel. Area Code: 505

Niger

Location: Western Africa, landlocked
Area: 489,191 mi^2 (1,267,000 km^2)
Population: 9,438,000 (Urban: 17%)
Literacy: 28%
Capital: Niamey, 392,165
Government: Provisional military government
Languages: French, Hausa, Djerma, indigenous
Ethnic Groups: Hausa 56%, Djerma 22%, Fulani 9%, Taureg 8%, Beriberi 4%
Religions: Muslim 80%, Animist and Christian 20%

Currency: CFA franc
Tel. Area Code: 227

Nigeria

Location: Western Africa
Area: 356,669 mi^2 (923,768 km^2)
Population: 102,850,000 (Urban: 39%)
Literacy: 51%
Capital: Lagos (de facto), 1,213,000; Abuja (designated), 250,000
Government: Provisional military government
Languages: English, Hausa, Fulani, Yorbua, Ibo, indigenous
Ethnic Groups: Hausa, Fulani, Yoruba, Ibo, others
Religions: Muslim 50%, Christian 40%, Animist 10%
Currency: Naira
Tel. Area Code: 234

Norway (Norge)

Location: Northern Europe
Area: 149,405 mi^2 (386,958 km^2)
Population: 4,340,000 (Urban: 73%)
Literacy: 99%
Capital: Oslo, 470,204
Government: Constitutional monarchy
Languages: Norwegian, Lapp, Finnish
Ethnic Groups: Norwegian (Scandinavian), Lapp
Religions: Lutheran 89%, other Protestant and Roman Catholic 4%
Currency: Krone
Tel. Area Code: 47

Oman ('Umān)

Location: Southwestern Asia
Area: 82,030 mi^2 (212,457 km^2)
Population: 2,163,000 (Urban: 13%)
Literacy: 20%
Capital: Muscat, 30,000
Government: Monarchy
Languages: Arabic, English, Baluchi, Urdu, Indian dialects
Ethnic Groups: Arab, Baluchi, Zanzibari, Indian
Religions: Ibadite Muslim 75%, Sunni Muslim, Shiite Muslim, Hindu
Currency: Rial
Tel. Area Code: 968

Pakistan (Pākistān)

Location: Southern Asia
Area: 339,732 mi^2 (879,902 km^2)

Population: 132,330,000 (Urban: 35%)
Literacy: 35%
Capital: Islāmābād, 204,364
Government: Federal Islamic republic
Languages: English, Urdu, Punjabi, Sindhi, Pashto
Ethnic Groups: Punjabi, Sindhi, Pathan, Baluchi, others
Religions: Sunni Muslim 77%, Shiite Muslim 20%
Currency: Rupee
Tel. Area Code: 92

Panama (Panamá)

Location: Central America
Area: 29,157 mi^2 (75,517 km^2)
Population: 2,705,000 (Urban: 53%)
Literacy: 89%
Capital: Panamá, 411,549
Government: Republic
Languages: Spanish, English
Ethnic Groups: Mestizo 70%, West Indian 14%, white 10%, Amerindian 6%
Religions: Roman Catholic 85%, Protestant 15%
Currency: Balboa
Tel. Area Code: 507

Papua New Guinea

Location: South Pacific islands
Area: 178,704 mi^2 (462,840 km^2)
Population: 4,342,000 (Urban: 16%)
Literacy: 52%
Capital: Port Moresby, 193,242
Government: Parliamentary state
Languages: English, Motu, Pidgin, indigenous
Ethnic Groups: Melanesian, Papuan, Negrito, Micronesian, Polynesian
Religions: Roman Catholic 22%, Lutheran 16%, United Church 8%, Anglican 5%
Currency: Kina
Tel. Area Code: 675

Paraguay

Location: Central South America, landlocked
Area: 157,048 mi^2 (406,752 km^2)
Population: 4,890,000 (Urban: 53%)
Literacy: 90%
Capital: Asunción, 502,426
Government: Republic
Languages: Spanish, Guarani
Ethnic Groups: Mestizo 95%, white and Amerindian 5%

Religions: Roman Catholic 90%, Mennonite and other Protestant
Currency: Guarani
Tel. Area Code: 595

Peru (Perú)

Location: Western South America
Area: 496,225 mi^2 (1,285,216 km^2)
Population: 24,305,000 (Urban: 72%)
Literacy: 82%
Capital: Lima, 371,122
Government: Republic
Languages: Quechua, Spanish, Aymara
Ethnic Groups: Amerindian 45%, mestizo 37%, white 15%
Religions: Roman Catholic
Currency: Sol
Tel. Area Code: 51

Philippines (Pilipinas)

Location: Southeastern Asian islands
Area: 115,831 mi^2 (300,000 km^2)
Population: 74,070,000 (Urban: 54%)
Literacy: 94%
Capital: Manila, 1,598,918
Government: Republic
Languages: English, Pilipino, Tagalog
Ethnic Groups: Christian Malay 92%, Muslim Malay 4%, Chinese 2%
Religions: Roman Catholic 83%, Protestant 9%, Muslim 5%, Buddhist and others 3%
Currency: Peso
Tel. Area Code: 63

Poland (Polska)

Location: Eastern Europe
Area: 121,196 mi^2 (313,895 km^2)
Population: 38,870,000 (Urban: 65%)
Literacy: 99%
Capital: Warszawa (Warsaw), 1,644,500
Government: Republic
Languages: Polish
Ethnic Groups: Polish (mixed Slavic and Teutonic) 98%
Religions: Roman Catholic 95%
Currency: Zloty
Tel. Area Code: 48

Portugal

Location: Southwestern Europe
Area: 35,516 mi^2 (91,985 km^2)
Population: 9,889,000 (Urban: 36%)
Literacy: 85%
Capital: Lisbon, 807,167
Government: Republic
Languages: Portuguese
Ethnic Groups: Portuguese (Mediterranean)
Religions: Roman Catholic 97%, Protestant 1%
Currency: Escudo
Tel. Area Code: 351

Puerto Rico

Location: Caribbean island
Area: 3,515 mi^2 (9,104 km^2)
Population: 3,817,000 (Urban: 73%)
Literacy: 89%
Capital: San Juan, 426,832
Government: Commonwealth (U.S. protection)
Languages: Spanish, English
Ethnic Groups: Puerto Rican (mixed Spanish and black)
Religions: Roman Catholic 85%, Protestant and other 15%
Currency: U.S. dollar

Qatar (Qaṭar)

Location: Southwestern Asia
Area: 4,412 mi^2 (11,427 km^2)
Population: 562,000 (Urban: 91%)
Literacy: 76%
Capital: Ad-Dowḥah (Doha), 217,294
Government: Monarchy
Languages: Arabic, English
Ethnic Groups: Arab 40%, Pakistani 18%, Indian 18%, Iranian 10%
Religions: Muslim 95%
Currency: Riyal
Tel. Area Code: 974

Romania (România)

Location: Eastern Europe
Area: 91,699 mi^2 (237,500 km^2)
Population: 22,715,000 (Urban: 55%)
Literacy: 97%
Capital: Bucureşti (Bucharest), 2,064,474
Government: Republic
Languages: Romanian, Hungarian, German
Ethnic Groups: Romanian (mixed Latin, Thracian, Slavic, and Celtic) 89%, Hungarian 9%
Religions: Romanian Orthodox 70%, Roman Catholic 6%, Protestant 6%
Currency: Leu
Tel. Area Code: 40

Russia (Rossija)

Location: Eastern Europe and Northern Asia
Area: 6,592,849 mi^2 (17,075,400 km^2)
Population: 150,500,000 (Urban: 76%)
Literacy: 98%
Capital: Moskva (Moscow), 8,801,500
Government: Federal republic
Languages: Russian, Tatar, Ukrainian
Ethnic Groups: Russian 82%, Tatar 4%, Ukrainian 3%, Chuvash 1%
Religions: Russian Orthodox, Muslim
Currency: Ruble
Tel. Area Code: 7

Rwanda

Location: Eastern Africa, landlocked
Area: 10,169 mi^2 (26,338 km^2)
Population: 8,064,000 (Urban: 6%)
Literacy: 58%
Capital: Kigali, 232,733
Government: Republic
Languages: French, Kinyarwanda, Kiswahili
Ethnic Groups: Hutu 90%, Tutsi 9%, Twa (Pygmy) 1%
Religions: Roman Catholic 65%, Animist 25%, Protestant 9%
Currency: Franc
Tel. Area Code: 250

St. Kitts and Nevis

Location: Caribbean islands
Area: 104 mi^2 (269 km^2)
Population: 41,000 (Urban: 42%)
Literacy: 98%
Capital: Basseterre, 14,725
Government: Parliamentary state
Languages: English
Ethnic Groups: Black 94%, mixed 3%, white 1%
Religions: Anglican 33%, Methodist 29%, Moravian 9%, Roman Catholic 7%
Currency: East Caribbean dollar
Tel. Area Code: 809

St. Lucia

Location: Caribbean island
Area: 238 mi^2 (616 km^2)
Population: 157,000 (Urban: 48%)
Literacy: 67%
Capital: Castries, 11,147
Government: Parliamentary state
Languages: English, French
Ethnic Groups: Black 90%, mixed 6%, East Indian 3%

Religions: Roman Catholic 90%, Protestant 7%, Anglican 3%
Currency: East Caribbean dollar
Tel. Area Code: 809

St. Vincent and the Grenadines

Location: Caribbean islands
Area: 150 mi^2 (388 km^2)
Population: 117,000 (Urban: 47%)
Literacy: 96%
Capital: Kingstown, 15,466
Government: Parliamentary state
Languages: English, French
Ethnic Groups: Black 82%, mixed 14%, East Indian 2%, white 1%
Religions: Anglican 42%, Methodist 21%, Roman Catholic 12%, Baptist 6%
Currency: East Caribbean dollar
Tel. Area Code: 809

Samoa

Location: South Pacific islands
Area: 1,093 mi^2 (2,831 km^2)
Population: 170,000 (Urban: 21%)
Literacy: 97%
Capital: Apia, 34,126
Government: Constitutional monarchy
Languages: English, Samoan
Ethnic Groups: Samoan (Polynesian) 93%, mixed European and Polynesian 7%
Religions: Congregational 50%, Roman Catholic 22%, Methodist 16%, Mormon 8%
Currency: Tala
Tel. Area Code: 685

Sao Tome and Principe (São Tomé e Príncipe)

Location: Western African islands
Area: 372 mi^2 (964 km^2)
Population: 135,000 (Urban: 47%)
Literacy: 73%
Capital: São Tomé, 5,245
Government: Republic
Languages: Portuguese, Fang
Ethnic Groups: Black, mixed black and Portuguese, Portuguese
Religions: Roman Catholic, Evangelical Protestant, Seventh Day Adventist
Currency: Dobra
Tel. Area Code: 239

Saudi Arabia (Al-'Arabīyah as-Su'ūdīyah)

Location: Southwestern Asia

Area: 830,000 mi^2 (2,149,690 km^2)
Population: 19,065,000 (Urban: 80%)
Literacy: 62%
Capital: Ar-Riyāḍ (Riyadh), 1,250,000
Government: Monarchy
Languages: Arabic
Ethnic Groups: Arab 90%, Afro-Asian 10%
Religions: Muslim 100%
Currency: Riyal
Tel. Area Code: 966

Senegal (Sénégal)

Location: Western Africa
Area: 75,951 mi^2 (196,712 km^2)
Population: 9,142,000 (Urban: 42%)
Literacy: 38%
Capital: Dakar, 1,490,450
Government: Republic
Languages: French, Wolof, Fulani, Serer, indigenous
Ethnic Groups: Wolof 44%, Fulani 23%, Serer 15%, Diola 6%, Malinke 5%
Religions: Muslim 94%, Christian 5%
Currency: CFA franc
Tel. Area Code: 221

Seychelles

Location: Indian Ocean islands
Area: 175 mi^2 (453 km^2)
Population: 75,000 (Urban: 55%)
Literacy: 58%
Capital: Victoria, 23,000
Government: Republic
Languages: English, French, Creole
Ethnic Groups: Seychellois (mixed Asian, African, and European)
Religions: Roman Catholic 90%, Anglican 8%
Currency: Rupee
Tel. Area Code: 248

Sierra Leone

Location: Western Africa
Area: 27,925 mi^2 (72,325 km^2)
Population: 4,815,000 (Urban: 36%)
Literacy: 21%
Capital: Freetown, 469,776
Government: Republic
Languages: English, Krio, Mende, Temne, indigenous
Ethnic Groups: Temne 30%, Mende 30%, other African
Religions: Muslim 30%, Animist 30%, Christian 10%
Currency: Leone
Tel. Area Code: 232

Singapore

Location: Southeastern Asian island
Area: 246 mi^2 (636 km^2)
Population: 2,904,000 (Urban: 100%)
Literacy: 89%
Capital: Singapore, 2,904,000
Government: Republic
Languages: Chinese (Mandarin), English, Malay, Tamil
Ethnic Groups: Chinese 76%, Malay 15%, Indian 6%
Religions: Taoist 29%, Buddhist 27%, Muslim 16%, Christian 10%, Hindu 4%
Currency: Dollar
Tel. Area Code: 65

Slovakia (Slovenská Republika)

Location: Eastern Europe, landlocked
Area: 18,933 mi^2 (49,035 km^2)
Population: 5,448,000 (Urban: 59%)
Capital: Bratislava, 441,453
Government: Republic
Languages: Slovak, Hungarian
Ethnic Groups: Slovak 86%, Hungarian 11%, Gypsy 2%
Religions: Roman Catholic 60%, Protestant 8%, Orthodox 4%
Currency: Koruna
Tel. Area Code: 42

Slovenia (Slovenija)

Location: Eastern Europe
Area: 7,820 mi^2 (20,253 km^2)
Population: 2,053,000 (Urban: 64%)
Literacy: 99%
Capital: Ljubljana, 233,200
Government: Republic
Languages: Slovenian, Serbo-Croatian
Ethnic Groups: Slovene 91%, Croat 3%, Serb 2%, Muslim 1%
Religions: Roman Catholic 96%, Muslim 1%
Currency: Tolar
Tel. Area Code: 386

Solomon Islands

Location: South Pacific islands
Area: 10,954 mi^2 (28,370 km^2)
Population: 406,000 (Urban: 17%)
Capital: Honiara, 30,413
Government: Parliamentary state
Languages: English, indigenous
Ethnic Groups: Melanesian 93%, Polynesian 4%, Micronesian 2%

Religions: Anglican 34%, Roman Catholic 19%, Baptist 17%, United Church 11%
Currency: Dollar
Tel. Area Code: 677

Somalia (Soomaaliya)

Location: Eastern Africa
Area: 246,201 mi^2 (637,657 km^2)
Population: 7,921,000 (Urban: 26%)
Literacy: 24%
Capital: Mogadishu, 600,000
Government: None
Languages: Arabic, Somali, English, Italian
Ethnic Groups: Somali 85%, Bantu
Religions: Sunni Muslim
Currency: Shilling
Tel. Area Code: 252

South Africa (Suid-Afrika)

Location: Southern Africa
Area: 471,010 mi^2 (1,219,909 km^2)
Population: 42,235,000 (Urban: 51%)
Literacy: 76%
Capital: Pretoria (administrative), 525,583; Cape Town (legislative), 854,616; Bloem
Government: Republic
Languages: Afrikaans, English, Sotho, Tswana, Zulu, others
Ethnic Groups: Black 75%, white 14%, mulatto (coloured) 9%, Indian 3%
Religions: Black Independent 19%, Dutch Reformed 14%, Roman Catholic 10%
Currency: Rand
Tel. Area Code: 27

Spain (España)

Location: Southwestern Europe
Area: 194,885 mi^2 (504,750 km^2)
Population: 39,485,000 (Urban: 77%)
Literacy: 96%
Capital: Madrid, 3,102,846
Government: Constitutional monarchy
Languages: Spanish (Castilian), Catalan, Galician, Basque
Ethnic Groups: Spanish (mixed Mediterranean and Teutonic)
Religions: Roman Catholic 99%
Currency: Peseta
Tel. Area Code: 34

Sri Lanka

Location: Southern Asian island
Area: 24,962 mi^2 (64,652 km^2)
Population: 18,185,000 (Urban: 22%)

Literacy: 88%
Capital: Colombo (designated), 612,000; Sri Jayawardenapura (seat of government), 10
Government: Socialist republic
Languages: English, Sinhala, Tamil
Ethnic Groups: Sinhalese 74%, Ceylon Tamil 10%, Moor 7%, Indian Tamil 6%
Religions: Buddhist 69%, Hindu 15%, Muslim 8%, Christian 8%
Currency: Rupee
Tel. Area Code: 94

Sudan (As-Sūdān)

Location: Eastern Africa
Area: 967,500 mi^2 (2,505,813 km^2)
Population: 30,480,000 (Urban: 25%)
Literacy: 27%
Capital: Al-Khartūm (Khartoum), 473,597
Government: Provisional military government
Languages: Arabic, Nubian and other indigenous, English
Ethnic Groups: Black 52%, Arab 39%, Beja 6%
Religions: Sunni Muslim 70%, indigenous 25%, Christian 5%
Currency: Dinar; Pound remains legal tender
Tel. Area Code: 249

Suriname

Location: Northeastern South America
Area: 63,251 mi^2 (163,820 km^2)
Population: 433,000 (Urban: 50%)
Literacy: 95%
Capital: Paramaribo, 241,000
Government: Republic
Languages: Dutch, Sranan Tongo, English, Hindustani, Javanese
Ethnic Groups: East Indian 37%, Creole 31%, Javanese 15%, black 10%, Amerindian 3 %, Chinese 2%
Religions: Hindu 27%, Protestant 25%, Roman Catholic 23%, Muslim 20%
Currency: Guilder
Tel. Area Code: 597

Swaziland

Location: Southern Africa, landlocked
Area: 6,704 mi^2 (17,364 km^2)
Population: 982,000 (Urban: 31%)
Literacy: 67%
Capital: Mbabane (administrative), 38,290; Lobamba (legislative)
Government: Monarchy
Languages: English, siSwati

Ethnic Groups: Swazi 97%, European 3%
Religions: African Protestant and other
  Christian 60%, tribal religionist 40%
Currency: Lilangeni
Tel. Area Code: 268

Sweden (Sverige)
Location: Northern Europe
Area: 173,732 mi^2 (449,964 km^2)
Population: 8,848,000 (Urban: 83%)
Literacy: 99%
Capital: Stockholm, 674,452
Government: Constitutional monarchy
Languages: Swedish, Lapp, Finnish
Ethnic Groups: Swedish (Scandinavian)
  92%, Finnish, Lapp
Religions: Lutheran (Church of Sweden)
  94%, Roman Catholic 2%
Currency: Krona
Tel. Area Code: 46

Switzerland (Schweiz, Suisse, Svizzera)
Location: Central Europe, landlocked
Area: 15,943 mi^2 (41,293 km^2)
Population: 7,064,000 (Urban: 61%)
Literacy: 99%
Capital: Bern, 136,338
Government: Federal republic
Languages: German, French, Italian,
  Romansch
Ethnic Groups: German 65%, French 18%,
  Italian 10%, Romansch 1%
Religions: Roman Catholic 48%,
  Protestant 44%
Currency: Franc
Tel. Area Code: 41

Syria (Sūrīyah)
Location: Southwestern Asia
Area: 71,498 mi^2 (185,180 km^2)
Population: 14,610,000 (Urban: 52%)
Literacy: 64%
Capital: Dimashq (Damascus), 1,549,932
Government: Socialist republic
Languages: Arabic, Kurdish, Armenian,
  Aramaic, Circassian
Ethnic Groups: Arab 90%, Kurdish,
  Armenian, and others 10%
Religions: Sunni Muslim 74%, other
  Muslim 16%, Christian 10%
Currency: Pound
Tel. Area Code: 963

Taiwan (T'aiwan)
Location: Eastern Asian island
Area: 13,900 mi^2 (36,002 km^2)
Population: 21,585,000 (Urban: 71%)
Literacy: 86%
Capital: T'aipei, 2,706,453
Government: Republic
Languages: Chinese (Mandarin), Taiwanese
  (Min), Hakka
Ethnic Groups: Taiwanese 84%,
  Chinese 14%, aborigine 2%
Religions: Buddhist, Confucian, and
  Taoist 93%, Christian 5%
Currency: Dollar
Tel. Area Code: 886

Tajikistan (Tojikiston)
Location: Central Asia, landlocked
Area: 55,251 mi^2 (143,100 km^2)
Population: 5,975,000 (Urban: 32%)
Literacy: 98%
Capital: Dušanbe, 582,400
Government: Republic
Languages: Tajik, Uzbek, Russian
Ethnic Groups: Tajik 62%, Uzbek 24%,
  Russian 8%
Religions: Sunni Muslim 80%, Shiite
  Muslim 5%
Currency: Ruble
Tel. Area Code: 7

Tanzania
Location: Eastern Africa
Area: 364,900 mi^2 (945,087 km^2)
Population: 29,075,000 (Urban: 24%)
Literacy: 59%
Capital: Dar es Salaam (de facto),
  1,096,000; Dodoma (legislative), 85,000
Government: Republic
Languages: English, Swahili, indigenous
Ethnic Groups: African 99%
Religions: Animist 33%, Muslim 33%,
  Christian 33%
Currency: Shilling
Tel. Area Code: 255

Thailand (Prathet Thai)
Location: Southeastern Asia
Area: 198,115 mi^2 (513,115 km^2)
Population: 60,630,000 (Urban: 20%)
Literacy: 93%
Capital: Krung Thep (Bangkok), 5,620,591
Government: Constitutional monarchy
Languages: Thai, indigenous
Ethnic Groups: Thai 75%, Chinese 14%

Religions: Buddhist 95%, Muslim 4%
Currency: Baht
Tel. Area Code: 66

Togo

Location: Western Africa
Area: 21,925 mi^2 (56,785 km^2)
Population: 4,489,000 (Urban: 31%)
Literacy: 43%
Capital: Lomé, 500,000
Government: Provisional military
government
Languages: French, Ewe, Mina, Kabye,
Dagomba
Ethnic Groups: Ewe, Mina, Kabye, others
Religions: Animist 70%, Christian 20%,
Muslim 10%
Currency: CFA franc
Tel. Area Code: 228

Tonga

Location: South Pacific islands
Area: 288 mi^2 (747 km^2)
Population: 110,000 (Urban: 41%)
Literacy: 100%
Capital: Nuku‘alofa, 21,265
Government: Constitutional monarchy
Languages: Tongan, English
Ethnic Groups: Tongan (Polynesian)
Religions: Methodist 47%, Roman
Catholic 16%, Free Church 14%, Church
of Tonga 9%
Currency: Pa'anga
Tel. Area Code: 676

Trinidad and Tobago

Location: Caribbean islands
Area: 1,980 mi^2 (5,128 km^2)
Population: 1,272,000 (Urban: 72%)
Literacy: 97%
Capital: Port of Spain, 50,878
Government: Republic
Languages: English, Hindi, French, Spanish
Ethnic Groups: Black 41%, East Indian 41%,
mixed 16%, white 1%
Religions: Baptist 40%, Anglican 19%,
Methodist 16%, Church of God 11%
Currency: Dollar
Tel. Area Code: 809

Tunisia (Tunisie, Tunis)

Location: Northern Africa
Area: 63,170 mi^2 (163,610 km^2)
Population: 8,960,000 (Urban: 57%)

Literacy: 57%
Capital: Tunis, 596,654
Government: Republic
Languages: Arabic, French
Ethnic Groups: Arab 98%, European 1%
Religions: Muslim 98%, Christian 1%
Currency: Dinar
Tel. Area Code: 216

Turkey (Türkiye)

Location: Southeastern Europe and
southwestern Asia
Area: 300,948 mi^2 (779,452 km^2)
Population: 63,020,000 (Urban: 69%)
Literacy: 79%
Capital: Ankara, 2,559,471
Government: Republic
Languages: Turkish, Kurdish, Arabic
Ethnic Groups: Turkish 80%, Kurdish 20%
Religions: Muslim
Currency: Lira
Tel. Area Code: 90

Turkmenistan (Türkmenistan)

Location: Central Asia, landlocked
Area: 188,456 mi^2 (488,100 km^2)
Population: 4,116,000 (Urban: 45%)
Literacy: 98%
Capital: Ašchabad, 412,200
Government: Republic
Languages: Turkmen, Russian, Uzbek
Ethnic Groups: Turkmen 73%, Russian 10%,
Uzbek 9%, Kazakh 2%
Religions: Muslim 87%, Eastern
Orthodox 11%
Currency: Manat
Tel. Area Code: 7

Uganda

Location: Eastern Africa, landlocked
Area: 93,104 mi^2 (241,139 km^2)
Population: 19,790,000 (Urban: 13%)
Literacy: 56%
Capital: Kampala, 773,463
Government: Republic
Languages: English, Luganda, Swahili,
indigenous
Ethnic Groups: Ganda, Nkole, Gisu, Soga,
Turkana, Chiga, Lango, Acholi
Religions: Roman Catholic 33%,
Protestant 33%, Muslim 16%, Animist
Currency: Shilling
Tel. Area Code: 256

Ukraine (Ukrayina)

Location: Eastern Europe
Area: 233,090 mi^2 (603,700 km^2)
Population: 51,940,000 (Urban: 70%)
Literacy: 98%
Capital: Kyyiv (Kiev), 2,635,000
Government: Republic
Languages: Ukrainian, Russian, Romanian, Polish
Ethnic Groups: Ukrainian 73%, Russian 22%
Religions: Ukrainian Orthodox, Ukrainian Catholic
Currency: Karbovanets
Tel. Area Code: 380

United Arab Emirates (Al-Imārāt al-'Arabīyah al-Muttahidah)

Location: Southwestern Asia
Area: 32,278 mi^2 (83,600 km^2)
Population: 2,992,000 (Urban: 84%)
Literacy: 71%
Capital: Abū Ẓaby (Abu Dhabi), 242,975
Government: Federation of monarchs
Languages: Arabic, Farsi, English, Hindi, Urdu
Ethnic Groups: South Asian 50%, native Emirian 19%, other Arab 23%
Religions: Sunni Muslim 80%, Shiite Muslim 16%
Currency: Dirham
Tel. Area Code: 971

United Kingdom

Location: Northwestern European islands
Area: 94,249 mi^2 (244,101 km^2)
Population: 58,410,000 (Urban: 90%)
Literacy: 99%
Capital: London, 6,574,009
Government: Parliamentary monarchy
Languages: English, Welsh, Scots Gaelic
Ethnic Groups: English 82%, Scottish 10%, Irish 2%, Welsh 2%
Religions: Anglican 47%, Roman Catholic 9%, Presbyterian 3%, Methodist 1%
Currency: Pound sterling
Tel. Area Code: 44

United States

Location: Central North America
Area: 3,787,425 mi^2 (9,809,431 km^2)
Population: 265,130,000 (Urban: 76%)
Literacy: 97%
Capital: Washington, 606,900
Government: Federal republic
Languages: English, Spanish
Ethnic Groups: White 84%, black 12%, Asian 3%
Religions: Baptist and other Protestant 56%, Roman Catholic 28%, Jewish 2%
Currency: Dollar
Tel. Area Code: 1

Uruguay

Location: Eastern South America
Area: 68,500 mi^2 (177,414 km^2)
Population: 3,236,000 (Urban: 90%)
Literacy: 96%
Capital: Montevideo, 1,251,647
Government: Republic
Languages: Spanish
Ethnic Groups: White 88%, mestizo 8%, black 4%
Religions: Roman Catholic 66%, Protestant 2%, Jewish 2%
Currency: Peso
Tel. Area Code: 598

Uzbekistan (Ŭzbekiston)

Location: Central Asia, landlocked
Area: 172,742 mi^2 (447,400 km^2)
Population: 23,345,000 (Urban: 41%)
Literacy: 97%
Capital: Taškent, 2,113,300
Government: Republic
Languages: Uzbek, Russian
Ethnic Groups: Uzbek 71%, Russian 8%, Tajik 5%, Kazakh 4%
Religions: Muslim 88%, Eastern Orthodox 9%
Currency: Som
Tel. Area Code: 7

Vanuatu

Location: South Pacific islands
Area: 4,707 mi^2 (12,190 km^2)
Population: 175,000 (Urban: 19%)
Literacy: 53%
Capital: Port-Vila, 18,905
Government: Republic
Languages: Bislama, English, French
Ethnic Groups: Ni-Vanuatu (Melanesian) 92%, European 2%, other Pacific Islander 2%
Religions: Presbyterian 37%, Anglican 15%, Roman Catholic 15%, other Protestant
Currency: Vatu
Tel. Area Code: 678

Vatican City (Città del Vaticano)

Location: Southern Europe, landlocked (within the city of Rome, Italy)
Area: 0.2 mi^2 (0.4 km^2)
Population: 1,000 (Urban: 100%)
Literacy: 100%
Capital: Città del Vaticano, 1,000
Government: Monarchical-sacerdotal state
Languages: Italian, Latin, other
Ethnic Groups: Italian, Swiss
Religions: Roman Catholic
Currency: Lira
Tel. Area Code: 39

Venezuela

Location: Northern South America
Area: 352,145 mi^2 (912,050 km^2)
Population: 21,845,000 (Urban: 93%)
Literacy: 90%
Capital: Caracas, 1,822,465
Government: Federal republic
Languages: Spanish, Amerindian
Ethnic Groups: Mestizo 67%, white 21%, black 10%, Indian 2%
Religions: Roman Catholic 96%, Protestant 2%
Currency: Bolivar
Tel. Area Code: 58

Vietnam (Viet Nam)

Location: Southeastern Asia
Area: 127,428 mi^2 (330,036 km^2)
Population: 74,360,000 (Urban: 21%)
Literacy: 88%
Capital: Ha Noi, 905,939
Government: Socialist republic
Languages: Vietnamese, French, Chinese, English, Khmer, indigenous
Ethnic Groups: Kinh 87%, Hao 2%, Tay 2%
Religions: Buddhist, Taoist, Roman Catholic, indigenous, Islamic
Currency: Dong
Tel. Area Code: 84

Yemen (Al-Yaman)

Location: Southwestern Asia
Area: 203,850 mi^2 (527,968 km^2)
Population: 15,025,000 (Urban: 34%)
Literacy: 38%
Capital: Ṣanʻāʼ, 427,150
Government: Republic
Languages: Arabic
Ethnic Groups: Arab, Afro-Arab, south Asians
Religions: Muslim, Jewish, Christian, Hindu
Currency: Rial
Tel. Area Code: 967

Yugoslavia (Jugoslavija)

Location: Eastern Europe
Area: 39,449 mi^2 (102,173 km^2)
Population: 11,135,000 (Urban: 57%)
Literacy: 89%
Capital: Beograd (Belgrade), 1,136,786
Government: Republic
Languages: Serbo-Croatian, Albanian
Ethnic Groups: Serb 63%, Albanian 14%, Montenegrin 6%, Hungarian 4%
Religions: Orthodox 65%, Muslim 19%, Roman Catholic 4%
Currency: Dinar
Tel. Area Code: 381

Zambia

Location: Southern Africa, landlocked
Area: 290,586 mi^2 (752,614 km^2)
Population: 9,569,000 (Urban: 43%)
Literacy: 73%
Capital: Lusaka, 982,362
Government: Republic
Languages: English, Tonga, Lozi, other indigenous
Ethnic Groups: African 99%, European 1%
Religions: Christian 50-75%, Muslim and Hindu 24-49%
Currency: Kwacha
Tel. Area Code: 260

Zimbabwe

Location: Southern Africa, landlocked
Area: 150,873 mi^2 (390,759 km^2)
Population: 11,450,000 (Urban: 32%)
Literacy: 78%
Capital: Harare, 681,000
Government: Republic
Languages: English, Shona, Sindebele
Ethnic Groups: Shona 71%, Ndebele 16%, white 1%
Religions: Mixed Christian and Animist 50%, Christian 25%, Animist 24%
Currency: Dollar
Tel. Area Code: 263

Traveler's Personal Diary

Contents

Calendar **242**

Weights, Measures, and Formulas **244**

Names and Addresses **246**

Travel Notes **248**

Itinerary **253**

Financial Worksheet **254**

Personal Information **256**

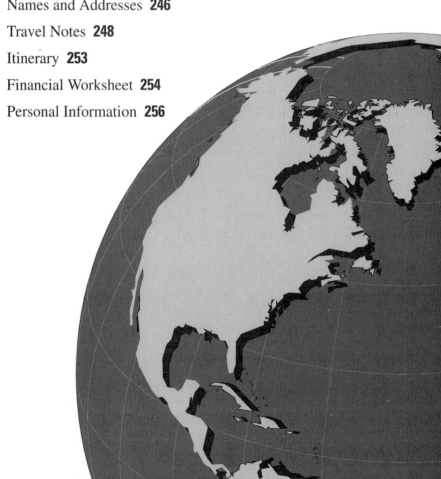

Calendar

1997

January

S	M	T	W	T	F	S
			1	2	3	4
5	6	7	8	9	10	11
12	13	14	15	16	17	18
19	20	21	22	23	24	25
26	27	28	29	30	31	

February

S	M	T	W	T	F	S
						1
2	3	4	5	6	7	8
9	10	11	12	13	14	15
16	17	18	19	20	21	22
23	24	25	26	27	28	

March

S	M	T	W	T	F	S
						1
2	3	4	5	6	7	8
9	10	11	12	13	14	15
16	17	18	19	20	21	22
23	24	25	26	27	28	29
30	31					

April

S	M	T	W	T	F	S
		1	2	3	4	5
6	7	8	9	10	11	12
13	14	15	16	17	18	19
20	21	22	23	24	25	26
27	28	29	30			

May

S	M	T	W	T	F	S
				1	2	3
4	5	6	7	8	9	10
11	12	13	14	15	16	17
18	19	20	21	22	23	24
25	26	27	28	29	30	31

June

S	M	T	W	T	F	S
1	2	3	4	5	6	7
8	9	10	11	12	13	14
15	16	17	18	19	20	21
22	23	24	25	26	27	28
29	30					

July

S	M	T	W	T	F	S
		1	2	3	4	5
6	7	8	9	10	11	12
13	14	15	16	17	18	19
20	21	22	23	24	25	26
27	28	29	30	31		

August

S	M	T	W	T	F	S
					1	2
3	4	5	6	7	8	9
10	11	12	13	14	15	16
17	18	19	20	21	22	23
24	25	26	27	28	29	30
31						

September

S	M	T	W	T	F	S
	1	2	3	4	5	6
7	8	9	10	11	12	13
14	15	16	17	18	19	20
21	22	23	24	25	26	27
28	29	30				

October

S	M	T	W	T	F	S
			1	2	3	4
5	6	7	8	9	10	11
12	13	14	15	16	17	18
19	20	21	22	23	24	25
26	27	28	29	30	31	

November

S	M	T	W	T	F	S
						1
2	3	4	5	6	7	8
9	10	11	12	13	14	15
16	17	18	19	20	21	22
23	24	25	26	27	28	29
30						

December

S	M	T	W	T	F	S
	1	2	3	4	5	6
7	8	9	10	11	12	13
14	15	16	17	18	19	20
21	22	23	24	25	26	27
28	29	30	31			

1998

January

S	M	T	W	T	F	S
				1	2	3
4	5	6	7	8	9	10
11	12	13	14	15	16	17
18	19	20	21	22	23	24
25	26	27	28	29	30	31

February

S	M	T	W	T	F	S
1	2	3	4	5	6	7
8	9	10	11	12	13	14
15	16	17	18	19	20	21
22	23	24	25	26	27	28

March

S	M	T	W	T	F	S
1	2	3	4	5	6	7
8	9	10	11	12	13	14
15	16	17	18	19	20	21
22	23	24	25	26	27	28
29	30	31				

April

S	M	T	W	T	F	S
			1	2	3	4
5	6	7	8	9	10	11
12	13	14	15	16	17	18
19	20	21	22	23	24	25
26	27	28	29	30		

May

S	M	T	W	T	F	S
					1	2
3	4	5	6	7	8	9
10	11	12	13	14	15	16
17	18	19	20	21	22	23
24	25	26	27	28	29	30
31						

June

S	M	T	W	T	F	S
	1	2	3	4	5	6
7	8	9	10	11	12	13
14	15	16	17	18	19	20
21	22	23	24	25	26	27
28	29	30				

July

S	M	T	W	T	F	S
			1	2	3	4
5	6	7	8	9	10	11
12	13	14	15	16	17	18
19	20	21	22	23	24	25
26	27	28	29	30	31	

August

S	M	T	W	T	F	S
						1
2	3	4	5	6	7	8
9	10	11	12	13	14	15
16	17	18	19	20	21	22
23	24	25	26	27	28	29
30	31					

September

S	M	T	W	T	F	S
		1	2	3	4	5
6	7	8	9	10	11	12
13	14	15	16	17	18	19
20	21	22	23	24	25	26
27	28	29	30			

October

S	M	T	W	T	F	S
				1	2	3
4	5	6	7	8	9	10
11	12	13	14	15	16	17
18	19	20	21	22	23	24
25	26	27	28	29	30	31

November

S	M	T	W	T	F	S
1	2	3	4	5	6	7
8	9	10	11	12	13	14
15	16	17	18	19	20	21
22	23	24	25	26	27	28
29	30					

December

S	M	T	W	T	F	S
		1	2	3	4	5
6	7	8	9	10	11	12
13	14	15	16	17	18	19
20	21	22	23	24	25	26
27	28	29	30	31		

Calendar

1999

January

S	M	T	W	T	F	S
					1	2
3	4	5	6	7	8	9
10	11	12	13	14	15	16
17	18	19	20	21	22	23
24	25	26	27	28	29	30
31						

February

S	M	T	W	T	F	S
	1	2	3	3	5	6
7	8	9	10	11	12	13
14	15	16	17	18	19	20
21	22	23	24	25	26	27
28						

March

S	M	T	W	T	F	S
	1	2	3	4	5	6
7	8	9	10	11	12	13
14	15	16	17	18	19	20
21	22	23	24	25	26	27
28	29	30	31			

April

S	M	T	W	T	F	S
				1	2	3
4	5	6	7	8	9	10
11	12	13	14	15	16	17
18	19	20	21	22	23	24
25	26	27	28	29	30	

May

S	M	T	W	T	F	S
						1
2	3	4	5	6	7	8
9	10	11	12	13	14	15
16	17	18	19	20	21	22
23	24	25	26	27	28	29
30	31					

June

S	M	T	W	T	F	S
		1	2	3	4	5
6	7	8	9	10	11	12
13	14	15	16	17	18	19
20	21	22	23	24	25	26
27	28	29	30			

July

S	M	T	W	T	F	S
				1	2	3
4	5	6	7	8	9	10
11	12	13	14	15	16	17
18	19	20	21	22	23	24
25	26	27	28	29	30	31

August

S	M	T	W	T	F	S
1	2	3	4	5	6	7
8	9	10	11	12	13	14
15	16	17	18	19	20	21
22	23	24	25	26	27	28
29	30	31				

September

S	M	T	W	T	F	S
			1	2	3	4
5	6	7	8	9	10	11
12	13	14	15	16	17	18
19	20	21	22	23	24	25
26	27	28	29	30		

October

S	M	T	W	T	F	S
					1	2
3	4	5	6	7	8	9
10	11	12	13	14	15	16
17	18	19	20	21	22	23
24	25	26	27	28	29	30
31						

November

S	M	T	W	T	F	S
	1	2	3	4	5	6
7	8	9	10	11	12	13
14	15	16	17	18	19	20
21	22	23	24	25	26	27
28	29	30				

December

S	M	T	W	T	F	S
			1	2	3	4
5	6	7	8	9	10	11
12	13	14	15	16	17	18
19	20	21	22	23	24	25
26	27	28	29	30	31	

2000

January

S	M	T	W	T	F	S
						1
2	3	4	5	6	7	8
9	10	11	12	13	14	15
16	17	18	19	20	21	22
23	24	25	26	27	28	29
30	31					

February

S	M	T	W	T	F	S
		1	2	3	4	5
6	7	8	9	10	11	12
13	14	15	16	17	18	19
20	21	22	23	24	25	26
27	28	29				

March

S	M	T	W	T	F	S
			1	2	3	4
5	6	7	8	9	10	11
12	13	14	15	16	17	18
19	20	21	22	23	24	25
26	27	28	29	30	31	

April

S	M	T	W	T	F	S
						1
2	3	4	5	6	7	8
9	10	11	12	13	14	15
16	17	18	19	20	21	22
23	24	25	26	27	28	29
30						

May

S	M	T	W	T	F	S
	1	2	3	4	5	6
7	8	9	10	11	12	13
14	15	16	17	18	19	20
21	22	23	24	25	26	27
28	29	30	31			

June

S	M	T	W	T	F	S
				1	2	3
4	5	6	7	8	9	10
11	12	13	14	15	16	17
18	19	20	21	22	23	24
25	26	27	28	29	30	

July

S	M	T	W	T	F	S
						1
2	3	4	5	6	7	8
9	10	11	12	13	14	15
16	17	18	19	20	21	22
23	24	25	26	27	28	29
30	31					

August

S	M	T	W	T	F	S
		1	2	3	4	5
6	7	8	9	10	11	12
13	14	15	16	17	18	19
20	21	22	23	24	25	26
27	28	29	30	31		

September

S	M	T	W	T	F	S
					1	2
3	4	5	6	7	8	9
10	11	12	13	14	15	16
17	18	19	20	21	22	23
24	25	26	27	28	29	30

October

S	M	T	W	T	F	S
1	2	3	4	5	6	7
8	9	10	11	12	13	14
15	16	17	18	19	20	21
22	23	24	25	26	27	28
29	30	31				

November

S	M	T	W	T	F	S
			1	2	3	4
5	6	7	8	9	10	11
12	13	14	15	16	17	18
19	20	21	22	23	24	25
26	27	28	29	30		

December

S	M	T	W	T	F	S
					1	2
3	4	5	6	7	8	9
10	11	12	13	14	15	16
17	18	19	20	21	22	23
24	25	26	27	28	29	30
31						

Weights, Measures, and Formulas

Distance

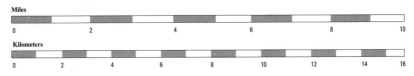

Miles

Kilometers

Miles to Kilometers: Multiply number of miles by 1.6
Kilometers to Miles: Multiply number of kilometers by .6

Liquid Measurement

Imperial Gallon

1 Gallon
4.5 Liters

2.64 Quarts
3 Liters

.5 Gallon
2.3 Liters

1 Quart
1.1 Liters

U.S. Gallon

1 Gallon
3.8 Liters

.5 Gallon
1.9 Liters

1 Quart
.9 Liter

The Imperial/Canadian gallon is based on the Imperial quart, which is approximately one-fifth larger than the U.S. quart.

The following measurements are approximate for easy conversion.

1 Imperial gallon = 4.5 liters
1 Imperial gallon = 1.2 U.S. gallons
1 liter = .22 Imperial gallon
5 Imperial gallons = 6 U.S. gallons

Temperature

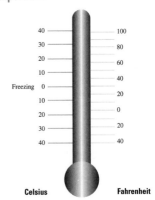

Celsius   **Fahrenheit**

Comparative Thermometer Readings

Fahrenheit to Celsius:
Subtract 32 from the number of Fahrenheit, then multiply by 5/9.

Celsius to Fahrenheit:
Multiply the number of Celsius by 9/5 and add 32.

Speed

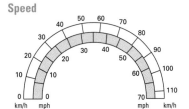

30 mph is maximum speed limit in most U.S. towns. The metric equivalent is 50 km/h.

50 mph is maximum speed limit on many rural two-lane roads in U.S. In metrics, 80 km/h.

55 mph is maximum speed limit on U.S. interstate highways. In metrics, 90 km/h.

60 mph is maximum speed allowed on access-controlled highways in Canada. The metric equivalent is 100 km/h.

Measures

Linear
1 inch = 2.540 centimeters
1 foot = .305 meter
1 yard = .914 meter
1 mile = 1.609 kilometers
1 meter = 39.37 inches
1 meter = 3.28 feet = 1.094 yards
1 kilometer = .621 mile
1 mile = 1,760 yards = 5,280 feet
1 yard = 36 inches = 3 feet
1 foot = 12 inches
1 span = 9 inches
1 hand = 4 inches
1 mile = 8 furlongs
1 furlong = 220 yards
1 nautical mile (knot) = 1.152 statute miles = 1.853 kilometers

Square/Area
1 sq. inch = 6.451 sq. centimeters
1 sq. foot = .093 sq. meter
1 sq. yard = .836 sq. meter
1 sq. centimeter = .155 sq. inch
1 sq. meter = 10.764 sq. feet = 1.196 sq. yards
1 sq. foot = 144 sq. inches
1 sq. yard = 9 sq. feet
An acre is equal to a square, the side of which is 208.7 feet
1 acre = 4,840 sq. yards = 43,560 sq. feet

1 sq. mile = 640 acres
1 sq. mile = 2.59 sq. kilometers
1 sq. kilometer = .386 sq. mile

Cubic/Volume
1 cu. inch = 16.387 cu. centimeters
1 cu. foot = .028 cu. meter
1 cu. yard = .765 cu. meter
1 cu. centimeter = .061 cu. inch
1 cu. meter = 35.314 cu. feet
1 cu. meter = 1.308 cu. yards
1 cu. yard = 27 cu. feet
1 cu. foot = 1,728 cu. inches
1 cord of wood = 4 x 4 x 8 feet = 128 cu. feet

Dry Measure (U.S.)
1 bushel = 1.245 cu. feet = 2,150.42 cu. inches
1 bushel = 4 pecks = 32 quarts = 64 pints
1 peck = 8 quarts = 16 pints

Liquid Measure (U.S.)
1 pint = 16 ounces = .473 liter
1 quart = 2 pints = 32 ounces
1 quart = .946 liter
1 gallon = 4 quarts = 3.785 liters
1 liter = 1.057 quarts

Miscellaneous
1 great gross = 12 gross = 144 dozen
1 gross = 12 dozen = 144 units
1 dozen = 12 units
1 score = 20 units
1 quire = 24 sheets
1 ream = 20 quires = 480 sheets
1 ream printing paper = 500 sheets

Weights

Avoirdupois
1 ounce = 28.35 grams
1 pound = .453 kilograms = 16 ounces
1 gram = .035 ounce
1 kilogram = 2.205 pounds
1 short ton = 2,000 pounds
1 short ton = .907 metric tons
1 long ton = 2,240 pounds
1 long ton = 1.016 metric tons
1 stone = 14 pounds

Troy
1 ounce = 20 pennyweights = 480 grains
1 pound = 12 ounces = 5,760 grains
1 carat = 3.086 grains
1 pennyweight = 24 grains = .05 ounce
1 grain troy = 1 grain avoirdupois = 1 grain apothecaries' weight

Mathematical Formulas
Diameter of Circle: circumference divided by 3.1416
Circumference of Circle: diameter multiplied by 3.1416
Area of Circle: square of radius multiplied by 3.1416 or square of diameter multiplied by .7854
Area of Triangle: base multiplied by ½ of height
Area of Parallelogram (including square): base multiplied by height
Surface Area of Sphere: square of diameter multiplied by 3.1416
Volume of Sphere: cube of diameter multiplied by .5236
Volume of Prism or Cylinder: area of base multiplied by height

Volume of Pyramid or Cone: area of base multiplied by ⅓ of height
Amount of Simple Interest: principle multiplied by rate of interest multiplied by time (in terms of years or fractions thereof)

Clothing Size Equivalents

Men's Suits and Overcoats
American: 36, 38, 40, 42, 44, 46
British: 36, 38, 40, 42, 44, 46
European: 46, 48, 51, 54, 56, 59

Women's Suits and Dresses
America: 8, 10, 12, 14, 16, 18
British: 10, 12, 14, 16, 18, 20
European: 38, 40, 42, 44, 46, 48

Shirts
American: 14, 14½, 15, 15½, 16, 16½ 17
British: 14, 14½, 15, 15½, 16, 16½, 17
European: 36, 37, 38, 39, 41, 42, 43

Men's Shoes
American: 7½, 8, 8½, 9½, 10½, 11½
British: 7, 7½, 8, 9, 10, 11
European: 40½, 41, 42, 43, 44½, 46

Women's Shoes
American: 6, 6½, 7, 7½, 8, 8½
British: 4½, 5, 5½, 6, 6½, 7
European: 37½, 38, 39, 39½, 40, 40½

Children's Clothes
American: 4, 6, 8, 10, 12, 14
British: Height (in) 43, 48, 55, 58, 60, 62
  Age 4-5, 6-7, 9-10, 11, 12, 13
European Height (cm) 125, 135, 150, 155, 160, 165
  Age 7, 9, 12, 13, 14, 15

Note : Size equivalents are approximate. Glove sizes are the same in every country.

Names and Addresses

Name

Address

City State Zip

Country

Telephone   (   )

FAX   (   )

Name

Address

City State Zip

Country

Telephone   (   )

FAX   (   )

Name

Address

City State Zip

Country

Telephone   (   )

FAX   (   )

Name

Address

City State Zip

Country

Telephone   (   )

FAX   (   )

Name

Address

City State Zip

Country

Telephone   (   )

FAX   (   )

Name

Address

City State Zip

Country

Telephone   (   )

FAX   (   )

Name

Address

City State Zip

Country

Telephone   (   )

FAX   (   )

Name

Address

City State Zip

Country

Telephone   (   )

FAX   (   )

Name

Address

City State Zip

Country

Telephone   (   )

FAX   (   )

Name

Address

City State Zip

Country

Telephone   (   )

FAX   (   )

Name

Address

City State Zip

Country

Telephone   (   )

FAX   (   )

Name

Address

City State Zip

Country

Telephone   (   )

FAX   (   )

Name

Address

City State Zip

Country

Telephone   (   )

FAX   (   )

Name

Address

City State Zip

Country

Telephone   (   )

FAX   (   )

Name

Address

City State Zip

Country

Telephone   (   )

FAX   (   )

Name

Address

City State Zip

Country

Telephone   (   )

FAX   (   )

Name

Address

City State Zip

Country

Telephone   (   )

FAX   (   )

Name

Address

City State Zip

Country

Telephone   (   )

FAX   (   )

Name

Address

City State Zip

Country

Telephone   (   )

FAX   (   )

Name

Address

City State Zip

Country

Telephone   (   )

FAX   (   )

Name

Address

City State Zip

Country

Telephone   (   )

FAX   (   )

Name

Address

City State Zip

Country

Telephone   (   )

FAX   (   )

Travel Notes

Travel Notes

Travel Notes

Itinerary

Date	Destination	Lodging	Address	Phone/FAX #

Financial Worksheet

Date:

Travel Fares

Meals

Lodging

Tips

Entertainment

Gifts

Other

Total

Currency Exchanged

Exchange Rate